nunity Justice

probation and criminal justi

EK LOAN

Edited by Jane Winstone and Francis Pakes

WILLAN
PUBLISHING

Published by

Willan Publishing
Culmcott House
Mill Street, Uffculme
Cullompton, Devon
EX15 3AT, UK
Tel: +44(0)1884 840337
Fax: +44(0)1884 840251
email: info@willanpublishing.co.uk
website: www.willanpublishing.co.uk

Published simultaneously in the USA and Canada by

Willan Publishing
c/o ISBS, 920 NE 58th Ave, Suite 300
Portland, Oregon 97213-3786, USA
Tel: +001(0)503 287 3093
Fax: +001(0)503 280 8832
email: info@isbs.com
website: www.isbs.com

First published 2005

ISBN 1-84392-128-6 (paperback)

British Library Cataloguing-in-Publication Data

A catalogue record for this book is available from the British Library.

Project management by Deer Park Productions, Tavistock, Devon
Typeset by PDQ Typesetting, Newcastle-under-Lyme, Staffordshire
Printed by T J International Ltd, Padstow, Cornwall

Contents

Figures and tables

Figures

Tables

To my children Jon, Andrew and Beth Winstone
and in loving memory of my father John Watts

To my daughter Katie Rose Pakes

Notes on contributors

Miranda Boone is a Senior Lecturer in Criminal Law and Criminology at the Willem Pompe Institute for Criminal Law and Criminology of the University of Utrecht, the Netherlands. Her thesis was on the subject of community sentences and she conducted research on different topics relating to criminal law and criminology. In particular, she wrote about sentences, prison systems and probation. Recently she co-edited a volume on criminal law and discretion. At present she is involved in a research project on the reorganization of the judiciary in the Netherlands.

Robin Fletcher is an associate researcher in the Criminology Department, Middlesex University. He is a retired Detective Superintendent, having served with the Metropolitan Police for 30 years. His research interests are the governance of crime, policing styles and systems, and the impact of multi-agency partnerships on crime reduction. He has published on the subjects of the impact of crime intelligence and the influence of community policing. He is currently researching the impact of the extended police family.

Dennis Gough is a Senior University Tutor in Community Justice Studies at the University of Portsmouth. He was formerly a senior probation officer with the National Probation Service. In addition to current developments regarding the National Offender Management Service, his other research interests are in child protection and the criminal justice system.

Nathan Hall is a Lecturer at the Institute of Criminal Justice Studies at the University of Portsmouth. His main research interest lies in hate crime, a subject he has researched extensively, particularly in relation to criminal justice responses in England and Wales and in the United States. His first book, *Hate Crime*, is being published by Willan Publishing in 2005. He is currently involved in comparative research on the policing of hate crime in London and New York.

Ruth M. Hatcher is a Lecturer in the Forensic Section of the School of Psychology at the University of Leicester. Her main research interest lies in the evaluation of offending behaviour programmes delivered to offenders within community settings. In particular she is interested in attrition from such programmes and the reasons for it. She is currently involved in a Home Office-funded national evaluation of offending behaviour programmes within the Probation Service of England and Wales.

Carol Hayden is a Reader in Applied Social Research at the Institute of Criminal Justice Studies, University of Portsmouth. Her research focus is on children in trouble, whether this is at home, in school or in the community. She has researched and published widely on children excluded from school and children in the care system, including evaluating interventions designed to help these children. She is currently writing a book on this theme.

Clive Hollin is Professor of Criminological Psychology in the Department of Psychiatry, Division of Forensic Mental Health, at the University of Leicester. He has worked as a prison psychologist, as director of rehabilitation in the Youth Treatment Service and as a consultant forensic psychologist at Rampton Hospital. He has published widely in the field of criminological psychology, particularly with reference to the management and treatment of offenders. He is co-editor of the journal, *Psychology, Crime and Law*.

Chris Lewis is a Senior Research Fellow at the Institute of Criminal Justice Studies, University of Portsmouth, and a consultant in criminology. He is particularly interested in criminal justice policy and was for many years a senior civil servant in the Home Office Research Department. His main current interests are research and statistics of crime, especially organized crime, gun crime and crime in Africa; offender programmes; prosecution systems and diversity issues.

Barry Loveday is a Reader in Criminal Justice at the University of Portsmouth. His main area of research is local policing and local police service delivery. He has written extensively on this and on issues relating to the performance, management and accountability of the police. He is a member of the Local Government Association's Safer Communities Advisors Panel, in which capacity he is currently advising local authorities on the implications and opportunities provided by the Police Reform Agenda now being pursued by central government. He has been extensively involved with the work of Crime Reduction Partnerships established with the Crime and Disorder Act 1998.

James McGuire is Professor of Forensic Clinical Psychology and Director of Clinical Psychology Training at the University of Liverpool. He has conducted research in prisons, probation services, and other settings on aspects of the effectiveness of intervention with offenders and related topics. He carries out psycho-legal work for courts and tribunals, and has been involved in a range of consultatative work with criminal justice agencies in the United Kingdom and other countries. His current research projects include evaluation of community-based offending behaviour programmes, a systematic review of violence prevention, and factors influencing treatment outcome in addictions.

Nikki McKenzie is a Senior Lecturer at the Institute of Criminal Justice Studies at the University of Portsmouth. Her main research interests lie in youth crime, youth justice and restorative justice. Nikki volunteers as a chair youth offender panel member with the Wessex Youth Offending Team, which she has done since 2002. She is currently completing her PhD on Family Group Conferences within the UK Youth Justice System.

Mike Nash is Deputy Director of the Institute of Criminal Justice Studies at the University of Portsmouth. His main research interests lie in the field of dangerousness, criminal justice policy, and professional cultures. He has written extensively in the field and Blackstone Press published his first book, *Police Probation and Protecting the Public*, in 1999. He is currently working on a new book on public protection and the criminal justice process.

Mike Nellis is Professor of Criminal and Community Justice in the Glasgow School of Social Work, University of Strathclyde. He is a former social worker with young offenders and has been closely involved in the training of probation officers. He has written extensively on the changing nature of the probation service, the promotion of community penalties, the significance of electronic monitoring and the cultural politics of penal reform (including the use of prison movies and prisoner's autobiographies). His most recent book (edited with Eric Chui) was *Moving Probation Forward* (Longmans 2003).

Francis Pakes is Principal Lecturer at the Institute of Criminal Justice Studies at the University of Portsmouth. His main research interest lies in comparative criminal justice. He has written extensively on criminal justice in his native country, the Netherlands. He published his first book, *Comparative Criminal Justice*, with Willan Publishing in 2004. He is currently involved in comparative research into legalization of euthanasia and assisted suicide as well as in the area of psychology and law.

Aaron Pycroft is a Senior Lecturer at the Institute of Criminal Justice Studies at the University of Portsmouth. He is a regional coordinator delivering the BA(Hons) Community Justice Studies programme. Prior to working at Portsmouth University Aaron worked for 15 years in the non-statutory sector as a practitioner and operational and senior manager within the field of substance abuse. He has worked extensively with DATs, PCTs, Housing Associations, criminal justice agencies and local authorities in developing and providing services. His main research interests are alcohol and drug issues, multiple needs, and multi-agency working.

Jacki Tapley is a Senior Lecturer at the Institute of Criminal Justice Studies at the University of Portsmouth. Her main research interests lie in victimology and the role of victims in the criminal justice system. Prior to joining the Institute, Jacki worked as a probation officer in Dorset. She has retained her links with Dorset and is a member of the Dorset Criminal Justice Board Consultative Committee and has undertaken research on the Board's behalf to assist in the development of local services for victims and witnesses. She is currently involved in collaborative research with academics from the United States and Australia focusing on young people's attitudes towards domestic violence and the current development of domestic violence legislation.

Jane Winstone is a former probation officer currently working as a Principal Lecturer at the Institute of Criminal Justice Studies at the University of Portsmouth leading the programme for the delivery of the probation officer qualification. Her main research interest lies in youth penology and she is currently evaluating delivery strategies in a young offender institution. Her long-standing involvement in community justice had led to a specific interest in mentally disordered offenders.

Chapter I

Community justice: the smell of fresh bread

Francis Pakes and Jane Winstone

> I am passionate about tackling anti-social behaviour in our
> communities. It is about respect for other people. It's about
> decency. It's about hardworking families who play by the rules
> not suffering from those that don't. It's everything that strong
> communities should stand for, protecting the vulnerable, sticking
> up for what is right.

These are the words of Tony Blair in a speech delivered on 28 October
2004. 'Community' is without doubt one of New Labour's most prolific
buzzwords, and unsurprisingly it has attracted a good deal of academic
interest. The term community features in the title of many a recent book
on criminal justice policy in the New Labour Era, including Crawford's
Crime Prevention and Community Safety (1999), Matthews and Pitts's (2001)
Crime, Disorder and Community Safety, as well as *Crime Control and
Community*, edited by Hughes and Edwards (2002). In addition, there is
the collection edited by Bottoms, Gelsthorpe and Rex on *Community
Penalties* from 2001. There is no doubt that in both policy and in academic
circles, community is the place to be.

This book arguably boarded the same bandwagon as it carries
'community justice' as its title and was beset by the same difficulty: that
community justice is hardly less vaguely defined than its even more
fashionable cousin, community safety. To us, community justice
comprises working with offenders, crime prevention, community safety
as well as working with victims and vulnerable groups. In addition, it is
also about revisiting the concept of 'justice' and exploring whether the

current arrangements can or will deliver community justice for some or all sections of what we understand to be 'community'.

The problem with the term, as with many other community buzzwords, is that it is part aspirational, part symbolic. Separating the wheat from the chaff is therefore no mean feat. Clear and Karp (1999) are clear about the value of the ideal of community justice. They argue that community justice is primarily about restoring the damage to victim and community rather than about punishing offenders. This vision is closely aligned to restorative justice. The ideal type represents a localized form of justice that supports effective and communicative communities whose propensities for self-governance are harnessed. Working in partnership is vital and so is the inclusion of schools and civic and religious organizations in enhancing community cohesion and informal social control (Clear and Karp 1999, 2000). Being both cohesive and inclusive, these communities are yearning to be empowered by the state to be involved with justice proper. Their sense of justice is one that centres on rehabilitation, in putting right the wrongs of the crime and the damage it inflicted on victim and community, and by bettering the offender in order to prevent re-offending. The ideal community fits the ideal of community justice, but suffers from the caveat that communities, by their very nature are both inclusive and exclusive, a point to which we return later.

The principles of community justice have been outlined as follows. First, the community is the ultimate consumer of criminal justice. Rather than offenders, or even victims, it is communities that the system ought to serve. Second, community justice is achieved in partnership at a local level. Third, it is problem focused: problems are addressed rather than cases processed. The extent to which these principles actually inform practice in Britain, or anywhere else for that matter, is highly debatable. At this point it is as inevitable as it is a cliché to lament the politicalization of the field of community justice. There is indeed an oft-noted disparity between the imagination and positive energy associated with community justice and the administrative 'one size fits all' reality of local implementations.

Deconstructing community

The symbolism associated with usage of the term 'community' is pervasive and widespread. To take a rather obvious example, the controversial Anti-Social Behaviour Act 2003 is filled to the brim with references to communities. The government's anti-social behaviour plan that carries the slogan 'Putting communities first' was published in November 2003 under the title *Together Tackling Anti-Social Behaviour*. It contains 99 references to community and communities. In his foreword, then Home Secretary David Blunkett used the term no less than ten times in a piece that is no more than 600 words long – few sentences, let alone paragraphs, have no reference to community in some shape or form.

There is something immensely compelling about the term community. It is associated with a naive immersion in togetherness: as it were, primitive man sitting round a fire after a successful hunt, what Rosenberg calls a 'warm circle' (in Bauman 2001: 10). Bauman emphasizes the naturalness of community as a self-explanatory state of belonging, of knowing to be surrounded by like-minded people. As social animals, being part of one all-embracing community appears to be our Garden of Eden. It is something we like to think we once had and we are forever trying to get it back.

Community is possibly the most native of social arrangements (Bauman 2001). In today's society, the fact that community is so often talked about is possibly a sign of trouble. 'Never was the word community used more indiscriminately and emptily than in the decades when communities in the sociological sense became hard to find in real life' (Hobsbawm 1994: 428). Communities are not what they used to be, or at least not how we collectively like to remember them.

What constitutes the essence of community? Redfield (1971) lists three criteria. The first is distinctiveness. The archetypal community is clearly set apart from others. It is clear who is included and who is not and its boundaries are beyond question, understood by both members and non-members. Second, the essential community is small; all members know each other and are often in each other's sight. Ontologically, the difference between 'us' and 'them' is that you are familiar with the sight of the members of your own community whereas the rest of the world is a stranger. Communication among insiders is all-embracing whereas interactions with others are scarce and superficial. The third defining feature is self-sufficiency. The community does not really need the outside world; at once there is pristine unity and splendid isolation (Redfield 1971). It can be added that communities provide a 'cradle to grave' sense of belonging. A further characteristic of such archetypal communities would be their self-governance. All of this, of course, harks back to Durkheim's conception of *mechanical solidarity* (cited in Giddens 1971), which is a form of social cohesion where people live and work within a tightly constrained radius and where roles, values and beliefs are prescribed and adhered to throughout the generations.

3

The problem, as Durkheim was the first to recognize, is that we no longer live in a mechanical-type society. We inhabit a society where difference, not similarity, is the distinguishing factor, which Durkheim labelled *organic solidarity*. This presupposes that social cohesion arises not from the acceptance of a common set of beliefs and sentiments, but from a complex system of interdependence which recognizes the pursuit of individual goals, provided they are legitimate and socially sanctioned. The modern technological world requires a fragmentation of living and working arrangements; concepts of family, that cornerstone of community, have undergone radical changes as the demands of modern living have restructured values, roles, ideals and economic arrangements. Unity and togetherness are no longer a 'given' commodity of social life; they need to be worked at, harnessed, cherished and protected. We are all members of all sorts of diluted communities that with varying levels of success try to fulfil our need to belong. Communities, so indiscriminately alluded to in political rhetoric, come in any number of shapes and sizes, a notion understated in the field of criminal justice policy:

> The need to 'define' or 'profile' communities is often regarded by practitioners to be a luxury which has little relevance to doing their jobs. Yet, many efforts to galvanise, develop and work with 'the community' end in failure precisely because this has not been done. The challenges facing high crime neighbourhoods, their connections with globalisation and other broader socio-economic change (for example with increasing individualism and changing patterns of trust), the competing interests and demands among different groups of people, the fact that different localities have different 'community careers' (Bottoms and Wiles 1986) and characteristics, and diverse, different and often competing needs which eschew the often formulaic and standardised agency approaches – is rarely understood by practitioners. (Foster 2002: 175)

Running the risk of identifying discursive types of community to death, we can distinguish the following types of late modern communities.

First there is the idea of community that represents a nostalgic indulgence. It refers to the spurious memory of a community that never was and typically represents an idealized version of our parents' or grandparents' time, using phrases such as, 'During the war we all stood together', and 'Nobody locked their houses when I was young'. Young notes that the feeling of 'paradise lost' seems ubiquitous:

Politicians of all persuasions, from social democrats to conservatives, share a preoccupation with the notion of returning to the past, or rekindling the half-warm memories of family, work and community. (Young 1999: 49)

Although widespread throughout Western civilization, there is something particularly British about how deep this notion has permeated popular discourse. Television was, allegedly, much better 30 years ago, and so were trains, teachers, and grandma's cakes. Often forgotten are the hardships, insecurities and worries of the time.

The second type is the oft-bemoaned divided community. We reserve this term for communities occupied by members of a limited set of mutually exclusive groups. Cohesion within these groups might be high, but interactions between the groups are shallow and often hostile. The division often occurs along religious lines where, say, Protestants and Catholics live side by side but lead by and large separated lives. These communities are multi-level: there is hardly a community at all as such, given that the different groups frequent their own religious, social and cultural institutions whilst failing to engage meaningfully with each other. At the same time, however, enclaves might be thriving, and the mere presence of 'outsiders' within the community boundaries might serve to increase members' sense of belonging within their group as both in-group and out-group sentiments are likely to be enhanced (Hogg and Abrams 1988). This can be understood as the 'siege mentality'; community spirit is only apparent when the members perceive themselves to be threatened by a hostile outside force. We see this in the current focus upon fear of crime and anti-social behaviour, which is used as a device to engender community spirit where none apparently existed before.

More indicative of the post-modern era are disintegrated communities in which cohesion does not really extend beyond the front door. These are the communities to which the maxim 'There is no such thing as community' applies best. People in these typically urban neighbourhoods tend to have a wide variety of backgrounds and the population tends to be young and transient. When policy-makers refer to 'our communities' they do not tend to have these in mind.

Gated communities tend to be in affluent neighbourhoods and have sharply defined physical boundaries. They are also called propriety communities as they are often set on private land. These communities tend to have private security arrangements in place, such as CCTV and access restrictions, and are also characterized by low crime rates and high levels of fear. Such communities offer the possibility for a more extreme form of stratification: 'us' and 'them' defined by the power literally to buy into such schemes. Having said that, it has been alleged that the sense of belonging within such communities is not particularly high: members feel more bound by the legal than by the social contract (Blakely and Snyder 1999). Davis (1990) also emphasizes the need felt by the middle classes to be insulated, both spatially and socially, from underclass undesirables. Urban planning and city design are increasingly geared to keep the underclass, and the disorder they are feared to inflict, out of sight of the middle classes.

Policy-makers also tend not to refer to virtual or otherwise despatialized communities. Increasingly, internet-based groups engage in interactions that give rise to what we might call communities. Distance-learning students engage with each other and their course via online learning centres. Chess aficionados play in online leagues and tournaments and first-time mothers share experiences via chat-rooms and user groups. Community no longer requires proximity.

It is worth mentioning the phrase 'communities of choice'. We might decide to send our children to public school, to become a school governor or to take part in the organization of a local five-a-side league, the reward of such actions being admission into a social structure that, as long as it is defined loosely enough, constitutes a community. Belonging is increasingly optional and our wish to become immersed in a social entity with its inevitable code of conduct and formal or informal social control, is offset against the demands that the community might place on us and the freedom that will be lost as a result. Of course, the luxury of choice is primarily reserved for the more affluent cushioned by an economic comfort zone; evicted tenants and excluded pupils will find the issue of choice by and large an anathema.

These are obviously crude descriptions: few would recognize their neighbourhood in any of these discursive community types. The fact remains that the use of the term community is simply over-stretched to the point that it hardly serves any purpose at all. It is like a supermarket spreading the smell of fresh bread throughout their store: it is a 'feel-good' factor, hinting at the way things used to be when the world was smaller and less bewildering.

Community justice and community spirit

The enthusiasm for anything with 'community' added to it is exemplified by the reception of New York City's so-called community courts. The Red Hook Community Justice Center was launched in Brooklyn in 2000. Since then, a number of similar courts have been established throughout the USA. The idea is that a single locus exists that serves as the hub for a variety of community justice efforts. A single-sitting judge can hear family, civil or criminal cases concerned with what are often termed 'quality of life' crimes. Solutions include mediation, restitution and community service orders with drug training and education programmes also available. Part of the Center is an unconventional youth court. Youths receive about 30 hours of training to serve as either judge, juror or prosecuting attorney, and they gain school credits for their participation. It is described as a true jury of peers, but it must be emphasized that this Youth Court deals with only about 100 minor cases a year and invariably when the guilt of the person is not at issue. At present it is too early to say whether such community centers represent a new level of the institutionalization of community justice. It is, however, safe to say that the idea appeals: after the marketing successes of zero tolerance policing (Pakes 2004), it seems that New York City has again produced a winner. In the time-honoured tradition of US/UK strategic harmonization, Liverpool is already piloting a community justice centre based on the Red Hook example.

Another idea from the United States that has been enthusiastically received, at least by the former Home Secretary David Blunkett, is that of community prosecution. Community prosecution represents a shift of perspective away from prosecuting officials being primarily reactive servants of the court, and towards them becoming proactive servants of communities (Etheridge 2003). It might involve assigning prosecuting officials to specific areas, or schools. It also might involve giving community leaders a say in sentencing, or the furtherance of community impact statements being heard in court.

Few would dispute that when it comes to effective crime reduction strategies, the local level is usually their natural habitat. However, they need to be informed by the reality that communities are likely to be composed of 'lightly engaged strangers' (Hancock and Matthews 2001: 110). The suspicion is that policy is based on an assumption of what communities are like, rather than on what actually happens in neighbourhoods up and down the country.

So what is the state of Britain's communities today? To what extent are neighbourhoods actually classifiable as communities? The Home Office Citizenship Survey allows us at least a glimpse of how matters stand (Muntan and Zurawan 2004). The survey looks at levels of civic participation, such as contacting a local councillor or attending a public meeting, informal volunteering (giving unpaid help to non-family members) and formal volunteering (giving unpaid help through groups, clubs or organizations). Whereas only a small minority (3 per cent) are actually involved in civic participatory activities, 37 per cent indicated that at least once a month they were engaged in informal volunteering, for example giving advice, looking after property or pets, transporting people, babysitting, cooking, cleaning, or shopping. Formal volunteering is done by 28 per cent and tends to concern education, sports and exercise, religion, hobbies and social clubs.

The report also looks at the relation between relative deprivation (at area level) and active community participation, which is the amalgamation of civic participation, informal and formal volunteering. At first sight there appears to be no relation between civic participation and relative deprivation. Similarly, in the sphere of informal volunteering, the differences between the most and least deprived areas are only moderate. If these data can serve as a measure for social cohesion (although they seem to be too general to do that convincingly), then the most deprived areas are hardly distinguishable on these indicators. A substantial difference, however, occurs with formal volunteering, where a difference of 15 percentage points was found between the least and most deprived areas.

The idea of working-class communities in which people 'look after each other' in a way lost by society's higher echelons is not confirmed by these data. Nor does it confirm the notion of deprived areas as hostile barren lands in which it is everyone for themselves. In terms of social cohesion, it would almost seem as if the rich and the poor have it in more or less equal amounts. Foster (2002) has indeed argued that in seemingly defeated and highly disorganized neighbourhoods there are often well established and understood mechanisms of social organization, in which networks of criminal activity might be embedded, challenging the assumption that crime always sides with disorder, and once more demonstrating that offenders and victims are never wholly separate entities.

It is arguable that these survey data give additional support for what Hancock and Matthews (2001) claim is evidence that people in communities do not merely pass in the night, but that some level of community-oriented activity is at least reasonably widespread. However, the suggestion that many urban areas consist mainly of relative strangers is likely to be remain unchallenged. You may not know your neighbour's name or even face but you might write to your MP, sign a petition, or water the plants of a colleague who lives down the road. It offers no evidence to back up Blunkett's idea of close-knit homogeneous communities of law-abiding citizens, sick to the back teeth of the rotten apples in their midst. It only shows that there is some degree of community spirit within a broad locality. Reports of the death of community are, therefore, obviously exaggerated. The survey, however, hardly allows us to assess it as having a good bill of health.

The Active Communities survey particularly looks at the 'us' part of the community equation. Jock Young (1999) is particularly concerned with what community does to outsiders. After all, community cohesion is greatly served by the exclusion of outcasts. This exclusion is usually physical and the preferred arrangement is simply not to have criminals, vandals, witches and monsters among us. Young refers to the establishment of a 'cordon sanitaire' (Young 1999) around communities that serves as a protective layer, keeping out the riff-raff and conveniently ignoring the fact that most individuals are more likely to be abused, beaten or killed by someone who is familiar than by a stranger.

The usage of the term community becomes altogether more sinister when its powers of exclusion are considered. As an example of how the community discourse increases the leverage on keeping outcasts at bay we look at two measures to tackle anti-social behaviour. These are dispersal orders and Anti-Social Behaviour Orders (ASBOs). Dispersal orders can be given in areas designated by a senior police officer for a period of six months when there are reasonable grounds to believe that members of the public have been intimidated, harassed, alarmed or distressed as a result of the presence or behaviour of groups of two or more persons in public places, and that anti-social behaviour is a significant and persistent problem in the relevant locality. Such a designation gives police officers additional powers. They may disperse any group, and direct people in any group to leave the area, as long as they do not live there, and to not return with 24 hours. The penalties for not complying can be a stiff fine (up to £5,000 pounds), or a maximum of three months' imprisonment (Anti-Social Behaviour Act 2003).

It will be interesting to see, from the research that will emerge, who it is that is dispersed and where they are dispersed from and to. It is potentially an excellent tool to protect middle-class areas from trouble overflowing from nearby estates. Anti-Social Behaviour Orders (ASBOs) have similarly increased the significance of the 'where' of anti-social behaviour. As is the case with dispersal orders, the criteria to be fulfilled in order to be eligible for ASBOs are defined with, as Foot called it, 'frightening vagueness' (Foot 2004). ASBOs typically forbid the recipient from exhibiting certain behaviours, such as vandalism, racist abuse or fare-dodging. Alternatively, or in conjunction, they can forbid the recipient from entering certain geographic areas, such as a shopping centre or a high street. Breach of an order is punishable with up to five years' imprisonment in the case of adults and up to two years' detention for juveniles.

9

The year 2004 saw a proliferation of imposed constraints on the freedom of the ASBO-ed: youths have been banned from city centres during school holidays; prostitutes have been forbidden to carry condoms; alcoholics have been ordered not to drink; an 11-year-old from Bradford cannot venture further than his own street (Wainwright 2004). There was also the headline-grabbing case of the farmer who got ASBO-ed for failing to control his pigs (Coates 2004). ASBOs and dispersal orders embody the power of exclusion, an issue about which NAPO has expressed concern (NAPO 2004, Fletcher 2005). That they are carried out with endless references to 'our communities' is telling, as what these measures tend to do is prevent the re-occurrence of incidents in places where communities have the social power to have the system work for them – instead of making sure that certain behaviours do not occur in the first place.

The contents of this book

This book examines community justice is its various guises. In its approach it takes the perspective of various criminal justice agencies, with particular focus on police and probation, as well as the perspective of a number of relevant groups within the criminal justice process, such as mentally disordered offenders, and victims. In addition, the role of non-criminal justice bodies such as schools, and non-statutory bodies such as faith-based organizations is also addressed. Several chapters deal with the newly established National Offender Management Service that is set to significantly alter the landscape in which community justice operates. Although NOMS is still at present in the process of finding its feet, several contributors discuss its possible or probable impact on community justice in England and Wales in the near future.

The early chapters explore the broad frameworks which inform community justice and current delivery arrangements. Chapter 2 outlines the politics of risk in relation to criminal justice and probation. Mike Nash sets out the political contexts in which risk assessment takes place and the near impossible demands being placed on probation in general and the probation practitioner in particular. Chapter 3 explores the values informing community justice and Mike Nellis debates whether a humanistic approach to criminal justice is disappearing along with the establishment of NOMS. He argues that 'punitive-repressive' or 'manage-rial-surveillant' versions of community justice may claim adherence to humanistic values whilst at the same time subverting their substance;

and that whilst informed by genuine moral deliberation, its parameters are too narrow to embrace humanistic considerations.

Chapter 4 considers how community justice has evolved from the perspective of the police. Robin Fletcher presents a historical overview of the ever-changing core roles of the police service, and outlines the current positioning of crime prevention and community safety within the police service and in relation to multi-agency arrangements. Chapter 5 focuses in greater depth on multi-agency crime reduction partnerships. Barry Loveday explores their genesis and functioning, in particular in relation to the role of the police within such frameworks. Issues such as differential levels of commitment to the partnership and the snag of non-coterminous boundaries are outlined and discussed. In another form of multi-agency arrangement, the political drive to establish seamless sentencing is discussed in Chapter 6, where Dennis Gough analyses the impact of the emergence of NOMS as the umbrella arrangement within which custodial and community sentences will be delivered in accordance with the Criminal Justice Act 2003. He assesses its likely effect upon probation work, as well as on probation culture and professional practice in working with offenders. Chapter 7 highlights the role of the Home Office in the delivery of community justice. Chris Lewis reviews the research base that has informed current strategies and the changing perspectives of the Home Office between 1995 and the present day with regard to What Works and other key initiatives.

From here the concern of the book turns to specific groups and the ways in which community justice can, is or will be implemented through voluntary and statutory agencies, policies and legislation. In Chapter 8, Aaron Pycroft debates the role of multi-agency work in dealing with people with multiple needs and in particular the work of faith-based organizations with regard to drug problems. In Chapter 9 Carol Hayden examines the role and potential of schools with regard to crime prevention, the links between educational factors and crime and the relationship between schools and the communities in which they are set. This highlights both the potential of schools to promote positive early experiences, which can act as protective factors for vulnerable young people but also the gap between these aspirations and the reality of deprivation which prevents individuals from an early age establishing a pro-social lifestyle. Chapter 10 specifically focuses on Anti-Social Behaviour and its impact on various groups. Ruth Hatcher and Clive Hollin outline issues of definition, measurement and the range of newly established measures in place to tackle it. Chapter 11 is concerned with youth justice. Nikki McKenzie examines the youth justice system and explores the current demonization of offending youngsters and the 'social construction of youth' in general. She considers the implementation of restorative justice, including referral orders, and presents some positive results, despite some of the anomalies of the ASBO. Chapter 12 has a focus on hate crime. Nathan Hall analyses the legislation in place to combat hate crime and the effectiveness or otherwise of probation programmes in working with hate offenders. In addition, he presents a typology of hate offenders and argues for probation workers to be better equipped to recognize and tackle hate within a wider range of offenders, rather than exclusively those labelled hate offenders by the courts. Chapter 13 targets another group that pose a particular challenge to criminal justice practitioners: mentally disordered offenders. Jane Winstone and Francis Pakes assess the position of mentally disordered offenders within criminal justice and conclude that the Mental Health Bill 2004 has little to offer to reduce the marginalization and negative stereotyping of this already disenfranchised group. Chapter 14 explores the role of victims in the criminal justice process. Jacki Tapley examines the measures put in place to achieve higher levels of confidence in the justice process as experienced by victims and looks at how political rhetoric relates to practical results.

Despite some of the pessimism expressed by previous authors, in Chapter 15 a positive note is sounded by James McGuire, who addresses the current state of provision for justice in the community for offenders, critically revisiting recent debates and re-positioning these in terms of the What Works delivery. The book concludes by offering an alternative perspective on community justice, as Miranda Boone analyses the transformation of the probation service in the Netherlands, a development with particular relevance to the UK in Chapter 16.

The state of community justice

As the contents of this book will demonstrate, community justice is part substance, part spin. Jacki Tapley, Nikki McKenzie and James McGuire describe developments that are encouraging, whilst Aaron Pycroft envisages a twenty-first century revival of the role of non-statutory agencies in the rehabilitative effort. Criminal justice is shown to be increasingly sensitive to the needs of various 'consumer groups' and has become increasingly concerned with recognizing vulnerability and treating it appropriately. On the other hand, contributors such as Nellis (Chapter 3), Winstone and Pakes (Chapter 13) and Loveday (Chapter 5), among others, list practical and, worse, principled problems with the current approaches taken. Not all is well in the world of community justice, and without doubt the strength of rhetoric promoting community justice is rather far removed from the reality of practice in the real world, probably nowhere more so than in the area of probation, as Mike Nash and Dennis Gough argue.

Achieving community justice in more than a token fashion is a daunting task. In this regard it is important to highlight the state of flux that has overcome the area. Whereas the pace of change in criminal justice policy has increased over several decades, New Labour probably hold the dubious honour of setting new standards here, passing more legislation in this field than any other previous government – from the Crime and Disorder Act 1998 to the Anti-Social Behaviour Act 2003, and with the Mental Health Act and the Management of Offenders Act quite possibly in the pipeline. Certainly the foreshadow of the latter has placed the world of probation in a state of limbo (Carter 2003), with its future particularly uncertain. The plethora of legislation over the past 12 years has inevitably created significant organizational change for the implementation of community justice, which has required revised philosophies, aims, structures and working styles. These have already posed quite overwhelming challenges for the system, which is still reeling from their ongoing impact. It now faces continued uncertainty as to its future shape, especially under NOMS. Retaining the motivation and support of the professionals will be the real challenge to Martin Narey, currently heading the initiative.

When it comes to delivering community justice, it is the people working in a professional, support or voluntary capacity who are affected; such radical changes without extensive prior consultation are likely to paralyse rather than empower the workforce. It also legitimizes a certain degree of pessimism: 'We will not know what will happen to community justice at this juncture, but we are sure it will not be good.'

As this book makes perfectly clear, there are many hurdles to overcome, particularly in a current political context where the fight against terror often overtakes local concerns, and where fear of crime easily gets divorced from risk of victimization *per se*. On the other hand, we need to stress that in the mosaic of agencies, platforms, partnerships and the like, positive messages do exist and need to be brought to the fore. Whereas the term 'community justice' is easily dismissed as New Labour's flavour of the month, the progress made under its umbrella in some areas (but, admittedly, not in all) is still something worth shouting about.

References

Bauman, Z. (2001) *Community: Seeking Safety in an Insecure World*. Cambridge: Polity Press.
Blair, T. (2004) Speech on Anti-Social Behaviour. Available online: *http://www.number10.gov.uk/output/Page6492.asp*.
Blakely, E.J. and Snyder, M.G. (1999) *Fortress America: Gated Communities in the United States*. Washington DC: Brookings Institution Press.
Blunkett, D. (2003) *Criminal Justice and the Community*. Paper given at Criminal Justice – Serving the Community, 7 July 2003.
Bottoms, A., Gelsthorpe, L. and Rex, S. (eds) (2001) *Community Penalties: Change and Challenges*. Cullompton: Willan.
Bottoms, A. and Wiles, P. (1986) 'Housing Tenure and Residential Community Crime Careers in Britain', in A. J. Reiss and M. Tonry (eds), *Communities and Crime*. Chicago: University of Chicago Press.
Carter, P. (2003) *Managing Offenders, Reducing Crime: A New Approach*. London: Home Office.
Clear, T.R. and Karp, D.R. (1999) *The Community Justice Ideal: Preventing Crime and Achieving Justice*. Boulder, CO: Westview Press.
Clear, T.R. and Karp, D.R. (2000) 'Toward the ideal of community justice', *NIJ Journal*, October: 20–29.
Coates, S. (2004) 'Pig owner hopes fence will save his bacon', *The Times*, 16 December 2004.
Crawford, A. (1998) *Crime Prevention and Community Safety: Politics, Policies and Practices*. Harrow: Longman.
Davis, M. (1990) *City of Quartz: Excavating the Future of Los Angeles*. London: Vintage.
Etheridge, J. (2003) *Community Justice in Action: The Baltimore City Pilot Programme*. Paper given at Criminal Justice – Serving the Community, 7 July 2003.
Fletcher, H. (2005) 'ASBOs – yet more powers', *NAPO News*, January, 165: 5.
Foot, M. (2004) 'ASBO Absurdities', *Guardian*, 1 December 2004.
Foster, J. (2002) 'People Pieces: The Neglected but Essential Elements of Community Prevention', in G. Hughes and A. Edwards (eds) *Crime Control and Community: The New Politics of Public Safety*. Cullompton: Willan, pp. 167–196.
Giddens, A. (1971) *Capitalism and Modern Social Theory: An Analysis of the Writings of Marx, Durkheim and Max Weber*. Cambridge: Cambridge University Press.
Hancock, L. and Matthews, R. (2001) 'Crime, Community Safety and Toleration', in F. Matthews and J. Pitts (eds) (2001) *Crime, Disorder and Community Safety*. London: Routlege, pp. 98–119.
Hobsbawm, E. (1994) *The Age of Extremes*. London: Michael Joseph.
Hogg, M.A. and Abrams, D. (1988) *Social Identifications: A Social Psychology of Intergroup Relations and Group Processes*. London: Routledge.
Hughes, G. (2002) 'Plotting the Rise of Community Safety: Critical Reflections on Research, Theory and Politics', in G. Hughes and A. Edwards (eds) (2002) *Crime Control and Community: The New Politics of Public Safety*. Cullompton: Willan, pp. 20–45.
Hughes, G. and Edwards, A. (eds) (2002) *Crime Control and Community: The New Politics of Public Safety*. Cullompton: Willan.
Matravers, A. (2003) *Sex Offenders in the Community: Managing and Reducing the Risks*. Cullompton: Willan.

Matthews, F. and Pitts, J. (eds) (2001) *Crime, Disorder and Community Safety*. London: Routledge.

Muntan, T. and Zurawan, A. (2004) *Active Communities: Headline Findings from the 2003 Home Office Citizenship Survey*. London: HMSO.

NAPO newsletter (2004) NAPO News, 1 October 2004, p. 12.

Pakes, F. (2004) *Comparative Criminal Justice*. Cullompton: Willan.

Redfield, R. (1971) *The Little Community*. Chicago: University of Chicago Press.

Wainwright, M. (2004) '11 year old confined to his own street', *Guardian*, 7 December 2004.

Young, J. (1999) *The Exclusive Society*. London: Sage.

Chapter 2

The probation service, public protection and dangerous offenders

Mike Nash

Late or post-modern society is characterized by 'risk' (Giddens 1990, Hudson 2001, 2003, Kemshall 2003). Societies are concerned with risk (or more accurately *increased* risk) because they believe that they lack the controls they once had over their lives. To a certain extent, the unexpected and unanticipated, in an age when we *think* we should have greater control, takes people back to a pre-modern form of existence where natural disasters and threats determined the parameters of risk. For example, in late summer 2004 a sudden river surge almost destroyed the Cornish coastal village of Boscastle. People felt powerless in the face of nature. Yet the paradox is that the sudden upturn in the scale and frequency of natural disasters would at least in part appear to be triggered by the 'advancement' of society and its outcomes, that is, global warming. Therefore, this sense of insecurity and risk is fuelled by a belief that events are beyond control, framed by a context where they *should* be in control.

Similar arguments can be deployed in thinking about the war on terror waged by President Bush in the United States. The world's most powerful nation is unable to offer its citizens the sense of safety and security they demand, and indeed are promised. The fragmentation of modern society, the decline of the nuclear family, the break-up of traditional communities all fuel the sense that the range and diversity of risk is increasing. In such a climate people seek guarantees, or at least promises, that these threats will be met and challenged, and that they will be reduced. The greater the sense of insecurity, the louder the demand for safety measures to be imposed. Governments of all hues respond to this public voice across the world, and the assessment and management of risk becomes a central feature of political life.

This wider sense of insecurity relating to global issues therefore impacts upon everyday matters such as fear of crime. As we will explain below, certain crimes and criminals promote an almost irrational fear and anxiety, way beyond the realistic risk posed to the public. Yet the media in particular focus on the spectacular and unusual, giving the impression that rare crimes are far more common than they are, and the chances of being victimized much greater than 'in the past' (but see Pearson 1983 for a discussion on recurring fears and visions of a previous golden age). However, just as governments have to respond to global risks, even though they are often powerless to do anything, so must criminal justice agencies respond to crime concerns. In so doing they become drawn into the same guarantee business as their political leaders. Risk management has thus become a core and overriding function for criminal justice agencies. Nevertheless, just as governments cannot prevent a natural disaster, so criminal justice agencies cannot prevent a recurrence of serious offending. They can only put in place measures that might help to manage the risk, to make it in essence seemingly more predictable. They need to try to anticipate behaviour that may well defy systematic assessment and prediction. The other side of the risk coin is blame – fail to predict or manage the risk and you will be blamed for getting it wrong. In such a climate it is easy to see that practitioners will seek all the assistance they can to 'get it right', even though getting it right with unpredictable offenders is a near impossible task.

It is clear that a climate of fear and insecurity will alter the way in which criminal justice practitioners work on a daily basis. This change in direction has probably been greater for the probation service than any other organization in the sector. Their concern with risk shifts its focus on the offender from one of rehabilitation to one of management and control (Hudson 2001). The process of managing risk becomes therefore a dominant feature of everyday practice. In probation terms this would include risk of re-offending (any offence) to the risk of repetition of serious and dangerous behaviour. The concern for those practitioners might be that the dominance of the risk agenda pervades all else, and even less serious offences become conflated into the global concerns of risk and insecurity.

This chapter will explore how concerns with risk and dangerousness have come to dominate probation practice and determined the ways in which probation officers work with other professionals. Fundamental to this consideration is the importance of context to practice. The context outlined above may appear to be a long way from the daily work of the probation officer. Yet working with risk and dangerousness has made probation practice more visible than ever and it is visible within a context that arouses great public anxiety. Therefore the risks associated with failure in probation practice are much greater than in a previous existence, when probation work was secretive and something of a mystery to the wider public.

Politics and risk

The growing concerns of the probation service with risk and dangerousness coincide with the politicization of this issue since the early 1990s. This period saw 'law and order' issues become a significant battleground between the major political parties in the UK, and indeed across much of the western world (Dunbar and Langdon 1998). It was the decision of the Labour Party under Tony Blair to re-invent itself as a hard-line party on crime which really forced the issue. As Labour and Conservative politicians sought to put distance between them, a general concern with crime and criminal justice steadily focused down to major concerns with serious and dangerous offenders, notably predatory paedophiles. Despite a lack of any real evidence that either the numbers of these offenders were growing, or that existing systems for managing them were failing, the media seized upon the issue. It did so at a time when political parties were parading their tough credentials, anxious to appease the press. Little was done to represent the real nature of the risk to an increasingly aware and concerned public.

Both government and opposition could therefore be accused of being complicit in inflating this issue for political ends. Dangerousness and the response to it was rapidly becoming a political football. The increased focus on serious and dangerous offenders is evident in a series of legislative and policy developments throughout the 1990s (from the 1991 Criminal Justice Act through to the 1998 Crime and Disorder Act via the Sex Offenders Act 1997). However, these efforts to toughen the response against a very small minority of offenders were to have much wider repercussions. The new response to dangerousness *was different* from previous patterns of working and to facilitate this a cultural shift was required. In enabling this cultural shift, the likelihood is that the organization's total response to offenders will also need to change. As we shall see below, this can mean a reconfiguration of approach and attitude, as well as of ethos and values. The avoidance of failure, which would increasingly be a public failure, therefore becomes very important to the organization.

The hardening of the political context meant that agencies within the criminal justice sector, especially traditionally 'soft' organizations such as the probation service, had to respond to the tough new regime. This process was not, however, an overnight one. Since the return of Margaret Thatcher as prime minister in 1979, the traditional ethos of the probation service has been under threat. That ethos, which had viewed offenders as themselves victims of a range of negative factors, was to become deeply unfashionable. The new right, both in the UK and the USA, were unsympathetic to offenders and increasingly uninterested in *explanations* for offending behaviour; they were more concerned with *condemnation*, increasingly less interested in evidence and more concerned with populism (Savage and Nash 1994).

For the probation service this had to mean a significant shift to the way in which it approached its work with offenders – if it was to maintain its position as a key criminal justice agency. A working style that sought to change behaviour in a non-condemnatory style, in which a degree of forgiveness and tolerance were present, was unlikely to survive in an atmosphere in which offenders were seen to be to blame for their actions. If the probation service were to survive in an increasingly hostile and punitive atmosphere it was likely that it would have to assume at least the language, if not the practice, of the 'new penology' (Feeley and Simon 1992). Its reluctance to engage in wholesale opposition to the changes proposed by the government suggested that organizational survival would be an increasing concern (Nash and Ryan 2003).

In practical terms, the legislative and policy changes were beginning to impact upon the daily practice of probation officers. National Standards, introduced by the 1991 Criminal Justice Act (CJA), were revised during the 1990s to further restrict the professional discretion of probation officers (Home Office 1995a). It could be argued that these standards were as much about sending out a new public message concerning the work of the probation service as it was about *improving* that work.

It must be remembered that the 1990s were a period in which the political stakes, particularly in law and order, were constantly being raised. Alternative agendas to that dominating the political field were unlikely to be acceptable to the government or the media. As such the victim increasingly assumed centre stage and, perhaps more importantly, certain types of victim rose to prominence. These 'deserving' victims were 'innocent' children, at risk from sex fiends and monsters – offenders who deserved no public sympathy at all! As Worrall (1997) indicates, the probation service had quietly and effectively worked with sex offenders for a number of years, but in the new climate their style of working was not restrictive or controlling enough. The change being visited upon the probation service might then have had more to do with symbolism than with major concerns about its effectiveness. It may have been that its language was considered inappropriate but its results were satisfactory. It should be remembered that the work described by Worrall came from an era when measurement of effectiveness was at best haphazard. Unfortunately the new era being ushered in would leave little opportunity for the old methods to be properly evaluated. It ought to be difficult to justify change without the evidence; however, the rapidity of change suggests that once more politics wins out over experience.

Organizational survival

The probation service, as many people understood it, was undoubtedly under threat. Tougher responses to the crime problem did not sit easily with a social work response to offenders. The service itself had undoubtedly responded to government concerns, for example, chief officers produced a document in 1988 entitled *More Demanding than Prison* (ACOP 1988). The content is easily deduced from the title, with the probation service determined to prove that it could be tough in the community when supervising offenders. Yet as we have seen throughout the 1990s the stakes were constantly being raised between government and opposition parties, in essence producing constant new and tougher demands on criminal justice agencies. As noted above, this political battle eventually focused down onto the issue of dangerous offenders and predatory sex offenders in particular. This issue became so politicized that it would inevitably impact upon all criminal justice agencies, although perhaps the probation service was to experience it more than others. The upshot of the political battle was that even meeting the new targets would instantly lead to the creation of others.

As we have implied above, the development of what has become known as the risk society is closely linked with fear of crime. As fear grows, invariably fuelled by media-fed moral panics, the pressure is on the government to *do something*. However, if serious consideration is given to trying to do something about possible future events, it is not difficult to see that this is essentially an impossible task. It is not possible to predict what people might do and when they might do it. This, however, is precisely what the public expect, and therefore is something that governments have to be seen to deliver. Doing something becomes being seen to do something, and that means actions that can be demonstrated. This is where one of the major changes for probation work would be located. Whereas in the past its work with serious offenders might have been relatively secretive (although perhaps also effective; see Coker and Martin 1985, Worrall 1997), it would now have to be much more accountable. Accountability would become ever more associated with shared risk assessment, a clear public message that probation officers were taking seriously the crucial public protection task.

Surviving through collaborating

It is important to grasp the importance of being able to demonstrate publicly that tasks are being carried out and that risk is being assessed (and managed, as we shall see below). To do this, two significant developments began to unfold in the 1990s. The first was the increasing use of risk assessment tools by probation officers and other criminal justice personnel, to predict the likelihood of future serious harm. The second was the development of multi and later inter-agency working with serious and potentially dangerous offenders. We will now consider both of these developments for the probation service.

We have made clear that being seen to tackle the problem of potentially dangerous offenders was an increasing political priority throughout the 1990s. Despite any significant evidence that the problem was worsening, political parties across the world appeared keen to parade their new tough credentials to the public. In the UK, Conservative government and Labour opposition fought themselves almost to a standstill over this issue. Dunbar and Langdon (1998) describe this as a process of trying to put 'clear blue water' between the protagonists. Although essentially a political battle, the effect of it was felt throughout the criminal justice sector. The probation service in particular, having been associated with a woolly and failing welfare approach, would have to change its ways if it wished to maintain its position at the 'centre stage' promised following the 1991 Criminal Justice Act. The problem for probation officers was that their claim to professional status rested, unfortunately for them, on a social work qualification. This was increasingly seen as an inappropriate response to serious and dangerous offenders and ultimately was abandoned by the Conservative govern-ment (Home Office 1995b). In the assessment and management of risk, the essence of probation practice, the casework interview, was no longer regarded as sufficiently rigorous to demonstrate to a concerned public that all attempts were being made to protect them. The risk society demanded greater evidence, almost as if the better the process the safer the outcome.

At this time 'evidence-based' ways of working were gaining consider-able support in Canada and North America and would become the mantra of the New Labour administration from 1997 onwards. The growing influence of psychologists and statisticians gradually saw the development of a range of risk assessment tools to assist professionals assess the risk of (initially) future re-offending and (later) future serious harm (for a discussion of the range of methods used see Kemshall 2001, 2003). The importance of these risk assessment tools was that they offered an alternative to the 'subjective' clinical interview, a method increasingly discredited in political circles. By utilizing scientific method it was suggested that the assessment would be more accurate, and less likely to be influenced by professionals' subjective feelings and experience. By producing a 'score' or level of risk, offenders could be classified and grouped according to risk and in so doing risk could be 'managed'. It is easy to see that this approach would be popular with politicians. Numbers could be produced relating to those who had been assessed and then tables produced of those falling within particular categories of risk. There would be clear evidence that this problem was being dealt with.

Yet, it is clear from a whole body of academic and practice evidence that the assessment of serious and dangerous behaviour is not as easy as these 1990s messages were indicating (Scott 1977, Prins 1988). The new actuarial methods gaining ascendancy throughout probation practice were based on studies that had examined very large offender groups. These large samples were, by definition, based upon the more common offence groups in which the offenders shared a number of similar characteristics. Dangerous behaviour is, in contrast, thankfully much less common. It is defined almost by an inability to discover patterns across groups of people, indeed the opposite occurs when patterns are sought *within* the individual behaviour of serial offenders. Therefore there is an inherent risk in an over-reliance upon statistical indicators as a means of assessment for very unusual and often highly individual behaviour.

A tension can therefore be seen in the assessment of potentially dangerous behaviour. That tension is caused by an acute political context, a need or demand to demonstrate that something is 'being done' and that this demonstration can be evidenced. As a result, pseudo-scientific assessment methods gain sway as they can produce a tangible, evidence-based score. Casework methods, under attack since the early 1980s, are seen as an inadequate response to potentially dangerous offenders and therefore the probation service increasingly and eagerly signed up to the actuarial agenda. Yet as we have already noted, the probation service had enjoyed success in its work with this offender group (Coker and Martin 1985) and had a body of accumulated experience in assessing and working with risk. It had not, however, the same body of evidence to prove it. The tension, therefore, is one between proving that a rigorous approach is being undertaken and the success or otherwise of the *outcome* of that approach. There needs to be a variety of approaches and it is important that the accumulated experience of the probation service is not lost in the rush to demonstrate rigour. As Kemshall (2001) indicates, a combination of actuarial and clinical methods is the most effective way forward, yet there is a danger that the clinical or casework expertise is already being lost.

In working with potentially dangerous offenders there is an over-whelming need to be aware of the trigger factors and context in which the dangerous behaviour takes place. This can, of course, be determined by analysis of the offender's history, their documentation and interviews with them. However, it is not enough simply to identify the triggers; they need to recognized in real life and responded to. Offenders will often, consciously or unconsciously, give out signals prior to any offending behaviour. The better the relationship between offender and probation officer, the more likely that process is to happen (Coker and Martin 1985). As Prins (1988) argues, working with potentially dangerous offenders necessitates 'thinking the unthinkable and asking the unaskable'. Not everyone can do this difficult and demanding task. It is an activity that is not easily bureaucratized. Much of the traditional experience of probation officers fits this task very well and should not be lost.

This point is important as the probation service increasingly shares its work with other criminal justice agencies. The use of standardized risk assessment tools across the agencies could lead to a dilution of agency difference and potentially of agency skills. These potential scenarios are highlighted when considering the difference between multi and inter-agency working (Crawford 1998). The latter implies a degree of closeness such that the differences between agencies become blurred and the distinctiveness of agency contributions possibly lost (for a discussion see Nash 1999a, 2004, Mawby and Worrall 2004). Yet the attractiveness of sharing a very considerable burden is easily understood. Since the 1980s a familiar Home Office message has been that crime cannot be solved by one agency (usually the police) working alone. Shared working would improve communication, avoid duplication and prevent potential gaps in provision.

For some while this ambition was to prove more idealistic than realistic. For example, a report by Her Majesty's Inspector of Probation (Home Office 1995c) had revealed reluctance on the part of some chief probation officers to share their information with the police service, and indeed some police officers had voiced concern over closer working with probation (Sampson and Smith 1992: 108). This position would not continue in the face of determined government efforts to join-up criminal justice agencies (see for example the change reported by HMIP three years later (Home Office 1998). For organizations such as the police service there was a new need to work more closely with others. The Sex Offenders Act of 1997 had given them new responsibilities to assess the risk presented by sex offenders, as well as the requirement to log and monitor them on the new sex offenders' register. The police service were therefore expected to undertake a much more active role at points in the criminal justice system in which they were less familiar. For example, sex offenders previously released from custody would have been almost exclusively the responsibility of the probation service. The Sex Offenders Act 1997 changed that and made this a much more public task than it had been previously for the probation service. The police were therefore happy to look for allies and assistance. For its part, the probation service, unused as it was to public exposure, welcomed the opportunity to work more closely with an organization that continued to enjoy good levels of public support. In a blame culture it was good to have as many friends as possible.

The structure for the risk assessment and management of potentially dangerous offenders therefore evolved during the 1990s and is now virtually fully developed across the UK. The advance in risk assessment tools, constructed in such a way that they could be used across the criminal justice sector, fostered the growth in multi-agency conferences (Nash 1999b, Kemshall and Maguire 2001, Maguire *et al* 2001). Taking much from the child protection model (Stevenson 1989) a core panel evolved, and increasingly an enlarged 'other agencies' sector became involved. These conferences, variously known as high-risk offender panels, potentially dangerous offender panels or serious and high-risk panels, were all concerned with assessing risk and managing the more serious cases in the community. They were to be convened at the major 'pinch points' such as before a court appearance, before release from custody or before transfer from another area. A scarcity of resources would mean that only the highest levels of risk would receive intensive intervention (for example, police surveillance or intensive community supervision). Yet, as we have noted above, in a blame climate it is quite likely that risk would be overestimated so as to avoid getting it wrong, or conversely, underestimated as there are insufficient resources to manage large numbers of high-risk offenders (Kemshall and Maguire 2001). Furthermore, entry points into the conference process, if offence-based, would throw up very large numbers and a filtering system was clearly needed – for example recent MAPPPA reports indicate that nearly 39,500 cases are monitored by MAPPPA (*Guardian*, 8 July 2004), and of course thousands more will have been filtered out of the system, but still would have consumed resources.

There are a variety of solutions to this problem, m
existence in various forms. One would be the contin
risk assessment tools to better identify levels of pot
by Kemshall (2001, 2003), the new Offender Assess
has been developed for use across the sector ar
actuarial and clinical information. It is undoubtedly an
previous tools but is time-consuming to complete. It is evident u.
faced with large numbers and limited resources, short cuts will be take..
(Maguire *et al* 2001). Out of this refinement of the risk assessment process
has come a separation of the high-risk category to include very high-risk,
or as the Home Office has called it, 'the critical few' (numbering just over
2,100 of the total figure noted above). This is a clear attempt to isolate
those offenders most likely, according to predictions, to engage in very
serious harmful behaviour, with a degree of imminence. Such a system
does allow a concentration and focus of resources. However, it should be
remembered that to get to the position of isolating the critical few, a good
deal of assessment work would have been undertaken at an earlier stage.
The development of first and second tier meetings, and classifications
such as 'risk aware', demonstrate that agencies are having to come to
terms with devoting considerable time and energy to reassure the public
that all is being done to protect them. At the same time, that reassurance
demands levels of resources that are simply not available and of course
diverts resources from other important tasks. Equally, a lack of
performance indicators in this important area of work for the police
has suggested that a lack of resources may be forthcoming (Knock *et al*
2002).

The climate in which public protection operates is one that is
intolerant of error. The pressure generated for agencies is enormous
and any mistake, or indeed an unrelated serious event, is likely to lead to
demands for greater protection, more rigorous assessment and greater
collaboration. The truth is that protection cannot be guaranteed but
politicians are reluctant to acknowledge this simple fact. The result is that
procedures will continue to be tightened as the demands for evidence-
based action continue unabated. The media focus on the critical few and
their very unusual behaviour will undoubtedly ensure a distorted future
for the probation service.

The parallels with the insurance industry are obvious. Insurance
premiums, based upon levels of risk determined by huge data sets, are
easily upset by natural disasters. These are by definition unpredictable
and largely replicate the situation with dangerous behaviour. As we have
indicated, unusual and rare behaviour is largely determined by a very
specific context. This offending is unique to the offender and it is difficult

ad across to other offender groups. It is then similar to a natural aster. Another feature of actuarialism is that the careful majority pay or the actions of the minority who are less concerned with protecting themselves or their property. A distorted concern with potentially dangerous offenders can equally impact upon the majority who are, in this instance, so-called 'ordinary offenders'. The dominant focus upon risk assessment will affect the ways in which practitioners work with all cases – it will set the tone for an agency. One result might be that all cases become inflated in terms of their risk and seriousness with the outcome being a more controlling and punitive regime. Another could be that certain categories of offender are no longer seen as the core business of an agency; it is clear from recent public messages concerning the probation service that this is becoming the norm. Lower-risk offenders, those that tend to fill the beds in prison, are increasingly seen as the responsibility of other agencies, in particular perhaps the voluntary sector. Public protection is becoming something of an exclusive club!

Justified loss of rights?

It should of course be remembered that the whole edifice of public protection is built upon the *possibility* that something might happen in the future. It may be based upon an event, or a pattern of events in the past, but it is by definition about predicting the future. This in itself may not appear to be too problematic, but it is the consequence of being predicted potentially dangerous that is very serious. This takes us into the issue of rights. What has become known as the first dangerousness debate (for example Floud 1982, Scott 1977, Hawkins 1983) was very concerned with the issue of offender rights. The concern centred upon the justification for limiting or removing the rights of offenders for what they *might* do in the future, rather than for what they *had* done in the past. If the basis of the legal process is that offenders are punished for their crimes and once punished cannot be punished again, a restriction of rights for *potential* behaviour appeared to be an infringement of natural law. The conclusions of several of the academic studies in the first dangerousness debate were that rights were important and that what has been termed the 'pre-emptive' strike (Morris 1994: 41) is morally wrong. However, an influential study by Floud and Young (1981) spoke of the 'just distribution of risk', meaning that it was justifiable to infringe an individual's rights if their previous behaviour effectively meant that they were a significant risk to others. This view would appear to be increasingly echoed in recent legislation both in the UK and North America.

If this view is accepted, the accuracy of the predictions upon which the assessment is based is paramount. We have, however, already seen that for this particular group of offenders such accuracy is unlikely. Society therefore has to decide, if it is interested in the issue of human rights, the accuracy levels it will accept before agreeing to remove those rights from offenders. If we really do live in a risk society marked by fear and anxiety, it is likely that we will be less tolerant towards offenders and more willing to see them lose rights. Although we can in no way accurately predict future behaviour, we appear prepared to accept this if previous behaviour causes us anxiety. The greater good of the wider community wins out over the (offending) individual. For critics such as Hudson (2001) this approach is more risk control than risk management. It echoes Garland's (2001: 181) view that certain offenders, such as sex offenders, are marked for life and as such remain beyond redemption. In the United States, attempts to challenge the infringement of rights caused by dangerousness legislation through the courts have been marked by failure. Indeed, the response of the state has been to describe dangerous behaviour, especially predatory sexual offending, as resembling a contagion. In such instances, the public good wins out and the contagion is isolated. The response of the British government to the foot and mouth outbreak in 2001 suggests how far society will go to rid itself of its plagues, eliminating even the unaffected in the process. If they sign up to this kind of agenda, probation officers are almost reversing a working philosophy that once centred almost exclusively upon rehabilitation. Their focus becomes one of monitoring and control with the stated intention of managing or isolating the risk posed by the offender. As Worrall (1997) and Young (1999) indicate, they become an agent of the 'exclusive society'.

In essence there is nothing inherently wrong about this practice. However, it may be that it is the 'how' rather than the 'why' that is important. The work of probation officers, over decades, has been to build a relationship with offenders and, by various means, work with them to help change their behaviour. This has come under serious criticism from all sides. Right-wing critics argue that it is too soft and liberal, that it befriends rather than challenges offenders. Such 'friendly' relationships are too cosy and tolerant of failure. This argument lay behind at least some of the rationale to change the nature of probation officers' qualifying training (Home Office 1995b). Other critics, from the left of the political spectrum, have criticized the intrusiveness of casework relationships and their bias and subjectivity. They are said to represent state violation of many basic human rights. However, evidence continues to support the value of a good professional relationship with offenders (see, for example, Burnett 2002, Rex 1999) whereas Coker and Martin

(1985) suggested that a good and trusting relationship was effective in monitoring the warning trigger factors for potentially dangerous behaviour. We have already seen in the work of Prins (1988) that offenders will often quite deliberately give off signals in the hope that they will be prevented from re-offending. These signals have to be recognized; and indeed, the offender will perhaps show them more willingly if the relationship is built upon trust. The probation officer has traditionally been the only operative within the criminal justice system working with offenders on this basis. It is a way of working that could become lost with the growth in inter-agency working and in a results and evidence led climate that demands tangible proof of what is being done. It will be unfortunate if this skill, or even the acknowledgement of the importance of these skills, is lost.

Undoubtedly the enhanced approach to partnership and multi-agency working will improve communication and ensure the efficient deployment of resources. Process should not win out over outcome, however. A recent case highlights the risks of believing that processes and procedures alone are a guarantee of safety. In March 2004 a man was convicted at Wolverhampton Crown Court for abusing boys in a pit dug beneath his floorboards at home. He was sentenced to life imprisonment. The significance of the case for our purposes occurred during the television interview given by a senior police officer following sentence (BBC Television News, 1 March 2004). He said that the offender had been 'well supervised' under the MAPPPA arrangements. This supervision had not, however, discovered the ongoing abuse of children in the pit beneath his lounge floor. Having the most efficient process available is no doubt invaluable, but knowing the offender as well as possible is priceless! Although serious reconviction rates under MAPPPA supervised cases remains very low, at 1 per cent, there remains a case for suggesting that procedure must be underpinned by professional skills and expertise.

Assessing and managing risk has become one of, if not the, most important task undertaken by probation officers. We have indicated that it is a time-consuming, resource intensive process. It has these features because of the innate difficulty of the task itself: attempting to make certainty out of uncertainty is inordinately difficult. Yet politicians and senior managers continue to play the game that safety, or greater safety, is achievable if all agencies work together, protocols become firmer and supervision more restrictive. This is a dangerous game to play, as any failure will inevitably lead to greater controls, new legislation and probably increased restrictions on professional discretion. Politicians will inevitably chase the unachievable, but perfect safety does not exist, just as the perfect assessment, prediction, and management process does not exist. In September 2004 the Home Secretary announced that persistent offenders and paedophiles would be tracked by satellite (piloted in three English counties, *Guardian*, 2 September 2004). Making use of the latest global satellite positioning technology, David Blunkett described this tracking as a prison without bars. Probation officers would have a key role in this new surveillance society – relationships at a distance? The belief in modern technology, in the power of science, has long held sway in criminal justice. The problem remains, however, that attempting to regularize human behaviour is difficult, and to regularize very unusual or abnormal behaviour next to impossible. Mantle and Moore (2004) argue that the best way to know about offending is to speak with offenders. This was essentially the skill that probation officers used to have. If they are distanced from this by process and technology, a gap may arise that will be difficult to fill in the future.

Dangerousness has become a conflated issue. It has assumed great political importance and as a result dominates the practice of criminal justice agencies. Not only does it have a net-widening effect in terms of the dominance of the risk agenda, but it also has an excluding effect. By this we mean that so-called less serious offenders are no longer seen as the legitimate territory of the probation service. The need to focus upon the most serious and potentially dangerous means that many other offenders are seen as ripe for passing over to other agencies. Thus the majority of offenders, those that spend most time in and out of prison, are increasingly seen as insufficiently serious for the probation service, the agency charged with public protection duties. Yet these offenders perhaps contribute most to the fear of crime, as their behaviour makes up the everyday crimes that make people feel at risk.

Conclusion

It is difficult to foresee what the future holds for the probation service in its work with potential dangerousness (as difficult as foreseeing dangerousness itself). In many ways the situation is always a calamity waiting to happen. An absence of disasters can be interpreted as the process working well, but this is not possible to prove. Nothing might have happened anyway. On the other hand, when the calamity does happen it will undoubtedly signal a system failure, demanding a change in policy and a further tightening of rules and regulations. It could be argued that the agencies have complied too much with an unrealistic central plan. However, it should be noted that organizational survival and financial support was often predicated upon meeting the challenges of the dangerousness agenda. The risk society is something that politicians have used to their advantage and in so doing undoubtedly contributed to its escalation. Yet, in 2004, an unlikely opponent to the idea was in evidence.

In a twist to the usual run of events, Oliver Letwin, the Conservative shadow home secretary, argued that concerns with risk had become too dominant and that people were living sheltered lives in fear (*Guardian*, 3 September 2004). In true political fashion he suggested 'courage' as a middle course; perhaps, if we were considering potential danger, 'reckless' would be more apt. If we strip out the politics, however, there may be a suggestion for the probation service that it should think carefully about putting all its eggs in one basket. It has had a unique position, working with a diverse range of offenders across the behaviour spectrum. Specialism *may* enhance skills but equally it opens up the prospect of deskilling in other areas. In such a politicized area it is dangerous in itself to limit one's position within the sector. Dangerousness may not be the political hot potato it has been – although who can really predict this?

We are not meaning to sound unduly pessimistic here. The probation service is rightly one of the key agencies working in public protection. It has a history of skilful and effective intervention, although in recent times its evidence base has been insufficiently robust. Undoubtedly the more open and regular sharing of information and agency collaboration in risk management is a significant step forward. It is also important that the probation officer's skill in building relationships and picking up on trigger factors and changes in behaviour remains paramount. Inter-agency working will undoubtedly enhance the process but this should not be at the expense of professional skills, which for the moment are seen as outmoded.

In essence the heat needs to be taken out of the dangerousness issue. If this can happen staff will be able to spend more time on the cases where they may be able to make a difference. The size of the potentially dangerous offender population needs to be reduced and should be defined by real behaviour and characteristics rather than politically constructed definitions which see the pool growing inexorably in size. Effective work with this group of people is painstaking and highly skilled. Staff involved need time and support from management and opportunities to train and reflect upon their work. If the volume of work continues at its present rate it will make this need for professional space more difficult to achieve. It has been argued that dangerousness is a political construction (Pratt 1997) and it now needs to be politically deconstructed.

References

ACOP (1988) *More Demanding than Prison.* Wakefield: Association of Chief Officers of Probation.

Burnett, R. (2002) 'The Case for Counselling as a Method for Working with Offenders', *Vista*, 7: 216–226.

Coker, J.B. and Martin, J.P. (1985) *Licensed to Live.* Oxford: Blackwell.

Crawford, A. (1998) 'Community Safety and the Quest for Security: Holding Back the Dynamics of Social Exclusion', *Policy Studies*, 19: 237–253.

Dunbar, I. and Langdon, A. (1998) *Tough Justice: Sentencing and Penal Policies in the 1990s.* London: Blackstone Press Ltd.

Feeley, M. and Simon, J. (1992) 'The New Penology: Notes on the Emerging Strategy of Corrections', *Criminology*, 30 (4): 449–474.

Floud, J. (1982) 'Dangerousness and Criminal Justice', *The British Journal of Criminology*, 22 (3): 213–228.

Floud, J. and Young, W. (1981) *Dangerousness and Criminal Justice.* London: Heinemann.

Garland, D. (2001) *The Culture of Control.* Oxford: Oxford University Press.

Giddens, A. (1990) *The Consequences of Modernity.* Oxford: Polity Press.

Hawkins, K. (1983) 'Assessing Evil', *British Journal of Criminology*, 23: 101–127.

Home Office (1995a) *National Standards for the Supervision of Offenders in the Community*, London: Home Office.

Home Office (1995c) *Dealing with Dangerous People: The Probation Service and Public Protection*, Report of a Thematic Inspection (HMIP). London: HMSO.

Home Office (1995b) *Review of Probation Officers Recruitment and Qualifying Training: Discussion paper by the Home Office.* London: Home Office.

Home Office (1998) *Exercising Constant Vigilance: The Role of the Probation Service in Protecting the Public from Sex Offenders*, Report of a Thematic Inspection (HMIP), London: Home Office.

Hudson, B. (2001) 'Human Rights, Public Safety and the Probation Service: Defending Justice in the Risk Society', *Howard Journal of Criminal Justice*, 40: 103–113.

Hudson, B. (2003) *Justice in the Risk Society.* London: Sage.

Kemshall, H. (2001) *Risk Assessment and Management of Known Sexual and Violent Offenders: A Review of Current Issues*, Police Research Series Paper 140. London: Home Office.

Kemshall, H. (2003) *Understanding Risk in Criminal Justice.* Maidenhead: Open University Press.

Kemshall, H. and Maguire, M. (2001) 'Public Protection, Partnership and Risk Penality: The Multi-agency Risk Management of Sexual and Violent Offenders', *Punishment and Society*, April 1 (2): 237–264.

Knock, K., Schlesinger, P., Boyle, R. and Magor, M. (2002) *The Police Perspective on Sex Offender Orders: A Preliminary Review of Policy and Practice*, Police Research Series Paper 155, London: Home Office, RDSD.

Maguire, M., Kemshall, H., Noaks, L. and Wincup, E. (2001) *Risk Management of Sexual and Violent Offenders: The Work of Public Protection Panels*, Police Research Series Paper 139. London: Home Office.

Mantle, G. and Moore, S. (2004) 'On Probation: Picked and Nothing to Say', *Howard Journal of Criminal Justice*, 43: 299–316.

Mawby, R.C. and Worrall, A. (2004) ' "Polibation" Revisited: Policing, Probation, and Prolific Offender Projects', *International Journals of Police Science and Management*, 6: 63–73.

Morris, N. (1994) 'Dangerousness and Incapacitation', in A. Duft and D. Harland (eds), *A Reader on Punishment*. Oxford: Oxford University Press.

Nash, M. (1999a) 'Enter the Polibation Officer', *International Journal of Police Science and Management*, 1(4): 360–368.

Nash, M. (1999b) *Police, Probation and Protecting the Public*. London: Blackstone Press.

Nash, M. (2004) ' "Polibation Revisited" – A Reply to Mawby and Worrall', *International Journals of Police Science and Management*, 6: 74–76.

Nash, M. and Ryan, M. (2003) 'Modernizing and Joining-up Government: The Case of the Prison and Probation Services', *Contemporary Politics*, 9: 157–169.

Pearson, G. (1983) *Hooligan: A History of Respectable Fears*. London: Macmillan.

Pratt, J. (1997) *Governing the Dangerous*. Sydney: Federation Press.

Prins, H. (1988) 'Dangerous Clients: Further Observations on the Limitation of Mayhem', *British Journal of Social Work*, 18: 593–609.

Rex, S. (1999) 'Desistance from Offending: Experiences of Probation', *Howard Journal of Criminal Justice*, 38, 366–83.

Sampson, A. and Smith, D. (1992) 'Probation and Community Crime Prevention', *Howard Journal of Criminal Justice*, 31, 105–19.

Savage, S.P. and Nash, M. (1994) 'Yet Another Agenda for Law and Order: British Criminal Justice Policy and the Conservatives', *International Criminal Justice Review*, 4: 378–51.

Scott, P. (1977) 'Assessing Dangerousness in Criminals', *British Journal of Psychiatry*, 131: 127–42.

Stevenson, O. (1989) 'Multi-Disciplinary Work in Child Protection' in O. Stevenson (ed.), *Child Abuse: Public Policy and Professional Practice*. Hemel Hempstead: Harvester Wheatsheaf.

Worrall, A. (1997) *Punishment in the Community: The Future of Criminal Justice*. London: Longman.

Young, J. (1999) *The Exclusive Society*. London: Sage.

Chapter 3

Dim prospects: humanistic values and the fate of community justice

Mike Nellis

Moral values and contemporary criminal justice

A degree of pragmatism is inevitable in the way we respond to crime and criminals. However, it is surely beyond argument that the pursuit of criminal justice should at least try to be a moral enterprise. The way that we respond to harmful individuals needs to be underpinned by discernible moral values; otherwise we are almost certain to treat them harshly, even cruelly, in ways that undermine our own claim to be decent and civilized. There is patently room for argument about the exact nature of those values, not least because there are various types of crimes and criminals, and different degrees of danger and harm. Nevertheless we must find as much consensus as possible as to what 'the right thing' to do actually is.

These issues have been part of the conversation of the centuries and will not vanish any time soon. New types and permutations of crime will emerge, legal, administrative and popular responses to crime will evolve, and new forms of punishment will arise as a result of broader cultural and technological changes. But the key idea here, that a society can be judged both by the way it criminalizes behaviour (the things it deems harmful, and the things it seeks to protect) and by the way it responds to those who break its laws (the nature of its controls and punishment), transcends particular contexts. It is an abiding touchstone of civilization.

I would like to think that the views expressed in the above paragraph were uncontentious, shared by contemporary policy-makers, by news media and the culture industry, and by criminal justice practitioners alike, but sadly, it is not so. The kind of moral values I have in mind, those which correspond to a humanistic vision, are patently in retreat, losing whatever grip they might once have had in the real world of crime control. I take humanism to be a belief system predicated on the absolute moral worth of all human beings, regardless of race, class, creed, colour or culture. It presents human beings, collectively and individually, as capable of great good, while acknowledging that under certain circumstances they are, collectively and individually, easily rendered capable of great evil. Humanism further assumes that human beings are easily made vulnerable to pain, physically and psychologically, especially but not only when young, and considers it an ethical imperative to create conditions under which the costs and consequences of this vulnerability are kept to a minimum. When human beings do act harmfully towards each other, the restraint of perpetrators is required. As importantly, if not necessarily as urgently, the causes and sources of harm must be ascertained, moral norms reaffirmed and every reasonable effort made to provide opportunities for the redemption of the perpetrator(s), regardless of the difficulty this might entail or the opposition it arouses.

There are both secular and faith-based versions of humanism (Margalit 1996, Norman 2004, Christie 2004, Gorringe 2004) and it may be that the faith-based ones will place greater emphasis on the importance of redeemability; rehabilitation (as the word is used in criminal justice debates) is a secular ideal distilled from an essentially religious idea of a person's intrinsic moral worth and latent moral capacity, and without a religious inflection it may seem an implausible and indeed unimportant ideal.

Politicians nowadays rarely appeal to humanistic values when they explain and justify new criminal justice legislation to the public, and in all honesty, such values may not resonate all that deeply with the public themselves. Certainly such values are regularly disparaged by the more populist news and current affairs media, treated as if they were nothing more than an apologia for leniency, a sure sign of pusillanimity in the face of danger and a lack of moral and political realism in anyone who expresses them. These media create a climate in which fear of crime is easily exploited by political parties who compete with each other to offer tough means of assuaging it. Politicians sometimes themselves create and amplify fears about crime in ways which outstrip even what some media have attempted. New Labour's four-year Strategic Plan for criminal justice (Home Office 2004), for example, explicitly conflates crime and terrorism and some of its proposals for 'ordinary crime' trade quite disreputably on anxieties about global security in a post-9/11 world.

Contemporary Home Office strategy is predominantly focused on the protection of the public, the reduction of crime and the enhancement of community safety, or at least the feeling of safety. These goals/ideas are largely presented in managerial terms, as pragmatic and self-evident social necessities. Entwined with them is a frequent reference to 'the proper punishment of offenders', and a somewhat less frequent reference to 'rehabilitation' which, at first sight, does add a humanistic dimension to the strategy. Public protection, proper punishment and rehabilitation, for all the tensions that exist between them can never be factored out in moral arguments about how best to respond to crime and criminals; all are relevant considerations, although there are also others, equally important, to which government attends much less. Difficulty arises when one starts to question *who* gets punished and *why*, the *means* by which public protection and community safety are to be created, and the *ways* in which offenders are to be punished and, indeed, rehabilitated (which can be done coercively, as in *A Clockwork Orange* (Burgess 1962)), in ways that vitiate the moral principles that notionally underpin the concept. New Labour, determined to be tough on crime, has shown a marked reliance on increased criminalization, the creation of an array of new criminal penalties and an approach to punishment which pays scant attention to proportionality in individual cases, or to social justice in general. It deploys an anti-criminal discourse which so demonizes offenders as a 'class' that hardly any of them could be taken seriously as candidates for rehabilitation and resettlement. Where rehabilitation is promoted it is often in formulaic, target-driven and micro-managerial ways that preclude expression of humanistic sentiments – genuineness, warmth and empathy – in face-to-face encounters with offenders. These are left out of the calculus of what matters. All these developments are packaged as the consequences of genuine moral deliberation, but the parameters of debate are often set too narrowly and too many humanistic values are excluded from consideration.

This chapter will affirm the importance of humanistic values, and the actions derived from them, in criminal justice and will suggest that the emerging ideas about community justice are, intellectually at least, the best vehicle for realizing them. It will not dwell at length on what community justice is or what it could become. That is the task of other chapters in the book, and there is clearly cogency in the idea. Nonetheless, whilst endorsing 'community justice' as an ideal I will emphasize just as strongly how much it goes against the grain of contemporary developments in criminal justice policy, and express doubts about realizing it in a sustained and systematic way. I would like to be more optimistic, but the times, I fear, are deeply uncongenial for humanistic community justice. I first drew this conclusion several years ago.

The (initial) community justice debate

I initially became interested in the idea of 'community justice' as a solution to the problem of 'social work values' in probation (Nellis 1995). In the aftermath of the 'punishment in the community' strategy, launched in the late 1980s by the Conservative government, the probation service in England and Wales embarked on a defiant affirmation of its traditional social work identity and its belief that rehabilitation of offenders was a principle to be upheld above all others. This seemed to me to be both an inappropriate response to 'punishment in the community' as it was (a strategy for reducing the use of custody via tougher community penalties) and an inadequate response to the very understandable fears of what 'punishment in the community' might become in the longer term (a wholly repressive crime control strategy in which rehabilitative considerations had no place). Articulating its identity and its mission in terms of 'social work values' would, I believed, result in the marginalization of the probation service. Such values, or at least the language in which they were expressed, had little cachet with either politicians or the public; they made the probation service sound as though it was not fully cognizant of the harm crime did to communities. Ironically, in its actual practice, the probation service was becoming increasingly aware of this, becoming more demanding in its approach to offenders, and (largely as a result of feminist perspectives on domestic violence) becoming more cognizant of the needs and rights of crime victims. But the language in which it was expressing itself was lagging behind practice, and not doing justice to it. I thought at the time that a cluster of ideas built around the core concept of community justice would be a solution to this, insofar as it would give the service a clearer public identity and a language credible enough to counter the worst excesses of what the Home Office was seeking to impose on it, in a way that social work language was not.

The cluster of ideas included restorative justice, community safety and anti-custodialism (which I later renamed 'hostility to custody'). The emerging discourse on restorative justice enabled a reasonably even-handed approach to the needs, rights and interests of both offenders and victims. It made concern for victims central to the probation enterprise, but not at the expense of rehabilitating offenders. By co-opting the emerging discourse on community safety into 'probation values' I conceded that the overriding aim of criminal justice was the protection of the public and the prevention of victimization, not the rehabilitation of individual offenders, important as that remained. Anti-custodialism was intended to capture the idea that imprisonment should always be used as a penalty of last resort, but was perhaps a little too close to abolitionism, hence my softening of the phrase. These ideas aroused both positive and negative comments at the time. Emboldened, I went on to suggest that 'community justice service' was a genuinely apt new name for the probation service, fearing that the Home Office (who were then insisting on a name change) would choose something far less palatable (Nellis 1998, 1999). Some of those who opposed this idea were probation traditionalists who felt that probation was such a time-honoured and still internationally respected term that it should never be jettisoned.

I eventually came to understand 'community justice' both normatively, as an ethos rather than a particular set of practices, and descriptively, as a strategy which blended the hitherto separate spheres of 'alternatives to prison' and 'crime prevention' into a single, operational entity (Nellis 2000). I valued the term 'community' because it simultaneously denoted a sense of place, the idea of local, devolved responsibility and the inherent interconnectedness of people. Effective crime reduction and effective resettlement of reforming offenders seemed to depend on local agencies and officials having sufficient autonomy and discretion to mobilize resources and create systems and cultures that suited their particular circumstances. 'Justice', I believed, was the moral heart of all debate about how we respond to crime, an indispensable ideal however much we might argue about its substance, which was already being used to designate workers in this field, as in 'youth justice'. As a concept, settling on what 'justice' meant was logically prior to settling questions about punishment. It also forced account to be taken of victims as well as offenders, and in terms of semantics alone it made it difficult to avoid the perennially hard questions about the relationship of criminal justice to social justice. The juxtaposition of these two terms, 'community' and 'justice', and the connotations of each, thus seemed to be a significant improvement on 'social work' as a way of articulating probation's evolving mission, and one that the Home Office might plausibly be persuaded of. It was not to be.

At the time of my initial thinking about community justice I was not aware of the powerful contribution made in this field by Todd Clear and his associates in America (Karp 1998, Clear and Karp 1999, Karp and Clear 2002). A subsequent reading of it amply confirmed my sense that community justice could indeed be a potent idea to organize around, and made redundant such plans as I had had to elaborate the concept more fully. I had, however, been influenced by the communitarian ideas of American writer Amitai Etzioni (1993), which were briefly influential within New Labour. Etzioni, drawing on traditions of civic republican writing in America, and on Jewish social philosophy, mounted a powerful critique of the atomization of American society and the social problems attendant upon loss of integrated, normative communities. He was as equally and deeply critical of the way in which untrammelled market forces created atomization and the egotism that lay behind so much crime, as he was of the way America had allowed its prison population to rise to such alarmingly high levels. Only a restoration of informal social controls at community level could both inhibit crime and make the use of imprisonment less necessary. To this end he recommended policies that emphasized both rights and responsibilities, distancing himself from the traditionally rights-oriented liberalism. This was the aspect of communitarianism that New Labour latched onto, but their attraction to Etzioni collapsed when they realized that he placed far more emphasis on the development of character and personal virtue; a long-term solution via socialization was at odds with the government demands for quick results and the managerial approach that they felt would bring them about. Ontologically, the genuinely humanistic emphasis in Etzioni's communitarianism was deeply at odds with commercially derived managerialist ideology, which had a far stronger hold over New Labour (McLaughlin, Muncie and Hughes 2001, Nash and Ryan 2003).

Community justice in (official) practice

Given the dropping of Etzioni, there is faint irony in the fact that New Labour's single experiment (to date) with community justice does owe something to the influence of his communitarianism in America itself. The North Liverpool Community Justice Centre began operation in December 2004, jointly run by the Home Office, the Lord Chancellor's Department and the Attorney General's Office. It has been inspired by the Red Hook court, established to deal with drug-related and violent crime in Brooklyn, New York (see also Pakes and Winstone, this volume). This has been deemed successful at increasing public support for, and interest in, local community justice processes, for constructive use of community sentences and for reducing the local murder rate. It has expanded from its original brief to deal with drug-using thieves and burglars and to hear property and domestic violence cases, and now includes a youth court in which 10–16-year-olds serve as jurors in peer trials – the latter being something that has surfaced elsewhere in the USA (and not emulated here in Britain).

The North Liverpool scheme consists of a court backed up by an array of support workers who will address the types of crimes that most concern local residents, for example vandalism, petty theft, drunk and disorderly behaviour and prostitution, and the drug and alcohol use that often underpins them. The support workers will consist of police, crown prosecutors, probation and youth offending teams. The court itself will be run by a judge rather than, as would have been more likely in the past, a magistrate or team of magistrates. Crucially, and distinctively, the court will take account of the views of local people, acquired through public 'meet the judge' evenings, as to how locally apprehended offenders should be dealt with; victims in particular will be enabled to meet the offender and express their views. The aim is to give some semblance of ownership to a local community as to how criminal justice is done in its area, but it remains to be seen how autonomous and responsive it can actually be within existing and anticipated sentencing frameworks. The judge appointed to pioneer this work has expressed hopes that his court will be less formal than other courts, but has nonetheless used the same zero-tolerance language regarding enforcement that pervades the rest of the community supervision world.

There is an obvious paradox about this initiative. The North Liverpool Community Justice Centre could just as easily be understood, not as a policy transfer from the United States, but as a reinvention of the locally based justice once administered by magistrates' courts and their probation officers. For the government to have described it thus would, however, have been at odds with its hostile attitude towards probation, which it seemingly regards as anachronistic and without credibility in criminal justice debate. Linking the North Liverpool scheme to an evolving probation tradition would have entailed public acknowledge-ment that there was something worth defending about probation, something worth carrying forward. New Labour eschews this, preferring instead to detraditionalize community supervision, of which the apotheosis has been the creation of the National Offender Management Service (NOMS), which, by merging prisons and probation into a single 'correctional service', in effect abolishes probation.

Despite its provenance, however, the North Liverpool Community Justice Centre warrants support. Its standing within New Labour's criminal justice policy as a whole is ambiguous, and there is no indication that it is the harbinger of any more such projects. In itself, it seems at odds with the marked neglect of localism within NOMS (which will be regionally organized), but it does represent a worthwhile attempt to realize a credible version of community justice, and should be watched with interest. It may work in that particular area, but if community justice is to mean anything substantial and become the basis of a humanistic reform movement, and a credible challenge to prevailing trends in criminal justice, it must be modulated to suit all the settings where crime occurs – racially tense provincial towns and inner cities, workless peripheral estates and alcohol-saturated town centres. It must offer viable local solutions to everything from hate crime to binge-drinking and its associated violence. It must avoid the sentimentality with which humanism can sometimes be tainted by its friends and enemies alike, and must understand both the nature of much contemporary crime and the appeal of the vindictive punishments that are being called forth to deal with it.

The problem of transgressive criminality

Contrary to the rational choice theorists of criminality for whom there is no such thing as society (or 'community'), globalized market forces and the egotistic, hedonistic cultural ideals that are related to them underpin and shape a great many criminal careers, at local level, even if some of the players themselves are unaware of it. Crime is a quintessentially capitalist enterprise, a business, a way of making a living, a form of work, a means to achieve a certain sort of lifestyle and status and – not by any means at odds with this – an opportunity to indulge a certain temperament, to be a consumer of illicit goods and pleasures. There are hierarchies of status, competence and capacity, and tensions associated with class and ethnicity, within and across criminal organizations and networks, just as there are in the 'legitimate' business world, which segues impercept-ibly into the illegitimate one. If it makes commercial sense to do so, some people work in both simultaneously: 'the duality of the criminal-business-man identity ... is a crucial device in structuring the identities of those practitioners engaging in local leisure markets' (Hobbs 1995: 117).

Criminal networks are amorphous, with solid enduring cores and more transient peripheries, where personnel may regularly change. Some people are involved in criminal activity full time and long term, others are involved only sporadically and temporarily, depending on patronage, talent, temperament, interests, opportunities and luck. What the more enduring participants have in common, as Hobbs describes them, is a certain set of values, a certain mentality – which those on the periphery, if they wish to get on, may seek to adopt and reproduce:

> Not only does the straight world not offer them the same financial rewards as the criminal life, it also does not offer the same *frisson* of excitement and exclusivity, as they share with their peers the ambience of spontaneity, autonomy, independence and resource-fulness that constitutes their outlaw status. They have no preten-sions to legitimacy, and there is little ambiguity concerning their lifestyle. When all is right in their world they stand out from the

majority of citizens who are [seen as] 'a greedy mob of mug punters simply asking to be taken'. They consider that they have seen through the system – they are above the piffling mundanities of everyday life and stand apart from its petty aspirations. (Hobbs 1995: 116)

The precise pattern and organization of criminality in a given locality may vary according to specific historical and geographical circumstances, but no contemporary community in Britain is without the influence, if not always the immediate physical presence, of businessmen-criminals. The root of their activity may lie well outside the particular locality in which their crimes first become visible; they are nodes in a chain of supply and demand. Demand, for example, for cheap labour in agribusiness and for sex workers in the leisure industry can both be satisfied by internationally connected people-traffickers, and their local agents, preying on people in failed states and collapsed economies many thousands of miles from the places in which they end up working. Conversely, top-of-the-range cars can be stolen to order from communities in Britain to supply customers elsewhere in Europe or in Asia. The intensity and scale of demand for illegal substances can create competition for profits and status among the suppliers, which in turn generates violence and taps into markets for illegal weapons. The demand for illegal substances (and alcohol) may be indirectly related to the banality and existential emptiness of the workaday world and in the absence of a culture of constraint – which consumerism corrodes – both, but especially alcohol, can fuel routine patterns of violence.

Such are the economics of contemporary criminality, with which community justice must reckon, if it can, if it is not to replicate the naivety and sentimentality of earlier humanistic interventions. It may well be that some young and young adults on the fringes of serious crime networks – low-level drug-dealers, proto-gangsters in particular neighbourhoods and drug-using burglars on particular estates – are amenable to community-oriented interventions specific to a given locality, but agencies involved in this should be under no illusions about the extra-communal forces that stimulate this activity. Over time they can regenerate new criminal networks to replace those that are broken up (not least because a new generation of kids may grow up with the same ambitions) and they persistently hold out an alternative value system, one that makes far more sense to excluded, lower-class youngsters than the nostrums of teachers, social workers and other crime control professionals. Local communities cannot be hermetically sealed; indigenous forces alone, whilst still important, never properly explain the styles and patterns of contemporary criminality. As Hobbs (1995: 106) puts it: 'the emergence of the market-place as the crucial dynamic within contemporary society stresses the redundancy of any analysis of serious crime that is restricted to the parameters of traditional neighbourhoods'.

Jock Young has developed a larger scale version of the market-creates-criminals argument, in an attempt to explain the visceral energy of underclass crime, the intensifying public concern about crime and anti-social behaviour and the manifestly vindictive, punitive 'turn' in criminal justice policy. He suggests that widening income differentials, increasing relative deprivation (a deepening sense of exclusion and humiliation among those with least options), the destabilizing impact of globalization on middle-class careers and traditions, leading to ontological insecurity and resentment towards perceived social inferiors who appear to abjure the self-discipline required to legitimate material success, lie at the root of these developments.

The criminality of the underclass is not simply a utilitarian affair involving the stealing of money or property or food or drink or drugs – although all of these elements are indeed part of the motivation. Violence is not just a simple instrument for persuading people to part with their cash, nor a management technique in the world of organized crime. Drug use is not a prosaic matter of being a pleasure of the poor – an alternative psychoactive experience to a gin and tonic or a light and bitter after a hard day at the office. Rather it involves all of these things, but above all it has a transgressive edge. For the transgressors are driven by the energies of humiliation – the utilitarian core is often there but around it is constructed a frequent delight in excess, a glee in breaking the rules, a reassertion of dignity and identity (Young 2003: 408).

Arguably this underplays the nihilistic, as opposed to the (rationally) hedonistic, elements in contemporary underclass crime, but Young is surely right to stress the emotionally driven character of much alcohol-fuelled fighting, gangland turf wars, domestic and sexual violence and seemingly 'senseless' property destruction. Those concerned with promoting community justice must surely take account of the kind of transgressive criminality that is being generated by contemporary economic and cultural arrangements, but whether a viable, local practical response to such crime is possible is a difficult question. Without a simultaneous strategy for increasing social justice and ameliorating inequality, the answer is probably 'no'.

The symmetry of Young's argument is perhaps its most intriguing aspect. Just as much lower-class criminal activity is driven by resentment at exclusion and humiliation, so state punishment is (at least in part) driven by the resentment and insecurities of the middle classes and the political elites who represent them. 'The punitive turn' of recent years Young writes (2003: 408), 'has a vindictiveness that goes beyond the principles of neo-classicism and deserved punishment'. There may well be a rational element (evidenced by managerialism) in contemporary crime control strategies, but 'there is [also] a vituperative quality pasted on the back of the rationale of control' (Young 2003: 408) which is more than mere rhetoric; it expresses the anger, fear and desperation of the once contented and stable. So just as market forces produce a type of offender and a criminal way of life upon which humanistic forms of community justice may not easily get a grip, so too do market forces shape the culture that responds to them.

Understanding the new punitiveness

Talk of a 'new punitiveness' in England and Wales (Pratt 2002) is understandable, but the idea needs unpacking nonetheless. It is not difficult to infer from the rising use of imprisonment (both increased admissions and longer sentences), and indeed of community penalties since the mid-1990s, that there has been a 'punitive turn' in Anglo-Welsh criminal justice. The initial emphasis under the early 1990s Conservative government on 'just deserts' was supplemented by a subsequent Conservative emphasis on incapacitation ('prison works'). Under New Labour the emphasis shifted decisively towards public protection, coupled with both the creation of many new criminal and imprisonable offences and a notional commitment to 'evidence-led' rehabilitative practices, based on the supposed efficacy of intervention programmes drawn from cognitive behavioural psychology. The introduction of Anti-Social Behaviour Orders (ASBOs) (which blurred traditional distinctions between civil and criminal penalties) and the national roll-out of innovative new penalties like electronic monitoring signalled significant transformations in the supervision of offenders in the community. The emergence of 'seamless sentences' in the Criminal Justice Act 2003, derived from a sentencing review and White Paper that had preceded it, betokened a weakening of a time-honoured polarity between custodial and community penalties. The advent of the National Offender Management Service (NOMS), which opens up the possibility of increased privatization of 'corrections', has taken place with astonishingly little public deliberation. All of these developments have, understandably, given rise to concern among individuals, organizations and interest groups who have traditionally subscribed to more humanistic (liberal) narratives of crime control. In a very real sense the shift has precipitated a crisis of values in criminal justice, which grows ever deeper.

To make sense of these various developments, and of the likely fortunes of community justice, requires a grasp of the three distinct and competing discourses that continue to pervade 'western European' penality (Peters 1988, Rutherford 1993, Feeley and Simon 1994, Cavadino, Crow and Dignan 2000, Scheerer 2000). There is no complete consensus on the characteristics and boundaries of the three discourses, but there is sufficient common ground among the various writers to suggest that they have discerned 'real' distinctions. For the purpose of this chapter I will use the terms 'punitive-repressive', 'surveillant-managerial' and 'humanistic-rehabilitative' to signify the ethos of each discourse. There are national variations among them, points of overlap between them, and tensions, inconsistencies and gradations of opinion within them, some commentators subscribing (quite reasonably) to parts of them but not all of them. These inflections and nuances do affect the precise way in which penal politics play out, but I am concerned here first with mapping the general contours of all three discourses, second with the probable and possible developmental trajectories of each one, and third with the more general impact that each has on the others.

Punitive-repressive discourse aims to maximize the delivery of pain to offenders. It tends to privilege the use of imprisonment, either for short periods to teach errant young people a lesson, or for natural life in the case of some murderers. Some within it subscribe to capital punishment, and sometimes corporal punishment. It can be both elitist or populist, although punitive elites in democracies often justify their sentiments by appealing to the allegedly visceral instincts of ordinary, decent citizens. The suffering of crime victims is invariably cited as a moral basis for inflicting equivalent or greater suffering on the offender. There tends to be no belief that offenders are reformable or redeemable, merely that they can be frightened (deterred) into law-abidingness or have their spirits broken, in or out of prison. The fiscal costs of punishment are largely dismissed as irrelevant, although it is imagined that costs would be reduced if prisons had 'no frills', that is, were made more austere. In the more recent past, community penalties have mostly figured in the punitive-repressive discourse as objects of derision. With the exception of corporal punishment, they have mostly been regarded as anodyne and inadequate measures, and if new forms of community punishment are to be introduced now they should be highly controlling, visibly humiliating, enforced on a zero-tolerance basis and always backed by imprisonment. Although a fair degree of this discourse is based on sound philosophical analysis and legal practice it is also from it that the baneful sentiment of 'populist punitiveness' (Bottoms 1995) is derived. This sentiment owes a great deal to media hype and to the vicissitudes of adversarial, opportunistic debate among political parties, but to deny that it has any roots in public opinion, and that it does not reflect genuine anger about certain types of crime, would be wishful thinking.

Managerial-surveillant discourse insists upon the application of technocratic rationality – the defining ethos of western modernity – to the growing (and otherwise unmanageable) problem posed by crime and criminals. Since the late twentieth century the body of knowledge called 'new public management' (NPM), glossed simply as 'managerialism' by a number of commentators, has given refined and sophisticated expression to it, at the macro, mezzo and micro levels of intervention. NPM imports concepts, practices and standards from the commercial world as part of a strategy for improving the efficiency and effectiveness of putatively ailing public services. It focuses primarily on the assessment and amelioration of certain pre-specified risks, mirroring the 'actuarialism' of the insurance industry. It embodies neoliberal values, favouring command and control structures, competition, commodification, and marketization. By setting tight targets and deadlines, specifying outcomes, constantly monitoring their attainment, perhaps penalizing their non-attainment, traditional organizational cultures can be 're-engineered'. Cost-efficiency becomes an end in itself, superseding values that may hitherto have given a transcendent purpose to an organization and motivated its professional staff. Surveillance (in the broad sense of information gathering and data processing) is integral to the operation of managerialism (Dandeker 1990, Jones 2000) and within such discourse new interventions like the electronic monitoring of offenders can gain particular credence. Within managerial discourse conventional understandings of moral judgement matter little; an attempt can be made to graft ethics on, but they are never central or intrinsic to it. All that matters is the manipulability, malleability and compliance of the objects of managerial intervention. If 'morality' means anything here it is nothing more than fidelity to the rules and procedures one is being required to comply with, whether one is a criminal justice employee or an offender. A good person is thus one who follows orders and achieves targets, nothing more, nothing less.

A whole tranche of human values – authenticity, empathy, kindness, compassion, the deeper sorts of respect, love, in short, the stuff that ethics is usually understood to consist of – are derogated by managerialism. This process is insufficiently acknowledged in public debate on the managerialization of public services generally, not just criminal justice. It is usually misrepresented by its own supporters as a positive good and often misrepresented by technocratically-inclined academics as less pernicious than it is. Even Feeley and Simon's (1994) term, 'actuarial justice', actually misrepresents processes that it otherwise depicts and analyses accurately, for 'justice' in the traditional normative sense (procedural fairness, ethically defensible, desert-based judgements) is precisely what atrophies when actuarial/managerial imperatives predominate. They inadvertently reduce 'justice' to little more than a synonym for processing offenders (or 'offender management'), making it harder to use the term to denote a vital moral ideal. Zygmunt Bauman (1989) has coined the word 'adiaphorization' to capture the socio-political process of expunging ethical considerations from managerial regimes. It is a rather ungainly term, but at present it is all we have to identify the process, and we should learn to use it.

Humanist-rehabilitative discourse has traditionally articulated a belief that criminality can be educated or counselled out of individual offenders, especially if certain kinds of practical help with employment, accommodation, addiction and family relationships are also offered, and if equality of opportunity prevails. At its most expansive, with reference to young people in particular, it encompasses the view that with appropriate support in families, schools and neighbourhoods, crime can actually be prevented from occurring. In its narrower, more reactive forms it concedes that offenders may have to be coerced, even imprisoned, but such constraints are only considered defensible in the service of higher moral ends, and their worst 'side-effects' are deliberately ameliorated to ensure attainment of those ends. The probation service built its mid to late twentieth-century identity around these beliefs, its interventions ranging from 'tough love' to psychologically based behavioural interventions. Latterly, restorative justice, citizenship and a commitment to human rights have been encompassed by this discourse, the latter reflecting the insight that humanistic values are largely unsustainable in the specific sphere of criminal justice if they are not also widespread, and firmly anchored, in civil society more generally. Such values can – and for popular consumption *must* – be expressed in secular language, but defences of restorative justice, for example, and the more general idea of an offender's inherent moral worth, are increasingly underpinned by theological arguments (Gorringe 2004). It is largely from resources in this discursive framework that a meaningful and morally worthwhile idea of community justice, even those versions that draw directly on communitarianism, must be drawn. Rehabilitation need not be abandoned, but it should be downgraded from being a principle above all others to being one important principle among several.

New Labour's substantive criminal justice policy is predominantly 'managerial-surveillant' (Fionda 2000, Carter 2003, Home Office 2004,

Tonry 2004). It is driven by a desire to reduce crime by a set amount *and* to avoid the unnecessary use of imprisonment and the high costs that this entails. Nonetheless, New Labour politicians still make very ready use of punitive rhetoric in their public pronouncements, partly in order to out-manoeuvre the Conservative Party, whose orientation (at least while in opposition) tilts more towards the 'punitive-repressive', and partly to appease its own punitive constituencies. Whilst nominally rational and quite possibly effective in their own terms, managerially-surveillant practices cannot always be made intelligible or palatable to an electorate schooled in, and perhaps more emotionally attuned to, the idea that *real* punishment must necessarily be retributive or vengeful in intent and painful in consequence, rather than effective. It is for this reason, for example, that electronically monitored curfews, whilst initially billed by government as a very tough community penalty, have not particularly been accepted as such in the media; being sentenced to stay at home for part of the day does not seem unduly onerous – onerous enough to be truly punitive – by everyone (Nellis 2004a, 2004b). Thus, whilst managerial-surveillant practices can and are pursued by stealth (at least as far as some audiences are concerned) punitive-repressive discourses are a genuine constraint on their development, sometimes frustratingly so to government, although they cannot say so publicly without alienating voters they need.

It is because there are real and obvious tensions between punitive-repressive and managerial-surveillant discourses (and often practices) that subscribers to the latter can sometimes pose as liberals, doing what they can to resist the excesses of populist punitivism, offering the only possible alternative to it. It is on this basis that many former supporters of humanistic-rehabilitative discourse have switched, with varying degrees of reluctance and enthusiasm, to a managerial-surveillant discourse, as the next best thing to their original ideal. This seems to have happened on a large scale in the probation service over the last ten years. But this switch is misleading, and dangerous, even if those who have made it do not realize it. Just because it is not as viscerally, aggressively punitive as populist punitiveness, that does not mean that there is nothing to fear from managerialism. Its regulatory potential is greater, its inhumanity more insidious. The logic of scorched earth managerialism, of the kind we have now, epitomized at the strategic level by NOMS, interminably restructuring organizations in a quest for an ever more chimerical vision of efficiency, is totalitarian; the meticulous, if disorienting, regulation of everything. It is here that Bauman's (1989) insight into adiaphorization is so important. Managerially driven interventions first of all suppress internal ethical considerations of the kind that are almost unavoidable in face-to-face encounters, but which are denied by managerialism. In addition they disregard external ethical standards that might place constraints on them, on the grounds that their mission is demonstrably superior, and not bound by those standards.

Conclusion: dimmed prospects for community justice

Where do these developments, trends and tendencies leave humanistic-rehabilitative discourse? Its institutional agents – professionals in the probation and youth justice services, various voluntary sector staff, the network of penal reform groups and several faith-based organizations – are undoubtedly threatened by both punitive-repressive and managerial-surveillant discourses, as articulated by various media and political champions. Both can – and do – claim that humanism is an anachronism in an era of volume crime, a moral luxury from a bygone age that is no longer adequate as a means of generating security and public confidence in a post-9/11 world: in essence that humanism is 'soft on crime'. Populist punitivists sometimes go further, and blame humanistic-rehabilitative discourse for *causing* (or at least aggravating) the ravages of crime in the first place, claiming, for example, that allowing offenders the alibi of poverty and dysfunctional families and permitting too many 'second chances' in court makes them worse. This strand of punitive-repressive discourse tends to portray humanistic-rehabilitative discourse as a kind of sentimental liberalism in which offenders are considered to be essentially benign, easily rehabilitated if only 'the system' gives them adequate support and ceases to oppress them. To the extent that there have been occasions in the past 20 years when probation officers have indeed given the impression that they subscribed to sentimental liberalism – defending a naive version of social work values, insisting on the primacy of rehabilitation as a criminal justice ideal – it might be said that they brought this criticism on themselves, and made it easy for their opponents. Perhaps, but it needs to be remembered that criticisms of humanitarian concern for offenders, even of the hard-headed variety, has a long history; populist punitivists in the 1990s would have sought to smear humanistic-rehabilitative discourse as sentimental liberalism regardless of whether probation had played into the stereotype.

The taint of sentimental liberalism, however, has undoubtedly stuck, and threatens to discredit and marginalize the entire edifice of humanistic-rehabilitative discourse. The problem with sentimental liberalism is the anodyne nature of its image of offenders. It denies how bad or harmful they can choose to be. It underplays the transgressive nature of much criminality and fails to grasp the nature of the economic and cultural forces that create it. To anyone who knows anything about the layers and circles of real criminals in a given community, sentimental liberalism never sounds equal to the challenge of dealing with them. Within the discourse as a whole there are ideas and understandings that are more adequate to the challenge, that do not rely on sentimental imagery and accept the limits of liberal emphasis on individual rights, but, for the time being at least, these have been eclipsed by the force of penal populism's caricature and by the apparent potency of managerial-surveillant arguments and practices. The most needful thing in contemporary criminal justice is to find a new way of articulating humanistic-rehabilitative discourse, otherwise we are locked into a future that will see the ascendancy of a soulless managerialism – the endpoint of which will be a new, more technologically sophisticated variant of totalitarianism. Managerialism will periodically be checked and impeded by outbursts of populist punitivism, but will not be eclipsed by them; rather it will absorb their vindictive energy and transform it into something equally repressive. It will thus withstand excoriation better than the ostensibly 'softer' humanistic-rehabilitative discourse, which under the weight of *both* its competitor discourses will be drowned out as a voice.

Therein lies the importance of community justice; intellectually and philosophically it represents the last best hope of reinventing and sustaining humanistic values in twenty-first century criminal justice in Britain. That said, I have tried to show here what community justice is up against, ideologically, and how weak its 'starting position' in contemporary debate actually is. Because of the dynamics outlined in this chapter, in relation to the origins of both transgressive crime and vindictive punishments, I do entertain the possibility that community justice may even – already – be a non-starter, that we have passed the point of no return, gone beyond the moment where any kind of humanism can be retrieved and refashioned into a real influence on the practice of criminal justice. 'Punitive-repressive' or 'managerial-surveillant' versions of community justice may of course develop, adopting the rhetoric whilst subverting the substance, but this would change nothing, except for the worse – not for the first time in penal history a promising reform would be co-opted and neutralized.

The trouble with such a stance, I recognize, is that it can be demoralizing; its very pessimism can assist the triumph of the forces to which one is opposed. But that, I think, is where we are. I can only hope that the impact of this book overall will prove me wrong, and lead to local experiments in humanistic community justice which, who knows, may eventually coalesce into something more significant. There is nothing to be lost by arguing and campaigning. Indeed it is desirable that we do. We may not win, or accomplish much, but we can at least choose how we lose.

References

Bauman, Z. (1989) *Modernity and the Holocaust*. Cambridge: Polity Press.
Bottoms, A. E. (1995) 'The Philosophy and Politics of Punishment and Sentencing', in C. Clarkson and R. Morgan (eds), *The Politics of Sentencing Reform*. Oxford: Clarendon Press.
Burgess, A. (1962) *A Clockwork Orange*. London: Heinemann
Carter, P. (2003) *Managing Offenders, Reducing Crime: A New Approach*. London: Cabinet Office.
Cavadino, M., Crow, I. and Dignan, J. (2000) *Criminal Justice 2000: Strategies for a New Century*. Winchester: Waterside.
Christie, N. (2004) *A Suitable Amount of Crime*. London: Routledge.
Clear, T. and Karp, T. (1999) *The Community Justice Ideal: Preventing Crime and Achieving Justice*. Oxford: Westview Press.
Dandeker, C. (1990) *Surveillance, Power and Modernity*. Cambridge: Polity Press.
Etzioni, A. (1993) *The Spirit of Community*. New York: Simon and Schuster. (English edition 1995, London: Fontana).
Feeley, M. and Simon, J. (1994) 'Actuarial Justice: The Emerging New Criminal Law', in D. Nelken (ed), *The Future(s) of Criminology*. London: Sage, pp. 173–201.
Fionda, J. (2000) 'New Managerialism, Credibility and the Sanitisation of Criminal Justice', in P. Green and P. Rutherford (eds), *Criminal Policy in Transition*. Oxford: Hart Publishing, pp. 109–130.
Gorringe, T. (2004) *Crime*. London: SPCK.
Hobbs, D. (1995) *Bad Business*. Oxford: Oxford University Press.
Home Office (2004) *Confident Communities in a Secure Society: The Home Office Strategic Plan 2004–08*. London: The Stationery Office, Cm 6287.
Jones, R. (2000) 'Digital Rule: Punishment, Control and Technology', *Punishment and Society* 2: 5–22.
Karp, D. (ed.) (1998) *Community Justice: An Emerging Field*. Oxford: Rowan and Littlefield.
Karp, D. and Clear, T. (eds) (2002) *What is Community Justice?* London: Sage.
Margalit, A. (1996) *The Decent Society*. Harvard: Harvard University Press.
McLaughlin E., Muncie, J. and Hughes, G. (2001) 'The Permanent Revolution: New Labour, New Public Management and the Modernisation of Criminal Justice, *Criminal Justice* 1: 301–318.
Nash, M. and Ryan, M. (2003) 'Modernising and Joining-Up Government: The Case of the Prison and Probation Services', *Contemporary Politics* 9: 157–169.
Nellis, M. (1995) 'Probation Values for the 1990s', *Howard Journal of Criminal Justice*, 34: 344–349.
Nellis, M. (1998) 'Community Justice: A New Name for the Probation Service?, *Justice of the Peace*, 25 April, 162 (17).

Nellis, M. (1999) 'Politics, Probation and the English Language', *Vista: Perspectives on Probation* 4: 233–240.

Nellis, M. (2000) 'Creating Community Justice', in S. Ballintyne, K. Pease and V. McLaren (eds), *Secure Foundations: Key Issues in Crime Prevention, Crime Reduction and Community Safety*. London. Institute for Public Policy Research, pp. 67–66.

Nellis, M. (2004a) ' "I Know Where You Live": Electronic Monitoring and Penal Policy in England and Wales 1999–2004', *British Journal of Community Justice* 2: 33–59.

Nellis, M. (2004b) 'Electronic Monitoring and the Community Supervision of Offenders', in A. E. Bottoms, S. Rex and G. Robinson (eds) *Alternatives to Prison*. Cullompton: Willan.

Norman, R. (2004) *On Humanism*. London: Routledge.

Peters, A. G. (1988) 'Main Currents in Criminal Law Theory', in Jan van Dijk *et al* (eds) *Criminal Law in Action*. Deventer: Kluwer, pp. 19–36.

Pratt, J. (2002) *Punishment and Civilization*. London: Sage.

Rutherford, A. (1993) *Criminal Justice and the Pursuit of Decency*. Oxford: Oxford University Press.

Scheerer, S. (2000) 'Three Trends into the New Millennium: The Managerial, the Populist and the Road Towards Global Justice' , in P. Green and A. Rutherford (eds), *Criminal Policy in Transition*. Oxford: Hart Publishing, pp. 243–260.

Tonry, M. (2004) *Punishment and Politics: Evidence and Emulation in the Making of English Crime Control Policy*. Cullompton: Willan.

Young, J. (2003) 'Merton with Energy, Katz with Structure; The Sociology of Vindictiveness and the Criminology of Transgression', *Theoretical Criminology* 7: 389–414.

Chapter 4

The police service: from enforcement to management

Robin Fletcher

The last quarter of the twentieth century saw a number of fundamental changes in the management of crime within our communities and one of the most visible was the way in which the police changed its philosophy from law enforcement to crime management. The traditional view of the police is that of a law enforcement agency tasked by the state to maintain the 'Queen's peace' and prosecute offenders. Whilst this will always be one of its core functions, it has also become an integral member of a multi-partnered 'responsible authority', created by the Crime and Disorder Act 1998, tasked with addressing broader social issues that are thought to be influential in the causation of crime and also anti-social behaviour.

The journey from 'law enforcer' to 'problem solver' evolved as sustained political, economic and social pressures questioned the ability of the police to deliver a service that fulfilled society's needs. The police have increasingly engaged in crime reduction programmes that deal not only with actual crimes but also with the fear of crime; concepts of community safety (Home Office 1991) that focus on crimes committed against the person rather than property; and the use of pre-emptive legislation (Crime and Disorder Act 1998) that encourages communities to become actively involved in protecting themselves through programmes of partnership crime prevention.

This chapter will examine how the police evolved (Matthews 1994) to accommodate these changes and identify some of the influences that were responsible. The delivery of community justice is, however, not implemented on a stand-alone basis; it involves multi-agency statutory and non-statutory arrangements and it should be borne in mind that as the functions of the police change, so too must the functions of these other service deliverers to accommodate this. To understand the context of these changes I will begin by examining the role of the police, acknowledging that they do not exist in isolation of other providers.

Functions of the police

Whilst 'policing' has a long history, dating back to the tenth century (Critchley 1978), the Metropolitan Police (MPS), formed in 1829, is recognized internationally as being the first 'modern' police organization to have crime prevention specified as a policing objective. The Home Secretary of the day, Sir Robert Peel, declared of the police: 'It should be understood at the outset, that the object to be attained is the prevention of crime ... To this great end every effort of the police is to be directed' (Critchley 1978: 52). Thus the primary role of the police was established, although the manner in which it was to be carried out changed in the fullness of time.

Having identified that the primary function of the police was to prevent crime the original process for achieving this was by highly visible patrols (Critchley 1978) that deterred 'ne'er do wells' by their mere presence (Reiner 1992, 1999). Constables were provided with a recognizable uniform that was symbolically 'preventative but not threatening' (Brogden, Jefferson and Walklate 1988: 4) and a hidden truncheon for defence. Thus policing established the principle that it was to be achieved through coercion and public support, or 'policing by consent', although Newman (1985: 260) reminds us that 'The police ... exist in part to apply authorised coercion when willing compliance is not forthcoming.'

Originally a constable's power of arrest was minimal, relying on the discretionary use of common law. Later these powers were added to by legislation that was enacted whenever a particular problem arose. It was not until the introduction of the Police and Criminal Evidence Act 1984 (PACE) that police powers of arrest, detention and accountability were rationalized under a single piece of legislation.

There was no 'master' plan of national policing but a 'higgledy-piggledy' (Boyle 1962: 596) approach that absorbed whatever problems had to be faced. This haphazard approach resulted in the police taking on many functions, which included 'inspectors of nuisance; weights and measures; diseases of animals, dairies and shops; contagious diseases; explosives and bridges; in the case of some borough forces, the running of fire and ambulance services' (Morgan and Newburn 1997: 76). These functions indicate the breadth of 'service' provision that police were expected to provide to the public. It was not until the latter half of the twentieth century that a more contemporary function of the police was established, which saw an increasing focus on law enforcement through 'order maintenance; crime control [and] environmental and traffic functions' (Morgan and Newburn 1997: 75).

Brogden et al (1988: 49) offer three theoretical perspectives to explain this haphazard approach:

1   The evolutionary theory: policing developed in response to increasing public disorder and rising crime.
2   The class-based theory: the changing social structure of the mid nineteenth century, and the rise of the industrial revolution, required a subordinate working class in order to staff the factories. The police were introduced to promote the interest of the dominant class.
3   The accidental theory: which considers the importance of local contingencies and unforeseen accidents that have no recognizable pattern.

The rationalization of police responsibilities into a service that we recognize today was driven by the Royal Commission of 1962, which reviewed police activity and recommended a change in the primary objective of the police (Critchley 1978: 298). Whilst Peel's policing philosophy made crime prevention the primary objective, the Commission adjudged this to be of secondary importance (Alderson 1979: 198). The Commission promoted the enforcement of law and order over other matters, measuring success through recorded crime statistics (Critchley 1978: 309), placing an emphasis on arrest, prosecution and short-term solutions.

Some tension appears to exist with this decision as the government-sponsored Cornish Committee (Home Office 1965) promoted crime prevention as a 'subject in its own right' (Weatheritt 1986: 45) to be developed in tandem with other policing duties. This dilemma was reasserted again in 1991 when a government White Paper described the role of the police simply as: 'The main job of the police is to catch criminals' (Home Office 1991: 5).

This focus on the police as prosecutors of criminal behaviour is understandable as they are the only agency equipped with the power to investigate and arrest all offenders, particularly when the use of force is necessary. But research has identified that crime is only a small element of the policing workload (Hough 1985) with the majority generally more concerned with community management and dealing with non-crime emergencies. This is due in part to the police being the only 24-hour service that is able to respond to any incident from unexpected childbirth, noise, family disputes, escaped animals and occasional incidents of crime (Morgan and Newburn 1997: 79). They are, in fact, an all-purpose social service and attempts to redefine their role more narrowly have been consistently undermined by this mosaic of functions in actual practice.

In recent years a number of reviews (ISTD 1993, Home Office 1993a, 1993b, 1995, Posen 1994) have tried to determine police core activity and define their role in modern society. The reason for these reviews was to establish police efficiency and effectiveness; internal and external accountability, and ways of reducing an increasing workload that appeared to prevent a focus on reducing rising crime rates. This was in addition for a need to respond to the government Financial Management Initiatives (FMI), introduced in 1982 (Morgan and Newburn 1997: 47) by the Thatcher government's drive to improve public service provision through intense financial scrutiny (Home Office circular 114/1983, Mawby 2002). Collectively these reviews caused the police to adopt new managerial systems (Crawford 1998), a variety of policing styles, localization of governance and greater cooperation with the community.

Professionalisation of the police

Until the middle of the twentieth century, the police had followed a traditional philosophy of policing that required intervention only to deal with those 'situations in which a citizen could request their attention, and problems on the street that officers could see required attention' (Brogden et al 1988: 4). Police were not encouraged to uncover crime unless it was called to their attention, and this was a main factor in the low crime reporting rate. The Royal Commission of 1962 considered that policing in this fashion was inefficient and no longer appropriate to society's needs (Oliver 1997). This view was partially driven by the public who were finding their voice on many social issues, of which crime was one.

To help improve the effectiveness of the police, the Commission recommended the creation of a central government Police Research and Planning Branch (Critchley 1978: 314) that could analyse crime problems and develop new methods of policing that would improve efficiency in tackling the increasing crime problem with inadequate resources (Critchley 1967, Weatheritt 1986). One of its first responses was to promote 'Unit Beat' policing (Home Office 1967, Emsley 1996), which effectively created a two-tiered policing system. This consisted of police officers who patrolled the community in vehicles, responding to incidents quickly, in a style often referred to as 'fire brigade' policing (McLaughlin and Muncie 1996: 55), and on a second level, resident police officers who patrolled on foot in an effort to maintain community contact (Emsley 1996). It was intended that these officers would retain the confidence of the community and maintain the necessary information flow that ensured local policing satisfied the requirements of the community. This two-tier system was eventually to have a negative impact on crime control within the community.

As frontline policing began to withdraw from the community, so the notion of patrol as a preventative method declined (Kettle and Hodges 1982, Weatheritt 1986). Officers were no longer gathering information that could warn of impending problems, or assist in solving those that had already occurred, nor were they able to support any informal control mechanisms that could reduce levels of anti-social behaviour (Wilson and Kelling 1982). Lea and Young's (1993) critique of policing recognized the dangers of marginalization by this process and argued the importance of maintaining a close relationship with the community.

The separation of police skills that began with the Unit Beat system later extended to other areas of policing, such as 'crime prevention', with the creation of specialist posts that took even more constables away from direct community contact. Crawford (1998) identified this as the beginning of an institutional change in police thinking that was seeking speedy solutions, which could be measured in simple terms, as proof of efficiency. It was a move that began with good intentions, but became swamped by a police 'action' culture (Reiner 1992) that sacrificed long-term holistic problem solving for instant measurable success.

Political and social influences

The 1960s was a time of major social change when the post-World War II welfare state experiment began to falter, leading to social disharmony and increasing conflict with the police. The first sign of this social change was a collapsing global market that caused Harold Wilson's Labour government to withdraw support for the inefficient and overstaffed nationalized industries. This was challenged by the powerful trade unions (Jefferson 1990: 32; Hall et al 1978: 272) through a series of strikes, causing national chaos with major power cuts and the introduction of a three-day working week. The friendly co-existence of the government and trade unions was coming to an end and this set up a collision course for future governments. The following Conservative Heath government fared no better, failing to stem the tide of rising inflation and increasing unemployment. Attempts to reduce the power of the trade unions included the introduction of the Industrial Relations Act 1971, to try to prevent the use of 'flying pickets' that were seen by the establishment as a deliberate and unnecessary act of confrontation. This caused much resentment among trade unionists and resulted in serious conflict with the police who were required to intervene (Lea and Young 1993) in these disputes. Subsequent aggressive and violent trade union activity was met by increasing levels of police 'force', which eventually led to the deployment of full riot equipment (Morgan and Newburn 1997). Using the police to intervene in trade disputes of this nature alienated them even further from the communities they would ordinarily patrol and identified them as an overt tool of the state.

Whilst the industrial and political conflicts of the 1970s dominated public perception on law and order issues, a more serious breakdown in police/public confidence began to emerge. During the 1950s and 1960s there had been an influx of immigrant families (Morgan and Newburn 1997) to supplement a workforce that had been decimated by World War II. On arrival in Britain they had taken up residence in many of the deprived inner-city areas where sub-standard housing, poor education and few employment opportunities existed (Saunders 1984, Fitzpatrick 1994, Thomas 1986). This created new social problems, one of which was an increase in the involvement of black youths in crime (Cohen 1972, Hall *et al* 1978), particularly within London.

At the beginning of the 1980s, crime in Brixton, south London, had risen to such levels that local senior police officers decided to use saturation tactics to stop and search young people who were thought to be potential offenders. The operation, known as 'Swamp 81' (Scarman 1981, Commission for Racial Equality 1981, Brake and Hale 1992, Lea and Young 1993), involved a large number of officers that had been supplemented by constables from other areas. The operation began on 6 April 1981 and within four days nearly 1,000 predominantly black youths were stopped and searched (McLaughlin 1996: 59), causing tremendous resentment (Reiner 1992, Lea and Young 1993). One factor for this dissent was the use of officers who did not work within the community and who failed to understand the importance of cultural issues, diversity and victimization. The result was a major street riot that had an unprecedented impact on the way in which the police were to evolve.

Police marginalisation

The introduction of the Unit Beat policing system had produced a generation of police officers who no longer understood the community in which they worked (Lea and Young 1993, Reiner 1994, McLaughlin 1996). This loss of contact had stopped the information flow that had enabled the police to hear and understand community concerns and build up a degree of trust that helped support the informal control mechanisms that exist within all communities. As Goldstein's (1990: 8) research was to show, successful policing involves 'a variety of informal methods' that require the full support and cooperation of the citizenry, who have to accept some responsibility in policing their community. Unit Beat policing did not help with this process. Even before 'Swamp 81', the police were not trusted or welcomed by the local community (GLC 1982), a position that was fuelled by local politicians who continually questioned police motives whilst calling for greater local accountability (Jefferson and Shapland 1994).

The subsequent inquiry (Scarman 1981) into the Brixton riot acknowledged that some attempts had been made to develop a police/community consultation process but that these had failed because both sides had stopped talking to each other, at a time when working together was of paramount importance (*Police Review*, 27 November 1981). To Scarman, to overcome this type of breakdown in communication required a statutory process that would force the three primary stakeholders – the community, the state and the police – to work together and share information. He believed that such cooperation would assist the police to focus attention on the small number of people who commit crime and disproportionally affect the quality of life of the community. The alternative method of trying to stumble across useful information (Lea and Young 1993) through the random use of stop and search tactics had already resulted in a major catastrophe that had to be avoided in the future.

Police as a multi-agency provider

As a result of increased tensions between the police and the community, Scarman recommended the creation of Police Community Consultation Groups (PCCG) for 'the prevention of crime, and the maintenance of an orderly society' by developing a 'two way flow of information' (Hope 1985: 27), a process intended to prioritize action and provide a degree of local accountability. This structure was later formalized within PACE.

PCCGs were formalized bodies of local councillors, members of the community and police who were expected to work together to develop appropriate policing initiatives that would reduce crime, the fear of crime and prevent further riotous confrontations. This was to be achieved by exchanging information that would identify community priorities and help the police to develop tactical responses that were acceptable to the community. However, these groups soon became forums in which statutory agencies, primarily the police, sought to legitimize their actions (Crawford 1998), whilst the community members used it as an accountability process (Fletcher 2000) to supervise police action. The ability of these groups to develop useful information was eventually challenged by the Crime and Disorder Act 1998 which accused them of being 'a rather narrow group of people, who often pursue sectional interests' (CDA para. 3.51), and recommended that they be excluded from the public consultation process.

Whilst the creation of PCCGs was a legislative requirement, the police, along with other public agencies, began to reassess their ability to provide an adequate service to the public. The police accepted the need to adopt a less aggressive policing style that would enable them to re-engage with the community and return to the idealism of a mythical 'Golden Age' (Elmsley 1996: 170) when the community supported the police. It was at this time that politicians and public began to demand that the police return to the more traditional 'community policing' style that pervaded the 'old days', even though this style of policing still has to be defined. Although the police were able to re-organize and restructure their resources, they were unable to find the simple 'community' of the 1950s, described by Johnston (1997: 186) as 'communities of collective sentiment', but instead uncovered a more complex group of 'communities at risk' that had a diverse set of values.

As a result of this revelation two fundamental changes in policing philosophy occurred. First, the police began to engage in social engineering programmes that no longer focused on the offender, but sought to tackle causational issues, many of which were beyond their remit. Second, it accepted that the police alone could not prevent all crime, and a wider view of crime control had to be embraced. To this end the government promoted a new policing philosophy (Home Office circular 8/84, Tilley 1992, Liddle and Gelsthorpe 1994) that required a multi-agency approach, which would holistically address community problems and positively impact the quality of life of the citizens.

The role of crime prevention, as a specialist function, began to be taken seriously by the UK government in the early 1960s following the findings of the Cornish Report (Home Office 1965), which made 71 recommendations. The report argued that crime could be reduced through situational prevention that concentrated on physical security systems, and this philosophy was to become the mainstay of Home Office thinking for many years. The original focus on situational measures was led by Ron Clarke, at that time the leading theorist in situational crime prevention, which concentrated on increased physical security as a means of preventing crime.

Despite the focus on situational prevention, the report also acknowledged that a multi-agency/partnership approach (Home Office 1965, para 233, 241–243, 246–247, 249) was an important part of the whole crime reduction process. However, many years were to pass before this became a reality.

To emphasize the specialist nature of crime prevention, the Home Office opened a Crime Prevention College (CPU) to train police officers in the art of situational prevention, which then became the main element of their prevention programmes. The CPU also began an intense programme of research and evaluation that soon became 'the major driving force' (Tilley 1991: 11) behind government thinking on crime prevention. It was not a central planning unit but acted in an advisory capacity with a prodigious output of official reports and statements, aimed at 'the elevation of crime prevention objectives to be the primary purpose of policing' (Weatheritt 1986: 49). It was a concept that appears encouraging to Weatheritt, who saw it as a 'sound base of informed rhetorical deliberation and activity' although others accuse it of indulging in 'administrative criminology' that promoted bureaucracy rather than pragmatic outcomes. In 1996, however, the CPU was merged with other 'parts of the criminal policy department' (Koch 1998: 75) to form the Crime Prevention Agency and to develop crime prevention policy for other agencies, in addition to the police, thus embracing a true multi-agency approach.

Crime prevention had by now moved beyond physical security and was embracing social, architectural and environmental issues that impacted community safety. The situational theories of Clarke (1997) had been added to by Newman's (1972) 'defensible space' theory, Jacobs (1961) description of urban planning and latterly Coleman's (1989) critique of public sector housing estates. Essentially these academic tomes argued that much of crime could be reduced at the architectural and design stages of urban building projects. A consequence of this theorizing was that police crime prevention officers were further trained in architectural design (Crawford 1998) so that they could advise local authority planning departments on aspects that might encourage criminal activity.

Despite the efforts of the Home Office (see Johnston, Shapland and Wiles 1993) to elevate crime prevention to a more central role in strategic police thinking, less than 1 per cent of its staff (Harvey et al 1989) are actively engaged in preventative strategies. Even worse is that those who are engaged in this type of work have found themselves in a marginalized role because, as Weatheritt (1986, in Graef 1989: 49) notes, it is not a 'glamorous specialism' and is of 'low status'.

Crime prevention models: the emergence of multi-agency perspectives

To try and explain why crime prevention is not recognized as a major crime control function Weatheritt (1986: 49) developed two histories of crime prevention. The first, the 'Home Office model', is identified with the growth of official reports, statements, departments and organizations, aimed at the elevation of crime prevention objectives to be the primary purpose of policing.

The second history, the 'police model', is a review of crime prevention 'behind the statements of intention' (Weatheritt 1986: 49) and is a less successful story. It focuses on the development of prevention activity by the police who were, at the time, considered to be the primary agency tasked with this work. There is an element of frustration in her review as she declares: 'Crime prevention has not become a part of mainstream policing and the specialist crime prevention service has been left to languish in something of a policing backwater' (Weatheritt 1986: 49). For Weatheritt crime prevention was a marginalized specialism that was not threaded through all police activity.

Since then, two other histories have emerged: the 'business model' and the 'community model'. The business model is important because it is influential on all of the other histories. It tells of the growth of private sector security in all its forms (Jones and Newburn 1997, Crawford 1998), and is concerned with making legitimate profit out of crime. It extends to the growth in the media markets, including the numerous factual television appeal programmes whose good intent has to be balanced by the increase of concern, if not fear, of crime among the watching public. It is also concerned with the use of private security companies to patrol public spaces, copying the deterrent factor of Peel's first constables, which is now being further legitimized by government support for quasi-police patrols in the form of 'community support officers' (www.homeoffice.gov.uk).

The community model is concerned with the development of crime prevention beyond the police, as a multi-agency partnership. It began in the mid 1980s with government recognition that crime is a problem for all. Changes in legislation have now spread the function of crime prevention, crime reduction and community safety across a wider forum, making it a statutory requirement for the police to work as equal partners with local authorities (Crime and Disorder Act 1998). The difference between this history and that of the Home Office model can best be understood by using Crawford's (1998) description of the differences between 'multi-tasking' and 'inter-tasking'. The first attempt at developing a multi-agency approach to crime prevention is an example of centralist government developing 'multi-tasking' reactivity without fully understanding the problems they sought to overcome. It was merely 'a coming together of various agencies, in relation to a given problem, without this significantly affecting or transforming the work that they do' (Crawford 1998: 174).

The community model recognized multi-tasking as a fragmented approach, which undoubtedly serviced the agenda of the participants, without necessarily assisting the community. From this beginning they progressed to a partnership approach which required inter-tasking, defined by Crawford (1998: 174) as 'those relations which interpret and thus affect normal internal working relations. They entail some degree of fusion and melding between agencies. They involved collaboration and interdependence.' More importantly, this new relationship often created new structures that challenged old practices and achieved solutions, which were not driven by organizational hidden agendas.

Much of this history has yet to be acted out, but it has raised the profile of crime prevention to new levels from which it is hoped safer communities will emerge, not as an isolated Cinderella (Weatheritt 1986: 45) waiting to be rescued but as a conquering hero cutting through the swathe of bureaucratic red tape to unite the forces of the community. Yet in true postmodernist thinking, it would be wrong to see each history as having developed in isolation. Each has evolved as an intricate part of the other, developing in response, and in some cases as a reaction to, the various theories and practices that have emerged in recent years. Successful crime prevention does not rely upon one theory, history or concept, it develops as a set of contexualized solutions to specific problems.

Partnership and social crime prevention

In the aftermath of the street violence and public disorder of the early 1980s, the government changed its crime reduction strategy as it reluctantly accepted the need to tackle many of the socio-economic factors that were beyond the remit of the police (Koch 1998). Their response was to circulate memo 8/84, which had been signed by officials from various government agencies including the Home Office, Departments of Environment, Education and Science, Health and Social Services and the Welsh Office (Home Office et al 1984, Koch 1998), calling on each government department to consider how they could help tackle crime. This circular became the driving force behind multi-agency activity and began the process of changing the focus away from situational towards social prevention. However, the first attempts at multi-agency cooperation saw various agencies working independently towards solutions that were driven by internal performance regimes (Hughes 1998, Adams 1998, Fletcher 2000). As a consequence agencies sometimes found themselves in conflict as they tried to impose a solution that was not in accord with other organizations.

This conflict raised issues of monitoring and evaluation as the government tried to show value for money. Eventually the government ordered a full evaluation of partnership activity (Home Office memo 4/ 90), which was conducted under the auspices of the Home Office Standing Conference on Crime Prevention, by a working group, that became known as the Morgan Report (Home Office 1991).

Partnership and social engineering

One of the first partnership initiatives to be developed by the police was Neighbourhood Watch (NHW), as an attempt to rebuild community bridges in the aftermath of the street riots of the early 1980s. It was a North American concept (Turner and Barker 1983) that soon involved 2.5 million people nationally in 42,000 schemes increasing to 130,000 schemes by 1995, with an indeterminate number of participants. Neighbourhood Watch began the process of changing policing philosophy from that of 'crime busters' to 'problem busters' (Bennett 1992: 26).

A criticism of this type of initiative was that it initially developed in those communities where formal/informal social structures, like tenant/ resident/community groups, already existed, whilst more vulnerable communities without recognizable structures were ignored (Skogan and Maxfield 1981), thereby servicing communities that had few crime problems but more importantly continuing to ignore those communities with whom the police needed to improve their dialogue. As a result these schemes became dominated by white middle-class values (Hussain 1988, Rosenbaum 1986), whose views were often used to counter those of the newly formed PCCGs that were developing more political agendas.

Although NHW was an exercise in social engineering by the police to produce a 'village community' in which community policing could flourish (Bennett 1992) situational crime prevention programmes dominated it. It was clearly too difficult for the few specialist police crime prevention officers to change social structures, so they initially used property marking, home security surveys and increased physical security as a way of 'selling' the NHW programme. Any positive social changes were more by accident than design, even though a review by Laycock and Tilley (1995) noted an increase in social intervention, even though it failed to reduce crime.

In the aftermath of the Scarman (1981) Report the 1980s became a halcyon time for developing social crime prevention activity. Home Office circular 8/84 was followed by circular 44/90, which created the 'partnership' forum in which a new generation of social engineering flourished.

Partnership and safer cities

The next government attempt to reduce crime through social engineering began in 1986 with the Five Towns Initiative, followed by the Safer Cities programme (Hughes 1998), which aimed to 'Reduce crime; Lessen the fear of crime; and create Safer Cities' (Crawford 1998: 52) by encouraging economic enterprise and community life. These were programmes that required the local authority, the police and other agencies to work together to identify local community problems through a crime audit and then develop strategies to solve them. But because of government (Hughes 1998) mistrust of the way in which local authorities had previously used financial aid, only limited funds were made available, with an expectation that it would be used to pump-prime other resources (Tilley 1992, Hughes 1998) from within the community and local businesses.

To ensure that political or hidden agendas would not usurp the Safer Cities programme, a neutral coordinator was introduced to override prejudices of the various agencies that were involved and help produce solutions that crossed the demarcation lines of those organizations (Tilley 1992). Whilst the idea of a neutral coordinator had some appeal, it brought other tensions. The introduction of an 'outsider' was challenged by some who believed that they would be incapable of understanding local culture, whilst others accused them of being lackeys of the government (Tilley 1992) and a new form of central control. The police believed they should be the primary coordinator as they had the most experience of crime prevention. The local authorities challenged this, believing that they controlled the resources that could have the greatest impact on improving community safety.

Although each scheme was coordinated by a neutral 'outsider', they were individually managed by an independent agency that was expected to consult with the local community. The agencies were chosen for their ability to analyse information gathered from a variety of sources and to produce a strategy that would have a long-term impact on crime and anti-social behaviour. They were also required to engage with the police, local authorities and other voluntary and statutory agencies in order to develop full partnership crime reduction projects. These relationships caused some tension, as each agency believed it should have led the programme or at least been more influential in deciding how projects were selected and financed (Tilley 1992).

In some local authority areas, the involvement of the police in these partnerships was considered to be extra difficult because of 'historical tensions' (Tilley 1992: 21), most notably those with a local authority that had a 'left-wing' bias. In London the police/local authority relationship was particularly difficult in some boroughs, causing new legislation to be passed that required local authorities to consult with the Commissioner of Police when promoting 'the prevention of crime or the welfare of victims in their area' (London Local Authorities Act 1989: S5.3).

To ensure a partnership approach was being made to tackle crime, the government later stipulated that bids for regeneration funding would only be considered if it could be shown that there had been a police involvement in the bidding process. Such action forced those local authorities that had refused to work with the police to overcome their various prejudices and create workable partnerships. This was particularly poignant as many of the areas with a serious regeneration problem, requiring the most extensive funding, were under the control of left-wing authorities and were probably the last organization that a 'right-wing' government would wished to be associated with.

Regardless of the political animosity between the dominant partners, these programmes came under attack for other reasons. Tilley's (1994) review of the Safer Cities programme identified a lack of leadership in many schemes and minimal support by the private sector, leading to poorly selected activities that were often badly funded and rarely evaluated. This view was reinforced by Liddle and Gelsthorpe (1994), whose later research also questioned the objectivity of many of the multi-agency partnerships. Another problem highlighted was the desire of the government to retain control, even when their declared intent was to localize. It is suggested by Hughes (1998) that the use of Crime Concern and NACRO to manage these programmes was the Home Office's way of maintaining indirect control, as they are all government sponsored quangos (quasi autonomous non-governmental organizations).

The Morgan Report: A new crime management ideology

By the start of 1990, it was clear that many agencies were engaged in partnership activity, but the lack of monitoring and evaluating called into question its impact. Consequently a review of all multi-agency activity was called for by the government, resulting in the Morgan Report (Home Office 1991), which made many radical recommendations. This was a far-reaching examination, which recognized that despite the obvious advantages of full partnership programmes, their objectives were rarely achieved, because agencies often performed to their own agendas.

The review identified that because crime prevention had remained almost exclusively within the remit of the police, it had become limited in its scope.

> The term 'crime prevention' is often narrowly interpreted and this reinforces the view that it is solely the responsibility of the police. On the other hand, the term community safety, is open to wider interpretation and could encourage greater participation from all sections of the community to fight crime. (Home Office 1991: 3)

By redefining crime prevention to a broader concept, Morgan hoped to re-engage the community in solving problems that were often due to a lack of informal control mechanisms that in earlier generations had prevented crime. However, being aware of the administrative functions of government reports, he then made several practical suggestions as to how this could be implemented.

The Morgan Report was a new crime management ideology that promoted greater community involvement, increased partnership activity and better leadership to provide locally supported holistic solutions. It recommended legislation be used to force the police, local authority and other statutory agencies to work together and, more radically, that the local authority should become the lead agency. To assist with this Morgan suggested a need for a local crime prevention coordinator to pull together joint agency activity. The Conservative government dismissed these suggestions due to financial cost, believing they would be responsible for funding this initiative. Its reticence was due to a financial policy that was trying to reduce local authority funding by capping expenditure. The employment of local crime prevention coordinators was, however, recognised as a positive suggestion and local authorities began to engage personnel for this function from within existing budgets.

Crime and Disorder Act 1998: Towards a stakeholder society

Whilst the government response was not encouraging, many of Morgan's recommendations were to emerge later in the Crime and Disorder Act 1998 (CDA) (see also Loveday, this volume). In reviewing the Morgan Report, Koch (1998: 43) identified five of recommendations that appear to be the basis for the CDA:

1   Local authorities and the police should have a joint statutory responsibility for crime prevention and community safety.
2   Community safety strategy should operate at the highest tier of local government.
3   Local authorities' involvement should be directed by a published Code of Practice.
4   Local partnerships should focus on young people and crime.
5   A coordinator with administrative support should be appointed in each unitary or county level local authority with direct access to chief executives and the local police commander. (Home Office 1991)

Although the Morgan Report failed to find favour with the Conservative Government, the opposition Labour Party embraced its philosophies with open arms. They promised to implement its findings when they returned to office and did so through the CDA. The Morgan Report, a new crime management ideology, promoted qualities that pervaded the New Labour movement's new political ideology called 'The Third Way' (Blair 1998). It was a concept that sought a 'stakeholder society' (Adams 1998: 150) that, whilst finding its theoretical base in management theory, promoted the idea of citizens being treated as customers of the state.

With regard to the particular problem of reducing crime and anti-social behaviour this concept drew from the theorizing of Etzioni (2000: 24), who considers the relationship between the community and the police also to be one of extreme importance. He states:

Public safety and community welfare benefit from the introduction of 'thick' community policing that entails much more than merely getting police officers on the beat. This involves the community in setting priorities for the police and in overseeing their conduct. And it requires involving the police in conflict resolution and in the protection of the overall quality of life. (Etzioni 2000: 24)

The moral positioning of Etzioni was shared by Blair who, as the leader of the New Labour Party, extolled the value of shared responsibility. Adams' analysis of Blair's philosophy considers this emphasis.

> Like those in the communitarian movement he [Blair] believes that people should start rebuilding communities by taking responsibility, and that, more generally, people should be responsible for their actions. There must be duties and obligations to match freedoms and rights. There must be a greater spirit of self-help and civic duty and a renewed emphasis upon the family. (Adams 1998: 149)

The CDA is the next logical step in reducing crime and anti-social behaviour for the benefit of the community. It places a statutory responsibility upon those agencies that have the power and resources to deter those who seek to cause disruption within the community, but more importantly places power in the hands of those who live within that community to determine how they should be policed.

Conclusion

In more recent times the once forgotten original objective of 'the prevention of crime' has been reintroduced into policing as a multi-agency process that requires the police to become a full partner in local, community-driven community safety and crime prevention activities. In pursuit of that process the police have embraced community policing methods in conjunction with situational and social crime prevention theories. This has developed a solid base on which to progress the legislative requirements of the Crime and Disorder Act 1998, which impose a statutory duty on the police to work towards a safer community.

References

Adams, I. (1998) *Ideology and Politics*. Manchester: Manchester University Press.
Alderson, J. (1979) *Policing Freedom*. Plymouth: Latimer Trend.
Bennett, T. (1992) 'Community Policing', *Criminal Justice Matters*, June, London: King's College.
Blair, T. (1998) *The Third Way: New Politics for the New Century*. London: Fabian Society.
Boyle, A. (1962) *Trenchard*. London: Collins.

Brake, M. and Hale, C. (1992) *Public Order and Private Lives*. London: Routledge.

Brogden, M., Jefferson, T. and Walklate, S. (1988) *Introducing Policework*. London: Unwin Hyman.

Clarke, R. (1997) *Rational Choice and Situational Crime Prevention: Theoretical Foundations*. Aldershot: Ashgate.

Cohen, S. (1972) *Folk Devils and Moral Panics: The Creation of the Mods and Rockers*. London, Routledge.

Coleman, A. (1989) 'Disposition and Situation: Two Sides of the Same Crime', in D.J. Evans and D.T. Herbert (eds), *The Geography of Crime*. London: Routledge.

Commission for Racial Equality (1981) *CRE's Submission under Part II of Lord Scarman's Enquiry into the Brixton Disorders*. London, CRE.

Crawford, A. (1998) *Crime Prevention and Community Safety*. London: Longman.

Critchley, T.A. (1978) *A History of the Police in England and Wales*, 2nd edition. London: Constable.

Emsley, C. (1996) 'The History of Crime and Crime Control Institutions c.1770–c.1945', in M. Maguire, R. Morgan and R. Reiner, (eds) *The Oxford Handbook of Criminology*. Oxford; Clarendon Press.

Etzioni, A. (2000) *The Third Way to a Good Society*. London: Demos.

Fitzpatrick, P. (1994) 'Racism and the Innocence of Law', in D.T. Goldberg (ed.), *Anatomy of Racism*. London: University of Minnesota Press.

Fletcher, R. (2000) 'An Intelligent Use of Intelligence', in A. Marlow and B. Loveday (eds), *After Macpherson*. Sheffield: Hallamshire Press.

GLC (1982) *Policing London: The Policing Aspects of Lord Scarman's Report on the Brixton Disorders*. London: GLC.

Goldstein, H. (1990) *Problem Oriented Policing*. London: McGraw.

Graef, R. (1989) *Talking Blues*. London: Fontana.

Hall, S., Chrichter, C., Jefferson, T., Clarke, J. and Roberts, B. (1978) *Policing the Crisis: Mugging the State and Law and Order*. London: Macmillan.

Harvey, L., Grimshaw, P. and Pease, K. (1989) 'Crime Prevention Delivery: The Work of the Crime Prevention Officers', in R. Morgan and D.J. Smith (eds), *Coming to Terms with Policing: Perspective on Policy*. London: Routledge.

Home Office (1965) *Report of the Committee on the Prevention and Detection of Crime* (Cornish Report). London: HMSO.

Home Office (1967) *Police Manpower, Equipment and Efficiency*. London: HMSO.

Home Office (1991) *Safer Communities: The Local Delivery of Crime Prevention Through the Partnership Approach* (Morgan Report). London: Home Office.

Home Office (1993a) *Police Reform: A Police Service for the Twenty First Century*, Cm 2281. London: HMSO.

Home Office (1993b) *Performance Indicators for the Police*. (Circular 17/93) London: HMSO.

Home Office (1995) *Review of the Police Core and Ancillary Tasks: Final Report*. (Posen Report). London HMSO.

Home Office, Department of Education and Science, Department of the Environment, Department of Health and Social Security, Welsh Office (1984) *Crime Prevention*, Home Office Circular 8/1984. London: Home Office.

Hope, T. (1985) *Implementing Crime Prevention Measures*, Home Office Research Study 86. London: HMSO.

Hough M. (1985) 'Organisation and Resource Management of the Uniformed Police', in K. Heal, R. Tarling and J. Burrows (eds), *Situational Crime Prevention*.

London: HMSO.

Hughes, G. (1998) *Understanding Crime Prevention*. Milton Keynes: Open University Press.

Hussain, S. (1988) *Neighbourhood Watch in England and Wales: A Locational Analysis*, Home Office Crime Prevention Unit, Paper 12. London: HMSO.

ISTD (1993) *Changing Police: Business or Service?* London: ISTD.

Jacobs, J. (1961) *The Life and Death of a Great American City*. Harmondsworth: Penguin.

Jefferson, T. (1990) *The Case Against Paramilitary Policing*. Milton Keynes: Open University.

Jefferson, T. and Shapland, J. (1994) 'Criminal Justice and the Production of Order and Control', *Journal of Criminology*, 34: 265–290.

Johnston, L. (1997) 'Policing Communities at Risk', in P. Francis, P. Davies and V. Jupp (eds), *Policing Futures*. Basingstoke: Macmillan.

Johnston, V., Shapland, J. and Wiles, P. (1993) *Developing Police Crime Prevention: Management and Organisational Change*, Police Research Group Paper 55. London: Home Office.

Jones, T., and Newburn, T. (1997) *Policing after the Act: Police and Magistrates Court Act 1994*. London: Police Studies Institute.

Kettle, M. and Hodges, L. (1982) *Uprising: The Police, the People and the Riots in Britain's Cities*. London: Pan.

Koch, B. (1998) *The Politics of Crime Prevention*. Aldershot: Ashgate.

Laycock, G. and Tilley, N. (1995) *Policing and Neighbourhood Watch*, Crime Detection and Prevention Series Paper 60. London: Home Office.

Lea, J. and Young, J. (1993) *What is to be Done about Law and Order?* London: Pluto Press.

Liddle, A.M. and Gelsthorpe L.R. (1994) *Inter-agency Crime Prevention: Organising Local Delivery*. Home Office Police Research Group Paper 52. London: Home Office.

Matthews, R. (1994) 'Crime Prevention, Disorder and Victimisation: Some Recent Western Experiences', *International Journal of the Sociology of Law*, 22: 87–104.

Mawby, R. (2002) *Policing Images, Policy, Communication and Legitimacy*. Cullompton: Willan.

McLaughlin, E. (1996) Police, Policing and Police Work, in E. McLaughlin and J. Muncie (eds), *Controlling Crime*. London: Sage.

McLaughlin, E. and Muncie, J. (1996) *Controlling Crime*. London: Sage.

Morgan, R. and Newburn, T. (1997) *The Future of Policing*. Oxford: Clarendon Press.

Newman, K. (1985) 'Police Bashers Risk to Labour Reputation. *Police Review*, October.

Newman, O. (1972) *Defensible Space, People and Design in the Violent City*. London: Architectural Press.

Oliver, I. (1997) *Police, Government and Accountability*. London: Macmillan.

Posen, I. (1994) *Review of Police Core and Ancillary Tasks*. Paper presented to ACPO Conference, March 1994.

Reiner, R. (1992) *The Politics of Police*. London: Harvester Wheatsheaf.

Reiner, R. (1994) 'Policing and the Police', in M. Maguire, R. Morgan and R. Reiner (eds), *The Oxford Handbook of Criminology*. Oxford: Clarendon Press.

Rosenbaum, D.P. (1986) 'The Problem of Crime Control', in D.P. Rosenbaum (ed.), *Community Crime Prevention: Does it Work?* London: Sage.

Saunders, D. (1984) *The West Indian Boys in Britain*. London, Grijelmo.

Scarman, L. (1981) *The Brixton Disorders 10–12 April 1981: Report of an Inquiry by the Rt. Hon. The Lord Scarman OBE.* London: HMSO.

Skogan, W.G. and Maxfield, M.G. (1981) *Coping with Crime: Individual and Neighbourhood Reactions.* London: Sage.

Tilley, N. (1992) *Safer Cities and Community Safety.* Home Office Police Research Group Paper 38. London: Home Office.

Thomas D.N. (1986) *White Bolts, Black Locks.* London: Billing and Sons.

Turner, B.W.M. and Barker, P.J. (1983) *Study Tour to the United States.* Metropolitan Police Internal Report.

Weatheritt, M. (1986) *Innovations in Policing.* London: Croom Helm.

Wilson, J. and Kelling, G. (1982) 'Broken Windows', *Atlantic Monthly*, March.

Chapter 5

Police and community justice in partnership

Barry Loveday

In what might be seen as one of the most positive legislative developments since the arrival of New Labour in 1997, the Crime and Disorder Act of 1998 has created statutory partnership arrangements across England and Wales to develop local crime reduction strategies. Although the 1998 legislation was to embrace a wide range of community justice issues, the central feature of the Act for police and local government was a new requirement to work with other agencies in partnership in developing local crime and disorder reduction initiatives.

The decision to develop new local partnerships can be traced back to the 1991 Morgan Report, *Safer Communities*. The Morgan Report, commissioned by the then Conservative administration was to consider the issue of how best to develop an effective crime prevention strategy. In what proved to be a source of embarrassment to the government, the Morgan enquiry concluded that the most effective way of improving crime prevention would involve local government in developing local strategies with the police and other agencies. This was not a message that the Conservative government, then waging war on the public sector, wanted to hear. In what became one of the Conservative government's best-kept secrets, it effectively sat on the report and refused to countenance the implementation of its primary recommendations. These would for the first time in years have served to enhance the role of local authorities.

Tony Blair's New Labour government was to alter this. In an early 'quick win' for New Labour, the Blair government committed itself to the full implementation of the Morgan Report recommendations. These were to form the basis of local Crime and Disorder Reduction Partnerships (CDRP), in operation since 1998. Although initially the 'lead' responsibility for the partnership was to be allocated to local authorities, it became apparent that the police service would only accept an arrangement within which that responsibility was shared with the police service.

Composition of the CDRP

As a result, the 'lead authorities' for the CDRP are made up of both the local authority and the police. The CDRP, represented at county council level by the chief executive and chief constable and at district level by the district authority chief executive and local police commander (a super-intendent), is statutorily responsible for sustaining and directing the partnerships consisting of a number of additional local agencies. Other than the local authority and police the partnership can be expected to include local health services, housing partnerships, the voluntary sector, probation service, the police authority, the Domestic Violence Forum, Youth Offending Teams (YOTs) and Drug Action Teams (DATs).

It is immediately apparent that both motivating and coordinating the work of so many members of a partnership presents a significant challenge. Effective leadership must be provided at the top, particularly by the local authority chief executive and police commander. Where such commitment is demonstrated it becomes possible for community safety officers – local authority employees – to implement a potentially effective crime reduction programme with the full support of partner agencies. Where this leadership is absent the successful delivery of service becomes more problematic.

There are further problems that can challenge effective partnership work at the local level. These relate to the advantages that arise where member agencies share coterminous boundaries, and corresponding disadvantages where this is not the case. This is compounded by the two-tier structure of local government in England and Wales, where all counties as well as all local district authorities are given CDRP responsibilities. This is not made easier by the fact that each tier is responsible for different services. This situation does not extend to the 'new' unitary local authorities based on largely urban areas, made responsible for the delivery of all local services in their towns and cities, yet problems with the coordination of strategic functions such as health, fire and police services may still arise. One possible long-term solution to the endemic lack of coterminosity that now confronts CDRPs could prove to be the creation of unitary authorities across England and Wales.

A further problem that has confronted CDRPs in the local delivery of crime reduction strategies has been intervention from central government in the determination of local service provision. The commitment by government to performance management and performance culture has generated a plethora of service targets and performance indicators, most of which have originated from Whitehall or the Cabinet Office. The impact of central government intervention presents a major challenge to the development of local crime reduction strategies that increasingly reflect the priorities of central government. The level of intervention experienced to date has made it difficult for some services to commit wholly to local strategic priorities unless these clearly overlap with those identified by central government. The problem of micro-management by the government has proved to be particularly problematic for the police service.

The crime audit process

The Crime and Disorder Act (CADA 1998) has required local agencies along with the police to record crime problems within their area. This requires all local services (particularly local authority services) to map every incident of which it is aware. As the local authority now shares with the police a statutory responsibility to reduce crime in the local area, it needs to be aware of the nature and extent of the crime problem within its boundary. One consequence of this has been the widespread introduction of geographic information systems (GIS) within the local authority for mapping crime and 'hot spots'.

The audit process also builds upon recorded crime statistics provided by the police and all crime data (where available) collected by other local services. Conducted on a three-yearly cycle, the audit forms the basis of the subsequent local crime reduction strategy. Data from local services could be expected to include all cases of criminal damage recorded by departments and the cost of repair. Housing associations, and local highways and amenities departments would be asked to provide details of running damage repair costs to their estate or to street furniture. Similarly, the local hospital trust would provide data relating to the number and nature of cases of assault with which it has dealt over the particular three-year period. Information would also be provided by Young Offender and Drug Action Teams, and the local social and youth service departments. As is evident from this process, the CDRP is heavily dependent on information recorded by member agencies. However, appropriate information may not always be held or recorded by them (Home Office 2002).

For example, for the crime audit the local education department and individual schools can expect to be requested to provide information concerning the incidence of permanent and temporary exclusions from schools, along with victimization rates in school or adjacent to it (see Hayden, this volume). This would include the incidence of school bullying – a matter that can be expected to assume a much higher profile, following the Pennell murder case in 2004 (Wainwright 2004). As with health trusts, however, there can be a tendency for schools not to record or acknowledge incidents that might generate negative local publicity.

Despite identifiable problems, the crime audit process now provides a more detailed information base concerning local crime and victimization patterns than before. Even with non-recording and/or non-disclosure by some agencies, the audit provides a more comprehensive database than previous dependence on police recorded crime statistics was ever likely to do. However, as originally devised the audit process could be seen as being overly orientated towards quantitative crime data collection and percentile reduction targets. This has been a particular characteristic of the crime data required by central government that might benefit from a future review.

One result of the current audit process is that it may not be sufficiently sophisticated to confront the more pervasive and complex problems, such as fear of crime or fear of victimization, that permeate many communities. The audit process may also prove less than effective in dealing with 'organizational cultures' with which the CDRP and community safety officers will inevitably be confronted. Whilst there has been a traditional academic interest in 'police culture' (e.g. Reiner 2000) within the CDRP, the problem of local bureaucratic cultures has yet to be fully acknowledged. This problem is complicated by the fact that within the local authority there may be not just one definable culture but a number of cultures that may differ between local service departments. This feature of the local authority world deserves further study by reference to specific departments such planning and highways or social services and housing, where commitment to the audit and CDRP strategy may differ substantially.

Whilst the crime audit process may face some resistance from local bureaucracies it does provide the opportunity to identify local community views about crime and disorder. All crime audits should involve public surveys of local residents and businesses. Many CDRPs will use either professional polling companies to conduct and analyse local public surveys or have developed their own postal surveys. Within each the aim is to ascertain local opinions and priorities. Many CDRPs will also make use of focus groups to engage with a variety of social groups and local associations within the community. The audit will also, by way of interview with a range of officers from CDRP agencies, identify the degree to which the partnership has been able to achieve its strategic objectives over the previous three years. This will relate to the work of the partnership, community safety policy and strategy implementation.

As a result the CDRP should reflect, within its audit, community concerns and priorities about crime and disorder. In relation to this it has been frequently found that 'disorder' rather than crime has been immediately identified as a priority issue for the community. This was not initially reflected within the priorities set by the Home Office for CDRPs and police forces. Until recently the government has been committed to reducing the incidence of 'volume crime', rather than responding to 'quality of life' issues that engage most communities.

Local crime reduction strategies

On completion of the audit process a local crime reduction strategy will be drafted. The strategy will address problems identified in the crime audit but will also include government crime priorities and targets as these are also likely to have some salience in the 'local' policing plan. The policing plan will percolate down to the local police 'basic command unit' (BCU), within which the local BCU commander will align CDRP priorities with those of the policing plan. Additionally the local CDRP is required to identify and target 'hidden crime', for example racial attacks, domestic violence and homophobic crime. These will usually be prioritized by the CDRP, which reflects a refreshing change from the past; these offences have long been very much part of the 'dark figure of crime', a result of both under-reporting and less than adequate recording procedures among police forces.

Thereafter the crime strategy is open to public consultation. This has proved to be a source of frustration, particularly when the public response has been less than overwhelming. However, sufficient local publicity can provide residents with information about the strategic aims of the partnership and local media coverage can be of assistance. Experience suggests, however, that the identification of 'hot spot' areas within specific estates are a matter of greater interest than local crime strategies (Fareham District Council First Crime Audit 1998/9). Local authority publications and free newspapers are used to circulate information, while a number of partnerships may use 'in-house' consultation with the main CDRP agencies as a primary platform within the consultation process.

One result of this can be that professional officers within the primary agencies who are members of the partnership will be also responsible for 'signing off' the local crime strategy. For this reason, among others, the government has raised the accountability of CDRPs as a matter of current concern (Home Office 2003a). As membership very often involves only professional officers, the accountability of the CDRP remains somewhat opaque. This matter assumes a greater salience when CDRP strategy can directly influence operational policing within the CDRP area.

Following consultation, the crime and disorder strategy provides the framework for the agencies within the partnership. It is led by the local operational 'crime and disorder team', a multi-agency team composed of community safety officers and the police. An example of a current crime and disorder strategy for 2002–2005 is shown below. The key aim of the strategy is to reduce crime and disorder, within which five priority areas are identified. These are:

- Targeted crime
- Drug and alcohol misuse
- Working with young people to reduce crime and disorder
- Domestic violence
- Anti-social behaviour.

Source: Hampshire Constabulary (2003)

Local strategies will reflect local concerns and can be expected to differ between partnerships. However, one common feature has been that public concern over anti-social behaviour remains a clear priority for many. Compliance with the crime reduction strategy (Section 17 of the Crime and Disorder Act 1998) requires all local service departments to consider the potential impact of their work on crime and disorder. Many planning departments within the local authority will now normally be expected to consult with a police architectural liaison officer. Similarly, highways departments may engage in consultation about changes or additions to street furnishing, particularly in relation to CCTV access and use.

Not all local service departments have proved to be equally assiduous in acknowledging or complying with Section 17 of the Crime and Disorder Act 1998. For various reasons some local departments have not proved fully committed to the crime reduction process and this has created a barrier to effective strategy implementation. A recent survey of local police commanders (Superintendents' Association 2003) highlighted the nature and extent of the problem faced by local crime and disorder teams. When asked within the survey the extent to which, in their experience, local partners and services had fulfilled their partnership role, most local police commanders indicated that few had done so (see Table 5.1 below).

Table 5.1 How completely partners have fulfilled their role

	Base	Completely (%)	Partly (%)	Not at all (%)
Local authority chief executive's office	210	58	38	2
Fire service	174	40	53	5
Police authority	146	40	53	6
Victim support	124	39	52	6
Local authority housing department	173	34	60	4
Probation services	192	26	60	11
For two-tier authority areas: county council	81	26	69	5
Local authority youth services department	183	25	67	7
Community groups and voluntary agencies	139	25	69	3
Social landlord/housing association	123	24	63	12
Local authority environmental health department	134	22	64	9
Local authority social services department	170	22	61	15
Local authority leisure and amenities department	114	18	70	11
Religious body	68	16	57	25
Local authority planning department	103	15	69	15
Local authority education department	182	15	70	13
Parish/community council	75	15	68	13
Business group or group promoting business interests	118	14	68	18
Health services, including primary care trust	195	11	60	26
Crown Prosecution Service	81	11	47	40
Transport provider	49	10	43	43
Court service	93	8	56	32
Other	21	33	52	5

Source: Superintendents' Association (2003)

The survey highlighted a situation where just a third of local BCU commanders believed that local government departments were fulfilling their role. Most commanders believed that local departments did not pull their weight. As these departments included environmental health, social services, leisure and amenities, planning, housing and local education departments, this perception might be considered a matter of concern. These are in fact the very departments that can be expected to exercise the greatest influence in the success of any local CDRP crime reduction strategy.

The survey identifies the problem that whilst the crime and disorder strategy is of central importance to the crime and disorder team (particularly the police), this view may be not be shared among local service departments, for whom it is of only peripheral professional interest (or relevance) (O'Byrne 2001). Yet, as is now recognized, the police cannot implement an effective community safety policy without support from local service departments. Additionally the use by the police of their enforcement powers alone is unlikely to be sufficient to achieve local crime reduction objectives (O'Byrne 2001). For the police to begin to develop a 'problem solving approach' to crime (problem orientated policing), effective partnership with local authority departments is essential. Professional experience suggests that crime reduction strategies within a community safety framework promise more success than either the old professional policing model or a crime control approach that were once on offer (O'Byrne 2001).

It is clear that the 'crime' problem the local community experiences is likely to be more effectively resolved within a partnership arrangement than by unilateral law enforcement by the police. As a survey of local commanders demonstrated, the primary problem confronting most police BCUs concerned 'alcohol-related disorder' and anti-social behaviour (see Table 5.2).

Table 5.2 Crime prevalence compared with the national average

Base: All respondents (223)	Above average (%)	Average (%)	Below average (%)
Volume crime	33	31	34
Serious/violent crime	34	25	39
Drug dealing	28	42	27
Race/hate crime	14	25	58
Witness intimidation	10	30	56
Organized criminal networks	17	28	52
Gang warfare and related killings	14	10	72
Alcohol-related disorder (e.g. from nightclubs/pubs)	30	52	16
Domestic violence	28	61	8
Traffic offences, including road traffic accidents	15	64	18
Anti-social behaviour	29	59	10

Source: Superintendents' Association (2003)

The nature and prevalence of crime identified in the survey suggests that most crime is local and involves primarily a threat to the quality of life of residents. Often dismissed in the past as 'minor crime', it significantly impacts on perceptions of personal safety and fear of crime within local communities, and represents one of the most profound current challenges to both the local CDRP and the police. Yet the ability of local police forces to respond to this challenge is increasingly compromised by pressure from central government to determine national (and therefore local) policing priorities.

Police priorities and the National Policing Plan

Under the Police Reform Act 2002 new powers were given to the Home Secretary to create a National Policing Plan within which the Minister is able to determine police priorities across the country over a three-year period. Within the current National Policing Plan (2004–2007), a number of key priorities have been identified by the government. These range from requiring police to provide a 'citizen focused service' to tackling 'volume crime', whilst also combating 'serious and organised crime both across and within force boundaries' (Home Office 2003b).

Additionally the police are required to encourage 'community engagement'. Another key priority is identified as 'countering terrorism and the threat of terrorism' (Home Office 2003b: 13). Recent police operations in relation to the terrorist threat have served to demonstrate the significant impact of national policing priorities on local policing. In line with national police priorities and using their powers under the Terrorism Act (2000), since 2001 28 police authorities across the country have been involved in operations that have led to 562 arrests of suspects under this Act.

Yet to date, of the 562 arrests 280 were subsequently released without charge. A further 152 of those arrested were either charged under legislation other than the 2000 Terrorism Act or 'released into the custody of immigration'. One example of the police response to 'terrorism' was provided by Greater Manchester Police in April 2004 when a series of anti-terror raids were carried out which led to the arrest of 10 people on suspicion of the commission, preparation or instigation of acts of terrorism. Subsequently all were to be released without charge (Travis 2004a). Clearly the police are torn between international tensions and local concerns.

National priorities identified by the government have had immediate consequences for CDRPs. The Anti-Social Behaviour Act 2003 gives the police new powers in relation to the use of Anti-Social Behaviour Orders (ASBOs). Within Section 30 of the Act police are able to 'disperse' groups of people deemed to be engaged in acts of anti-social behaviour, to determine geographic areas which may not be used by those identified as being involved in acts of anti-social behaviour, and to impose curfew orders on those so involved. While the imposition of ASBOs must have the support of the local authority, the Home Secretary (and Prime Minister) remain committed to their much wider application. The use of the ASBO may, however, allow the police to fulfil an additional national key priority identified within the National Policing Plan: 'tackling anti-social behaviour and disorder'. Once again the 'nationalization' of the use of the ASBO can be expected to have implications for the local CDRP and its own determination of local priorities.

One further problem that has arisen in relation to policing priorities concerns the introduction of the police National Intelligence Model (NIM). The NIM, which under the 2003 National Policing Plan all police forces are required to adopt, identifies three levels of crime that reflect the seriousness of the offence. Level 1 relates to local and minor crime while levels 2 and 3 relate to cross-border crime and national/international crime.

The National Policing Plan 2003 highlights the need for all police forces to meet the challenge of tackling serious and organized crime (level 2 and 3 crime) that occurs across force boundaries. Within the National Policing Plan it is stated that 'levels 2 and 3 of the NIM must be a key priority for all forces' (Home Office 2003b: 24). The national requirement on the part of the Home Secretary for all forces to prioritize 'organized and other serious crime' does not appear to be in accord, however, with the nature and reality of the majority of crime confronting most BCU commanders. This, as the 2003 survey demonstrates, remains overwhelmingly a 'level 1' crime problem (see Table 5.2 above).

Basic command units and delegated responsibility

CDRPs are increasingly subject to pressures to conform to national police agendas. Their ability to fulfil their responsibilities properly can become more problematic as a result. As the Superintendents' Association has argued, local commanders are under increasing pressure to achieve centrally determined targets and objectives that often seem not to be in alignment with community perceptions of local crime priorities (Super-intendents' Association 2003).

A further problem for BCU commanders relates to delegated responsibilities and budgets within the police force. Currently all BCUs are subject to individual inspection by Her Majesty's Inspectorate of Constabulary (HMIC). It is evident however that while commanders are made responsible for the performance of the BCU (largely in terms of achieving nationally set performance targets) they usually do not have the resources to effect any real change at a local level. Although recent changes to Home Office police grants means that some funding now goes direct from the Home Office to the BCU, there is a continuing problem with local BCU budgets. As a survey of all current BCU commanders demonstrated only a minority of these officers had any real control over police funding. The 2003 Superintendents Report showed that many commanders had either only 'partial' or 'no control' over significant elements of the police budget (see Table 5.3).

Table 5.3 The decisions BCU commanders can make without reference to Force HQ and what control they have over the budget

Base: All respondents (223)	Responsibility (%)	Full control of budget (%)	Partial control of budget (%)	No control (%)
Office equipment	87	80	18	2
Operations support	38	23	37	40
Vehicle fleet	27	21	49	30
Crime support	21	16	34	50
Management info	42	20	37	43
IT	22	14	58	27
Property management	22	10	61	29
Human resources	32	22	43	35
Police pay	13	32	24	43
Training	29	14	57	29
Overtime budget	77	79	20	1
Officer staffing levels	37	26	36	38
Civilian staffing levels	42	38	34	29
Maintenance	52	32	52	15
Allowances, e.g. vehicle and telephone	50	14	58	27
Income generation, e.g. selling police time to football grounds	49	40	39	21

Source: Superintendents' Association (2003)

The survey shows that the only area where BCU commanders had full control of the budget proved to be 'office equipment'. Thereafter BCU responsibilities and control of the budget markedly diverged. In those areas where functions would impact BCU management and performance most, the local commander had only limited responsibility. This was most marked in relation to 'officer staffing levels', where just over a quarter of respondents (26 per cent) stated that they had full control of the budget (Superintendents' Association 2003).

The issue of local delegation of budgets cannot be considered in any detail here. It is sufficient to note that current arrangements surrounding the non-delegation of budgets to BCU commands by police headquarters can be expected to impact on the ability of local commanders to influence the work of the CDRP. Under current funding arrangements there appears to be little that they can realistically bring to the 'partnership table'. This may only serve to highlight further police dependence on local authority services in the pursuit of local CDRP crime reduction strategies.

This conundrum for the BCU commander is discussed in the Superintendents' Association report *Moving Policing Forward* (Superintendents' Association 2004). It argues that current funding arrangements for BCUs are haphazard with a wide divergence of practice across the country. Whilst some BCUs are given 'significant devolvement of funds' and flexibility in their use, others have budgets that are 'dictated and controlled at force level with only the most limited devolvement available' (Superintendents' Association 2004: 5).

The report found that even where BCUs enjoy significant devolvement it was not uncommon for funds to be withdrawn at short notice 'to pay for force priorities'. This served to hinder short and medium-term priorities that had been agreed with partners 'for actions to achieve the local crime and disorder reduction plan' (Superintendents' Association 2004: 5). One result of this has been a diminution of trust between BCU commander and their partners (Superintendents' Association 2004: 5). Alternative sources of funding, which attempt to tap into central funding streams, are based on competitive bidding and require the allocation of BCU staff to prepare bids. Many of these prove to be unsuccessful. Experience has led the Superintendents' Association to argue the case for direct funding to the BCU and access to other partnership funds, which would lead to local commanders having the 'financial wherewithal' to enjoin with partners to solve local community safety problems.

The Superintendents' Association has therefore argued for direct funding to the BCU to a statutory minimum level. This might begin to provide local commanders with the flexibility to determine their spending 'in line with agreed local priorities' (Superintendents' Association 2004: 5). The problem of non-delegation of budgets within one of the primary CDRP agencies may have impeded the successful development of partnership arrangements to date. Further reform of police funding may still be necessary if this problem is to be resolved.

Partnership boundaries

Funding is not the only problem confronting the police partnership role within the CDRP. As was identified within an early Home Office progress report on CDRPs, where different agencies operate within different geographical boundaries 'difficulties of various kinds arise for partnerships' (Home Office 2002: 20). The lack of coterminosity has meant that it is difficult to disaggregate data or make meaningful comparisons between services in the same CDRP area. This remains an ongoing problem. Outside of unitary authorities, the lack of coterminosity between local BCU commands and local authority boundaries can be particularly problematic. In the counties a police commander can be made responsible for a number of CDRPs operating within the BCU area. The problem is compounded by the small size of some district authorities that cannot justify or support a BCU. As yet HMIC does not require the collection of data concerning the presence or absence of coterminous boundaries, despite the recognized value of this in improving police effectiveness (O'Byrne 2001).

As HMIC is concerned with improving efficiency and effectiveness, and is responsible for the collection of data on police performance, the evident failure to identify 'coterminosity' as a factor impinging on performance might be thought anomalous. In the absence of direction from HMIC it is also the case that police forces are able to change BCU boundaries unilaterally (usually through amalgamation of existing BCUs) and this often only serves to compound the problem.

Reorganized (and usually enlarged) BCUs within which local commanders are able to exercise less managerial discretion are, ironically, justified by police headquarters with reference to improving BCU efficiency. One consequence of the redrawing of BCU boundaries is a greater difficulty in sustaining the local CDRP partnership. Currently this does not appear to be a matter of great concern to either chief police officers or HMIC.

Yet the current trend towards the creation of larger BCUs can be significant for those responsible for their management. Within such large units it is unlikely that the BCU commander can provide the 'visible direct leadership style' thought necessary to enhance police performance (Superintendents' Association 2004: 7). As noted BCUs now exist with 1,400 staff, and proposals are in place to raise this figure to 2,000. If these changes are introduced, BCUs would be bigger than most county police forces. Arguing that a BCU should not exceed 400 staff, the Superintendents' Association has stated that where BCU size goes above that 'it is questionable whether the BCU Commander can provide the visible direct leadership style' that is now required (Superintendents' Association 2004).

The problem of non-coterminous boundaries was clearly addressed by the Superintendents' Association. It has argued in favour of shared boundaries and has stated that:

> The requirement to engage in partnership working makes coterminosity the most critical single factor in determining whether a BCU is likely to deliver effective local policing. (Superintendents' Association 2004: 4)

The report claimed that the more closely aligned the boundaries of respective partners proved to be, then the more effectively the partners could combine in the delivery of community safety. It acknowledged that where BCU commanders are required to work with multiple partnerships that are in turn required to work with more than one BCU commander, 'an inevitable confusion follows in respect of resourcing and responsibility'. It was not rare for a BCU commander to work with two or more partnerships whose strategic aims were 'at best misaligned and at worst conflicting' (Superintendents' Association 2004: 4).

Local agency boundaries

There may be agencies, such as Local Criminal Justice Boards and the Crown Prosecution Service, whose boundaries are never likely to be coterminous with those of the local authority or BCU. For the probation service the structural changes implemented by NOMS may provide additional challenges. There are, however, a number of important agencies responsible for the delivery of local services, which immediately impact on the delivery of CDRP crime reduction strategies, where shared boundaries could well be established. These would include all local authority departments, primary care trusts, probation, Drug Action Teams (DATs) and the Youth Justice Board. Some agencies are already sharing common boundaries, as are, for example, the DATs that have recently (2004) been amalgamated with the local CDRP.

The problem of non-coterminous boundaries between local authorities and BCUs clearly needs to be addressed. Within the counties the situation is made worse by the two-tier system where strategic services are the responsibility of the county whilst local services are the responsibility of the districts. Because of the small size of many districts, one BCU will often be required to work with a number of district councils, thus creating the problems identified earlier by the Super-intendents' Association.

One example of the problem associated with two-tier local government can be seen in Warwickshire, where a small county police force of 1,000 officers work within two BCUs and are responsible for five district councils. In the absence of a unitary structure it is difficult to develop effective partnership arrangements successfully. At county council level, strategic services will need to be represented on each local district CDRP besides participating at a county level. This suggests that future local government reorganization may need to consider the opportunities arising from an expanded unitary authority arrangement that brings an end to the current two-tier divide.

The Soham case and Humberside Police boundaries

The need for closer local service collaboration within shared boundaries has been demonstrated in a number of recent high-profile murder investigations. In both the Victoria Climbie and Soham murder cases it was apparent that the failure of local police to record and share information, or establish effective partnership arrangements, had contributed to these tragedies. In the Soham case it was evident that the failure of social services to pick up on, record and fully communicate to Humberside Police information concerning Ian Huntley's earlier criminal activities contributed significantly to Huntley's ability to obtain a school caretaker's job at Soham, Cambridgeshire (Bichard 2004).

The Bichard Inquiry stated that there was a clear need to 'reaffirm the guidance in "Working Together to Safeguard Children" so that the police are notified as soon as possible when a criminal offence has been committed or is suspected of being committed' (Bichard 2004: 14). The failure on the part of social services may have been compounded by the lack of shared boundaries between social services and Humberside Police. Following the abolition of Humberside as a county it was replaced by a number of unitary authorities including those based on the rural areas of North Lincolnshire – Scunthorpe and Grimsby – that from 1974 formed part of Humberside County. Reform did not, however, extend to redrawing police boundaries, and the new unitary authorities in Lincolnshire were required to liaise with Humberside Police whose boundaries were not correspondingly restructured. It was evident to some commentators that ready communication might not be easy to establish or sustain between the 'new' unitary authorities and a police force HQ across the Humber (Brown 2004).

As was to be argued, despite continued lobbying by the local MP for North Lincolnshire to redraw police boundaries, Home Secretary, Michael Howard refused to accept the case that North Lincolnshire should be covered by the Lincolnshire police force. As the MP was to argue later:

> Among other reasons [justifying this change] it seemed a recipe for disaster that these new Lincolnshire local authorities' social services departments should have to liaise with a police force headquartered in another county. (Brown 2004)

Of consequence was the lack of surprise on Brown's part concerning the later identification within the Bichard Inquiry Report of systematic and corporate failing in the senior management of Humberside Police, which did little to encourage effective communications between the force and surrounding local authority social services departments (Brown 2004). Altogether the Soham case only served to reinforce the argument for clear, identifiable communications between public services based on shared coterminous boundaries.

Partners in targeting and reducing crime?

Since their creation, the government has set CDRPs clear targets in relation to crime reduction. Most recently the Home Secretary has identified the reduction of 'volume crime' as a primary target for both the CDRP and police forces. Volume crime concerns acquisitive or property crime and encompasses burglary and theft of or from motor vehicles. Although the targets set by government have often been met, what precise impact such target-setting has had on successive reductions in acquisitive crime remains unclear. This issue is complicated by the research conducted by Simon Field in 1990. This suggested that a clear link between the business cycle and the nature of offending could be identified.

As Field's research concluded, when employment rises and with it disposable income, the police can expect a corresponding fall in acquisitive crime but increase in violent crime. With any rise in unemployment (particularly among the young) the cycle would be reversed, with acquisitive crime rising and violent crime falling (Field 1990). The business cycle identified by Field may have some application to current crime trends in England and Wales, particularly as property crime continues to fall (Home Office 2004).

It does so against a background of significantly increased employment opportunities and an expanding economy that over the last five years has seen a dramatic fall in the number of unemployed, particularly among the young. Interestingly, as recorded crime statistics demonstrate, the fall in property crime has been more than matched by a rise in violent crime (Home Office 2004).

Quarterly figures for recorded crime during 2003 saw a 17 per cent rise in violent crime against the person over the year. Whilst new methods of recording offences used by the police may explain some of this rise, it was also accepted that much of the problem surrounding the incidence of violent crime related to young people and their use of disposable income for the purchase of alcohol. This has been matched by the growth of the 'night time economy' (NTE), within which large, themed pubs, bars and clubs compete for business particularly in terms of alcohol sales. Responding to the problem of violent crime many police forces have decided to target 'binge-drinking' in towns and cities in an attempt to reduce the number of alcohol-related assaults. The Home Office now estimates that alcohol is the primary cause of approximately half of all violent crime and connected to 70 per cent of late-night admissions to hospital Accident and Emergency departments (Bennetto 2004).

The changing trends in offending may, as Field suggests, accurately reflect changes within the economy rather than any success by the government or police. It also suggests that increased disposable income and the use of alcohol primarily by the young will continue to impact on the quality of life of others, particularly in relation to alcohol-induced anti-social behaviour. Under the Anti-Social Behaviour Act 2003 the police have new dispersal powers, but against this must be balanced the effect of the Licensing Act 2004 that will significantly extend licensing hours and may, as a result, increase competition between licensees. How the CDRP responds to this development will be of interest, particularly if the police are given new crime reduction targets relating to violent crime.

The excessive consumption of alcohol or 'binge-drinking' among the young may be a problem that can at best be managed rather than solved. The use by police and local authorities of new powers under the 2004 Licensing Act in relation to licensees who break the law might prove to be of only limited success in comparison with the current size and financial importance of the NTE to the UK drinks industry (Travis 2004a, 2004b). It could offer a real test of the efficacy of local partnerships, as any success will require leadership and a close cooperation and understanding between the primary partners within the CDRP.

Conclusion

To date the decision by New Labour to implement the primary recommendations of the Morgan Report in establishing local partnerships may be judged both timely and appropriate. However, tensions may increasingly surround these partnerships. One relates to the fact that often community safety strategies involve long-term objectives, where quick 'wins' are not realizable particularly where these relate to 'social crime prevention' objectives. This can easily conflict with a party political process that inevitably highlights short-term gains.

Additionally, government commitment to what it sees as effective solutions to immediate problems of anti-social behaviour may not be shared or accepted within partnerships. The implementation of the Anti-Social Behaviour Act 2003 has occurred at a time when the CDRP has amalgamated with the DAT. There may not, as a result, be a shared perception as to either its value or utility particularly in relation to the dispersal powers given to the police under the Act.

A further tension has arisen from the comprehensive application across the public sector of a performance management approach where great emphasis is placed on measurable short-term targets and objectives. These are often set within a highly political context and may be designed for immediate public (media) consumption rather than to improve the effectiveness of public services. The resulting 'gaming' by public services has been recently identified in a highly critical report by the Audit Commission (Audit Commission 2003). It found that many public services 'manage' performance measures to achieve the targets set for them rather than improve effective service delivery. This has already impacted on most public services making up the partnership.

One further impact of performance management has been that individual public service targets set by the central government are seen as paramount by those services, rather than the targets or objectives set for them by the CDRP. Centrally set performance targets can always be expected to have high salience for public services. This has been most clearly evidenced in health and education 'services' over the operational life of the CDRP.

The government's commitment to performance management and measurable targets presents a continuing challenge to the CDRP particularly in terms of the implementation of long-term crime reduction strategies. Within these measurable results are of course unlikely to be immediately available. Evidence suggests, however, that the long-term success of crime reduction partnerships may ultimately depend on the extent to which government releases public services from central performance measures. This would allow partners making up the CDRP the discretion to identify and respond to local crime and disorder priorities. It must remain a matter of speculation, however, as to when (or whether) locally determined crime reduction strategies, developed independently of central government, will find either favour or support from New Labour.

References

Audit Commission (2003) *Targets in the Public Sector*. Audit Commission: Public Sector Briefing 2003.

Bennetto, J. (2004) 'Alcohol takes the blame for soaring levels of violent crime among young men', *Independent*, 30 July 2004.

Bichard (2004) *A Public Inquiry Report on Child Protection Procedures in Humberside Police and Cambridgeshire Constabulary*. London: TSO (Stationery Office).

Brown, M. (2004) 'Soham proves the need for a national police force', *Independent*, 23 June 2004.

Field, S. (1990) *Trends in Crime and their Interpretation*. London: HMSO.

Hampshire Constabulary (2003) *Isle of Wight BCU Service Plan 2004/5*. Hampshire Constabulary.

Home Office (1991) *Safer Communities: Report of the Morgan Inquiry*. London: HMSO.

Home Office (2002) *Crime and Disorder Reduction Partnerships: Round One Progress*. Police Research Series Paper 151. London: HMSO.

Home Office (2003a) *Building Safer Communities*. London: HMSO.

Home Office (2003b) *National Policing Plan 2004–2007*. London: HMSO.

Home Office (2004) *Criminal Statistics England and Wales*. London: HMSO.

Loveday, B. and Reid, A. (2003) *Going Local: Who Should Run Britain's Police?* London: Policy Exchange.

O'Byrne, M. (2001) *Changing Policing: Revolution not Evolution*. Lyme Regis: Russell House Publications.

Reiner, R. (2000) *The Politics of the Police* (3rd edition). Oxford: Oxford University Press.

Superintendents' Association (2003) *Factors that Impact on Basic Command Unit Performance*. London: BMRB Social Research International.

Superintendents' Association (2004) *Moving Policing Forward – Proposals for the Future*. Superintendents' Association.

Travis, A. (2004a) 'Low Number of Convictions does not Tell the Whole Story, Insist Police', *Guardian*, 5 August.

Travis, A. (2004b) 'Drinking Fuels Big Rise in Violent Crime', *Guardian*, 29 April.

Wainwright, M. (2004) 'Boy Killer Unmasked as Bully', *Guardian*, 28 July.

Chapter 6

'Tough on probation': probation practice under the National Offender Management Service

Dennis Gough

This chapter considers the creation and impact of a unified correctional agency, the National Offender Management Service (NOMS), upon the National Probation Service and the community supervision of offenders. This merger between the prison service and probation service has, with hindsight, been looming since the birth of the New Labour criminal justice modernization programme and the consultation document *Prisons Probation – Joining Forces to Protect the Public* (Home Office 1998).

The chapter debates the impact the creation of NOMS will have on the traditional position the probation service has held in the criminal justice system. Principally, it argues that the loss of a singular, identifiable probation service is critically important for the criminal justice system as a whole. It will remove from the system a critical force, an organization with a proud history of identifying and working against discrimination. It removes a singular organization with a history of challenging sentencers to deal with offenders in respectful, just and social inclusionary ways in the community. It highlights the change to probation values from being anti-incarceration to viewing custodial sentences as having a role to play in the rehabilitation process, in the creation of a seamless sentence of custody and community (Home Office 2001).

Finally, alternatives to the punitive stance will be outlined. This will address recent research into desistance from crime, and introduces the notion of 'tough' punishment as being a communicative enterprise (Duff 2003). This reinstates the traditional probation officer skills of building engaging and constructive relationships with offenders within a community context as a future paradigm.

The announcement to Parliament on 6 January 2004 of a unified correctional agency took observers by surprise in view of the absence of any extensive prior consultation (Dobson 2004: 144). Actually, for those who wished to see it, the signs of such a policy development had been present with the creation of a National Probation Service in 2001 and the establishment of coterminous boundaries between some key agencies. This was, with hindsight, a stepping stone whereby the probation service was readied for the birth of a correctional service after unequivocal opposition to such a merger when it was originally proposed in 1997. Correctionalism relates to what McNeill (2004) defines as looking

> to the individual for the causes of criminality and locates responsibility for crime solely with individuals. It characterises the criminal as one of a deficient/or dangerous group (classified by risk) from whom society must be protected ... The primary focuses of practice are the enforcement of punishment and the management of risk. (McNeill 2004: 241)

When considering the impact of such a merger, with notable exceptions (see Nellis, this volume) the main focus of academic and professional attention has to date been directed at technical and economic issues. These include value for money, contestability around the delivery of particular services to offenders, and the potential benefits of a seamless custodial sentence supported by the distribution of shared resettlement paperwork through the prison and probation silos. Whilst these factors are undeniably important in the creation of NOMS, the lack of attention given by policy-makers regarding the fundamental idea of a *cultural and political* union of the probation service and the prison service has been noteworthy. Indeed, the cultural divide between the two agencies could be said to have been ignored in the quest for efficiency and value for money (Carter 2003: 5). This is, despite the fact that the *Prisons–Probation Review* (Home Office 1998: 7–8) had identified 'continuing conflict of identities and working cultures' as a key obstacle to amalgamation. In the creation of NOMS the central issue for the probation service has become nothing less than the transformation of its very nature.

The proposed merger and accompanying legislative changes to custodial and community supervision will reconfigure traditional probation values and ethical stances. By removing the traditional custody–community split and emphasizing the rehabilitative and punitive ethos of both, the probation service's traditional hostility to incarceration will have to be reconfigured. The merging and forming of new cultures that embrace incarceration under a unified correctional agency will occur if short-term custodial sentences are to be embraced by probation practitioners. Convincing probation practitioners of the usefulness of imprisonment is a tricky task, considering that traditionally probation officers have viewed incarceration as a criminogenic factor. For a large number of probation officers, a merger with the prison service is almost like sharing your bed with the enemy, an uneasy association of pro-social modelling and 'racist gladiator games' (*Observer*, 27 June 2004). Government hopes regarding the rehabilitative ethos of the prison sentence concentrate solely on what custody can be made to do, and not what custody takes away from individuals in terms of self-respect, and alienation to the powerful socializing effects of family, employment and society.

Correctionalism under NOMS

Under the provisions of the Criminal Justice Act (2003), stand-alone, short-term custodial sentences of under 12 months, where previously the offender was released without supervision, have been abolished. They are replaced with provisions that combine the custodial sentence with community-based post-release supervision by NOMS. In an attempt to redress the revolving-door syndrome of offenders serving half a prison term only to be released without supervision or control, Halliday (Home Office 2001) proposed Custody Plus, a new short-term custodial sentence of under 12 months where sentencers would prescribe the length of time to be served in the custodial environment (between two and 13 weeks) and time to be served in the community (Roberts and Smith 2004: 186). Clearly the government's aim here is to make shorter custodial sentences less destructive and reduce the 60 per cent reconviction rate within two years of release, that rightly concerned Halliday (Home Office 2001: 126).

The government has adopted two further short-term custodial sentences to complement Custody Plus. The Intermittent Custodial Sentence allows a custodial element of between 14 and 90 days to be served at the weekend or in the evening, with a community based licence served in the remainder of the week. The custodial element of the Suspended Sentence Order is held in reserve or suspended, subject to the offender's compliance with community supervision and adherence to conditions imposed (Roberts and Smith 2004: 186). Hence, all new short-term custodial sentences contain community based supervision upon release from prison, where interventions are drawn from the same generic menu as for community only based sentences.

The apparent abolition of ineffective short-term custodial sentences is to be commended. Explicit in Halliday's idea of seamless sentence and end-to-end management of offenders is the importance of continuity of treatment interventions whilst in prison and in the community. However, in practice, the 'seamlessness' of the seamless sentencing is not easily achieved.

The plan is that regional offender managers commission interventions in both arenas of prison and probation. Treatment outcomes that start in the custodial environment are then built upon in the community under post-release supervision, possibly with the same treatment provider. Such an approach might enhance the chances of improving substance misuse treatment outcomes. However, less has been said regarding NOMS' ability to integrate the key cognitive-behavioural accredited programmes across the two sectors of prison and probation. The majority of such programmes are based on sequential learning, and any missed sessions need to be completed in order for the offender to progress through the programme. Short-term custodial sentences such as Custody Plus, where the custodial element could be as little as two weeks, seem ill-prepared to begin rehabilitation in such a short time period. Furthermore, the chances of an offender being released from custody to continue a programme of sequential learning such as Enhanced Thinking Skills, in the community without disruption will be slim, both in terms of planning and resources. A crucial challenge to the seamless treatment of offenders therefore is NOMS' ability to move beyond ensuring that assessments are not repeated to ensuring that work started in custody is not wasted with the offender waiting for similar programmes to start in the community.

The government's proposals amount to a blurring of traditional conceptions of custody and community. The old 1991 Criminal Justice Act distinctions between different types of community penalties disappear, as does the fundamental distinction between the custodial and community based sentences related to the seriousness of the offence. The notion that the custodial sentence signalled the court's ultimate punishment for the offender, whilst community supervision was the environment for rehabilitative work, is altered by short-term custodial sentences which now promise both. Roberts and Smith (2004) question whether the new short-term custodial sentences should be regarded as a traditional community sentence with additional conditions of short periods of imprisonment.

These debates suggest that something fundamental is occurring in terms of the philosophy of punishment, signalled by a change in the domains in which punishment is implemented. It is also worth remembering that sentencers have, up until now, been shown to be consistently drawn towards the more punitive sentencing alternatives.

For example, the rise in sentencers' use of the Combination Order, a creative mix of punishment and unpaid labour; this disposal was intended mainly for use in the Crown courts, yet most came from magistrates' courts, raising serious concerns about net widening (see Mair, Sibbit and Crisp 1994). Whilst the NOMS sentencing arrangements are intended to reduce prison numbers in the long term, similar strategies implemented in New Zealand and Finland resulted in the opposite outcome – a rise in prison numbers (Coyle 2004: 16–17). This must surely sound a warning for the UK initiative and is yet another issue to be addressed if the aims of NOMS are to be successfully carried through.

Changes to short-term custodial sentences, and the resultant blurring of the custodial–community distinction, will have a profound effect on the role of probation intervention and in working with offenders to change behaviour. The National Probation Service will work more closely with prisons, to develop and 'market' community based disposals based increasingly upon community incapacitation and exclusion. This is aimed at increasing sentencer confidence in tough new community supervision that aims to 'protect the public', despite the fact that previous attempts to improve sentencer confidence in community penalties generally resulted in increasing the severity of those penalties (Hedderman, Ellis and Sugg 1999). Supervisory practices involving the control and restraint of individuals via tagging on home arrest, electronically monitored exclusion zones and lie detector testing will be commonplace. Community penalties will have to control offenders' lives to an ever greater authoritarian degree with all disposals focused around punishment rather than rehabilitation.

Generic community penalties will emerge with a plethora of additional enforceable conditions to appear tougher and more demanding. As such a supervisory relationship will be based on the authoritative power of the probation officer over the offender. Indeed, it is likely that the monitoring and surveillance inherent in community supervision will become an end in itself as technology develops to the point at which the information on compliance or non-compliance takes precedence over all other contact with an offender. Ultimately the vision is that the supervision process could become akin to moving a chess piece around the board, with the offender manager permitting certain moves and behaviour but not others. This, rather than a working relationship where supervision agendas are skilfully negotiated, shared and agreed, will define the law enforcement role of the probation officer.

Historically, the probation service's key values were the promotion of community based supervision based on a belief in the benefits of anti-incarceration. Explicit in this rehabilitative approach has been the value of longer-term objectives in working alongside offenders to change their thinking patterns, their moral outlook and subsequent behaviour within the community context. The probation service's optimistic outlook was that all offenders with the appropriate services and guidance could change their behaviour. It is worrying that in abandoning its traditional anti-incarcerative value base, probation officers may begin to propose short-term custodial sentences in order to manage short-term risk factors, or avoid community waiting lists for drug treatment rather than offering alternatives to them.

The risk is that by blurring the boundaries between the separate aims of punishment and rehabilitation, we end up with the 'worst of both worlds'. Probation officers may come to view prison as a positive experience, with bursts of incarceration being the norm – with all its social exclusionary potential to perpetuate the offending behaviour cycle; and, of course, prison numbers may well rise, so more people will be affected. Within the community, the probation officer's role then becomes solely concerned with the public protection agenda and carrying on the custodial intervention and control in the community rather than providing a distinguishable alternative to incarceration.

The new punitivism

Current political discourse implies a future vision of community supervision where punishment, community control and surveillance are seen as central drivers of community supervision. This emphasis and reconfiguration of the creative mix really builds upon the challenges posed by the 2003 Act in terms of selling community based sentences to sentencers within a market place of attractive custodial penalties. In selling community supervision on its ability to get tough with offenders, effective technology and policing are emphasized as primary, whilst the therapeutic relationship between probation officer and offender is relegated or ignored altogether. This view of using technology to manage and exclude offenders, was expressed by the then Home Secretary David Blunkett (cited in Cowan 2004: 1) when he stated that 'the new technology will allow the development and promotion of the tough community sentences which are vital if we are to prevent re-offending and give non-violent offenders a chance to serve an effective sentence in the community.'

So, in order to promote community supervision to both sentencers and the public, the non-violent, non-sexual offender has to receive a punitive penalty. Oddly, despite the public's view of rehabilitation as the primary aim of sentencing, they also see prison as the best way to achieve this (Home Office 2001: Appendix 5): a net-widening impact of greater scrutiny, control and swifter enforcement practices for all offenders, irrespective of seriousness and risk. This is congruous to Rose and Hutton's analysis of late modern society being divided into the affluent, the comfortable, and the underclass (cited in Nellis 1999). The underclass are the permanently excluded individuals whose behaviour is constrained and controlled by government agencies, including the probation service, rather than subjected to any serious efforts at social inclusion.

This is where use of the term 'community' becomes devious: it is often used to suggest at best a caring, welcoming place for offender rehabilitation and reintegration to take place. Rather, here it is in effect a prison-esque setting of restraint and punishment. For instance, the Home Secretary Blunkett's initiative for the probation service in delivering 'prison without bars' in the community by the use of satellite technology is a contemporary illustration of the primacy of control and surveillance in political discourse and policy development (Cowan 2004). By extending the prison environment's control and surveillance into the community, Blunkett perceived technology as effective in reducing crime by 15 per cent. There is no reference to the longer-term need to change behaviour. Indeed, when satellite tracking is said to be effective with domestic violence offenders, no mention is made of the newly accredited domestic violence programme designed to change pro-violent attitudes in the longer term. Elsewhere, Blunkett also minimized the prospect of behaviour change by probation officers:

> believing that offenders in the community will reduce their re-offending through occasional interviews with probation officers is ... naive. Therefore, in the community we have introduced vigorous supervision with much more use of electronic tagging and demanding sentences. (Home Office 2004: 9)

This political pessimism and sense of resignation regarding the ability of probation officers to effect behaviour change, despite the promotion of the What Works initiative, is also reflected in Prime Minister Blair's statement that:

> you cannot change a person into something else – let's be realistic – but what has to happen is that the penalty they are paying for being a nuisance becomes more of a hassle to them than to stop being like that. (Blair in Roberts 2004: 12)

This reflects a view of offenders as rational choice actors susceptible to deterrence rather than socially excluded, impoverished or damaged individuals, with little prospect of an improvement in their circumstances.

Blair and Blunkett clearly viewed the supervision process as insufficiently controlling. They promoted the use of 'at a distance' surveillance techniques to maximize the management of the individual and reduce offending by concentrating efforts on reducing the opportunities to offend. It is apparent that by 'talking up' the prison service's ability to perform positive rehabilitative roles, incarceration becomes a substance misuse detoxification unit without a waiting list (HMCIC 2004: 29) or, ironically, an environment to rescue an offender from a pro-criminal peer group in the community. Community supervision is alternatively promoted not on its strength in engaging in rehabilitative work but in its ability to replicate the traditionally prison-based strengths of surveillance and incapacitation, but within a community context. Seamlessness has come to mean that both the prison and probation environments under the NOMS framework will provide various blends of the same thing, with each entering into the other's traditional areas of function and strength.

Roles and responsibilities

Key to the success of Carter's end-to-end management of offenders is the ability of the practitioner to manage interventions whilst the offender is in the custodial or community arena. It is also clear that the vast majority of probation officers will become national offender managers and will be responsible for the assessment, supervision planning and enforcement of court sentences. The offender intervention remit and rehabilitative work with offenders is to be split from this task and opened up for contestability with the private and not for profit sectors (Carter 2003: 33). This division in roles and responsibilities gives rise to a number of concerns.

First, offender management and interventions will be managed separately; this will further distance case managers from rehabilitation, thus creating a purchaser/provider split that directly matches an enforcement/rehabilitation split. There is a potential, here at least, that the offender manager role assumes a narrow managerial focus of community enforcer and surveillance officer, with little room for individual motivation or a working relationship based on mutual respect and persuasion. Whether national offender managers prioritize tough enforcement practice, or focus on their role in support of rehabilitation, becomes critical in determining whether individually tailored offender interventions continue or the offender becomes another drop-out from the programme of intervention with the 'gains made by the offenders prior to breach proceedings sacrificed on the altar of tough mindedness' (Hedderman and Hough 2000: 5).

With regard to contestibility, concern is also raised regarding the proposal that within five years the core role of offender managers (i.e. the supervision and management of offenders) is to be subject to contestability with private and not for profit sectors (Garside 2004: 7). By taking on the central offender management role, the benefits to offenders from flexible, creative and client-centred interventions from the non-statutory sector will be compromised by the current managerialism inherent in the supervisory process. Offenders will surely miss out on accessing services from the voluntary sector that are outside the ideological and political constraints of the criminal justice system, and/or that are not seen as sufficiently repressive or punitive in order to gain sentencer approval. For non-statutory organizations with healthy service user participation philosophies, this would presently necessitate a move away from client-centred practice to create their own domains of power between criminal justice professional and offender. It may also eventually impact on their funding, creating heavy dependence on criminal justice money and therefore incorporation within the extending corrections–industrial complex (Ellis and Winstone 2002).

Does punitivism work? Messages from research

There is an assumption throughout current political discourse and policy initiatives that crime reduction can be effectively achieved through deterrence and retribution. Significantly, the 2003 Criminal Justice Act requires any courts to have regard to the purposes of sentences which include the reduction of crime: 'the reduction by deterrence' (Criminal Justice Act 2003, Part 12, Chapter 1, Section 142).

Despite this new punitivism, however, academic research has questioned the impact of deterrence to reduce crime in a simple cause and effect way. After evaluating deterrence research, McGuire (2002: 5) concludes that studies of sentence severity and recidivism do not show any 'unambiguous link between the severity of penalties and recidivism outcomes'. Moreover, McGuire (2002) observes that the likelihood of re-offending is little influenced by the sentences imposed on offenders and many as being 'impervious' to the effects of criminal sanctions (McGuire 2002: 5). There is no magic bullet, either for deterring offending individuals, or by setting a punitive example to others. It would certainly be more fruitful to focus on improving detection certainty than to rely on any marginal increase in deterrence through 'toughening' sanctions (Bottoms 2004; von Hirsch *et al* 1999). It is also very clear in the Halliday Report's own evidence (Home Office 2001: 117) that sentencers and all other criminal justice professionals (with the exception of solicitors) saw general deterrence as a minor consideration for the purposes of sentencing. Deterrence is likely to be far more effective for those individuals who have a great deal to lose by the criminal sanction. The core probation officer caseload of persistent offenders have little or nothing to lose in this respect and hence the deterrent threat is assessed as having no discernible treatment effect (Hedderman and Hough 2004).

Turning to the crime reduction potential of community incapacitation, McGuire cites research by Petersilia and Turner (1993 cited in McGuire 2002) which found no favourable treatment impact between those offenders who had received an intensive form of supervision, increased surveillance and electronic monitoring, and those who were not made subject to this intensive form of supervision. As a result McGuire (2002) concludes that 'turning up the heat' by increased monitoring and restrictions on offenders has no beneficial effect in reducing criminal behaviour, yet this is exactly what sentencers tend to do when presented with the chance (Mair, Sibbit and Crisp 1994, Hedderman, Ellis and Sugg 1999).

The perceived relationship between tougher enforcement of community penalties and lower reconviction rates has also been to the forefront in terms of the toughening up of such supervisory processes through deterrence. The reasoning appears to be that if offenders are aware that the probation service is a 'law enforcement agency' (Home Office 2000) and that it responds to non-compliance by returning the offender to court with a threat of imprisonment, offenders will comply with the court order, and indeed the threat of a custodial sentence will deter them from criminal behaviour. Alternatively, Hedderman and Hough's (2004) findings from their research into this area are:

> Our own view is that offenders under probation supervision typically have a long history of insensitivity to deterrent threat – whether made in the home, the classroom, in the youth justice system or in the adult courts. (Hedderman and Hough 2004: 163)

In trying to ascertain whether tougher enforcement action 'worked' to reduce crime, the Association of Chief Officers of Probation (ACOP) found that tough enforcement action in one probation area, when compared to a probation area with less robust enforcement practice, did not correlate to any reduction in re-offending rates (see Hedderman and

Hough 2004 and Ellis 2000). The evidence for the effectiveness of enforcement is insubstantial: see, for instance, May and Wadwell (2001) based on only two probation services. However, evidence of the lack of a clear causal relationship between enforcement and reconvictions is easier to come by. As Hearnden and Millie (2004: 55) state:

Offenders exposed to tough enforcement regimes have reconviction rates that are no different from those in more lenient probation areas. In other words, those areas which have departed most from the Standards have not paid a price in terms of reconviction rates.

The acid test for the NOMS 'project' is perhaps to come up with a compliance system that is more creative and based on evidence of What Works. The danger is that it will be far easier to stick to simplistic managerialist enforcement (and now compliance) targets within a multi-agency environment. Examples of this type of approach are already easy to find and have shown no progression in the requirement for evidence-based practice (see, for example, Probation Circulars 24/00 and 43/2004).

Whilst the measurable and tougher enforcement agenda is firmly entrenched into contemporary probation practice, without conclusive evidence as to its effectiveness in reducing offending rates academic discourse is ever more critical of the relationship between community penalties, tough enforcement action and the probation service's remit to reduce re-offending. The number of Community Rehabilitation Orders that have run their full course and completed the programme of intervention has decreased steadily from 70 per cent in 1993 to only 57 per cent in 2003 (Probation Statistics 2003). In 2003, only 24 per cent of Drug Treatment and Testing Orders ran their full course and 31 per cent were breached for failure to comply with requirements. The tensions probation officers feel towards their enforcement role have been reflected upon in the literature. Academics such as Ellis (2000) and Hearndon and Millie (2004) question the effectiveness of a mechanistic and adminis-trative enforcement practice designed to predominantly reassure sentencers and politicians that the service can appear tough with offenders. Key to this new sense of disquiet are the messages from research that offenders who begin programmes of cognitive-behavioural treatment and who subsequently drop out of such treatment are actually at a far higher risk of re-offending in the future than those offenders who never took part in the treatment in the first place (see Hedderman 2004).

Research by Cann et al (2003) indicates that the higher reconviction rates for drop-outs from accredited programmes in the prison system comprised the 2.5 per cent treatment effect found on those offenders who actually completed the programme of intervention. The detrimental effect found for drop-outs more than cancelled out the beneficial effect for those who managed to complete their programme. The higher reconviction rate for programme drop-outs was 28.7 per cent compared with 23.8 per cent for those in the comparison group who did not undertake the accredited programme. Significantly in this respect, a preoccupation with enforcement and breach does nothing to address how practitioners can ensure the high attendance or completion rates that are essential to secure a reduction in recidivism (Underdown 2000).

Taking such research findings into account, contemporary community supervision, characterized by tough enforcement practice and significant non-completion of the intervention programme, may only replicate the current concerns regarding the revolving door of short-term prison sentences: but under NOMS, the offender manager is holding the door. The beginnings of a realistic approach to achieving compliance and the reduction of re-offending has found its way into the *Joint Inspection Report into Persistent and Prolific Offenders*, where the mechanistic enforcement agenda was found wanting with this 'hard to reach' group of offenders. The report calls for a more creative, proactive form of supervisory practice, citing outreach work as successful (HMCIC 2005). Indeed, sentencer dissatisfaction with community supervision for persistent and prolific offenders may not be easily reduced to a demand for tougher punishment, but rather dissatisfaction with the probation service's ability to intervene effectively with this offender group. Whilst 33 per cent of persistent offenders were sentenced to custody, 31 per cent of the offender group received a financial penalty and only 8 per cent a Community Rehabilitation Order. This lack of confidence in community supervision, as opposed to the use of financial penalties is even more remarkable in view of recidivism rates as high as 96 per cent for some young adult persistent offenders (HMCIC 2005).

The end of the probation service: an end to critical debate?

Historically, the probation service has assumed a unique role within the criminal justice system. Indicative of this historical role has been the service's concern with the excessive punitive use of incarceration as a form of punishment, and especially regarding the impact of labelling the individual as prisoner. The creation of a unified correctional service could signal the final end to the traditional humanistic, penal reductivist critical pulse in the heart of the community justice process (see Nellis this Volume). By merging with the prison service under NOMS, the probation service faces an extension of 'command and control' central governance and standardized services to offenders, courts and community. It may be, with the blurring of the custodial and community divide in sentencing, and the absence of a questioning and critical value base within the criminal justice system, that probation officers' traditional anti-custodialism will diminish and custody will be proposed as an effective way to both punish and rehabilitate.

Duff (2003: 188) offers an alternative to social work or punitivism. He refers to punishment as a 'communicative enterprise'. This is his supervisory paradigm which tries transparently to persuade the offender not to offend again in the future. It aims to confront the offender with the effects of his or her offending behaviour and challenges them to face up to the need for behaviour and attitudinal change. Furthermore, Duff's ideal sees the role of the probation officer (or future offender manager) to be a mediator between offender, their victims and the community in which they both live. Hence the supervisory relationship is tough and burdensome, as it brings home to the offender how his or her behaviour has transgressed community values and how engaging in behaviour change can achieve the goals of penance, moral concern for others and future reconciliation with the community (Duff 2003: 187–188). The probation officer is not seen as traditionally on the offender's side in Duff's ideal, but rather is seen to speak for the wider community when supervising the offender in a morally plausible conception of community punishment. Duff's communicative punishment ideal resonates with victims and has value in securing public and sentencer confidence in the generic community sentence of the future. It transcends merely being restrictive, and acting tough with offenders.

It is clear that the probation service has to respond to the changes in society and penal landscape at the beginning of a new century. Indeed, the move to the creation of NOMS and the increasing prioritization of economics, risk avoidance, and surveillance are a symptom of what Garland (1996) has called the crisis in penal welfarism and a move to a new form of crime control model. Modernization and progression, although not necessarily the same thing, are beyond reproach. As society becomes more complex and solutions to criminality and punishment increasingly adopt new forms and value bases, the service cannot cling to its altruistic value base and swim against the tide for fear of increasingly being sidelined as a social work dinosaur of the past. It is unrealistic to argue for a return to the probation service of history, of an alternative to punishment by the court, of special pleading or conditional mercy. But in repositioning the probation service we are in danger of killing some of its historic defining characteristics.

References

Bottoms, A. (2004) 'Empirical Research Relevant to Sentencing Frameworks', in A. Bottoms, S. Rex and G. Robinson (eds), *Alternatives to Prison: Options for an Insecure Society*. Cullompton: Willan.

Cann, T., Falshaw, L., Nugent, F. and Friendship, C. (2003) 'Understanding What Works: accredited cognitive skills programmes by adult men and young offenders.' Home Office Research Findings 226.

Carter, P. (2003) *Managing Offenders, Changing Lives: A New Approach. Report of the Correctional Services Review*. London: Strategy Unit.

Cowan R. (2004) 'Welcome to the Prison without Bars', *Guardian*, 3 September.

Coyle, A. (2004) 'Lessons from Abroad', in *Safer Society*, 21, Summer. NACRO.

Dobson, G. (2004) 'Get Carter', *Probation Journal*, 51 (2): 144–154.

Duff, R.A. (2003) 'Probation, Punishment and Restorative Justice: Should Altrusim Be Engaged in Punishment?', *Howard Journal of Criminal Justice*, 42 (2): 181–197.

Ellis, T. (2000) 'Enforcement Policy and Practice: Evidence-Based or Rhetoric Based', *Criminal Justice Matters*. 39, Spring: 6–8.

Ellis, T., and Winstone, J. (2002) 'The Policy Impact of a Survey of Programme Evaluations in England and Wales: Towards a New Corrections – Industrial Complex?' in J. McGuire (ed.) *Offender Rehabilitation and Treatment*. Chichester: Wiley.

Garland, D. (1996) 'Probation and the Reconfiguration of Crime Control', in R. Burnett (ed.), *The Probation Service: Responding to Change*, Proceeds of the Probation Studies Unit, First Colloquium. Oxford: Oxford University Press.

Garside, R. (2004) 'Who Delivers and Why it Matters', *Safer Society*, 21. NACRO.

Hearndon, C. and Millie, A. (2004) 'Does Tougher Enforcement Lead to Lower Reconviction?', *Probation Journal*, 51 (1): 48–58.

Hedderman, C., Ellis, T. and Sugg, D. (1999) *Increasing Confidence in Community Sentences: The Results of Two Demonstration Projects*, Home Office Research Study 194. London: Home Office.

Hedderman, C. and Hough, M. (2004) 'Getting Tough or Being Effective: What Matters?', in G. Mair (ed.), *What Matters in Probation*. Cullompton: Willan.

Hedderman, C. and Hough, M. (2000) 'Getting Tough or Being Effective: What Matters?', in G. Mair (2004) *What Matters in Probation*. Cullompton: Willan Publishing.

Hedderman, C. and Hough, M. (2000) 'Tightening Up Probation: A Step Too Far?', *Criminal Justice Matters*, 39, Spring: 5.

HMCIC (Her Majesty Chief Inspector of Constabulary *et al*) (2005) *Joint Inspection report into Persistent and Prolific Offenders*. HMI.

Home Office (1998) *Prisons–Probation Review Final Report*, Chapters 2 and 3. downloaded from http://www.homeoffice.gov.uk/docs/ppr2.html, 15 January 2005.

Home Office (2000) *National Standards for the Supervision of Offenders in the Community*. London: Home Office.

Home Office (2001) *Making Punishments Work. Report of a Review of the Sentencing Framework for England and Wales*. (Halliday Report) London: Home Office.

Home Office (2004) *Reducing Crime, Changing Lives*. London: Home Office.

Mair, G., Sibbit, R. and Crisp, D. (1994) *The Combination Order – An interim report*. Home Office Research and Planning Unit (unpublished).

May, C. and Wadwell, J. (2001) *Enforcing Community Penalties: The Relationship Between Enforcement and Reconviction*. Home Office Research Study 155. London: Home Office.

McGuire, J. (2002) 'Integrating Findings from Research Reviews', in J. McGuire (ed.), *Offender Rehabilitation and Treatment. Effective Programmes and Policies to Reduce Reoffending*. Chichester: Wiley.

McNeill, F. (2004) 'Supporting Desistance in Probation Practice: A Reply to Maruna, Porter and Carlvalho', *Probation Journal*, 51 (3): 241–247.

Nellis, M. (1999) 'Towards "The field of Corrections": Modernizing the Probation Service in the Late 1990's', *Social Policy and Administration*, 33 (3) September: 302–323.

Roberts, J. and Smith, M.E. (2004) 'Custody Plus, Custody Minus' in M. Tonry (ed.) *Confronting Crime: crime control policy under New Labour*. Cullompton: Willan.

Roberts, S. (2004) ' Government Strategy: Increasing Community Safety or Courting the Decent Majority' in *Criminal Justice Matters*, No. 57 Autumn: p12–14.

Underdown, A. (2001) 'Making "What Works" work: Challenges in the delivery of Community Penalties' in A. E. Bottoms, L. Gelsthorpe and S. Rex (eds) *Community Penalties: change and challenges*. Cullompton: Willan.

von Hirsch, A., Bottoms, A. E., Burney, E. and Wikström, P. O. (1999) *Criminal Deterrence and Sentence Severity: An Analysis of Recent Research*. Oxford: Hart Publishing.

Chapter 7

Working for community justice: a Home Office perspective

Chris Lewis

This chapter considers recent developments in policy and research on the treatment of offenders from the point of view of the Home Office. It will start with a brief history of the present, after which it will consider how the views and priorities of the Home Office have changed from 1995 onwards until the present day. Finally, this chapter will offer a look to the future, as well as the context surrounding the instigation and implementation of the National Offender Management Service (NOMS).

History of What Works in treatment of offenders in probation

During 2004 four important accounts of how practice in England and Wales has changed since 1990 were published, each taking a different point of view. They were written by James McGuire, George Mair, Christine Knott, and Gemma Harper and Chloe Chitty. We will review these publications in turn before moving on to the state of affairs from 1995 onwards.

James McGuire is a leading international expert on what works in the treatment of offenders and understands the issues from a practical point of view. He highlights the importance of environmental factors and socialization but also of personal factors such as the individual's cognitive and emotional development. His book goes into the detail of the research foundations of factors that lead to offending, and of the development of offender behaviour programmes; it gives a psychological perspective to such concepts as retribution, deterrence and incapacitation, and looks at the main practical applications of psychology in sentencing. He takes us back to the 1970s in a good degree of detail, where poor research had led to the conclusion that 'nothing works', and describes the development of large-scale studies or meta-analyses in the 1980s and 1990s that restored the potential of offender programmes to the forefront of policy and practice development in North America. He also goes through what works best with different types of offenders (McGuire 2004).

Professor George Mair has been a senior researcher in the Home Office Research Unit and as an academic is now able to look at the policy implementation area from the outside. He subtitles his chapter 'A House Built on Sand?' and makes the case that the benefits of rehabilitating offenders through treatment have been overemphasized. He stresses the importance of key Home Office individuals influencing policy in this area, over-hasty implementation of programmes and the lengthy period before evaluations appeared showing that programmes were not as successful as they might have been. He concludes that 'current [2003] conditions do not appear to be very encouraging for the What Works initiative', and hopes that 'balanced reflective work which uses traditional skills but is not afraid to try out new methods characterises the probation service of the 21st century' (Mair, 2004b: 31).

Christine Knott has a more measured approach (Knott 2004), as befits someone still engaged at the highest level in the National Offender Management Service (NOMS) in managing offenders. She starts with the Home Office Effective Practice initiative of 1998 (Home Office 1998b), quickly moves through effective practice principles, the What Works strategy of 2000, structural changes, and the Offender Assessment System (OASys), to an account of where the policy had got to by mid-2003, including lessons learned and likely future directions. She is more positive than Mair, saying 'figures show that we have been able to make a difference' and that despite major changes proposed following the Carter Report, 'we have a great deal of success on which to build and a wealth of talent and skill within the Probation Service to see improved services to offenders that ultimately create a safer and a better society' (Knott 2004: 27).

Gemma Harper and Chloe Chitty (Harper and Chitty 2004) are senior researchers in the Home Office working on the evidence base for the impact of corrections on re-offending. Their review of 'what works' pulls together all the research evidence and much of the policy context of the period 1999 to 2004. It is essential reading to appreciate the current position of the Home Office regarding how far the prison and probation services and the Youth Justice Board can actually reduce offending. It also calls for a more robust basis for research in this area, a feature we will return to later in this chapter.

The Home Office perspective in 1995

The Home Office perspective in 1995 can be characterized as follows:

- There were 50-plus probation areas dealing with community justice. Many of these areas had different boundaries from other agencies, making it difficult to liaise with the police or the courts. They were controlled locally, but a central Home Office unit had much financial control. There was no head of the probation service, certainly not the head of the Home Office Probation Unit, who was always a professional civil servant, with often no previous experience of probation. Some guidelines were set centrally, but there was no central advice or assistance on offender programmes.

- Her Majesty's Inspectorate of Probation was located within the Home Office. Its traditional role was to inspect and improve the service. From around 1995, it became clear that the chief inspector was keen to extend his activities towards leading the probation service into embracing change, particularly as far as effective practice was concerned. There was no body of people more qualified to do this, but there was also no authority to do anything more than attempt to exert influence.

- The probation service was sidelined under the (then) Home Secretary who had concentrated on the police service, and on increasing the prison population as a deterrent to crime, despite the probation service claiming to know better how to deal with offenders than the prison service. However, this did not result in an improvement in recidivism, and reconviction rates after a community sentence were the same as those following prison. Although the probation service was in no danger of being abolished, it was certainly out of favour and struggling for funds.

- In a similar fashion, the Home Office Research Directorate was regarded as trying to promote offender-friendly initiatives out of fashion with those in power. Research itself was structured in a very old-fashioned way, statistics were separated from research and all police and much prison research were carried out in organizations separate from the research directorate. Although Chris Nuttall, the head of research, had the charisma and North American experience spoken of by Mair (2004b), he had no secure base from which to expect success for the policies that he espoused on offender treatment. Research funding was constrained and the very existence of the research directorate in its then form was thought to be under threat, especially if the Conservative government were to be returned.

- In contrast, the prison service was coping well with increasing numbers, and at the same time pushing ahead with developing, accrediting and implementing offender programmes, following the North American model. By 1995 they had set up the Offending Behaviour Programme Unit in Prison Service HQ and were working towards setting up two panels: the Sex Offenders Treatment Accreditation Panel (SOTAP) and the General Accreditation Panel (GAP) for other offender programmes.

Thus in 1995, the development of offender programmes in the probation service was left to individual areas, with little central direction, finance, accreditation or pressure for programmes to show that they were achieving their aim of reducing reconviction rates.

Developments after the 1997 election

The 1997 election returned a New Labour government. This made little difference at first. Many criminal justice policies were similar to previous ones and there was no extra money for new developments until 1999. Moreover, New Labour concentrated on their crime prevention initiatives that had been trailed in their manifesto, with their main aim to set up local crime prevention partnerships. However, there were some areas of development. Between 1995 and 1999 several changes placed the Home Office in a much better position to be able to respond to government when, as was predicted by some, it would attempt to reduce crime by spending more money on the treatment of offenders.

The research unit merged with the statistical departments into thematic areas in 1996 to give more strategic emphasis to the development of probation and prison research. This led to the publication of a study that listed the different criminal justice policies that 'worked' in reducing crime (Nuttall, Goldblatt and Lewis 1998). The study covered all social areas save drug treatment and basic skills provision. Thus, effectiveness of probation policies was confined to a share of the 20 pages dealing with offenders (Vennard and Hedderman 1998). Many aspects, particularly implementation and training, were not covered in any detail. Neither did the research attempt to analyse whether programmes that were developed in different jurisdictions could be transferred to England and Wales, or whether they would need to be changed.

As part of its role to encourage the best standards of management and probation practice, the Probation Inspectorate commissioned a study in 1997 of effective practice in the probation service (Ellis and Underdown 1998). The authors looked at evaluation results available for programmes operating since October 1992. Returns were made by 43 areas on 210 potentially suitable programmes. The survey provided an account of the incidence and quality of outcome evaluation. After several stages of enquiry, the barriers to successful evaluation became clear, and eventually only 11 studies were identified as having some value as case examples of good evaluation practice. Given the lack of any central direction or funding this was not entirely surprising. The HMIP work also developed key criteria for assessing programme quality: targeting, eligibility and assessment, staffing, programme design, programme delivery, case management, evaluation and monitoring. This work had considerable policy impact (see Ellis and Winstone 2002).

Following this report, which the chief inspector called one of the most important reports that it had ever produced, HMIP published their guide to Effective Practice (Home Office 1998b) to seek to address issues of professional practice, operational management and best practice in monitoring and evaluating. This was an important document that focused not only on central practice but also on the day-to-day experience of many probation officers delivering effective offender programmes in their local areas.

In July 1997 a Prisons–Probation Review was set up to consider ways in which the better integration of the two services could improve their efficiency and performance. This included implications for the structure, organisation, management and working practices, human resources, funding and legislation governing the functions of those services. This recommended (Home Office 1998a) that prison and probation should remain separate but that probation services should coincide with the 42 police areas. It also recommended that much planning for the prison and probation services ought to be carried out in common; in particular there should be a more effective management of offender programmes, including common approaches to risk assessment and management, accreditation of offender programmes and to research and evaluation. Many Home Office personnel felt that the question of whether the prison and probation services should be merged into a corrections service such as existed in several other countries had simply been postponed rather than rejected permanently.

At the same time a comprehensive spending review (CSR) resulted in the Home Office getting around some £200 million of the new money that the New Labour government made available from 1999. A single output measure of reducing crime was set as a criterion for how this new money should be allocated to criminal justice agencies. This led to a long 'wish list' of new initiatives that agencies felt could gain them more resources. Most of the money went to the more powerful agencies such as the police, whether or not the proposals were backed by evidence. In areas such as prisons and probation, money tended to be made available where evidence of reducing crime could be produced. Working with offenders was one of these areas.

Although, in retrospect, this all seems rather well planned, the truth was that the considerable success of the CSR was a great surprise to most. It partly reflected the lack of any other forward thinking in Home Office areas such as Immigration. The CSR thus led to large investments in programmes across the justice system. Civil servants and justice services alike were unprepared for the demands that were about to be made on them. This was not only the need to respond to greater investment in programmes, but to bring both the structures and the human resources of agencies up to date and in line with other agencies.

In the probation area, this amounted to the following:

- The National Probation Service would be set up as soon as possible.
- Local services would be merged into 42 areas.
- A joint accreditation system for offender programmes would be set up.
- An offenders' assessment system, again jointly with prisons, was to be set up.
- Money was available for pilot offender programmes from April 1999.
- Evaluation was vital and to be built in from the start.

In addition, all other criminal justice services were expected to deliver reductions in crime, all staff would be trained in new systems, all investment programmes would need to be evaluated and all IT systems would be brought up to date. The emphasis on evaluation and on good IT systems created great demands on staff. These were impossible to deliver in the short term. In fact, it was not really until 2004 that the need for a coherent structure for evaluation was fully set down by the Home Office (Harper and Chitty 2004).

We shall return to the effect of this political pressure to deliver reductions in crime. For the moment, we look in more detail at the area of accreditation, and how this pushed forward the work of the probation and prison services on offender programmes.

Accreditation

The accreditation panel for correction programmes was one of the first new structures to be set up. It was a relaunch of the Prison Service panels to add community programmes to reduce re-offending with offender programmes. It was known as the Joint Accreditation Panel (JAP), later the Correctional Services Accreditation Panel (CSAP) and was a non-departmental public body funded by the Home Office. It has come in for some criticism (see Mair 2004a).

The first thing to note is that JAP was much better funded than most non-departmental public bodies. The daily rate for members was £500, nearly twice what most other bodies paid, and reflected the need to do a lot of preparation in advance of the meetings. With at least ten days work a year this was a useful amount of payment and reflected the large amount of money available for new initiatives. However, it contrasted with the more economic approach of the Treasury when funding the new National Probation Service (NPS). Four years on, spending reviews for 2005–2007 have cut down the money available in real terms with a reduction in the scale of CSAP activities. For example, the 2003–2004 report laments the fact that very few panel member visits to prisons and probation areas are likely to be able to be afforded in 2004–2005 (CSAP 2004).

The 1999 levels of funding encouraged a large number of applications for JAP. The first chairman was Sir Duncan Nichol, ex-head of the NHS, who had then become a professor researching health delivery. Such an important chair was invaluable to the JAP when dealing with ministers and high officials. Sir Duncan provided a welcome sense of strength and continuity until 2004 when he moved to be the chair of the Parole Board. Existing prison service panel members who applied were taken on to the new panel. This had the advantage of having a group who knew the ropes well but it skewed the expertise towards those familiar with sex offender/drug treatment programmes. It also resulted in a number of panel members from North America but none from the European mainland. All JAP members had good background knowledge of the evidence base on which offender programmes were based as well as a firm belief that such programmes could be successful. They had less experience of the pitfalls of implementing such programmes.

Those on the selection committee were keen to follow a diversity agenda but few of the younger applicants had the experience required. A good proportion of JAP was female but despite several of those short-listed being from minority ethnic communities all these dropped out before interview. A large number of Home Office, prison and probation service members were co-opted to the JAP, representing research, the inspectorates, funders, policy-makers and gatekeepers to the system. The end result was a white, middle-aged panel, slanted to certain types of experience, heavily academic/civil service based. There was a particular lack of working practitioners and members from minority communities. Finally, although well funded, it was not well funded enough to be able to employ a staff of experts in addition to the secretariat.

Within these constraints, the panel planned to work along the lines in Figure 7.1. There was very little consultation with the prison or probation services on the way of working and indeed the panel had been working for over a year before the NPS came into existence.

Figure 7.1 Ways of working of the Joint Accreditation Panel

> - Nearly all applications were came to JAP via gatekeepers in the prison and probation services.
> - A series of tight parameters was set for programmes to obey.
> - The panel met twice a year, for a week at a time.
> - Little activity took place between meetings.
> - Applications were essentially paper ones.
> - Because of the amount of work, sub-panels were set up to deal with the large number of applications.

The panel's ways of working led to the consequences shown in Figure 7.2. In retrospect, some of these probelms might have been foreseen, but the pressure of ongoing work meant that it would take fully three years before the rougher edges of the panel's way of working were rubbed off.

Figure 7.2 Unintended consequences of the panel's ways of working

> - Probation service gatekeepers placed emphasis on putting together a portfolio of programmes that covered the various type of offender for which work was needed. They were thus able to veto any applications that fell outside their own ways of thinking, or seemed to be 'too experimental'. Although this did not happen to any significant extent, it was an important criticism made from the start.
> - A programme that 'failed' at one panel meeting could not be resubmitted for six months.
> - Because of the large number of programmes that needed to be accredited to make up the proper portfolio, small sub-panels dealt with most applications.
> - There were few site visits to see the programmes in action. In fact there were few discussions between those proposing programmes and the panel.
> - Because of the need to accredit programmes then in their infancy in the UK, accreditation was given without there being full evidence that they would actually work in their present context.
> - Full account could not be taken of the likely implementation difficulties.

Ministers placed a lot of faith in accredited programmes. The probation service, which had no accredited programmes in 1998, was expected to deliver 20,000 accredited programmes by 2003 plus 30,000 persons being dealt with in accredited community systems by 2005. Most Home Office officials and probation officers felt it unlikely that such rapid expansion could be achieved.

The criteria used by the JAP to judge offender programme applications were derived from the various meta-analyses carried out in North America, and were similar to those that had been used in the prison panel for several years (see Figure 7.3).

Figure 7.3 Panel criteria

- A clear model of change.
- Proper selection of offenders.
- Targets should be a range of dynamic risk factors.
- Effective methods should be used.
- There should be a skills orientation.
- The sequencing, intensity and duration of the programmes should be appropriate.
- Engagement and motivation should be addressed.
- The programmes should involve some form of continuity with what happens afterwards, either while still on probation or in the community.
- Programme integrity should be maintained.
- The programmes should be monitored and evaluated.

These criteria were set out clearly in guidelines produced by the JAP with notes to help applicants. Although this was an attempt to be helpful to those applying, to some people this increased the feeling of too academic an approach.

Another feature of the panel's work was that programmes were strictly defined as 'those that have been proved to be effective with offenders' (JAP 2002: 24). This was interpreted as cognitive-behavioural methods with the addition of structured therapeutic communities for prisons. Other programmes that were based on existing research or had a testable theory were allowable, but were not encouraged and very few came forward. In addition, the panel did not concern itself with the more bread-and-butter ways of dealing with offenders such as improving their life skills through basic (or higher) skills education, or drug treatment that was not cognitive-behavioural based. Although there were often other accreditation mechanisms for such work, this again made the panel seem more remote from the day-to-day work of the correctional services, which began to place more emphasis on such basic programmes. JAP was also criticized for not concerning itself with special programmes for sub-groups such as women or ethnic minorities.

The panel also worked closely with those developing and funding systems in the correctional services. Although this was realistic, in order to influence the development of programmes and to follow the main problems with trying to deliver such a large change, this closeness was also criticized and with hindsight could have been managed better.

The panel achieved its main aims of accrediting a portfolio of programmes. It also gradually modified its way of working and communicating its results in a more positive way, partly as a result of earlier criticisms. This was especially the case after the appointment of the second panel in 2003.

Each year the panel produces an annual report (see CSAP 2004) that lays out the successes of the panel and its ways of working. The 2004 report summarized progress over the first five years, during which time JAP/CSAP accredited a number of general offending programmes, mostly for use both by the probation service and in prisons (see Figure 7.4).

Figure 7.4 General offending programmes accredited

• Enhanced Thinking Skills (ETS) • Think First • Reasoning and Rehabilitation • Priestly One-to-One • Cognitive Skills booster

In October 2003 the panel recognized a programme especially for women: the Women's Acquisitive Crime programme, following pilot work in South Wales, Hertfordshire and the West Midlands.

Figure 7.5 shows the more specialist programmes that have also achieved accreditation status. The panel has also accredited the Democratic Therapeutic Community Core Model as well as the first accredited integrated system for enhanced community punishment. This latter accreditation covered the whole of a sentence, rather than the more usual concept of providing an additional element to a sentence. It was meant to be a way of delivering the sentence in order to enhance the likelihood of reducing re-offending on the part of those subject to it. This accreditation of more complex phenomena, such as integrated systems, was a recognition that the panel needed to be more realistic about what it was accrediting and hence encouraging to be used. It also recognized that good programmes implemented in an unfavourable environment are unlikely to work.

Figure 7.5 Sex offender, violence and substance misuse programmes accredited

- Community – sex offender group programme
- Thames Valley – sex offender group work programme
- Northumbria – sex offender group programme
- Prison service – sex offender treatment family of programmes*

- Controlling anger and learning to manage it
- Cognitive self-change programme
- Healthy Relationships Programme (HRP)*
- Integrated Domestic Abuse Programme (IDAP)

- ASRO, prism, drink impaired drivers
- RAPt Substance Abuse Treatment Programme*
- FOCUS*
- Action on Drugs*
- STOP*
- The Lancaster castle 12-step prison partnership programme*
- P-ASRO*
- North east area (formerly Garth and Wymott) therapeutic community programme*
- Ley prison programme*

*Only in prisons

Other learning features of the panel over the first five years are shown in Figure 7.6.

Evaluation of offender programmes

This chapter does not go into detail about the evaluation of offender programmes, as a good, detailed evaluation of the various projects under the What Works banner can be found in the collection of papers by Burnett and Roberts (2004). This reviews the overall picture since 1999, and considers in detail the assessment tools used, effective educational interventions, probation service interventions to address basic skills and educational needs, and emerging evidence about offending behaviour programmes including intensive supervision and surveillance and community service.

Figure 7.6 Developments in panel activities

- More site visits were made to find out exactly what went on in a prison or a probation service, although this has had to be cut back in 2004.
- The panel looked at the systems of audit used by the correctional services to ensure that the programmes and systems they accredited were being implemented properly, had management support, full monitoring, and staff were appropriately trained to run these programmes.
- Advice and guidance were given to programmes that were not yet accredited but were being developed.
- The diversity issue was placed at the forefront of panel thinking, including the plan to develop a set of diversity checklists to use alongside the accreditation criteria when considering programmes and integrated systems.
- For the panel appointed in 2003 members were chosen as experts in specific pre-defined areas.
- The panel also began to concern itself with the training of treatment managers and with the psychometric tests used in programmes.
- More involvement of the panel with research and data quality matters, especially with evaluation, the need to improve the research methodology and collecting information on key knowledge gaps.
- The need to develop closer relationships with NOMS, following the Carter Report.

More recent material on the evaluation of the cognitive behaviour projects of the Youth Justice Board is given in Feilzer (2004). A summary of the impact of corrections on re-offending from the point of view of the Home Office is given in Harper and Chitty (2004). This is the most important review of the literature since 1998 (Nuttall, Goldblatt and Lewis 1998) and supplies the research strategy that was lacking in that 1998 review.

The picture that has been reached at the end of 2004 can be summarized in the words of Roger Hood when introducing the Burnett and Roberts report, where he speaks of the report as sounding 'just the right mixture of cautious optimism and healthy scepticism' (Burnett and Roberts 2004: viii). In fact, although some evaluations have shown good reductions in reconviction rates through the use of offender programmes, others have shown only limited success and many evaluations have been inconclusive.

However, not everyone was as positive about offender programmes. Martin Narey, the chief executive of NOMS, probably gave the 'official' position in April 2004:

Research results from the cognitive skills programmes, whether delivered in prisons or the community are, to say the least, disappointing. Evidence of drug treatment is more hopeful, but the number of offenders who benefit in prison is too few and the numbers who drop out of treatment in the community are too many. Education is my great hope, providing as it does a route out of social exclusion for offenders. (Narey 2004)

Narey appeared a little more positive by November 2004, when he commented in the Harper and Chitty review that:

[This book] is positive in confirming that there is a sound theoretical basis for our programmes, and that for some programmes there is now good evidence that they do indeed reduce re-offending. But the report also sets us some major developmental challenges – for more powerful research methods that will give us a clearer picture, more sophisticated measures of impact, more complex interventions that tackle the mix of criminogenic factors present in each individual and the creation of offender management as an effective tool for targeting the right interventions in each case. (Harper and Chitty 2004: i)

Perhaps this slightly greater optimism stems from the latest results on reconvictions. The most recently published reconviction statistics give promising, if slightly mixed, results.

For adults the actual reconviction rate within two years for those starting community sentences or discharged from custody in the first quarter of 2001 was 53.7 per cent, significantly less than the predicted rate of 54.7 per cent. The actual rate for those starting community sentences alone was 51.2 per cent, which was lower than, but not significantly below, the predicted rate of 51.7 per cent (see Wilcox, Young and Hoyle 2004).

For juveniles the overall actual reconviction rate within 12 months for those dealt with in the first quarter of 2002 was 36.5 per cent, significantly less than the expected rate of 37.9 per cent. Statistically significant reductions were recorded for pre-court disposals, first-tier penalties as a whole, supervision orders and community penalties (Home Office 2004).

Other pre-court community disposals have proved to be promising. For example, a community sanction that could help reduce re-offending is the practice of ensuring that most cautioning contains a restorative element, usually derived from a structured dialogue between the offender, the victim and the police about the offence and its implications. Wilcox *et al* (2004) report promising results from Thames Valley, where this practice has been in force since 1998.

Why have expectations not been met?

None of this quite adds up to meeting the expectations around in 1998. So, all those working in the area of offender programmes need to ask why, over five years after the initiative was started, we are still at such an early of development. The answers seem to lie in three areas. First, the need, from 1999 onwards, to respond so quickly to the political imperative; second, the lack of a strategic approach to the research agenda; and, third, the central controlling mechanisms that discouraged local initiative. We will consider these in further detail.

Need to respond to the political imperative

Many problems came about in the period 1999 to 2004 as a direct result of trying to do too much. More widely, this can be seen as being the direct consequence of having a government in a hurry and civil servants unable to slow the process down. This manifested itself in three major ways:

- The establishment of national and local service standards, public sector agreements and performance indicators.

- The encouragement of partnership in service planning, and the setting up of new structures where these did not exist, e.g. the National Probation Service, the Youth Justice Board, Drug Action Teams, Crime Disorder Reduction Partnerships.

- Going ahead on a broad front and without full consultation with those stakeholders who had most to contribute to the discussion.

Criminal justice was not the only area of social policy where this happened. For a discussion of how this was followed in a similar way by the government in other social policy areas see Williams 2002.

Most stakeholders in the criminal justice area would have suggested an approach that was both more measured (slower) and more strategic. Perhaps get the structures right before setting the detailed parameters of performance and delivery. Three examples are:

- It would have been more sensible to set up the NPS first, and bed that in for a few years, before demanding delivery of a large number of offender programmes.

- The work of the Youth Justice Board, in developing its own programmes and its accreditation, assessment and evaluation could have been integrated with that for adults but this has still not happened.

- The development of the OASys assessment system took place in parallel with the piloting of the programmes for which it was an essential selection tool. This imposed a heavy burden on practitioners, especially as it was initially introduced without proper IT systems for its data capture.

It was also poor planning for the probation service to go from a position of having lots of programmes with little evaluation and no accreditation before 1999 towards a full-blown system of accreditation and evaluation, without some long transitional period. Moreover, it soon became clear that the government was keen not just to have pilot programmes, but to set targets for full-scale roll-out of offender programmes in a time period that made it likely that the evaluation would not fully have been completed.

Many recognized the likely pitfalls from the start, but the attraction of a lot of money becoming available was too great and a large industry of probation officers, managers, researchers, psychologists and academics was soon at work attempting to deliver all this.

It is to everyone's credit that so much has been delivered in five years. Proper planning would have set this development within a ten-year project plan, with guaranteed government support, and continued guaranteed funding within a secure and stable framework of governance for criminal justice. However, there is a polarization of UK politics that means there is a high probability that specific policies and structures introduced in one government will be supplanted in the next.

Moreover, the political pressure of the last 15 years has been one of continuous new initiatives. Both the advocates of offender programmes and the researchers evaluating them have yet to learn how to deliver within the realities of the changing political situation. The coming of NOMS, as a further element of change within which the treatment of offenders is now set, and has added yet another political imperative to be coped with, that of contestability, or achieving cost savings through expanding the private security industry or with voluntary or charitable groups.

Strategic approach to the research agenda

Research into probation had long been characterized by limited investment as a response to various policy initiatives, rather than being set in a more strategic context. The coming of more money in 1999 was welcome, enabling the Home Office to double their research effort. However, there was still no real strategic approach until 2002.

Research tended to be confined to the evaluation of pilot programmes. In the beginning, these programmes took a long time to be implemented, with sometimes researchers being around before offenders were placed on the programme. Output measures were confined to reconviction measures. Since the databases being used did not hold date of offence, but only date of conviction, the actual measurement of reconviction rates was awkward, which led to two years being necessary before robust measures of reconviction were available. Moreover, more sophisticated, and probably more realistic, measures of reconviction, such as the average time between convictions, or the severity of the offence for which convicted, were not attempted. The methodology used was not strong. Typically, comparator groups were used to compare with the treatment groups, but there were great difficulties in choosing comparator groups that were appropriate. The more defendable types of research, such as randomized control trials (RCTs), were discounted as being unlikely to be acceptable in a criminal justice context, despite the fairly widespread use of RCTs in North America, and a growing number of advocates of them in the UK, including the Royal Statistical Society (see Bird 2003). Although the Sherman typology of research evaluations was quoted in Nuttall *et al* (1998) it was not until Harper and Chitty (2004) that its full implications were recognized.

The various models for interpreting the effects of programmes on offending behaviour were oversimplistic in that they implicitly assumed that where programmes had an effect, it was a long-term one. In addition, two negative, if unintended, structural points concerning Home Office research came to light. First, different teams with different approaches carried out evaluations of probation and prison programmes. Not until 2002 did the two teams work alongside each other with the same research director. Second, another consequence of having a lot of money for 'what works' research was that the money for basic prisons and probation research was cut to the bone. This meant there was little new known about the context in which programmes were being implemented: for example, about how new structures had affected case management and how the new forms of training of practitioners were actually standing up to the new demands of the corrections services. Despite this, a lot of good work was carried out in the period 1999 to 2003 (see Burnett and Roberts 2004). However, a more strategic approach would have enabled research to be more directed, and possibly more usable results produced earlier.

This lack of a strategic approach has now been modified. Since 2002 the Home Office has brought 'what works' research on probation and prisons into the same section, the Correctional Services Accreditation Panel has set up a research sub-panel, working closely with the Home Office, and a strategic approach to research is now being pursued.

Harper and Chitty (2004) set out this strategic approach in terms of more severe sentencing, rising prison populations and the increase in community sentences that have characterized the last ten years. Five aspects are covered:

1   The methodological background to the research evidence.

2   Factors associated with offending.

3   The evidence associated with offender programmes.

4   The evidence associated with alternative approaches to integrating offenders in the community, considering what works with education, employment, accommodation, drugs and alcohol and mental health.

5   An assessment of evidence and quality of research needed to highlight improvements required in policy design, implementation and evaluation to determine the success of the National Offender Management Service.

Harper and Chitty acknowledge it is difficult to guarantee that programmes proved in North America will travel to this country as well as the weak research design that has contributed to the lack of knowledge about 'what works'. On research design they propose the scale in Figure 7.7. However, they also go far wider in proposing an integrated model to evaluate the impact of interventions (Figure 7.8). This structure is similar to that used by audit teams within the prison and probation services and involves looking at the climate where programmes are delivered, their cost-effectiveness, the quality of delivery, and a wider understanding of both long and short-term outcomes.

Figure 7.7 Scientific methods scale adapted for reconviction studies

Standard	Description
Level 1	A relationship between intervention and reconviction outcome *(intervention group with no comparison group)*.
Level 2	Expected reconviction rates* (or predicted rates) compared to actual rates for intervention group *(risk predictor with no comparison group)*.
Level 3	Comparison group present without demonstrated comparability to intervention group *(unmatched comparison group)*.
Level 4	Comparison group matched to intervention group on theoretically relevant factors, e.g. risk of reconviction *(well-matched comparison group)*.
Level 5	Random assignment of offenders to the intervention and control conditions *(randomised control trial)*.

*Expected reconviction rates can be generated using the Offender Group Reconviction Scale–Revised (OGRS–R), see Taylor (1999). This is a Home Office developed risk predictor instrument that assesses the likelihood of reconviction in the absence of any intervention.

Figure 7.8 An integrated model to evaluate the impact of offenders

Climate of delivery to be evaluated by interviews with staff and offenders
Cost-effectiveness to be evaluated by: • Cost per completion • Reconvictions saved • Recorded and unrecorded offences saved • Criminal justice system savings
Quality of delivery evaluated by: • Level of staff training and supervision • Selection of appropriate offenders • Adherence to the intervention guidance • Audit data
Treatment outcomes evaluated by (short-term): • Experience of intervention, e.g. offenders • Changes in offender behaviour • Psychological assessment • Progress during intervention
Treatment outcomes evaluated by (long-term): • Reconviction data • Offence-related behaviour data • Post-discharge follow-up to include: housing, employment, social support, substance misuse, etc.

Central control and local initiatives

A further problem of the development of offender programmes was the central control. The criticism of local initiatives (Ellis and Underdown 1998) was mainly one of lack of evaluation, rather than of programmes that did not work. A later paper describes how attempts to evaluate existing probation programmes foundered on the lack of individual probation services to coordinate and agree sufficiently on evaluation (Ellis and Winstone 2002). This resulted in individual services losing all independent control over their programme provision and the conclusion was that all programmes would only be funded if they were accredited. This led to poor feeling between the National Probation Directorate and local areas, which felt rather constrained in what they were able to do. This came out in various ways: in particular, some areas, with a high percentage of special groups, e.g. minority ethnic populations, felt that the centrally imposed programmes were just not right for many of their clients, and needed to be modified if they were to work.

Another important feature was whether programmes developed in North America could be translated to England and Wales. Certain aspects were changed as a matter of routine, e.g. the language used, and the case studies quoted were translated into British terms. In many cases, programmes were developed from scratch in British terms. However, the whole emphasis on the history and evidence coming from North America, and the fact that practitioners in North America had been carrying out such work for many years and were used to being trained for such activities, again led to the feeling among some British practitioners that foreign programmes were being imposed on them.

Local perceptions were made worse in some cases where locally developed programmes, which had been built up over several years, did not get accreditation, whereas 'foreign' programmes that had been rewritten for British conditions seemed to get accreditation more easily, even though they had never been run in England before.

In the eyes of many practitioners, this was all bound up with the growing centralization, not only of the probation service, with its national HQ in London, but of many other aspects of British governance during the 1997–2003 period. Practitioners saw the central control of what works in treating offenders in the same way as they saw what works in education and health being characterized by growing prescription in what local teachers, health staff and criminal justice practitioners were expected to do. Some were happy with the idea that their work was set by guidelines, as this enabled them to follow them rigidly. Others felt that local initiatives were being stifled.

The clash between central control and local action is also seen in the poor implementation of offender programmes that has been evidenced in recent Home Office research (Hollin *et al* 2004). The effectiveness of five structured Offending Behaviour Pathfinder programmes implemented by the National Probation Service in 2000–2001 was examined. A sample of over 2,200 offenders assigned to such programmes was followed up for between 12 and 18 months, in comparison with a similar group of over 2,600 offenders not allocated to the programmes. Reconviction outcomes were then compared.

The research found poor implementation evident:

- Only 54 per cent of offenders were appropriately targeted for the programmes they had been ordered to take.
- Only 35 per cent of offenders completed a programme as ordered.

The research also found that offenders designated to attend programmes had a higher risk of re-offending than the comparison group and at follow-up were more likely to have been reconvicted. However, offenders who completed a programme had a significantly lower rate of reconviction than the comparison group and non-completers, after taking risk levels into account. This later finding could mean that completed treatment reduces re-offending but the comparison control group design used in this study cannot rule out that this may be the result of a selection effect for those who completed programmes.

It will always take some time before a healthy balance between central control and local initiative is achieved and various mechanisms have been set up to deal with local worries. However, these mechanisms also had a bureaucratic feel to them, so that, although local feeling did have a formal way of being fed back to the centre, there was a local perception that their views were not always taken seriously, under the political pressure to deliver a large number of programmes in such a short time.

What can we expect in the future?

The environment in which programmes have been developed over the last few years has not been a stable one. Many of the reasons for the perception that programmes have not been as successful as was promised lie in the constant change in governance and strategy that have characterized the political process since 1997. The setting up of the National Offender Management Service (NOMS) at the end of 2003, which was due to bring together offender programme planning for the prison and probation services, initially added to this feeling of instability.

In one sense it was a natural conclusion of an ongoing political imperative to bring the two corrections services together. This is seen in the robust approach of the leadership of NOMS to the absolute necessity of more cooperation between the two services if re-offending is to be brought down. The head of NOMS has spoken of there being 'in most places, a miserable joining up of work with individuals in custody and after release' and of 'offenders who get off drugs in prison [and] return to addiction after release, sometimes on the same day' (see Narey 2004). Everybody recognizes the truth of this, despite the hard work of probation and prison services in the past.

The initial political pressure to get NOMS off the ground before the initial preparation and consultation had been fully carried out seems to have been resisted successfully by a combination of local corrections staff who want their voice to be heard and a NOMS management prepared to slow things down and rescue government from its impetuosity.

Another important feature of NOMS is the need to let the private security industry have more input into offender services. It was already apparent in 2002 that private security companies were managing a growing workload of offenders sentenced to various forms of electronic tagging as well as a small number of private prisons (see Ellis and Winstone 2002). By 2004 electronic tagging was being delivered to well over 10,000 offenders (Nellis 2005) and more private prisons will be opening in 2005. The likelihood of growth in the private security industry is now very strong but NOMS management seems to have persuaded ministers to go slow on this aspect as well. More recently, the NOMS has published its draft strategy for co-operating with the voluntary and community sector in managing offenders (see NOMS 2005).

The government intends to put their thinking on NOMS onto a statutory basis. In the Queen's Speech after the 2005 general election, it was announced that the Management of Offenders Bill would be introduced during the summer of 2005. If the Bill is similar to the one introduced in the previous session it will establish the aims of NOMS and extend the government's powers to direct the contracting out of probation services by probation boards; it will also impose a duty on probation boards to ensure a sentence plan is prepared for every offender who receives a custodial or community sentence. It is also likely to introduce sentencing changes that will work towards keeping the prison population at no more than 80,000, and extend the use of electronic monitoring.

The intention is thus to increase the use of the fine, to reduce the use of imprisonment and to increase the proportion of offenders who are supervised by the private or voluntary sector. It is unlikely that this will come about exactly as forecast and the main question at issue by 2007 is likely to be the extent to which the National Probation Service will be funded well enough to carry out the work that will flow from the provisions of this bill. Past experience shows that funding is unlikely to be sufficient.

Conclusion

The programmes described by James McGuire and Christine Knott and accredited by the CSAP (Figures 7.4 and 7.5 above) can reduce re-offending of those sentenced for criminal acts and hence lead to greater public security. There seems to be a growing awareness that more time is needed to collect the evidence of the extent to which this is likely to happen here, as distinct from North America, in the political, structural and funding context in which the prison and probation services will exist in the future. The British public will be well served by a greater investment in offender management if only because of the waste in lives of those unable to play their proper part in society because of the consequences of what is often youthful criminal activity, albeit extensive and very disruptive to society.

What is needed is an evidential base that sets down the various alternatives to reducing crime in terms of their cost-benefit to society, so that judgements can be made in the investments needed between education and early interventions, policing of crime and anti-social behaviour, situational crime prevention, restorative justice, intensive supervision and offender programmes, both cognitive and basic skills, and levels of custody. This will need to be followed by an attempt to get a broad consensus of the British public to recognize that much criminal behaviour can be changed for the better with appropriate interventions.

Whilst the strategy proposed for the Home Office in Harper and Chitty (2004) goes much further than previous attempts at evaluation, it does not place offender management quite where it should be, in the context of earlier interventions with children. For a useful discussion of the role and potential of crime prevention in schools see Hayden's chapter in this volume. This is due to the failure of another of the current government's political imperatives – their attempts to get government departments to work closer together. For the moment, the criminal justice system has to continue to go it alone.

References

Bird, S. (2003) *Performance Indicators: The Good, the Bad and the Ugly: Report of a Royal Statistical Society Working Party*, October 2003.

Burnett, R. and Roberts, C. (eds) (2004) *What Works in Probation and Youth Justice: Developing Evidence-based Practice.* Cullompton: Willan.

CSAP (Correctional Services Accreditation Panel) (2004) *Annual Report 2003–2004.* London: Home Office.

Ellis, T. and Underdown, A. (1998) *Strategies for Effective Offender Supervision: Report of HMIP What Works Project.* London: Home Office.

Ellis, T. and Winstone, J. (2002) 'The Policy Impact of a Survey of Programme Evaluations in England and Wales: Towards a New Corrections-Industrial Complex', in J. McGuire (ed.), *Offender Rehabilitation and Treatment Effective Programmes and Policies to Reduce Re-offending.* Chichester: Wiley.

Feilzer, M. (2004) *The National Behaviour of the Youth Justice Board's Cognitive Behaviour Projects.* Downloaded from www.youth-justice-board.gov.uk on 10 October 2004.

Harper, G. and Chitty, C. (eds) (2004) *The Impact of Corrections on Re-offending: A Review of 'What Works'*, Home Office Research Study 291. London: HMSO.

Hollin, C., Palmer, E., McGuire, J., Hounsome, J., Hatcher, R., Bilby, C. and Clark, C. (2004) *Pathfinder Programmes in the Probation Service: A Retrospective Analysis.* Home Office Online Report 66/04, London. Downloaded from www.homeoffice.gov.uk on 22 December 2004.

Home Office (1998a) *Final Report of the Prisons – Probation Review.* Downloaded from http://www.homeoffice.gov.uk/docs/pprcont.html on 6 October 2004.

Home Office (1998b) *Evidence Based Practice: A Guide to Effective Practice.* London: HM Inspectorate of Probation, Home Office.

Home Office (2004) *Juvenile Reconviction: Results from the 2001 and 2002 Cohorts*, Home Office Online Report 60/04. Downloaded from www.homeoffice.gov.uk on 4 December 2004.

Home Office (2005) *Press Notice*, 13 January. Downloaded from www.homeoffice.gov.uk on 15 January 2005.

Hood, R. (2004) 'Foreword' in R. Burnett and C. Roberts (eds), *What Works in Probation and Youth Justice: Developing Evidence-based Practice.* Cullompton: Willan.

JAP (Joint Accreditation Panel) (2002) *Third Report from the Joint Prison/Probation Accreditation Panel, 2001–2002.*

Knott, C. (2004) 'Evidence-based Practice in the National Probation Service', in R. Burnet and C. Roberts (eds) (2004) *What Works in Probation and Youth Justice: Developing Evidence-based Practice.* Cullompton: Willan.

Mair, G. (ed.) (2004a) *What Matters in Probation.* Cullompton: Willan.

Mair, G. (2004b) 'The Origins of What Works in England and Wales: A House built on sand?' in G. Mair (ed.), *What Matters in Probation.* Cullompton: Willan.

McGuire, J. (2004) *Understanding Psychology and Crime: Perspectives on Theory and Action.* Maidenhead: Open University Press.

Narey, M. (2004) *Parole Board Annual Lecture*, 6 April 2004. Downloaded from www.paroleboard.gov.uk/publications/MartinNarey.htm on 14 October 2004.

Nellis, R. M. (2005) 'Electronic monitoring and the community supervision of offenders' in A. Bottoms, S. Rex and G. Robinson, *Alternatives to Prisons: options for an insecure society.* Cullompton: Willan.

NOMS (National Offender Management Service) (2005) *Managing Offenders,*

Reducing Crime: The Role of the Voluntary and Community Sector in the National Offender Management Service. Downloaded from www.hmprisonservice.gov.uk/assets/documents/1000090DNOMS_VSUstrategy.pdf on 28 February 2005.

Nuttall, C., Goldblatt, P. and Lewis, C. (1998) *Reducing Offending: An Assessment of Research Evidence on Ways of Dealing with Offending Behaviour*, Home Office Research Study 187. London: Home Office.

Taylor, R. (1999) *Predicting Reconvictions for Sexual and Violent Offences Using the Revised Offender Group Reconviction Scale*, Home Office Research Findings 104. London: Home Office.

Vennard, J. and Hedderman, C. (1998) 'Effective Interventions with Offenders', in C. Nuttall, P. Goldblatt and C. Lewis (eds), *Reducing Offending: An Assessment of Research Evidence on Ways of Dealing with Offending Behaviour*, Home Office Research Study 187. London: Home Office.

Wilcox, A., Young, R. and Hoyle, C. (2004) *An Evaluation of the Impact of Restorative Cautioning: Findings from a Reconviction Study*, Home Office Findings 255, London: Home Office.

Williams, M. (2002) 'Why Doesn't the Government Respond to the Participating Public? *Vanguard Online*, December. www.vanguardonline.f9.co.uk/030101.doc.

Chapter 8

A new chance for rehabilitation: multi-agency provision and potential under NOMS

Aaron Pycroft

The backdrop to the following discussion is the creation of the National Offender Management Service. This multi-agency arrangement is the most significant development for the criminal justice sector in recent years. Generally, despite an acknowledgement of the complexities that need to be addressed in establishing NOMS, I am arguing in its favour. It represents a necessary evolution in both a theoretical and a practical sense in the state and civil society's arrangements for punishment and rehabilitation. In particular I am arguing that these arrangements have the potential to rediscover the importance of a common humanity at the heart of an increasingly harsh penal process, via the formal involvement of a wider range of community based organizations.

This chapter will explore some of the key issues involved in multi-agency working by setting the context for the development of the New Labour approach to the reform of the public sector and in particular to the criminal justice sector. I will use the issue of a multi-agency response to multiple needs to highlight the necessity of placing the offender (service user) at the heart of any multi-agency process. Central to my argument is the view that a rehabilitative ideal based upon a 'what works' agenda (see McGuire 1995) and its underpinning philosophy requires a greater democratization of the correctional services for the users of those services, and their key stakeholders. I will argue that the correctional services have much to learn from other organizations that are working with the same groups of people, and in ways that are crucial to the rehabilitative effort. It is the aim of this chapter to consider some of these issues from a broader perspective than that of either purely the probation or prison services. I will use the lens of my non-statutory experience to express my own understanding of community justice and to highlight some of the debates concerning the role of faith-based organizations (FBOs) within the delivery of public services. It will be argued that the interface between statutory and non-statutory agencies is the key to delivering flexible, and responsive services that meet the needs of individuals and communities. This will lead to a discussion concerning the role of professional power and expertise within the delivery of rehabilitative services and particularly the perceived challenge to the respective identities of the probation and prison services.

Contestability and the rational consumer

A multi-agency approach to service delivery is at the heart of New Labour's attempts to reform public services in general. Within these social policy debates there are key arguments about the best use of public resources, the role of the not for profit and for profit sectors in this delivery, as well as accountability and effectiveness. Within the criminal justice sector there are key arguments about the function and purpose of punishment and rehabilitation and the role of particular professional groupings within the delivery of community justice and the professional identities and value bases that inform practice (Nash 2004).

The Labour administrations since 1997 have committed themselves to an essentially utilitarian 'what works' evidence based agenda. This approach has seen the creation of National Service Frameworks (NSF), which are a key plank of policy in New Labour's social inclusion agenda. There is an emphasis on accountability and the meeting of targets to justify public investment. In the regulated market place, organizations whether statutory or 'contracted in', have to provide what is required or alternative providers will be found who can. This is the principle of contestability. In all of these NSFs there is an emphasis on local accountability (consider the creation of primary care trusts, the role of Drug Action Teams, Crime and Disorder Reduction Partnerships) and (except for criminal justice) the incorporation of service users into the planning, evaluation, and governance of those services. A part of the rationale for this approach is to ensure that service delivery is tailored and flexible enough to meet the needs of the people that it is serving, by the service providers being accountable to those people and benefiting from the insight that those users bring to bear.

In these areas of social policy and welfare provision there is a commitment to empowerment that recognizes individuals and groups as consumers who not only have rights and choice but are also repositories of expert knowledge that needs to be utilized to create more effective services. NSFs are a product of the 'Third Way' thinking associated with the early New Labour administration. They are a tool for state and civil society to work in partnership for the renewal of civil society (see Giddens 1998) and the regeneration of the political process. In the criminal justice sector New Labour has sought to find a way that encapsulates both enforcement and rehabilitation, hence the dictum 'tough on crime and tough on the causes of crime' (Blair 1993).

Whether intentional or not, what this statement does is to lay bare the tension that lies at the heart of the delivery of community justice in a liberal democracy. The 'tough on crime' dictum questions the relationship between punishment and rehabilitation, which are not one and the same thing. The aims of punishment are retribution and deterrence, whereas rehabilitation may be necessary after punishment but it is not an aim of punishment. A major conflict for the probation service in the past has been the tension between being both an agency of enforcement and punishment and an agency of rehabilitation. One of the interesting aspects of the NOMS arrangements is the potential for separating out the functions of punishment and rehabilitation, with the combined correctional service being responsible for enforcement and punishment, and other contracted agencies being able to focus on rehabilitation. Many non-statutory agencies who have a mission to advocate for their service users have been concerned by a clash in values between this role and the demands of enforcement, but potentially the new arrangements could lessen these tensions.

Central to the New Labour agenda is the highlighting of the notions of personal responsibility that are to be found within the neo-liberal tradition. Essentially this follows from the idea that individuals are rational and free and interact with each other to form society and the state to govern that society. Whilst there is this strong neo-liberal influence, the government's social inclusion agenda also recognizes that there are circumstances and structures that prevent individuals from making a contribution to society, and that the voices of the excluded need to be heard within the corridors of power. Therefore service user participation is a key aspect of NSFs; they require that service users are involved in organizations from the operational level, right up to board level. A service user perspective is essential in decision-making so that decisions are made in the interests of the communities that those organizations purport to serve. Organizations such as the National Treatment Agency for Substance Misuse, and the Housing Corporation, are putting a great deal of time and effort in engaging with service users at this level. Although there is not a commitment to this kind of empowerment within the probation service or the prison service, with the establishment of NOMS, organizations that are being run by and for their service users (who may be offenders) will be at the heart of the rehabilitative effort.

Scapegoating and social exclusion

It is interesting to speculate as to why New Labour has not carried this agenda into the criminal justice arena, given its own acknowledged links between social exclusion and crime. At one level there is the recognition by New Labour that its core voters in the urban centres suffer a disproportionate amount of crime and need the most protection from the effects of drug dealing and use, vandalism and a whole range of anti-social behaviour. This is a compelling argument: these problems would have been long ago addressed if they were affecting the leafy suburbs in quite the same way. However, at a more profound level is the concern that 'criminals' are being homogenized and scapegoated into a 'criminal class'. This is evident politically in the bidding wars between New Labour and the Conservatives over being tough on crime, but also more subtly within concepts of responsibility. Although there is a link between social exclusion and crime, New Labour will argue (in support of its core constituency) that not all people who experience social exclusion commit crime: this is logically and empirically true. However, implicit within this discussion is a concept that is akin to the notion of the deserving and undeserving poor: if you do not make the effort and take responsibility for your own actions then you cannot expect to receive any support or services from state or society. The work of Girard (1985) demonstrates how scapegoating can develop into a system of persecution. This persecution occurs when the differences of opportunity between groups are neutralized, that is, when dominant and less dominant groups find themselves on a perceived level playing field of opportunity. No one group is then privileged in terms of access to resources and life chances. With their hegemonic status threatened the dominant group will blame and seek to exclude the suspected agents of their misfortune. In this respect the UK has seen racist violence over issues concerning immigration and asylum. These exclusionary processes would seem to be inherent within society, and with regard to criminal justice it would seem that a political consensus between left and right has been built around the scapegoating of people who offend, irrespective of explanations for that offending. More punitive approaches have been adopted as a consequence.

The paradox here is that at a time when governments on both sides of the Atlantic are seeking to engage more faith-based organizations in the delivery of public services, many of these organizations would argue that the rights (human rights, not consumer rights) of their service users are at the heart of their service delivery. In the UK there are debates about whether it is appropriate to use faith-based organizations. Consider, for example, the debate over faith schools, and the criticism of Islamic schools not teaching wider community values. In the USA, where the constitution provides for a clear a separation between religion and state, various legal challenges are being made against the government and their plans to increase the use of faith-based organizations in the delivery of public services. However, despite any expansion of the role of faith-based organizations in service delivery, large numbers of people already use faith-based organizations, such as Alcoholics Anonymous and Narcotics Anonymous, as well as services provided by the Salvation Army and similar bodies. This is as true in America as it is in the United Kingdom. In the UK many faith-based organizations receive support through public monies, such as Supporting People for supported housing schemes, and grants and contracts to provide, for example, drug and alcohol services.

Visionaries and exclusionaries

Traditionally, faith-based organizations involved in the provision of welfare in the UK have been Christian. More recently faith groups have developed within the Hindu, Jewish and Islamic traditions, among others, to meet the specific needs of their communities. These arrangements are not simply social, cultural or environmental in nature, as faith-based approaches have an overarching contribution to make towards the overcoming of problems and behavioural change. For example, 12-step programmes, which grew out of the evangelical movements of the nineteenth and twentieth centuries (see Thom 1999), have some success in helping people to overcome addiction. Likewise there has been an interest in the role of Buddhism in dealing with addictions (Paramabandhu and Farmer 1994), as well as in the complementary roles of religion and behavioural therapy (Miller and Martin 1988). Additionally, approaches to restorative justice have taken an interest in various faith traditions from around the world that seek to overcome the punitiveness of western approaches (Strang and Braithwaite 2001).

Multi-agency working is hampered by the fact that different agencies have differing philosophies, theologies and values. At times these have the potential to cause great tension. This has been cited as one of the major difficulties for non-statutory community based organizations contracting with the state. Take, for example, Catholic teaching, which takes the view that it is the dignity of the person in themselves that constitutes the foundation of equality of all people. This dignity is the indestructible property of every human being. The Catholic, and indeed wider Christian, view is that a person is an absolute end in themselves, and cannot be used as a means to an end (see Waterhouse 1980). This view is derived from a natural law approach that dates back to Thomas Aquinas (1226–74), who argued that through the process of reason, divine truth is self-evident and therefore needs to be encompassed in secular law.

This view stands in contrast to those approaches that can be described in a generalized sense as utilitarian which the New Labour government has predicated its policies upon in its evidence-based 'what works' agenda. This approach is concerned more with outcomes than process, and the problem (from a natural law perspective) is that utilitarianism has little consideration for inalienable natural rights that stem from an absolute view of individual dignity.

In practice, the utilitarian approach to human rights argues that we are endowed with rights that are ceded to us by the state, through the democratic process, but that these rights can be taken away, they are not inalienable. Equality before the law and protection against the state for all individuals, and the avoidance of a tyranny of the majority over minorities are taken as prerequisites under the development of democratic and constitutional government. Compare this, for example, with the utilitarian approach taken by both Britain and the USA for the detention without trial for terrorist suspects at Guantanamo Bay and Belmarsh Prison. The respective governments argue that the end justifies the means but opponents argue that you cannot protect society by acting unjustly yourselves. These are profound issues that go to the heart of constitutional politics, and the relationships between individuals, society and the state. Moreover, they exemplify the depth of the philosophical divide between faith-based organizations and the state.

Given this potential for a clash of values, why would faith-based organizations want to engage with the state at all? In practice some do not, and would see the idea of contracting with an outside body as inhibiting their autonomy. However, the establishment of the new National Offender Management System (NOMS) might make this involvement more attractive to faith-based organizations. NOMS requires a full integration of the hitherto independent prison and probation services and the establishment of a regulated market place for independent (non-statutory) organizations to become increasingly involved in the delivery of services to offenders. With the introduction of a regulated social market into service provision there is an opportunity for a wider range of organizations who are committed to people and communities to become involved in the process. This is important because a traditional role of welfare organizations has been to advocate on behalf of their service users, and this advocacy process will now be at the heart of the criminal justice system. Faith-based organizations have the potential to provide a powerful counterbalance to the punitive elements within the system.

Complex realities

How do these issues relate to the reality of contemporary community justice? An examination of the context and development of faith-based organizations and other bodies committed to the rehabilitative ideal indicates that their missions are premised upon notions of empowerment and rehabilitation, which are associated with the old penal welfarism of 'assist, befriend and advise'. Within this tradition the starting point of community justice is the indivisibility of the individual, their circumstances and the context in which they live. This resembles a communitarian approach that sees the failure of an individual to fulfil their potential in life as a failure of the community. However, this approach does not have to absolve the concept of personal responsibility. A key question and a challenge for state and society is one of determining how best to encourage personal responsibility within the context of community, and how to deal with failures of personal and communal responsibility. An understanding of the impact of social exclusion gives a wider perspective that considers how these notions of responsibility might be linked to the processes of discrimination and exclusion within communities. To understand this complexity, and particularly the relationships between the individual and society, it is important not only to understand the sociological, social psychological and psychological processes that are occurring but also the impact of economics, and policy decisions at both national and local levels.

This government defines social exclusion on the basis of multiple needs and sees social exclusion as a matrix of concurrent needs or problems that prevent individuals or groups from participating in the benefits of society (SEU 2005). In the academic and professional literature this matrix of needs is sometimes referred to as poly problems, multiple needs, complex needs, or distal needs. In a medical sense it is understood as dual diagnosis, or from a criminal justice perspective this is interpreted through the concept of criminogenic need. The different labels reflect differing clinical, treatment and policy viewpoints, but whichever the label, the problems included are offending behaviour, drug and alcohol problems, mental health problems, psychological, relationship, housing, employment and educational difficulties.

There is a consensus among practitioners and researchers that individuals are presenting with more complex needs to health and mental health services, drug and alcohol services, as well as criminal justice agencies. Despite these realities this is an area that is under-researched and under-theorized. Fiorentine (1998) in particular discusses how 'taken for granted' concepts of multiple needs are crucially linked to service delivery and multi-agency working. He argues that in the substance misuse sector (in the USA, but this is also true for the UK) there is an assumption that to address substance misuse it is necessary to address what he describes as other distal needs, related to housing, health and employment. Services are arranged to do just that, which requires a large investment in those ancillary services and working arrangements. However, Fiorentine's research actually indicates little relationship between the resolution of distal needs and overcoming substance misuse.

The work of Fiorentine raises some crucial questions. For example, the National Treatment Outcome Research Study (Gossop, Marsden and Stewart 2001) demonstrates the prevalence of multiple needs/problems within people presenting to drug services but within the research methodology there is no claim to establish causality between the various factors. It may be that it is because these issues reflect the complexity of social reality that there has been an avoidance of research and theorization. This does not help the professional or indeed the service user who is trying to deal with a plethora of presenting problems. This should be an area for dialogue and research between academics, researchers and practitioners.

By assuming a relationship between multiple needs and social exclusion the New Labour approach has tried to address some of these issues by recognizing the complexity of presenting problems and the importance of the interface between residential and community settings, whether that be between hospital and social services, or prison and the probation service. Research such as the National Treatment Outcome Research Study continues to demonstrate the necessity of seamless services that avoid relapse to physical or mental ill health, substance misuse or offending behaviour. Organizations have to work closer together in the interests of their service users, and not of themselves or to maximize their professional standing.

The self as expert

Clinical realities and the inter-relatedness of social problems have challenged the monopolies of the public sector professions. Whilst professional skills are still very much in demand, the ways that professions are organized have changed. For example, as a manager in the non-statutory sector providing substance misuse services for a range of statutory agencies, I employed doctors, nurses and social workers. The criminal justice sector is not, nor should it be, immune to these developments. The changes in the probation service over the course of the last century have been well documented, and have been at the heart of debates concerning the shift in emphasis between punishment and rehabilitation. The challenge for the probation service has been to find a function and role that is legitimate to government, the judiciary and the public as well as achieving the aims of reducing re-offending. In seeking to achieve these ends the probation service has a long history of working with the voluntary sector. Given the links between offending behaviour and social exclusion, the work of the probation service has always been dependent upon those services provided by other agencies, and the expertise that they can provide. Since the 1980s some of these services have been provided under contract to the probation service, including programmes for domestic violence and drink impaired drivers' schemes. However, as Hefetz and Warner (2004) argue, contracting is a dynamic process that may involve contracting out and contracting back in. This is true with the establishment of the National Probation Service, which saw the delivery of these services being brought back in-house and the establishment of accredited programmes.

Considerations of the effectiveness of those contracted out programmes aside, it is important to consider these changes in the light of the threat to the profession of the probation officer. There has been debate concerning the passive way in which the profession seemed to accept the establishment of the national service, and the end of 'assist, befriend and advise' to become an agency of enforcement and punishment (Mair 2004). It has been argued that the future of the profession was dependent upon implementing these changes. Friedson (1970) argues that to be distinctively autonomous a profession requires the patronage of the state, which grants the profession a licence and mandate to control its own work. At the heart of this professional project are notions of technical and specialist knowledge, and the need for the probation service to demonstrate its own expertise. This specialist knowledge is to be found in the commitment to cognitive behavioural approaches that inform accredited interventions and the whole language of risk assessment.

Under traditional welfare models, expertise is attributed to individuals exercising roles informed by their professional status. Under this model it is the professional who diagnoses the individual and their needs, and decides upon and applies the proper treatment. This is a top-down medicalized approach, reflected in the approach of health, education, social work and criminal justice agencies. In contrast, other views of government (such as the liberal view) require that individuals become experts of themselves and adopt both an educated and a knowledgeable relation of self-care towards their minds and their behaviours, as well as that of the members of their own family (Rose 1996). Zibbell (2004) argues that this approach (which has been a consistent theme in government policy from Thatcher to Blair) then reconfigures the role of service-user, who becomes an expert. This is apparent in the drug and alcohol sector, where the National Treatment Agency (NTA) has invested time, money and energy in ensuring service-user consultation and participation in service governance and delivery. It is an integral part of Models of Care (The NSF for the Substance Misue Sector). Despite the fact that users of illegal drugs are by definition committing criminal offences, in the work of the NTA, through Drug Action Teams and others, the service-user identity is that of drug-user, consumer and expert of self. It is precisely this reconfiguration of role that provides the service-user with the opportunity to demand a participatory role in the administration of the services that they use. Across all the sectors of public policy and welfare provision, the biggest block to this participatory approach is that of professional power, which may be intimidated by the voices of articulate and empowered service-users.

A key part of the Third Way agenda is developing a sense of responsibility and citizenship by giving people a stake in the services that they use (Giddens 1998). If citizenship means the possession of legal rights, choice and participation, a decent income and geographical and social mobility then the offering of access to full citizenship, which has been denied via the processes of social exclusion, logically should lead to a pathway out of crime.

A study by Mercier and Alarie (2002) lends support to this conclusion. Researching deviance in relation to homelessness and drug abuse in general, individuals were asked to identify progress indicators of moving away from homelessness and drug abuse. The usual indicators were found, such as housing, financial situation, social relationships and mental health, but also (to the surprise of the researchers) notions of citizenship and social status were included. There would appear to be a direct correlation between a better control of anti-social behaviour with changes in the individual's relationship with society in so far as people who have been excluded are not continually scapegoated and labelled as offenders but are entitled to assume a position of influence within society.

Conclusion

Although multi-agency working is by its very nature complex, at times controversial, and heavily politicized it is conceptually and practically at the heart of social policy and public service provision. Whether for reasons of cost efficiency or for the purposes of capacity, building this approach, particularly in the form of utilizing the private and not for profit sectors, is set to continue. With regard to criminal justice the creation of NOMS presents a huge challenge to the prison and probation services in terms of their cultural and professional practices, identities and understandings. In particular there is concern over the increasingly punitive nature of the corrections system. However, these developments represent an evolution that provides opportunities as well as threats, with regard to a clear distinction between the purposes of punishment and rehabilitation. The majority of organizations who are committed to working within the NOMS framework will do so because they are committed to rehabilitation. At times a difference in values will bring them into conflict with the state, but essentially organizations who are experienced and committed to working with social exclusionary factors will be at the heart of the penal process advocating for their service users. One of the most interesting factors is that many of these organizations, working under the auspices of other lead agencies such as the Housing Corporation or the National Treatment Agency for Substance Misuse, will be working to full service-user involvement. At its best this involvement can often be a pathway for individual service users who have committed crimes to gain a foothold on a career ladder by gaining work experience on a voluntary or paid basis. Whilst there is concern over the changes to the probation service, it perhaps should be remembered that other agencies of rehabilitation with demonstrable specialisms and expertise will be engaging directly with the NOMS structure, and that these agencies may be far more representative of the people that they serve than has hitherto been the case.

References

Blair, A. (1993) 'Why Crime is a Socialist Issue', *New Statesman*, 29 (12): 27–28.

Fiorentine, R. (1998) 'Effective Drug Treatment: Testing the Distal Needs Hypothesis', *Journal of Substance Abuse Treatment*, 15: 281–289.

Friedson, E. (1970) *Medical Dominance*. Chicago: Aldine-Atherton.

Giddens, A. (1998) *The Third Way*. Oxford. Polity Press.

Girard, R. (1985) *The Scapegoat*. Baltimore. Johns Hopkins University Press.

Gossop, M., Marsden, J. and Stewart, D. (2001) *NTORS after Five Years (National Treatment Outcome Research Study: Changes in Substance Use, Health and Criminal Behaviour in the Five Years After Intake*. London: Department of Health.

Hefetz, A. and Warner, M. (2004) 'Privatization and its Reverse: Explaining the Dynamics of the Government Contracting Process', *Journal of Public Administration Research and Theory*, 14, 171–190.

Mair, G. (ed.) (2004) *What Matters in Probation*. Cullompton: Willan.

McGuire, J. (ed.) (1995) *What Works: Reducing Reoffending: Guidelines from Research and Practice*. Chichester: Wiley.

Mercier, C. and Alarie, S. (2002) 'Pathways Out of Deviance: Implications for Programme Evaluation', in S. Brochu, C. Da Agra and M. Cousineau (eds), *Drugs and Crime Deviant Pathways*. Aldershot: Ashgate.

Miller, W. and Martin, J. (1988) *Behavior Therapy and Religion: Integrating Spiritual and Behavioral Approaches to Change*. California: Sage.

Nash, M. (2004) 'Probation and Community Values', in J. Muncie and W. Wilson (eds), *Student Handbook of Criminal Justice and Criminology*. London: Cavendish.

Paramabandhu, G. and Farmer, R. (1994) 'Bhuddism and Addictions', *Addiction Research*, 2.

Rose, N. (1996) 'Governing "Advanced" Liberal Democracies', in A. Barry, T. Osbourne and N. Rose (eds), *Foucault and Political Reason*. Chicago: University of Chicago Press.

SEU (Social Exclusion Unit) (2005) What is social exclusion? Available on line: http://www.socialexclusion.gov.uk/page.asp?id=213

Strang, H. and Braithwaite, J. (2001) *Restorative Justice and Civil Society*. Cambridge: Cambridge University Press.

Thom, B. (1999) *Dealing with Drink: Alcohol and Social Policy, from Treatment to Management*. London. Free Association Books.

Waterhouse, H. (trans) (1980) *Pacem In Terris: Encyclical Letter of Pope John XXII on Human Rights and Duties*. London: Catholic Truth Society.

Zibbell, J. (2004) 'Can the Lunatics Actually Take Over the Asylum? Reconfiguring Subjectivity and Neo Liberal Governance in Contemporary British Drug Treatment Policy', *International Journal of Drug Policy*, 15: 56–65.

Chapter 9

Crime prevention: the role and potential of schools

Carol Hayden

> ... an effective crime prevention strategy lies outside the criminal justice system and in the fields of education and employment, through which fundamental economic, social and political inequalities can be challenged. (Muncie 2002: 158)

This chapter will review the arguments about the role and potential of schools as a site for crime prevention. It will consider the evidence about the scale and nature of problematic (and sometimes criminal) behaviour presented on the school site, by children and others. The chapter concludes with a look at the competing priorities for schools in relation to any crime prevention role.

Preventing crime is generally understood to be a complex process in which the role and potential of a wide range of agencies is now under review (Hughes, McLaughlin and Muncie 2002). It is often maintained that youth is the most criminogenic age. Young people are also the most common victims, particularly males (Muncie 2004). Offending behaviour during adolescence and young adulthood is widespread. Graham and Bowling (1995) found that half of males and a third of females aged 14–25 admitted that they had committed at least one offence at some time, although for the majority this was limited to one or two property offences. Victimization studies show that high proportions of young people are affected: for example a third of a national sample of 12–15-year-olds claimed to have been assaulted at least once in a six-month period; a fifth had been harassed by people of their own age, the same proportion had been harassed by an adult; a fifth had their property stolen (Muncie 2004). The Youth Justice Board (YJB) has commissioned an annual survey of secondary school age young people since 1999, through MORI (Market and Opinion Research International). These surveys explore the prevalence of offending among young people and compare young people in mainstream education to those attending facilities for pupils excluded from school. The 2004 YJB survey found that 26 per cent of mainstream school pupils had committed a crime in the last year, compared to 60 per cent of excluded pupils; 49 per cent of mainstream pupils had been a victim of any offence compared to 55 per cent of excluded pupils in the same time period (MORI 2004).

The opening quote from Muncie reflects a view that an *effective* crime prevention strategy has to deal with underlying and fundamental issues. Education and its connection to employment opportunities are key in this respect. The links between education and crime can be illustrated in a variety of ways. One of these is low levels of numeracy and literacy, which is striking among the prison population: nearly one in two (48 per cent) prisoners have difficulty with reading and two-thirds (65 per cent) have difficulties with working with numbers. Strong associations have been found between poor basic skills and the amount of self-reported contact with the police and offending (Parsons 2002).

The high prevalence of youth offending and victimization found in different ways in surveys and official statistics suggests the conclusion that primary crime prevention in the form of universal programmes in schools are an obvious component in the overall fight against crime. However, what is of most interest to policy-makers are the persistent and prolific offenders (2 per cent of men; 1 per cent of women) who account for about half of all offences committed (East and Campbell 1999). This group may not be containable in mainstream schools. Yet the role and potential of schools in crime prevention should be reviewed with varying levels of need in mind. Schools as universal service providers have the difficult task of ensuring effective targeting of help whilst avoiding the potentially negative impact of what might be seen as labelling. Sutton *et al* (2004) conclude that preventative services should be presented and justified in terms of children's existing needs and problems, rather than in relation to any future risk of criminality.

Crime prevention policies and measures may occur at the individual, situational or structural level and are carried out by many different agencies. Schools have a role to play on all levels. At the level of the individual, schools can enhance pro-social behaviour, personal achievement, the sense of being part of a wider community, as well as the opportunity to lead a productive and law-abiding life. Schools can promote parental interest and involvement in their child's education and achievement. In other words, schools can help to enhance many of the well-known 'protective factors' against criminal involvement. Furthermore, schools can provide the opportunity for social advancement and as such they are a vehicle for a route out of poverty and lack of opportunity and the temptation to follow a 'criminal career'.

On the other hand, schools are also a site where criminal, anti-social and abusive behaviour can occur, from both within and outside the community. Schools thus have to guard against 'outsiders' as well as develop a safe and orderly community within school itself.

Crime, inequality, anti-social behaviour and young people

The association between crime, anti-social behaviour and young people inhabits popular imagination and discourse. One-child 'crime waves', 'feral children' and similarly emotive headlines are common in the mass media. Individual cases, such as the killing of Jamie Bulger in 1993 by two ten-year-old boys truanting from school at the time have come to signify a more 'generalised crisis in childhood and a breakdown of moral and social order' (Muncie 2004: 5). This is not a new debate. The behaviour of young people has caused concern for some adults for as long as we have documented the issue. Jones (2001: 45) cites a 6,000-year-old inscription from an Egyptian priest proclaiming: 'our earth is degenerate – children no longer obey their parents'.

The inter-connection between social and economic inequalities (now more commonly located within the debates about social exclusion and neighbourhood renewal) and concerns about disorder and social control are well documented (SEU 2001a, 2001b). The specific links between disorder, crime and general neighbourhood decline were highlighted in New Labour thinking whilst still in opposition (Straw and Michael 1996). Thus what was once the domain of social welfare has become redefined in terms of the potential contribution to crime control (Hughes *et al* 2002). Schools as a place in which the vast majority of young people spend their teenage years become an obvious site for development in this context.

Much of the behaviour of young people that especially troubles adults is referred to as 'anti-social' (see also Hatcher and Hollin, this volume, McKenzie, this Volume). However, there are different interpretations of this term. Rutter *et al* (1998) use the term 'anti-social behaviour' in a very specific way, to cover behaviour that is a criminal offence, whether or not the behaviour results in detection or conviction. Their use of the term in relation to criminal behaviour is chosen in order to make the distinction between this behaviour and the various diagnostic categories used by clinicians when referring to behaviour considered to be outside the norm (such as conduct or oppositional disorders). Rutter *et al* remind us that the various clinical disorders are *not* synonymous with criminal behaviour, neither is criminal behaviour synonymous with social or psychological dysfunction. In contrast the Home Office (2003: 5) definition and use of the term is wider: 'it is behaviour which causes or is likely to cause harassment, alarm or distress to one or more people who are not in the same household as the perpetrator.' Examples of anti-social behaviour include graffiti, abusive and intimidating language, excessive noise, dropping litter, drunken behaviour in the street, and dealing drugs. Such behaviour is explicitly blamed for holding back the regeneration of the most disadvantaged areas and creating an environment conducive to crime.

The Home Office definition of 'anti-social behaviour' can be seen as a response to a more generalized concern about social disorder and the specific concern about young people in public places. For example, the British Crime Survey (BCS) found that 22 per cent of respondents perceived a high level of disorder in their neighbourhood, with a third (33 per cent) citing teenagers 'hanging around' the streets as a big problem (Home Office 2004). The Home Office definition of anti-social behaviour is important. Some of the behaviour viewed as 'anti-social' according to the Home Office and viewed as problematic by respondents to the BCS is not criminal, yet Anti-Social Behaviour Orders (ASBOs) can be served on children from the age of ten committing 'nuisance' activities. Breach of an ASBO is a criminal offence. These orders have been available since April 1999 and are used for adults as well as young people (see also Hatcher and Hollin, this Volume). The most common types of behaviour for which ASBOs have been served are 'general loutish and unruly conduct such as verbal abuse, harassment, assault, graffiti and excessive noise' (Home Office 2003: 11).

Acceptable Behaviour Contracts (ABC) are more recent; they constitute 'a written agreement between a person who has been involved in anti-social behaviour and one or more agencies whose role it is to prevent such behaviour' (Home Office 2003: 52). ABCs are designed for young people (10–18 years), and they can be effected more quickly than ASBOs and at lower cost (Stephen and Squires 2003). It is advocated that the ABC should be well publicized among young people, in particular within schools. Information from the education service about truancy and school exclusion is explicitly cited as a potential evidence source when identifying individuals for ABCs. Stephen and Squires note that 'not only can almost any behaviour potentially be regarded as "anti-social" but there is a much lower standard of "proof". A situation that can be viewed as "criminalisation by stealth".' (Stephen and Squires 2003: 11). As some of the behaviour that is the focus of ASBOs and ABCs is not criminal, the process could thus be argued to be having a 'net-widening' effect of bringing into the orbit of the criminal justice system young people who would not previously be in this situation.

Research evidence on persistence and desistance of anti-social behaviour (as defined by Rutter *et al* 1998) would indicate that the more serious and persistent forms can be detected as early as age three, in the form of oppositional and hyperactive behaviour. The distinction is made between 'adolescent-limited' and 'life course persistent' anti-social behaviour, although it is emphasized that 'nothing is cast in stone' and a range of life events and other opportunities and circumstances can play a part in helping anti-social behaviour to continue or cease (Rutter *et al* 1998: 307). Schools could be said to occupy this difficult terrain – they can help to ameliorate and reduce behaviour problems or in the worst circumstances they may emphasize and entrench their significance. The explicit involvement of schools in crime prevention programmes might be seen as further evidence of the 'net-widening' already referred to, or alternatively evidence of attempts at 'nipping problems in the bud'. There is clearly the potential for schools to occupy both positions simultaneously.

Risk and protective factors – the role of schools

The role and potential of schools in relation to crime prevention is a relatively neglected area in UK criminology, although school-related issues are often cited as part of the well known list of 'risk' and 'protective' factors for future criminality (Farrington 1996). According to Farrington, risks specifically relating to schooling include: low intelligence and school failure, and hyperactivity/impulsivity/attention deficit. More broadly Farrington notes that the prevalence of offending by pupils varies greatly between schools, although the mechanisms at work alongside the social mix of pupils attending schools are not sufficiently understood. Outside the school, other risk factors relate to poor socio-economic circumstances and community influences; poor parenting and family conflict; low levels of parental supervision, as well as individual temperament. Many of these factors have in turn been found to be associated specifically with truancy and school exclusion (Graham and Bowling 1995, Hayden 2002). Protective factors identified by Farrington (1996) include resilient temperament, warm affectionate relationship with at least one parent, parents who provide effective supervision, pro-social beliefs, consistent discipline and parents who maintain a strong interest in their child's education. McCarthy, Laing and Walker (2004: ix–x) caution against a simplistic interpretation of the concept of risk, noting that risks are 'context-dependent and vary over time and with different circumstances'. In particular, children vary in their resilience to difficult circumstances. Children with a stronger sense of attachment to other people, with a more positive outlook on life, more plans for the future and more control over their lives are more likely to demonstrate resilience.

The broader role of school in enhancing protective factors against adverse social circumstances and outcomes is well appreciated and more widely researched in American studies. American research has singled out the concept of 'school connectedness' as the most important school-related variable that is protective for adverse outcomes, such as substance use, violence and early sexual activity (Resnick, Bearman and Blum 1997). One study of over 83,000 pupils found that four attributes explained a large part of between school variance in school connectedness (McNeely, Nonnemaker and Blum 2002). These attributes were classroom management climate, school size, severity of discipline policies, and rates of participation in after-school activities. School connectedness was found to be lower in schools with difficult classroom management climates and where temporary exclusion was used for minor issues. Zero-tolerance policies (often using harsh punishments like exclusion from school) were associated with reports of pupils feeling less safe than in schools with more moderate policies. Pupils in smaller schools felt more 'connected' or attached to their schools than those in larger schools. Not surprisingly students who participate in extra-curricular activities report feeling more connected to school; they also achieve higher grades (McNeely *et al* 2002).

In Britain, a study by Rutter, Maughan, Mortimore and Ouston (1979) is often cited as the landmark study that showed that schools could 'make a difference', rather than simply reproduce existing social inequalities and divisions. Of specific interest here is the finding that school organization and ethos have an impact on rates of delinquency. The implications of studies like this have not been lost on New Labour. The priorities for the 1997 administration have been often quoted as 'education, education, education', with 'social inclusion' as a consistent broader policy objective seen throughout the public sector. In relation to schools this has included targets to reduce school exclusion (now abandoned) as well as increase attendance (still in operation) and a plethora of initiatives aimed at promoting social inclusion through education. A number of initiatives typify the uneasy tension between welfare and justice in New Labour's reforms, however, such as the increasingly hard line taken with parents whose children do not attend school regularly (the first parent was imprisoned in 2002) and proposals in relation to the drug testing of schoolchildren.

A wider role for schools?

It was clear from the start that New Labour saw a wider role for schools than what might be termed academic achievement and the acquisition of the credentials ultimately needed for employment. New Labour came into office at a time when there was widespread concern about exclusion from school and truancy and the growing evidence about their associations with criminal involvement. Indeed, the first report from the Social Exclusion Unit (SEU) focused on truancy and school exclusion (SEU 1998). Targets were set for a one-third reduction in school exclusion and truancy in a five-year period. *Social Inclusion: Pupil Support* (DfES 1999) was the guidance launched to replace the Tory guidance, *Pupils with Problems* (DfEE 1994), refocusing the debate away from the individual and towards broader social objectives. However, this attempt to refocus the role of schools came after a long period in which academic achievement, league tables and competition between schools had been engineered as a way of driving up academic standards in schools. Schools had been given a very clear message on how they would be valued, both by the school inspection system Ofsted and by the way parents interpreted league tables and consequently exercised their 'choice' of school. New Labour sought to maintain what it saw as the advantages of this system, overlaid with the broader mission of social inclusion. Pointing to the obvious tensions between the social inclusion and standards agendas, Loxley and Thomas (2001: 299) comment that 'an ungenerous observer might suggest that the government is trying to have its cake and eat it'.

Yet schools in Britain have long been acknowledged to have a wider remit than simply the transmission of specific forms of knowledge, not least the more explicit social control functions of promoting a certain kind of conformity and obedience to authority, as well as keeping children and young people 'off the streets' and occupied (Carlen, Gleeson and Wardhaugh 1992). Beyond these key roles are others that broadly come under the heading of individual well-being and the opportunity to socialize with peers. These objectives are summarized in Bloom's taxonomy (in Fitz-Gibbon 2000: 7), which characterizes schools as having three broad goals: cognitive, affective and behavioural. Cognitive goals are to do with academic learning. Affective goals relate to happiness, aspirations and satisfaction with school. Behavioural goals include regular attendance, paying attention in class and pro-social behaviour. Fitz-Gibbon (2000) notes how parents are often reported to be equally interested in affective and behavioural goals as well as cognitive attainment. The ideal school would maximize opportunities for these goals, recognizing that one affects another. Further, all of these goals interrelate with well-known protective factors against criminal involvement. Pupils who are happy and 'connected' to school are more likely to behave in 'acceptable' ways – attend, achieve and in turn have aspirations for a law-abiding future. It could be argued that the behavioural goals are fundamental to all of this, not least because in order to benefit from school in cognitive and affective terms, you have to attend school regularly in the first place!

School attendance: associations with criminal and anti-social behaviour

We have already noted that school-related issues are part of the range of risk and protective factors that surround children and young people. The inter-connection between school attendance, achievement and specifically school exclusion is now a well-rehearsed part of the debate about social exclusion and inclusion. Those who do not attend school regularly or full-time are known to come disproportionately from the more vulnerable groups in society and as we have already noted they are also known to be more likely to be involved in offending behaviour.

A number of key studies have found strong evidence of the association between school exclusion and offending (see Graham 1988, Graham and Bowling 1995). Graham and Bowling (1995: 42) conclude that exclusion 'is both a cause and a consequence of crime'. Other well-known reports in this field suggest that if children were in school they would not be committing crime (Audit Commission 1996). A Social Exclusion Unit report goes as far as seeing children not attending school as a 'significant cause' of crime (SEU 1998: 1). Studies (YJB 2002: 54) have shown that pupils playing truant are more than twice as likely to offend, compared with those who have not played truant (65 per cent and 30 per cent respectively). However, the YJB study also notes that pupils do not necessarily offend whilst playing truant: half said that they never offended whilst playing truant (48 per cent), and only one in ten (10 per cent) said they often did so. Excluded pupils were similarly more than twice as likely to report offending, compared with non-excluded pupils (64 per cent and 26 per cent respectively). Nevertheless, Berridge *et al* (2001) conclude in their study that the relationship between school exclusion and offending is complex, making absolute statements difficult.

Behaviour in schools

As we noted earlier, a key goal for schools has always been about socializing children and young people into pro-social patterns of behaviour and getting children to attend school regularly. There are other forms of problematic and aggressive behaviour in schools, such as bullying, that may also overlap with the issues explaining some truancy and exclusion. Early aggressive behaviour is strongly associated with later anti-social and criminal behaviour, and schools could be seen as well placed to detect such behaviour and help in its amelioration. Some forms of school-based behaviour involving the harassment of minority groups and bullying in schools is now viewed as a form of 'hate crime' by a number of police forces in the UK in their work with schools. It is already established that perpetrators of hate crimes in the community are most likely to be teenage boys, with relatively low levels of school achievement (Gadd 2004; see also Hall, this volume).

There are various ways in which we might try to estimate how big an issue problematic and aggressive behaviour is in schools. Some of this behaviour could be viewed as criminal, some could be seen as anti-social, whilst other behaviour may be simply part of the growing-up process and 'testing the boundaries' with adults. It should also be emphasized that some of the behaviour that is viewed as problematic in a school (such as 'disruptive' behaviour) may not be viewed in quite the same way in other settings. Differences in opinion are evident between parents and teachers about the extent to which a particular behaviour constitutes a problem severe enough to warrant school exclusion (Hayden and Dunne 2001). All the ways of estimating the scale of problem behaviour in schools are open to some criticism. It is also worth remembering that for many pupils, school is a place that is safer than home or the community. However, putting aside these concerns for a moment and taking note of some of the evidence available, it is difficult to escape the conclusion that schools are frequently the site for behaviour that is at the least anti-social and sometimes criminal, although not necessarily seen as such. The language within the education service when talking about very difficult pupil behaviour tends to be 'disruptive' or 'disaffected'. Although low-level disruption to lessons and harassment of teachers are a feature of surveys focusing on pupil behaviour (DES/WO 1989, Neill 2000, NAS/UWT 2003), it is evident that pupils are reported to be the most frequent victims of the more severe events – physical violence, bullying and harassment in schools, as Table 9.1 illustrates.

Table 9.1 Behaviour in schools (as reported by teachers)

Type of behaviour/problem	Frequency and % reporting, by teacher
Possession of offensive weapon (pupil)	3% weekly or monthly 9.2% termly 20.2% annually 33% 'ever'
Physical violence – direct threats (pupil to pupil)	43.4% weekly 19.3% monthly 83.2% 'ever'
Physical violence – threats to pupils from third parties (usually parents, less frequently former pupils)	16.1% weekly 14.5% monthly 52.7% 'ever'
Bullying and harassment – pupil to pupil	32.2% weekly 20.4% monthly
Damage to teachers' property	26.8% weekly 19.7% monthly
Physical violence – threats from pupils to teachers	5% weekly 5% monthly 25% termly or annually
Physical violence – threats to teachers from third parties (usually parents, less frequently former pupils)	7.9% termly 8.9% weekly 8.9 % monthly
Unwanted physical contact – towards teachers (pushing, touching)	8.2% termly 10.9% annually

Source: Adapted from Neill (2002: 2–4). Based on 13 LEAs, 2,575 responses.

Another survey conducted by a teaching union and focusing only on abuse against teachers, across 304 schools (primary, secondary and special) in the north-west of England, revealed 964 incidents of abuse against teachers in a two-week period in January 2003. About one in eight of these abuses (126 cases) involved what were termed 'physical assaults' (NAS/UWT 2003).

Research into personal safety and violence in schools (Gill and Hearnshaw 1997) provides a picture of what a random sample of 3,986 schools experienced in one school year. Selected findings from this research are presented in Table 9.2.

Table 9.2 Personal safety and violence in schools (at school level)

Type of incident	% schools reporting in last school year
Physical violence – pupil to staff	18.7% (member of staff – hit, punched or kicked) 2.9% (member of staff – hit with weapon or other object, stabbed or slashed)
Physical violence – pupil to pupil	50.7% (pupil – hit, punched or kicked) 6.9% (pupil – hit with weapon or other object, stabbed or slashed)
Weapons – carried by pupils, on school site	12.1% of schools
Theft with threats or actual violence	1.9% of schools

Source: Adapted from Gill and Hearnshaw (1997: 1–2). Based on 9% of schools nationally, 2,303 responses.

Tables 9.1 and 9.2 illustrate a worrying picture of the incidence of very problematic and sometimes criminal behaviour in schools. The surveys also highlight the different ways data may be collected (e.g. by individual teacher or by school), thus creating problems of comparability.

Pupil-based surveys come up with equally worrying, though varying, rates of prevalence of different types of bullying behaviour. Again there are problems of definition and comparability across surveys. For example, 'physical violence, pupil to pupil' (as referred to in Tables 9.1 and 9.2) may be one-off acts of aggression; they may on the other hand be more sustained. According to Smith (2002: 117–18) and based on Smith *et al* (1999), 'bullying is a subset of aggressive behaviours, characterised by repetition and power imbalance'. Bullying takes various forms – physical, verbal, social exclusion and indirect forms such as spreading rumours.

Table 9.3 Bullying surveys

Authors	Area	School type/age	Prevalence
Whitney and Smith (1993)	Sheffield (6,000 pupils)	Primary and Secondary	27% of primary and 10% of secondary pupils had been bullied; 12% of primary and 6% of secondary pupils had bullied others
Katz, Buchanan and Bream (2001)	UK (7,000 young people)	13–19 years	More than 50% had been bullied: 13% of boys and 12% of girls were bullied 'severely'

Bullying surveys produce fairly wide-ranging estimates depending on the way questions are asked and the timescale involved. Smith and Myron-Wilson (1998: 406) estimate that: 'around 1 in 5 children are involved in bully–victim problems' in the UK, with similar incidences reported in other countries. Furniss (2000) discusses whether some forms of bullying should be considered to be a crime, rather than as a school disciplinary matter. Furniss considers the issue both from the standpoint of existing legal provisions as well as from the point of view of the level of protection afforded to children. She points out that assaults on teachers (though less frequent than pupil-to-pupil assaults) are often reported to the police whereas in pupil-to-pupil cases, parents are expected to make the decision about whether or not to involve the police.

Permanent exclusion from school might be viewed as an indicator of teachers' limits to tolerance in relation to pupil behaviour. A large proportion of the reasons for permanent exclusion involve physically aggressive behaviour from pupils or behaviour that is highly disruptive of the learning of other pupils. When permanent exclusion figures are compared with surveys of teacher experience like the ones noted above, one might be surprised by the relatively small proportion of children who are permanently excluded – according to official statistics (see Table 9.4).

Table 9.4 Permanent exclusions

Year	All permanent exclusions
1990–1991	2,910
1996–1997	12,700
1999–2000	8,300
2000–2001	9,210
2001–2002	9,540
2002–2003	9,290

Source: Figures from www.dfes.gov.uk

However, it is important to appreciate that although these official figures for permanent exclusion represent a very small proportion of the school population (the rate of permanent exclusion was 1.3 per 1,000 school population in England or 0.13 per cent in 2002/2003), they are the tip of the iceberg in terms of disaffected and other difficult to manage behaviour in school. Fixed period exclusions (a matter of days usually) are much more numerous. The first available national data estimates 80,000 fixed period exclusions involving 62,000 individual pupils in the summer term of the 2003 school year (DfES 2004). Some pupils were subjected to more than one fixed period exclusion in this school term.

The most common single reason given for both permanent and fixed period exclusions is 'persistent disruptive behaviour' (20 per cent of all exclusions). Physical assault against an adult accounted for 12 per cent of permanent and 5 per cent of fixed period exclusions. Physical assault against a pupil accounted for 14 per cent of permanent and 16 per cent of fixed period exclusions (DfES 2004). Work conducted by the author for one urban education authority found records of exclusion for about 2 per cent of the whole school population in a one-year period; most of these were fixed period exclusions, for a matter of a day or so (Hayden 2000).

Official records of non-attendance involve a much bigger proportion of the school population. The reasons for non-attendance are varied, but in some cases at least they represent disaffection or disinterest in schooling and in others avoidance of work pressures or bullying. Schools record 'non-attendance', which covers authorized absence (for example through sickness) and unauthorized absence (which may include a range of situations including truancy and being a young carer). 'Truancy' suggests an active choice not to go to school and is thus a particular form of absence.

Table 9.5. Non-attendance: percentage of half days missed

	1995–1996	2002–2003
Authorized	6.9	6.13
Unauthorized	0.7	0.7

Source: Figures from www.dfes.gov.uk

Other estimates for children not attending school include half a million schoolchildren engaged in illegal work, of whom 100,000 are believed to truant from school daily in order to work (TUC/MORI 2001). The most commonly quoted figure in government announcements is 50,000 schoolchildren truanting from school on any school day (DfES 2002). Further, around 100,000 pupils were found to 'disappear' from the school roll between years 10 and 11 in a one-year period of monitoring (Ofsted 2003). There are a complex set of circumstances and reasons to explain why children are not in school or not benefiting from school. They all have their behavioural manifestations, although it tends to be the 'acting out' child that causes most consternation among teachers and parents because such behaviour demands attention.

Schools and their community as a site for crime

Schools are seen as a potential site for crime, as well as the site for crime prevention that has been the focus of much of this chapter. Enhanced security measures are a common feature of the school environment: CCTV, keypad entry systems and main gates locked for substantial periods of the day. Under the Safer School Partnerships guidance (DfES 2002), police officers are based in schools in areas with a high level of street crime. The police also have a role in the event of parallel criminal proceedings in cases of school exclusion where a serious allegation or event has occurred (DfES 1999).

The last section looked at behaviour in schools and the various ways the education service and educational research tends to measure the extent of the issue. Criminologists have a slightly different focus and many of the surveys conducted are more explicitly looking at the prevalence of offending behaviour and victimization of young people of school age. Self-report surveys conducted with school pupils provide us with a picture of young people's involvement in criminal activity in the community (see for example, Aye Maung 1995, based on BCS data, or the annual YJB survey, MORI 2004).

However, there is very little research explicitly focusing specifically on criminal acts committed on the school site, presumably because of the extreme sensitivity of such data and the difficulties of gaining access to undertake the research. One self-report study of a sample from 20 state secondary schools (3,103 respondents) in Cardiff found that one in five pupils reported involvement in one of five categories of offence on the school site in a one-year period. The proportion of pupils reporting offences were as follows: assault (13.2 per cent); vandalism (6.7 per cent); theft (6.0 per cent); robbery (0.7 per cent); breaking into school (0.7 per cent). Interestingly, this study reports varying levels of impact on offending behaviour in relation to individual and lifestyle factors, with school context exercising a different level of relative protection in relation to these factors (Boxford 2004). This sort of study is important in a number of ways: it illustrates the high level of offending that may be occurring in schools; it adds to the debate about the extent to which schools (in combination with other factors) can address these issues, and it reminds us that some of the acts dealt with as a within-school disciplinary issue could be seen as a criminal offence.

Despite enhanced security in schools, studies have found high proportions of pupils expressing real fears about being victimized in school: one third of pupils in a study by Noaks and Noaks (2000). Pupils expressed further fears about particular situations like school buses and unsupervised settings. Fears about travel or security in school were sufficient for between 3 and 5 per cent of pupils to miss school in another study (Kingery, Coggleshall and Alford 1998). Whatever the precise focus of these surveys, they all indicate a high prevalence of anti-social and potentially criminal behaviour in the lives of children of school age. This has led Phillips (2003) to comment upon the 'normalization' of aspects of abuse, harassment and violence in young people's lives. In particular, stealing, fighting and general aggression are reported to be common (Howard League 2002).

In a range of ways, schools are also a place where adults, parents and former pupils may vent their anger and frustration. There are various ways that we can estimate the scale of this sort of problem. Table 9.1 includes estimates of 'third party' incursions onto the school site, directed at either pupils or teachers. Sometimes people want to gain access to the school site for the purpose of vandalism and arson or theft of school property. Further, schools may also act as a site for 'professional perpetrators' to gain access to children (Sullivan and Beech 2002). Sullivan and Beech (2002) quote a BBC survey reported in 2000, that estimated that about 400 teachers in the UK were suspended each year, following allegations of abusing pupils.

The need for better security for schools, as well as screening of school staff, have been highlighted in the public imagination by events such as the Dunblane tragedy in which 16 children and their teacher were killed by an intruder (during the school day); the murder of head teacher Philip Lawrence at the school gates (at the end of the school day); and the murder of two primary age schoolgirls in Soham by the school caretaker (in the school summer holidays). Yet these are very different types of event, involving attacks on children, teachers and the whole school community. Research indicates that external threats to security, specifically intrusion to the school premises, are ranked higher as a concern by schools than internal threats from people within the school community (Lloyd and Ching 2003). Security firms now offer such schemes as SchoolWatch over the summer holiday period. Such firms tend to focus very much on property and damage from arson, vandalism and graffiti, rather than harm to people (see www.chubb.co.uk). The risk of arson and vandalism is known to be higher in deprived urban areas than elsewhere. Arson attacks against schools has declined from over 1,100 in 1994 to just under 800 in 2000. However, there has been an increase in the proportion of arson attacks occurring in school time. Around 250 of the 800 arson attacks in 2000 were during the school day when pupils are present (Arson Prevention Bureau 2002).

Table 9.6 Rates of school-time arson fires: English metropolitan areas compared with non-metropolitan areas

	Metropolitan areas	Non-metropolitan areas
Number (rate) of fires per 100,000 pupils	3.3	2.3
Number (rate) of fires per 100 schools	1.2	0.7

Source: Arson Prevention Bureau (2002)

Schools as a site for crime prevention

As we noted earlier, the prevalence of offending is known to vary greatly across schools and it is now well known that schools can make a difference, independently of socio-economic circumstances. Further, schools are an obvious site in which to influence the next generation *en masse*.

Overall schools clearly have wide potential for enhancing protective factors against criminal involvement. Schools can help foster pro-social behaviour and provide opportunities for a sense of personal achievement, school 'connectedness' and 'inclusion' in a community. Schools already provide positive opportunities for the great majority of young people, many of whom have committed a minor criminal offence and some of whom are at risk of more extensive criminal involvement. Schools are encouraged to involve and interest parents and carers in their children's education (thereby enhancing a protective factor against criminality); in policy terms this is often seen as a self-evidently 'good thing'. However, in all these areas, Rutter *et al* (1998: 233) conclude that good-quality evidence about both effects and the mechanisms at work is limited.

There are numerous 'whole school' and more targeted approaches to managing behaviour in schools in Britain, such as Assertive Discipline, Circle Time and Team-Teach. In-school units, mentors and Connexions advisors are also common. Further, schools are expected to have policies to deal with bullying, harassment and behaviour management more generally. Restorative justice approaches are more familiar in criminal justice settings but are also being used in school settings. Most initiatives involve outside facilitators offering restorative conferencing to schools in relation to bullying or where exclusion is being considered. Interest in the potential of restorative practices in schools is said to be growing and more initiatives are starting (Hopkins 2002); this is apparent in some of the Safer School Partnerships (discussed below).

Traditionally the role of the police in relation to schools has been as an additional teaching resource, for example in drugs education pro- grammes, which are well established in schools. Some in-school programmes have been based on quite substantial investment from police authorities, although the impact on pupil attitudes and behaviour is difficult to establish or attribute to the programmes as such (Downey, Keene and Wincup 2002). Yet police officers have admitted to an ambivalence about their role, as school visits also provide an opportunity for intelligence gathering (Walsh 2004). Current policy takes a more educative stance, developing from the view that drugs education should provide opportunities for pupils to develop their knowledge, skills, attitudes and understanding about drugs, as well as an appreciation of the benefits of a healthy lifestyle and so on. However, at the same time Blair has suggested the possibility of drug testing in schools, and indeed sniffer dogs are already used in some schools. Concern has been expressed at this possibility, not least because drugs like cannabis stay in the system longer than more harmful drugs like heroin and ecstasy (Walsh 2004). The American experience of drug testing in schools is not promising, because of civil liberties challenges, resistance from schools (reportedly 95 per cent of schools do not use the tests) and the lack of evidence of a reduction in drug use where the tests are used (Walsh 2004).

In recent years the role of the police in relation to schools has become more operational, as in 'truancy sweeps', where police officers work with the educational welfare service to get children back into school. Police also take an operational approach in Safer Schools Partnerships, a joint initiative between the Department for Education and Skills (DfES), the Youth Justice Board (YJB) and Association of Chief Police Officers (ACPO). Safer School Partnerships are part of a number of measures that link behaviour in and around schools to an explicit crime prevention programme. Partnerships are located in areas with high levels of street crime, or crime 'hot spots'. In these partnerships a dedicated full-time police officer is based in a secondary school and the feeder primary schools. Key objectives of this role include the prevention and reduction of crime, anti-social behaviour and related incidents around the school; tackling bullying and violence experienced by staff and students; truancy and exclusion; damage to the school buildings; and drug-related incidents (DfES 2002).

Good-quality evidence about the effectiveness of school-based programmes is generally lacking in the UK. Much of the available evidence is from the United States. For example, a recent meta-analysis of 165 studies of school-based prevention activities analysed the evidence available about the impact of activities ranging from individual counselling or behaviour modification programmes through efforts to change the way schools are managed. The analysis shows that school-based practices appear to be effective in relation to certain behaviours: reducing drug and alcohol use, school drop-out and attendance problems. In common with findings from prisons research, cognitive behavioural programmes were found to be consistently positive in effect. Non-cognitive behavioural counselling, social work and other therapeutic interventions showed consistently negative effects (Wilson, Gottfredson and Najaka 2001).

It is interesting in this context to note what children say. A Howard League (2002) consultation with 1,100 children reported three key issues that they identified to help prevent crime: activities and safe places to 'hang out'; police to stop viewing all young people as trouble and treat them with more respect; more initiatives (such as counselling and information on reducing crime) in schools and other places where children are more generally found.

Schools in and of the community, or schools as a fortress against the community?

Schools are one of our most expensive community resources and a major agent of socialization alongside the family. However, schools have an uneasy task if they make their crime prevention role explicit. Their potential in this respect is at once self-evident but also open to contention, misinterpretation and even potential misuse. Whilst some aspects of crime prevention (such as CCTV) and security measures may seem necessary against intruders, vandals and arsonists, they might also be open to other uses. Equally, the role of police in schools may be open to role conflict and move into crime detection, rather than prevention. 'Schools in and of the community' is a concept that requires some careful thought.

The evidence of widening social division in schooling in Britain is clear (Hayden 2000). Many would argue that the system of league tables and competition has played an important part in bringing this about. This tends to mean that 'sink' schools are apparent in most cities, their catchment areas usually coinciding with the poorest, most 'socially excluded' areas of the city. It is a challenge in such circumstances to be a school 'in and of the community', rather than act as a fortress against the negative influences in the community. For schools to be a community resource they have to be open and available to the community in a way that does not conflict with the needs of the current cohort of children and young people getting their chance to do well at school. If schools are open to a community they may also be more open to the risks in that community.

Table 9.7 Competing priorities for schools

The majority: no or minor criminal involvement	⟷	The minority: persistent and prolific offenders (especially for reintegration programmes)
Victims	⟷	Perpetrators
Academic achievement	⟷	Social inclusion
The current cohort of children and young people	⟷	The needs of parents and the wider community
Schools as welcoming and open places	⟷	Risk reduction
Schools as a fortress against the community	⟷	Schools in and of the community

In terms of their role and potential in crime prevention, schools have to balance a number of competing priorities. None of the competing priorities shown in Table 9.7 is necessarily mutually exclusive, but all are nevertheless priorities about which it is difficult to arrive at a consensus. For schools in general (rather than only schools in the most deprived areas) to achieve a better balance in relation to these priorities we would need a fundamental rethink about the funding, staffing and evaluation of schools. The role and potential of schools in relation to crime prevention is a relatively easy case to make. The bigger questions remain: such as, to what extent do we as a society want to see schools in general prioritizing a crime prevention role; or whether this role should only be prioritized in 'crime hot spots' for schools in challenging circumstances. Also, there is a need for a more realistic look at educational provision for young offenders of school age, both inside the secure estate and once they leave. In relation to the latter group we need to consider urgently whether reintegration to mainstream school provision is realistic and fair to all concerned.

In conclusion, schools are clearly potential sites for crime as well as crime prevention. They are generally protected and protective environments, compared with life in many communities. Children and young people spend a great deal of time in school and schools are a crucial agent of socialization, as well as one of the main community organizations to which most people have a connection at some point in their lives. The potential of schools to foster pro-social behaviour and attitudes, as well as enhance protective factors against criminal involvement, is well appreciated. The key issue for policy and practice is how to realise fully this potential.

References

Arson Prevention Bureau (2002) *School Arson: Education under Threat*. Available on-line: www.arsonpreventionbureau.org.uk.

Audit Commission (1996) *Misspent Youth*. London: Audit Commission.

Aye Maung, N. (1995) *Young People, Victimisation and the Police*, Home Office Research Study 140. London: HMSO.

Berridge, D., Brodie, I., Pitts, J., Porteous, D. and Tarling, R. (2001) *The Independent Effects of Permanent Exclusion from School on the Offending Careers of Young People*, RDS Occasional Paper 71. London: HMSO.

Boxford, S. (2004) *Schools and the Problem of Crime: The Importance of School Context*. Paper presented at the British Society of Criminology Conference, University of Portsmouth, 6–9 July 2004.

Carlen, P., Gleeson, D. and Wardhaugh, J. (1992) *Truancy: The Politics of Compulsory Schooling*. Buckingham: Open University Press.

DES/WO (Department for Education and Science/Welsh Office) (1989) *Discipline in Schools: Report of the Committee of Enquiry Chaired by Lord Elton*. London: HMSO.

DfEE (Department for Education and Employment) (1994) *Pupils with Problems*. London: HMSO.

DfES (Department for Education and Skills) (1999) *Social Inclusion: Pupil Support*. London: HMSO.

DfES (2002) *Safer School Partnerships: Guidance*. Issued jointly by the DfES, Home Office, YJB, Association of Chief Education Officers, ACPO. London: DfES.

DfES (2004) Permanent and Fixed Period Exclusions, Summer Term 2002/2003. Experimental statistics first release. 29 July, ESR 01/2004. Available online: http://www.dfes.gov.uk/rsgateway/DB/SFR/, accessed on 12 October 2004.

Downey, S., Keene, J. and Wincup, E. (2002) *Getting It Right: Understanding and Evaluating an Evolving Partnership Education Programme*. Reading, Canterbury: Universities of Reading and Kent.

East, K. and Campbell, S. (2001) *Aspects of Crime: Young Offenders 1999*. London: HMSO.

Farrington, D. (1996) *Understanding and Preventing Youth Crime*. York: York Publishing Services Ltd/Joseph Rowntree Foundation.

Fitz-Gibbon, C. (2000) 'Education: Realising the Potential', in H.T.O. Davies, S.M. Nutley and P.C. Smith (eds), *What Works? Evidence-based Policy and Practice in Public Services*. Bristol: The Policy Press, pp. 69–92.

Furniss, C. (2000) 'Bullying in Schools: It's Not a Crime – Is It?' *Education and the Law*, 12: 9–29.

Gadd, D. (2004) 'Hate and Bias Crime: Criminologically Congruent Law? A Review of Barbara Perry's *Hate and Bias Crime: A Reader*. *The Australian and New Zealand Journal of Criminology*, 37: 144–154.

Gill, M. and Hearnshaw, S. (1997) *Personal Safety and Violence in Schools*. Department for Education and Employment Research Report, RR21. London: DfEE.

Graham, J. (1988) *Schools, Disruptive Behaviour and Delinquency*, Home Office Research Study 96. London: HMSO.

Graham, J. and Bowling, B. (1995) *Young People and Crime*. Home Office Research Study 145. London: HMSO.

Hayden, C. (2000) 'Exclusion from School in England: The Generation and Maintenance of Social Exclusion', in G. Walraven, C. Parsons, D. van Veen and C. Day (eds), *Combating Social Exclusion through Education*. Leuven-Appledoorn: Garant/EERA, pp. 69–82.

Hayden, C. (2002) 'Risk Factors and Exclusion from School', in E. Debarbieux and C. Blaya (eds), *Violence in Schools and Public Policies*. Paris: Elsevier Science, pp. 85–102.

Hayden, C. and Dunne, S. (2001) *Outside, Looking In: Children and Families' Experiences of Exclusion from School*. London: The Children's Society.

Home Office (2003) *A Guide to Anti-Social Behaviour Orders and Acceptable Behaviour Contract*. London: HMSO.

Home Office (2004) Anti-Social Behaviour. Available online www.homeoffice.gov.uk/crime/antisocialbehaviour/index/html, downloaded on 30 May 2004.

Hopkins, B. (2002) 'Restorative Justice in Schools', *Support for Learning*, 17, 144–149.

Howard League (2002) 96% of Teenagers are Victims of Crime. 11 April. Available online: www.howardleague.org/press/2002/11402.html, downloaded on 2 July 2004.

Hughes, G., McLaughlin, E. and Muncie, J. (eds) (2002) *Crime Prevention and Community Safety*: New Directions. London: Sage Publications in association with the Open University.

Jones, S. (2001) *Criminology*, 2nd edition. Trowbridge: Butterworth.

Katz, A., Buchanan, A. and Bream, V. (2001) *Bullying in Britain: Testimonies from Teenagers*. East Molesey: Young Voice.

Kingery, P., Coggleshall, M. and Alford, A. (1998) 'Violence in School', *Psychology in the Schools*, 35, 247–258.

Lloyd, R. and Ching, C. (2003) *School Security Concerns*. Department of Education and Skills Research Report RR419. London: DfES.

Loxley, A. and Thomas, G. (2001) 'Neo-Conservatives, Neo-Liberals, the New Left and Inclusion: Stirring the Pot, *Cambridge Journal of Education*, 31: 291–301.

McCarthy, P., Laing, K. and Walker, J. (2004) *Offenders of the Future? Assessing the Risk of Children and Young People becoming involved in Criminal or Antisocial Behaviour*, Department of Education and Skills Research Report RR545. London: DfES.

McNeely, C.A., Nonnemaker, J.M. and Blum, R.W. (2002) 'Promoting School Connectedness: Evidence from the National Longitudinal Study of Adolescent Health, *Journal of School Health*, 72: 138–146.

MORI (Market and Opinion Research International) (2004) *MORI Youth Survey 2004*. London: Youth Justice Board.

Muncie, J. (2002) 'A New Deal for Youth? Early Intervention and Correctionalism', in G. Hughes, E. McLaughlin, and J. Muncie (eds), *Crime Prevention and Community Safety*: New Directions. London: Sage Publications in association with the Open University, pp. 142–162.

Muncie, J. (2004) *Youth and Crime*, 2nd edition. London: Sage Publications.

NAS/UWT (National Association of School Masters/Union of Women Teachers), (2003) *NAS/UWT Report on Violence and Indiscipline*. Available on line: www.tea-chersunion.org.uk, accessed on 27 March 2003.

Neill, S.R.St J. (2000) *Unacceptable Pupil Behaviour. A Survey Analysed for the National Union of Teachers*. Warwick: Institute of Education, University of Warwick.

Noaks, J. and Noaks, L. (2000) 'Violence in School: Risk, Safety and Fear of Crime', *Educational Psychology in Practice*, 16, 69–73.

Ofsted (2003) *Education Not Fully Meeting the Needs of the Most Vulnerable Pupils at Key Stage 4*, Press Release, NR 2003-69, 10 June 10. Available on line: www.ofted.go-v.uk/news.

Parsons, S. (2002) *Basic Skills and Crime: Findings from a Study of Adults Born in 1958 and 1970*. London: Basic Skills Agency.

Phillips, C. (2003) 'Who's Who in the Pecking Order?', *British Journal of Criminology*, 43: 710–728.

Resnick, M.D., Bearman, P.S. and Blum, R.W. (1997) 'Protecting Adolescents from Harm: Findings from the National Longitudinal Study on Adolescent Health', *Journal of the American Medical Association*, 278: 823–832.

Rutter, M., Giller, H. and Hagell, A. (1998) *Antisocial Behaviour by Young People*. Cambridge: Cambridge University Press.

Rutter, M., Maughan, B., Mortimore, P. and Ouston, J. (1979) *Fifteen Thousand Hours: Secondary Schools and their Effects on Children*. Shepton Mallet: Open Books Publishing.

SEU (Social Exclusion Unit) (1998) *Truancy and Exclusion from School*. London: Cabinet Office.

SEU (2001a) *A New Commitment to Neighbourhood Renewal*. London: Cabinet Office.

SEU (2001b) *Preventing Social Exclusion*. London: Cabinet Office.

Smith, P.K. (2002) 'School Bullying, and Ways of Preventing It', in E. Debarbieux and C. Blaya (eds), *Violence in Schools and Public Policies*. Paris: Elsevier Science, pp. 117–128.

Smith, P.K. and Myron-Wilson, R. (1998) 'Parenting and School Bullying', *Clinical Child Psychology and Psychiatry*, 3, 405–417.

Smith, P.K., Morita, J., Junger-Tas, J., Olweus, R., Catalano, R. and Slee, P. (eds) (1999) *The Nature of School Bullying: A Cross-national Perspective*. London and New York: Routledge.

Stephen, D. and Squires, P. (2003) *Community Safety, Enforcement and Acceptable Behaviour Contracts: An Evaluation of the Work of the Community Safety Team in the East Brighton 'New Deal for Communities' Area*. Brighton: Health and Social Policy Research Centre, University of Brighton.

Straw, J. and Michael, A. (1996) *Tackling the Causes of Crime: Labour's Proposal to Prevent Crime and Criminality*. London: Labour Party.

Sullivan, J. and Beech, A. (2002) 'Professional Perpetrators', *Child Abuse Review*, 11: 153–167.

Sutton, C., Utting, D. and Farrington, D. (2004) *Support from the Start: Working with Young Children and their Families to Reduce the Risks of Crime and Anti-social Behaviour*, Department of Education and Skills Research Report 524. London: DfES.

TUC/MORI (2001) *Half a Million Kids Working Illegally*. 21 March 21. London: TUC.

Walsh, C. (2004) *Drug Testing in Schools*. Paper presented at the British Society of Criminology Conference, University of Portsmouth, 6–9 July 2004.

Whitney, I. and Smith, P.K. (1993) 'Bullying in Junior/Middle Schools', *Educational Research*, 35, 3–25.

Wilson, D.B., Gottfredson, D.C. and Najaka, S.S. (2001) 'School-based Prevention of Problem Behaviours: A Meta-Analysis', *Journal of Quantitative Criminology*, 17: 247–272.

Winchester, R. (2003) 'We Don't Want No Education', *Community Care*, 23–29 January: 26–28.

Wolke, D.F.H. (1999) Research Report submitted to the ESRC, September.

YJB (Youth Justice Board) (2002) *Youth Study*. London: Youth Justice Board.

Chapter 10

The identification and management of anti-social and offending behaviour

Ruth M. Hatcher and Clive R. Hollin

On 10 September 2003, the Home Office's Anti-Social Behaviour Unit conducted a one-day audit of reports of anti-social behaviour within England and Wales. The research incorporated information collected by the police, local authorities, housing associations, voluntary organizations, the British Transport Police, the fire brigade, and the health services. In the chosen 24-hour period, 66,107 reports of anti-social behaviour were filed, amounting to one report of anti-social behaviour every two seconds (Home Office 2003b).

The government estimates that the anti-social behaviour within our communities costs the taxpayer a substantial £3.4 billion a year (Home Office 2003a). In addition to this significant economic cost, there is also evidence of high psychological and emotional costs to the victims following experience of such acts. Shaw and Pease (2002) have highlighted that the cumulative effect of exposure to even minor instances of anti-social behaviour can result in the victim's experience of psychological damage, sleep disturbance, and emotional trauma. Thus, when the economic, social and individual costs of anti-social and criminal behaviour are considered, it becomes obvious why tackling such behaviour has become an item that ranks high on the political agenda.

Over the years there has been a variety of attempts to combat the related issues of anti-social and offending behaviour. With the introduction of the Anti-Social Behaviour Act 2003, followed by the inauguration in June 2004 of the National Offender Management Service, the Home Office has set out a vision to provide 'the tools for practitioners and agencies to effectively tackle anti-social behaviour'

(Home Office 2004a), with the aim of 'end to end management of offenders, whether they are serving sentences in prison, the community or both' (Home Office 2004c).

Given this political policy, the procedures that flow from it will demand attention to two areas by the relevant criminal justice agencies. First, how can criminal justices agencies seek to identify anti-social behaviour? Second, once recognized, how can it be managed within community settings? The issues raised by these two questions will be addressed in this chapter.

What is anti-social behaviour?

The starting point is one of definition: if a given behaviour is to be managed, then there must be agreement on what it constitutes. The Criminal Justice Act 1998 defines an anti-social act as behaviour 'that caused or was likely to cause harassment, alarm or distress to one or more persons not of the same household as himself'. This broad definition encompasses a wide range of behaviours, such as using and selling drugs, harassment, graffiti, verbal abuse, damage to property, excessive noise, alcohol abuse, prostitution, intimidation, and criminal behaviour. Such a broad definition of this problem behaviour can be seen to be allied to the view that anti-social behaviour is a subjective concept and as such is based on individual perception (Harradine, Kodz, Lemetti and Jones 2004). In other words, what is viewed as anti-social by one individual may not be judged to be so by another. Therefore variations between the communities within which we live may mean that some acts are tolerated, or even sought after, within one environment, but are seen as anti-social within another. For example, the recreational use of marijuana may be viewed by some communities as alarming and so, following the above definition, as constituting an anti-social behaviour. However, other communities may see the use of marijuana in a neutral or desirable light.

Armitage (2002) argues that there are difficulties with a 'catch all' definition, such as the one posited by the Criminal Justice Act. The issue is that the definition is grounded in the *consequences* of the act, rather than the characteristics of the act itself. This approach to definition provides the potential not only for variation in interpretation, but also for confusion concerning to which agencies the behaviour should be reported. Indeed, it would appear that using this type of definition means that the same act could be construed as anti-social or not depending on the views of the observer.

In recognition of the heterogeneity of anti-social behaviour and the ensuing conceptual confusion (Rutter, Giller and Hagell 1998), there have been recent attempts to create a typology of anti-social behaviours (Harradine *et al* 2004). The typology advanced by Harradine *et al* aims to 'provide a practical framework and . . . a guide to the types of behaviours that local practitioners may want to include in a definition of anti-social behaviour' (Harradine *et al* 2004: 4–5). Based on the range of definitions already in use, as well as responses from British Crime Survey participants, this typology concentrates on the anti-social act itself, rather than its consequences, and is purely descriptive. Within the definition, anti-social behaviour is categorized into one of the following four categories: (1) misuse of public space, including begging, drug misuse and dealing, abandoning cars; (2) disregard for community/personal well-being, including noise, rowdy behaviour and hoax calls; (3) acts directed at people, including intimidation and harassment on the grounds of race, sexual orientation, gender, religion, disability or age; (4) environmental damage, including criminal damage, vandalism and littering.

It is apparent that a definition of anti-social behaviour is neither straightforward nor clear-cut. There are a wide variety of acts that may be perceived as anti-social behaviour and the heterogeneity of the concept makes it difficult to define. On the other hand, the definition of criminal behaviour can be perfectly straightforward in adopting the position, as stated by Williams (1955): 'A crime is an act that is capable of being followed by criminal proceedings, having one of the types of outcome [punishment, etc.] known to follow these proceedings' (Williams 1955: 21). Thus, the term 'anti-social behaviour' encapsulates a range of acts, which might or might not be construed as criminal. For example, some kinds of behaviour, such as bullying and harassment, which Goldstein (2002) refers to as 'low level aggression', could result in a criminal prosecution but are generally viewed as anti-social. One the other hand, behaviours such as being rude, shouting insults and hanging round streets could be viewed as anti-social under the Criminal Justice Act's definition, but whether these individual acts would be reported to the police and result in criminal proceedings is doubtful. However, the term 'criminal behaviour' is unambiguous in that it refers to behaviours that, by definition, are prohibited by criminal law. As might be expected, it is clear that there is a strong connection between anti-social behaviour and crime. Taylor and Gottfredson (1986) have reported correlations between the two behaviours as high as 0.63.

If resources are to be directed to managing anti-social and criminal behaviour, then some level of understanding of the extent of the issue is important. This takes us to the matter of measurement: how can the amount of anti-social and criminal behaviour be estimated?

Measurement of anti-social behaviour

The highlighted problem in defining anti-social behaviour naturally impacts on the ability to measure the volume of such behaviour over time. If there is little agreement on what acts constitute anti-social behaviour then finding a way to measure the incidence and frequency of such behaviours is inevitably problematic.

Harradine *et al* (2004) have proposed that there are three ways of collecting data on anti-social behaviour: through witness and victim reports, logging of incidents, and public perceptions. They propose that the utilization of these methods will depend upon the objective of the data collection exercise in hand. Different approaches can be useful in measuring anti-social behaviour in different circumstances, say according to type of behaviour or geographical areas.

The three approaches to measurement are each discussed below.

Report data

This first type of data collection relies on counting the number of reports made to the appropriate agencies over a certain time period. Hence, information from the police, social services, local authorities, housing associations, fire service, and other such organizations is collated. The collection and systematic organization of this type of information can provide a one-off snapshot of anti-social behaviour within a particular time-frame. Alternatively, if such information is routinely collected it can be used to establish patterns of anti-social behaviour within particular locations.

The most recent example of data collected from reports was the Anti-Social Behaviour Unit's one-day count of reported anti-social behaviour in September 2003 (Home Office 2003b). As mentioned above, in order to build up a national picture, local organizations counted the number of reports of anti-social behaviour that they received over a period of 24 hours. Over 65,000 acts of anti-social behaviour were reported nationally in this one-day period, the majority relating to litter and rubbish, criminal damage or vandalism, vehicle related nuisance, and nuisance behaviour (51.4 per cent).

Whilst this method of data collection can be useful to local Crime and Disorder Reduction Partnerships and Community Safety Partnerships in providing approximations of cost and indications of particular problems, the method is not without disadvantages. The utilization of different measuring and recording techniques between national and local agencies can result in *ad hoc* results. Furthermore, it is suspected that a significant proportion of anti-social behaviour is not even reported to the appropriate agencies due to fear of recriminations or because of lack of confidence in the agencies tasked to deal with it (Hunter, Nixon and Parr 2004). Indeed, British Crime Survey respondents who admitted experiencing problems related to anti-social behaviour were unlikely to report such behaviour. In all, 80 per cent of respondents who had experienced problems with drunk or rowdy behaviour and 46 per cent with noisy neighbours had not made any kind of complaint to the appropriate agencies (Wood 2004).

Whilst the lack of reporting would result in an underestimate in the count, there is also the risk that overlapping data may do the contrary and overestimate the number of anti-social acts. For example, some incidents may have been reported by different people to a single authority on more than one occasion, meaning that one act of anti-social behaviour would be counted more than once. In addition, some anti-social behaviour or acts could be reported to more than one agency: for example, graffiti may be reported to the police for them to investigate as a criminal damage offence, or to the local authority because it is deemed to be unsightly and needs removing. In such cases, again, one act would be recorded more than once in the count of anti-social behaviour reports.

Incident data

In an effort to eliminate the problems of overlapping data and multiple counting of anti-social acts, data relating to specific incidents of anti-social behaviour can instead be used to measure the problem. Harradine *et al* (2004) propose a number of sources for this method of counting, including police recorded crime figures on low-level crime, CCTV recordings, and street, visual, or community audits of observable signs of anti-social behaviour. This method of data collection allows the estimation of the frequency of specific types of anti-social behaviour, perhaps within specific locations at specific times. This method may be useful for evaluation or the monitoring of the incidence of specific behaviours at a given time and place, but it is unlikely to provide a general picture of the prevalence of a multi-faceted construct such as anti-social behaviour. The problem in establishing a clear definition of anti-social behaviour also means that this method is not without its limitations. With little consensus on which precise acts or behaviours constitute anti-social behaviour, it is likely that different organizations could produce different counts from observing the same place on the same day.

Public perception data

Surveys such as the British Crime Survey or local crime surveys attempt to solve the problems inherent in incident data by collating information relating to public perceptions of anti-social behaviour within their communities. This method of measurement therefore relies on the subjective nature of the construct of anti-social behaviour and allows respondents to define the behaviour, rather than forcing a definition on the data collection. In surveys, participants are generally sampled from the general public and are asked about their own experiences of certain behaviours, their perceptions of the behaviour, and its consequences within their area of residence. This type of measurement can provide rich data and allows comparisons between groups of respondents of, say, different age, gender, and locality.

Public surveys have reported concern among respondents over anti-social behaviour within their local neighbourhoods (Kershaw 2001). The latest British Crime Survey therefore attempted to explore further these public perceptions (Wood 2004). The survey found that the majority of respondents said that they had not seen an improvement in anti-social behaviour over the preceding two years: speeding traffic and teenagers hanging around the area were reported as being the biggest problems. However, those respondents living in 'hard-pressed areas' – characterized by low-income families, a large proportion of resident in council properties, high-rise developments and inner city estates – were more likely than those in more affluent areas to report anti-social behaviour within their locality. There was also a qualitative difference in the profile of behaviours reported by the hard-pressed and affluent areas: those in affluent areas complained of speeding traffic, whilst drug use and drug dealing was characteristic of the reports of those living in the less affluent districts.

Whilst there are definitional and measurement issues associated with understanding the parameters of anti-social behaviour, the critical point lies in the way we respond to anti-social behaviour. The way we respond to anti-social behaviour is important at three levels: first, for the sake of those who have been victimized; second, to try to prevent future victimization; third, to attempt to prevent offenders following a pathway to more serious criminal behaviour. Following the last point, what do we know about the characteristics of those who commit anti-social and criminal acts?

Understanding anti-social and offending behaviour

There are many ways to address the issue of understanding anti-social and offending behaviour. To illustrate the issues, two approaches that are currently receiving attention, longitudinal studies and risk-needs assessment, are discussed.

Longitudinal studies

One way to look for factors associated with the onset and maintenance of anti-social behaviour is to conduct 'life-span' or *longitudinal* research. This type of research has grown in sophistication in recent years and has informed theory and practice in criminology and crime prevention (Farrington 2003). One of the main points to emerge from the longitudinal studies is that much juvenile crime is 'adolescence limited' – the majority of young people who behave in an anti-social and criminal manner (and lots of young people do) will 'grow out of crime' by the age of 18 years (Moffitt 1993). Now, while this 'growing out' is true for the majority of young people, some will continue their offending while progressing to adulthood. Moffitt (1993) draws on this evidence to make the distinction between 'adolescence limited' and 'life-course persistent' offenders. The findings from longitudinal research studies allow identification of the factors associated with longer-term offending. It follows that knowledge of these factors is important in informing both theory and practice.

There are several major longitudinal studies in the literature, carried out in different countries (e.g. Kyvsgaard 2003, Moffitt *et al* 2001). In England, the *Cambridge Study in Delinquent Development* is a longitudinal study that began in 1961 with a cohort of 411 young males, then aged 8–9 years, and is continuing with over 90 per cent of the sample still alive as they reach their early fifties (Farrington 2002). The data gathering for the Cambridge Study has involved access to official records, repeated testing and interviewing of the males, their parents, peers, and teachers. Whilst the Cambridge Study has produced a great deal of information, however as the participants are all males the outcomes do not, say, apply to females.

Interestingly, the official convictions recorded for the young men corresponded reasonably well with self-reported delinquency. This match means that there can be a high degree of confidence when making comparisons of the worst offenders with the other men in the study. The force of making these comparisons is to identify the developmental characteristics of the juveniles that have predictive value with regard to offending as an adult. The main predictive factors, encompassing individual, family, and economic features, are summarized in Table 10.1.

Table 10.1 Child and adolescent predictors of adult offending

1	Antisocial childhood behaviour, including 'troublesomeness' in school, dishonesty and aggressiveness.
2	Hyperactivity-impulsivity-attention deficit, including poor concentration, restlessness, risk-taking and impulsivity.
3	Low intelligence and poor school attainment.
4	Family criminality as seen in parents and older siblings.
5	Family poverty in terms of low family income, poor housing; and large family size.
6	Harsh parenting style, lack of parental supervision, parental conflict, and separation from parents.

Source: After Farrington (2002)

The Cambridge Study, like other longitudinal studies, shows that certain adverse features in early life are associated with the onset of anti-social and criminal behaviour. It also seems that these adverse features and developmental problems may be concentrated in certain families. Farrington, Barnes and Lambert (1996) studied 397 families and found that half of the total convictions across all the families were accounted for in just 23 families.

Risk–needs assessment

In risk-needs assessment with offenders, the theory is that there are aspects of an individual's life – such as their attitudes to crime, their relationships, and their financial circumstances – that are known to be associated with their criminal behaviour. These aspects of an individual's life that are associated with their offending are called *criminogenic needs* and, as such, are *risk factors* for future offending (Andrews and Bonta 2003). The aggregate of an individual's criminogenic needs forms their overall risk level for future offending.

Following this theoretical approach, several risk–needs assessment schedules have been developed. For example, the Level of Supervision Inventory (LSI) was originally developed by Andrews (1982) and later renamed the Level of Service Inventory; a revised version (LSI-R) was published by Andrews and Bonta (1995). Completed through file review and interview, the LSI-R assesses ten criminogenic factors: criminal history, education and employment, financial situation, family and marital relationships, accommodation, leisure and recreation, companions, alcohol and drug problems, emotional and personal problems, and attitudes and orientation to crime. The LSI has been shown to be a practical form of assessment to use with a range of offender populations and performs well in both identifying need and risk prediction (Hollin, Palmer and Clark 2003). There are several similar assessment schemes currently in use, such as OASys and ACE (Robinson 2003), to inform assessment with offenders.

One function of both the longitudinal research and risk–needs assessment is to highlight those areas at which preventative measures may be directed with maximum effect. In the following section we consider the range of preventative measures than have been put into operation.

Initiatives to address anti-social and offending behaviour

Society's response to anti-social behaviour can, and does, take a number of routes, with criminal prosecution the most obvious. However, the reporting of anti-social behaviour does not always result in criminal, or even civil, court action, although these routes are available if felt appropriate. NACRO (2003: 1) has advocated a 'Balanced approach to anti-social behaviour', that should encompass interventions which include prevention, education and enforcement on individual, group and universal levels.

Prior to the Crime and Disorder Act 1998, anti-social behaviour was dealt with by civil proceedings under the Housing Act 1996, the Environment Protection Act 1990, the Noise Act 1996, or through injunctions against the anti-social individual. In addition, there were criminal law solutions under the Protection from Harassment Act 1997 and the Public Order Act 1986. Despite these numerous options, there were loopholes within the legislation that led to a general dissatisfaction with the existing arrangements. For example, the majority of the legislation listed above was not available to use against juveniles, who are often the perpetrators of the very behaviour that this legislation aims to combat. In addition, much anti-social behaviour, when considered in isolation, is not deemed to be serious enough to bring about legal proceedings. It is the cumulative nature of small anti-social acts that creates the greatest impact on the community, but the laws could only be directed towards individual instances of behaviour that were often deemed too trivial to pursue.

The Crime and Disorder Act 1998 and the Anti-Social Behaviour Act 2003 therefore provided local authorities and the police with a number of preventative and enforcement measures. Further, these measures could be used with juveniles and against the perpetrators of cumulative sub-criminal acts in order to intervene to reduce the risk of further offending. Some examples of the intervention schemes operation in England and Wales will be discussed to illustrate current practice.

Prevention: Youth Inclusion Programmes and Acceptable Behaviour Contracts

As seen above, perpetrators of anti-social behaviour may lead lives that result in increased exposure to the risk factors associated with anti-social behaviour and so increase the likelihood of anti-social acts. For example, in a review of Anti-Social Behaviour Orders it was found that almost one in five of those proposed for such an order had problems with drugs and one in six had problems with alcohol (Campbell 2002b). In recognition of this type of issue, preventative measures have been developed that attempt to reduce anti-social behaviour by tackling the problems seen to be associated with the behaviour. Thus, rather than trying to prevent the anti-social behaviour by enforcing set conditions, the aim of these measures is to address the factors that are assessed as contributory to the behaviour. If successful, such measures should reduce anti-social behaviour and divert these individuals away from a life of anti-social and criminal behaviour.

There are numerous examples of preventative interventions running at both local and national levels within England and Wales. In the broad field of prevention, the distinction is made between three different levels of prevention, which can be applied to anti-social behaviour: (1) *primary* preventative measures that are directed across society as a whole to eliminate totally the development anti-social behaviour; (2) *secondary* prevention measures that target those groups within society seen to be most at risk of developing anti-social behaviour; (3) *tertiary* prevention that focuses on the individual known to have previously behaved in an anti-social manner.

Youth Inclusion Programmes (YIPs), run by Youth Offending Teams, were introduced in 2002 in order to tackle anti-social behaviour and crime among youths within the community. These programmes, which tend to operate within the most deprived and high crime estates within England and Wales, target high-risk youths through inter-agency information sharing. Thus, within the framework above they are an example of a *secondary* prevention strategy. In this approach, local agencies such as the Youth Offending Team, police, social services, schools, and local education authorities are charged with identifying risk factors relevant to the young people they know. Those individuals who are deemed the highest risk – that is, those assessed to have the highest level of risk factors for anti-social and offending behaviour – are targeted for the YIP.

Youth Inclusion Programmes attempt to engage the 'top 50' high-risk individuals within the community in positive activities for at least five hours per week. These activities can include sport, health and drugs education, motor projects, family projects, and arts, culture and media. In addition, they aim to provide information and educational material such as career guidance and educational assistance. Running alongside these activities are mentoring programmes that aim to provide positive role models to support and advise the selected young people. Drawing on the growing 'what works' literature, especially in relation to responsivity and dosage (Bernfeld, Farrington and Leschied 2001), YIPs attempt to target the intervention with regard to the individual needs of the person involved. Thus local areas, whilst given guidance, have been given a free hand to decide which particular activities to include within their programmes.

Financed jointly by the Youth Justice Board and local agencies, Youth Inclusion Programmes have produced some mixed early evaluation results in relation to their ambitious targets (Mackie, Burrows and Hubbard 2003). Through the introduction of YIPs the aims were: to reduce arrest rates of those targeted by the programme by 60 per cent, to reduce truancy and school exclusion rates by 33 per cent, and to reduce recorded crime in the targeted community area by 30 per cent.

Of the national sample of 5,508 young people who have been identified locally as being within the 'top 50' at-risk individuals, an impressive 4,050 (73.5 per cent) have voluntarily engaged in the projects provided by the YIP (Mackie, Burrows and Hubbard 2003). In addition, those in the top 50 that have attended YIP activities have reduced their arrest rates by 65 per cent compared to the time preceding their involvement in the YIP. Furthermore, when those completing YIPs have been arrested, this has been for a less serious index offence than before their engagement with the YIP.

On viewing this information in isolation it would seem that the YIPs are already achieving their aim in relation to arrest rates, after only two years in operation. However, further data reported by Mackie, Burrows and Hubbard (2003) have shown large reductions (44 per cent) in the average arrest rate of those 'top 50' individuals who did *not* engage in a YIP. It seems that the YIP cannot take sole responsibility for the impressive reductions in the arrest rates of its attendees. Other explanations for these findings could be changes in the police's arresting practices, or changes in local situations, or even growing out of crime.

The findings in relation to the second and third aims of reductions in truancy and crime within the area have not been encouraging. Truancy has actually been seen to increase by an average 40 per cent and crime within YIP-targeted communities has actually risen by 5.8 per cent, after adjustments for changes in national recording and changes in local crime.

Acceptable Behaviour Contracts are designed to serve as early warnings to individuals that their behaviour is unacceptable, without the need for court intervention. An Acceptable Behaviour Contract is a written voluntary agreement between an individual who is deemed to have been involved in anti-social behaviour and the agencies that are tasked with dealing with such behaviour. Whilst Acceptable Behaviour Contracts are generally used with young people they can also be used with adults.

The individual who has been acting in an anti-social manner is invited, in the case of a juvenile with their parents or legal guardian, to attend a meeting with local agencies in order to discuss their problem behaviour. The outcome of this meeting is an agreed list of conditions that the individual is to adhere to for the following six months. Similar to Anti-Social Behaviour Orders, these conditions can encompass geographical restrictions, the prohibition of damage to property, and graffiti and verbal abuse of others (Bullock and Jones 2004). Tailored to the individual, these contracts are not legally binding; however, if breached they can be used to evict the family from council or registered social landlord premises. Further, they can form the basis of evidence that can be presented to the court in support of an application for an Anti-Social Behaviour Order.

The Acceptable Behaviour Contracts scheme has been running in the London Borough of Islington in London since 1999 and has been evaluated using both qualitative and quantitative methods (Bullock and Jones 2004). Whilst the numbers of anti-social acts were seen to reduce during the contract, they were by no means eradicated. A proportion of the people who signed a voluntary Acceptable Behaviour Contract continued to commit the anti-social acts that were contained within their contract. It is therefore not surprising that 43 per cent of the contracts were breached, some of them three or more times. With practitioners reporting a lack of available resources to monitor the scheme, it is feasible that the breach rate was actually significantly higher with further undetected breaches.

The latest statistics suggest that local Crime and Disorder Reduction Partnerships (CDRP) have been increasingly using Acceptable Behaviour

Contracts in their attempts at early intervention (Home Office 2004c). One in four CDRPs reported using Acceptable Behaviour Contracts in the past year, with the national total of contracts reaching over 5,000. Indeed, representatives from Mid-Bedfordshire stated that within the local area, contrary to what was found in Islington, 'over 120 acceptable behaviour contracts have been served; this is a 95 per cent success rate' (Home Office 2004c: 18).

The use of Youth Inclusion Programmes and Acceptable Behaviour Contracts demonstrates how difficult it is to work at the secondary prevention level. They also illustrate how problematic it is in practice to produce unequivocal evidence of the effectiveness of an intervention.

Enforcement: Anti-Social Behaviour Orders and Parenting Orders

It is apparent from the above that whilst prevention programmes can be designed and implemented, continuing to engage those at risk is not guaranteed. Accordingly, measures have been introduced to enforce the individual's compliance with preventative measures. Two examples of such interventions are Anti-Social Behaviour Orders and Parenting Orders.

Anti-Social Behaviour Orders (ASBOs), introduced under the Crime and Disorder Act 1998, were designed to complement existing procedures for dealing with anti-social behaviour and to bridge some of the loopholes mentioned above. Available as a sanction against any individual aged ten years or over, they are civil orders that can be applied for by local authorities and/or the police (and since the Anti-Social Behaviour Act 2003 in conjunction with registered social landlords, the British Transport Police, housing action trusts and county councils if necessary) against anyone who has displayed anti-social behaviour, in order to deter and prevent the escalation of further anti-social acts. On passing an ASBO the court will specify certain conditions, such as preventing the individual from entering a geographical area or associating with other named people, for a minimum of two years. As the ASBO is a civil order, the standard of proof required within the case is concordant with civil cases and is hence judged on the balance of probabilities, rather than the stricter beyond reasonable doubt requirement of criminal cases.

The latter point has been one of contention, especially as breach of the civil order can result in a criminal conviction and possibly imprisonment of up to five years. Civil rights groups, such as Liberty, have attacked the introduction of ASBOs, stating: 'They subvert the criminal justice system by attempting to tackle criminal behaviour and impose criminal-level penalties through the civil courts – on the basis that someone has "probably" committed the offence' (Liberty 2002).

There has also been concern over the identification to the general public of juveniles who are subject to ASBOs. Concern has been expressed over the naming and shaming of anti-social individuals based on evidence assessed on the balance of probabilities and potentially through the use of hearsay evidence. Previously, the court would use the Child and Young Person's Act to dispose of people under the age of 18 years. This procedure prevented the names and addresses of these individuals being reported in the press. However, the government has been firm in its view that the recipients of ASBOs, whether juvenile or adult, should be named to aid in the prevention of further anti-social behaviour: 'There should be a presumption in favour of publicising the identity of the defendant in order to ensure as far as possible that the ASBO will be effective in preventing further anti-social behaviour. It cannot be in the interest of justice or public order for an ASBO to be issued with little prospect of breaches being noticed' (the Home Secretary cited in *Guardian*, 2001).

A Home Office review in 2002 found that the majority of ASBOs that had been ordered were against men (84 per cent) and people under the age of 21 years (74 per cent). Practitioners reported that they were concerned over the time it takes for an ASBO to get through court, the amount of resources needed, and the cost of taking action through ASBOs (Campbell 2002a). The overall total average cost of an ASBO was found to be £5,350 and it took more than 13 weeks from the date of application to the order being imposed by the court. In addition, the uptake of the orders varied considerably across the country with some areas choosing not using them at all. In those areas that did use ASBOs over one-third of orders (36 per cent) were breached within nine months of receiving the order, some of them up to five times.

A further intervention for anti-social behaviour that works on the principles of enforcement is that of the Parenting Order. Based on the research evidence that shows that a lack of parental supervision has associations with criminal behaviour (Graham and Bowling 1995), a Parenting Order is placed on the parents of a child who has displayed anti-social or criminal behaviour where it is deemed that the order will prevent further such behaviour. Whilst there are options for working with parents without the need for court intervention which follow similar principles to the Acceptable Behaviour Contracts described above, when the parent is unwilling to cooperate with local agencies an application to the court can be made for an order to be granted under civil jurisdiction.

A Parenting Order consists of two elements: the first and core element being the requirement of attendance at a parenting programme that can last up to three months. The parenting programme aims to provide parents with the skills necessary to respond to the needs of their child. This intervention can take the form of a cognitive behavioural programme, mentoring, parenting advice, individual family therapy, functional family therapy, solution focused therapy, family group conferencing, and group based programmes (Home Office *et al* 2004).

The second element of a Parenting Order is an individualized collection of specific controls that the parent must exercise over their child for the following 12 months. As under an Anti-Social Behaviour Order, these can vary from a curfew to ensuring attendance at school. If a parent fails to carry out the conditions of a Parenting Order without reasonable excuse, they can be prosecuted and a criminal offence can be recorded against them. The court can impose a fine of up to £1,000 in addition to a community order, a curfew order, or an absolute or conditional discharge.

Whilst associations such as the National Association of Head Teachers welcome such enforcement, the high-profile prosecutions and, on occasion, prison sentences for the parents of anti-social juveniles has provoked argument concerning the use of Parenting Orders. The idea that the parents can ultimately be criminalized because of acts committed by their child is not one with which some campaign groups, such as Barnardo's, find agreement. They argue that such measures could result in more financial and emotional poverty within the very groups that need support and education to prevent further anti-social and criminal behaviour.

In addition, from August 2002, the police were given the power, under the Criminal Justice and Police Act 2001, to issue fixed penalty notices for anti-social behaviour within four pilot areas. Previously these fines of either £40 or £80 were applicable only to persons over the age of 18 years for certain acts. Thus, offences resulting in a £40 fine included wasting police time or giving false report, sending false message, knowingly giving false alarm to a fire brigade, and using threatening words or behaviour likely to cause alarm, harassment or distress. Offences resulting in a £80 fine included being drunk in a highway, other public place or licensed premises, throwing fireworks in a thoroughfare, trespassing on a railway, throwing stones at trains or other railway traffic, buying or attempting to buy alcohol for consumption in a bar or licensed premises by a person under 18 (the offence is for the adult buying the alcohol for an underage person), disorderly behaviour while drunk in a public place, and consumption of alcohol in designated public place. However, the Anti-Social Behaviour Act 2003 extended these fines to acts of graffiti and fly-posting, as well as to people aged 16 and 17 years. The Home Office reports that over 20,000 notices such as these have been issued to perpetrators of anti-social behaviour (Home Office 2004c). An early evaluation of the pilot areas (Spicer and Kilsby 2004) found that the majority of fixed penalty notices were given for causing harassment, alarm or distress (49 per cent) or 'disorderly behaviour while drunk' (41 per cent).

The basis of enforcement lies in the notion of deterrence. The concept of deterrence is central to the criminal justice system in many western societies. The foundation of deterrence lies in having measures in place that force people to behave in a social manner for fear of the punitive consequences should they do otherwise. While fine in theory and with popular appeal, it is altogether less clear that criminal justice measures based on deterrence actually have the intended effect (Hollin 2002). There is a strong argument that effective measures to prevent crime need to be constructive rather than destructive in nature.

Conclusion

It is evident that anti-social and criminal behaviour is part of the fabric of society and is not going to go away. It follows that we need to have in place policies and procedures that will allow for the management of anti-social acts in order to reduce their likelihood and protect against their effects on victims. As seen in this chapter – from definitional issues to determining what works in effective crime reduction – none of this is simple. Nonetheless, as the human sciences advance so our understanding improves, translating understanding into policy remains the challenge of the day.

References

Andrews, D.A. (1982) *The Level of Supervision Inventory (LSI): The First Follow-up.* Toronto: Ontario Ministry of Correctional Services.

Andrews, D.A. and Bonta, J. (1995) *LSI-R: The Level of Service Inventory-Revised.* Toronto: Multi-Health Systems.

Andrews, D.A. and Bonta, J. (2003) *The Psychology of Criminal Conduct*, 3rd edition. Cincinnati, OH: Anderson Publishing.

Armitage, R. (2002) *Tackling Anti-social Behaviour: What Really Works*, NACRO Community Safety Practice Briefing. London: NACRO.

Bernfeld, G.A., Farrington, D.P., and Leschied, A.W. (eds) (2001) *Offender Rehabilitation in Practice: Implementing and Evaluating Effective Programs*. Chichester: Wiley.

Bullock, K. and Jones, B. (2004) *Acceptable Behaviour Contracts Addressing Antisocial Behaviour in the London Borough of Islington*, Home Office Online Report 02/02. London: Home Office.

Campbell, S. (2002a) *A Review of Anti-social Behaviour Orders*, Home Office Research Study 236. London: Home Office Research Development and Statistics Directorate.

Campbell, S. (2002b) *Implementing Anti-Social Behaviour Orders: Messages for Practitioners*, Home Office Research Findings 160. London: Home Office Research and Development Directorate.

Dodd, T., Nicholas, S., Povey, D. and Walker, A. (2004) *Crime in England and Wales 2003/4*, Home Office Statistical Bulletin 10/04. London: Home Office.

Farrington, D.P. (2002) 'Key Results from the First Forty Years of the Cambridge Study in Delinquent Development', in T.P. Thornberry and M.D. Krohn (eds), *Taking Stock of Delinquency: An Overview of Findings from Contemporary Longitudinal Studies*. New York: Kluwer Academic/Plenum Publishers.

Farrington, D.P. (2003) 'Developmental and Life-course Criminology: Key Theoretical and Empirical Issues – the 2002 Sutherland Award Address', *Criminology*, 41: 221–255.

Farrington, D.P., Barnes, G.C. and Lambert, S. (1996) 'The Concentration of Offending in Families', *Legal and Criminological Psychology*, 1: 47–63.

Goldstein, A.P. (2002) *The Psychology of Group Aggression*. Chichester: Wiley.

Graham, J. and Bowling, B. (1995). *Young People and Crime*, Home Office Research Study 145. London: Home Office.

Guardian (2001) 'Shame faced', *Guardian*, 24 October.

Harradine, S., Kodz, J., Lemetti, F. and Jones, B. (2004) *Defining and Measuring Anti-social Behaviour*, Home Office Practice and Development Report. London: Home Office.

Hollin, C.R. (2002) 'Does Punishment Motivate Offenders to Change?', in M. McMurran (ed.), *Motivating Offenders to Change: A Guide to Enhancing Engagement in Therapy*. Chichester: John Wiley and Sons.

Hollin, C.R., Palmer, E.J., and Clark, D. (2003) 'The Level of Supervision Inventory-Revised Profile of English Prisoners: A Needs Analysis', *Criminal Justice and Behavior*, 30: 422–440.

Home Office (2003a) *Together: Tackling Anti-social Behaviour: Action Plan*. London: Home Office.

Home Office (2003b) *Together: Tackling Anti-social Behaviour: The One-Day Count of Anti-social Behaviour*. London: Home Office.

Home Office (2004a, 30 September) *Anti-Social Behaviour Act*. Available online: http://www.homeoffice.gov.uk/crime/antisocialbehaviour/legislation/asbact.html#-Dates.

Home Office (2004b, 30 September) *Reducing Crime, Changing Lives*. Available online. http://www.probation.homeoffice.gov.uk/output/page214.asp.

Home Office (2004c) *Together: Tackling Anti-social Behaviour – One Year On*. London: Home Office.

Home Office, Youth Justice Board and the Department for Constitutional Affairs. (2004) *Parenting Contracts and Orders: Guidance*. London: Home Office.

Hunter, C., Nixon, J. and Parr, S. (2004) *What Works for Victims and Witnesses of Antisocial Behaviour*. Sheffield/London: Sheffield Hallam University/ASB Unit, Home Office.

Kershaw, C., Chivite-Matthews, N., Thomas, C. and Aust, R. (2001) *The 2001 British Crime Survey: First Results, England and Wales*. Home Office Statistical Bulletin 18/01. London: Home Office.

Kyvsgaard, B. (2003) *The Criminal Career: The Danish Longitudinal Study*. Cambridge: Cambridge University Press.

Liberty (2002, 30 January) *Extending Anti-social Behaviour Orders Misses the Point*, Liberty Press Release. London: Liberty.

Mackie, A., Burrows, J., Hubbard, R. (2003) *Evaluation of the Youth Inclusion Programme: An Evaluation of Phase One of the Programme*. The Youth Justice Board for England and Wales (online publication).

Moffitt, T.E. (1993) Adolescence-limited and Life-course-persistent Antisocial Behavior: A Developmental Taxonomy. *Psychological Review, 100*, 674–701.

Moffitt, T.E., Caspi, A., Rutter, M., and Silva, P.A. (2001) *Sex Differences in Anti-social Behaviour: Conduct Disorder, Delinquency, and Violence in the Dunedin Longitudinal Study*. Cambridge: Cambridge University Press.

NACRO (2003) *A Balanced Approach to Anti-social Behaviour: A Summary of Interventions*, Community Safety Practice Briefing. London: Nacro.

Robinson, G. (2003) 'Implementing OASys: Lessons from research into LSI-R and ACE', *Probation Journal, 50*: 30–40.

Rutter, M., Giller, H. and Hagell, A. (1998) *Antisocial Behaviour by Young People*. Cambridge: Cambridge University Press.

Shaw, M. and Pease, K. (2002) 'Minor Crimes, Trivial Incidents: The Cumulative Impact of Offending', *Issues in Forensic Psychology, 3*: 41–48.

Spicer, K. and Kilsby, P. (2004) *Penalty Notices for Disorder: Early Results from the Pilot*, Home Office Research Findings 232. London: Home Office.

Taylor, R.B. and Gottfredson, S.D. (1986) 'Environmental Design, Crime, and Prevention: An Examination of Community Dynamics', in A.J. Reiss and M. Tonry (eds), *Crime and Justice: A Review of Research, Communities and Crime*. Chicago: University of Chicago Press.

Wood, M. (2004) *Perceptions and Experience of Antisocial Behaviour: Findings from the 2003/4 British Crime Survey*. Home Office Online Report 49/04. London: Home Office.

Williams, G. (1955) 'The Definition of Crime', in J. Smith and B. Hogan (eds), *Criminal Law*, 2nd edition. London: Butterworths.

Chapter 11

Community youth justice: policy, practices and public perception

Nikki McKenzie

In the context of dealing with issues surrounding the offending behaviour of youths, it is necessary to understand that the term community justice has, since the change of government in 1997, become synonymous with restorative justice. Howard Zehr states that:

> Restorative Justice sees things differently . . . crime is a violation of people and relationships . . . It creates obligations to make things right. Justice involves the victim, the offender and the community in a search for solutions which promote repair, reconciliation, and reassurance. (Zehr 1990: 181)

This approach is somewhat different from the way that youth justice services have dealt with the causes of crime as well as the young people themselves. However, in terms of whether it meets the principles of community justice it can be suggested that it does so, and perhaps more effectively than community justice in the adult sphere.

Nellis (2001, cited in Nellis and Gelsthorpe 2003: 237) suggests that the key components of community justice are 'the creation of community safety, the reduction of custody and the promotion of restorative justice', all of which should be understood within the realms of anti-oppressive practice. It is apparent that the inclusion of risk-based decision-making involved in the evidence-based approach to working with young people (Raynor 2001) and a multi-agency approach has allowed for community safety issues to become a significant factor in the assessment of and working with young offenders. It is also evident that current youth justice legislation has sanctioned the development and use of restorative justice. Nevertheless it is debatable whether there has indeed been a reduction in the use of custody in preference to community justice and community penalties, given that the latest Audit Commission Report (2004) indicates that the juvenile prison population has remained stable. Notwithstanding this, the youth justice system has no doubt made great advances in offering practice that is inclusive of young people and their families as well as the wider community and victims, but a practice that is based on setting and meeting targets, and in the process criminalizes young people at an earlier stage.

This chapter will draw upon an academic/practitioner's view of the youth justice system and will reflect upon the system's ability to embrace effective practice and to incorporate the principles of restorative and community justice. It will consider whether the youth justice system offers empowerment to all its participants, the effectiveness of using restorative justice when there is little or no victim input, and debate whether the introduction of restorative justice is mainly a means for the state to relinquish responsibility. Finally, it will consider the extent of youth crime, in particular focusing on public perception and the introduction of the Anti-Social Behaviour Order as a means to control 'evil' young people. This discussion will be contextualized within the parameters of the current political climate.

The youth justice system and the political context

The historical background of the youth justice system and the welfare versus justice debate has been well documented and as such will not be covered here in any detail (see Brown 1998, Smith 2003, Haines and Drakeford 1998, Pickford 2000). However, with the change of government in 1997 some of the problems relating to the running and effectiveness of the system, identified by Straw and Michael's *Tackling Youth Crime: Reforming Youth Justice* (1996) and the Audit Commission's *Misspent Youth... Young People and Crime* (1996), would be eradicated. It was anticipated that New Labour, who had been bequeathed 18 years of Thatcher/Major neo-liberalistic policy, would 'represent a "third way" one distinct from old traditions and beyond the old taxonomies of "left" and "right"' (Heffernan 2000: xii). However, this was not to be, particularly in relation to law and order.

In the run-up to the 1997 general election, supporters of New Labour were mystified by the party's new-found toughness on law and order. Many felt that this was a vote-winning artifice and that, once in government, the party would opt for the recognized more compassionate, understanding attitude of the 1970s (Pitts 2000). This was not to be realized. It soon became apparent that New Labour's rhetoric would indeed become fact and that they would not only be tough on the causes of crime but even tougher on offenders. Their manifesto claimed that *they* were now the 'party of law and order' and that they would pursue the 'heavy handed' measures dealing with sex offenders and sentencing that the Conservative Party recommended (Savage and Nash 2001).

It should be acknowledged that part of the Conservative legacy was the new public managerialist approach taken to governing public policy. Here it was envisaged that New Labour would offer a 'third way' style of management and that many of the Conservative methods would be pushed aside for a less radical and neo-liberal approach. However, *Tackling Delays in the Youth Justice System* (1997), which made proposals to introduce a swift administration of justice for young offenders, offered an insight into the management approach that New Labour were now adopting:

> The government believes that financial penalties could provide an effective incentive to better performance. (Home Office 1997a: 14)

New Labour, rather than reverting back to old Labour ways, or in fact offering a new way to manage the public sector, in particular law and order, was opting for the new public management stance: it was a case of 'New Labour in Conservative clothing'.

What was different with New Labour, however, was that they liked what managerialism had to offer in relation to 'what works', 'joined-up solutions', 'empowerment', and 'communitarian' devolution of power to 'local people' aspirations (Pitts 2000: 7). The Crime and Disorder Act 1998, the first major piece of legislation implemented by New Labour, established the setting up of multi-agency teams (Youth Offending Teams), through greater emphasis on partnerships and the introduction of restorative justice. Youth Offending Teams are comprised of representatives from the police service, probation service, health service, education, social services, connexions, and often include reparation providers, such as Crime Concern, to deliver a range of interventions and programmes that will ensure that young people 'face up to the consequences of their crimes and learn to change the habits and attitudes which led them into offending and anti-social behaviour' (Home Office 1997b: 27–28).

The Crime and Disorder Act 1998 (CDA) and the Youth Justice and Criminal Evidence Act 1999 (YJCEA) were the culmination of an intense period of consultation and evaluation of the youth justice system by both the Labour government (Straw and Michael 1996) and the Audit Commission (1996). The political rhetoric had a strong focus on parental responsibility, communitarianism and restorative justice, which should be seen as a progressive move towards the reintegration of young offenders back into society. However, it is apparent that the Labour government was responding to crime as the Conservatives did, by adopting a crime control and punishment attitude, and by embracing a New Right philosophy, directing responsibility back to the community and the family. The changes in the youth justice system and the introduction of new orders, although providing the overdue reform of the system has, to some degree, meant that young people are becoming criminalized at an earlier point. This is particularly the case where the cautioning system has been replaced with reprimands and final warnings and where the Anti-Social Behaviour Order appears to have become the answer to all evils.

Although a restorative justice approach is a positive move to encourage young people to take responsibility for their offending behaviour, it is perhaps the case that the government's *laissez-faire* attitude is going too far and as a consequence they are perpetuating an already highly charged blame culture. Brown (1998) suggests that the murder of James Bulger by two ten-year-old boys in 1993 rocked the foundations of our beliefs and equanimity with the world around us and changed the very notion of childhood. Any form of deviation from social expectations by this age group challenges our sense of social order and this has resulted in a suspicion of youth and a readiness to blame young people for all the ills of society.

Notwithstanding this, the government, through the changes in policy and the overhaul of the youth justice system (see Smith 2003, Haines and Drakeford 1998), have found a way, through the introduction of restorative justice, of including and empowering citizens and young people within a system that traditionally has not tolerated them. However, to what degree do citizens understand that they have a say in the youth justice system or are aware of the changes that have taken place?

Restoration via referral orders

The new orders in the CDA (1998) and the YJCEA (1999) have allowed not only for young offenders and their families to have a voice within the youth justice system but also for the victim and wider community to receive reparation and restitution for offences committed against them. However, it must be acknowledged that restorative justice requires the system in which it is working to be patient and accepting of the delays that inevitably occur when all these individuals are involved. Unfortunately this is not the case in a system such as in England and Wales that advocates a swift administration of justice. When used within a punitive system its implementation might lead to distortions.

Restorative measures are often seen as an alternative to punishment, but as Duff (1992, in Walgrave 2001) argues, restorative sanctions and processes should be seen as 'alternative punishments' rather than 'alternatives to punishment'. Both Duff (1992) and Daly (2001) argue that all hard burdens imposed and accepted under pressure should be considered as a punishment, and thus restorative justice should be considered to be essential to crime control as it provides 'hard treatment' (Walgrave 2001). What has developed in England and Wales is the maximalist (Bazemore and Walgrave 1999) version of restorative justice. The maximalist version is oriented towards conducting justice through restoration as an alternative to the punitive or rehabilitative justice systems that are presently in existence. According to McCold (1999) there is a possibility for restorative justice to become punitive if coercive judicial sanctions are included but disguised as restorative measures. He believes that all coercive interventions are punishments and therefore restorative justice should reject them.

In the UK the Labour government has recognized the benefits that may be offered through the use of restorative justice, but McCold's (1999, in Walgrave 2001) notion that there is a possibility that it could become punitive is emerging as a reality. With the introduction of the referral order (see Crawford and Newburn 2003) and the reparation order (see Leng, Taylor and Wasik 1998), an alternative brand or 'neo-restorative justice' has been introduced. Young people are sentenced to these orders by the court and *have to* become involved in the process, rather than having the choice to.

This is not the case with all types of restorative justice being used within England and Wales, but in most instances there is some element of coercion to take part in the intervention. This undermines the principles of restorative justice and threatens the effect of the outcome. It is also commonly the case that the 'ordered' restorative justice interventions, such as the referral order and reparation order, have little or no victim involvement. As such this form of restorative justice is a specific brand that fails to have any real personal impact upon victims. Although this can be seen as problematic it should be acknowledged that as long as the victim is having a choice of whether to be involved in the process, whether they choose to take part or not, there needs to be respect for their choice and a recognition that this particular brand of neo-restorative justice has taken place. As a consequence of the lack of victim involvement within an initiative, it is necessary for community representatives, in the case of the referral order, or restorative intervention providers/Youth Offending Teams officers, in the case of reparation orders, to portray the view of the victim. This is not necessarily a problem with the referral order as true restorative justice principles advocate community involvement. But to have only a professional view of how the victim of a crime may feel should be considered a watered-down version and a half-hearted effort at achieving inclusivity and empowerment.

The referral order, which shows the Labour government's commit-ment to restorative justice as a means of reducing and preventing youth offending, is a new primary sentencing disposal for all 10–17-year-olds who plead guilty and are convicted for the first time by the court. The only other options for disposal open to the magistrates for these types of offenders will be an absolute discharge, custody or a hospital order. The length of the referral order is determined by the severity of the offence and can be made for a minimum of three months and a maximum of 12 months. The length of the order should be proportionate to the offence and it is the responsibility of the court to specify the length for which the contract will have effect and to order a parent/guardian to attend a so-called youth offending panel with the young person if he or she is under 17 years of age. This new approach is intended to do the following.

- Ensure that the most serious offenders continue to be dealt with in a criminal court to provide punishment, protect the public and prevent re-offending.

- Provide an opportunity for less serious offending to be dealt with in a new non-criminal panel enforced by a criminal court.

- Involve young people more effectively in decisions about them – encouraging them to admit their guilt and face up to the consequences of their behaviour.

- Involve the victim in the proceedings, but only with their active consent and focus on preventing behaviour. (Home Office 1997a)

The youth offender panel is made up of one member of the Youth Offending Team and at least two members of the local community, who undergo training and may have some expertise or interest in dealing with young people. The panel is governed by the principles of restorative justice, defined as restoration, responsibility and reintegration (Home Office 1997a). In order to encourage the restorative nature of the process other people may be invited to the panel meeting, on a strictly voluntary role. This may include:

- the victim or a representative of the community at large
- a victim supporter
- a supporter of the young person, but not their solicitor
- signers and interpreters if required
- anyone else that the panel considers to be capable of having a 'good influence' on the offender (Newburn *et al* 2002).

The aim of the panel is to agree a contract with the young person and their family. The contract will include programmes, delivered predominantly by the YOT, designed primarily to prevent further offending. It also provides measures of reparation either directly to the victim or indirectly to the wider community.

Traditionally the criminal justice system has tended to ignore the wants or needs of the victim and assumed that the victim's interests are the same as those of the wider public, which are served by the crown. Cayley observes that 'modern criminal justice has stressed the aggrandizement and edification of the state, rather than the satisfaction of victims' (Cayley 1998: 217).

The integration of a victim perspective within the criminal justice system, through the use of restorative justice, has evoked considerable debate among academics (Crawford 2000, see also Tapley, this volume). The feasibility of using restorative justice as a method that gives victims a voice within a criminal justice system that is 'intrinsically bound up with state coercion and is not necessarily the appropriate cradle of redistributive justice' (Crawford 2000a: 10) has been well documented (see Crawford 2000b, Reeves and Mulley 2000, Shapland 2000, Erez 2000, Walgrave 2000, Morris and Young 2000, Johnstone 2002). Ashworth (2000: 185) also places the victim movement into the political climate, stating that there is some confusion, as greater penal severity and integrating the victim perspective seem to go hand in hand. However, with regards to integrating a victim perspective within the criminal justice system, working under a managerialist philosophy the victim perspective is caught up in the same auditable performance outcomes as the rest of the players in the criminal justice system.

The establishment of the youth offender panel was an attempt, by the government, to clarify their position within the welfare versus justice debate through the delivery of a 'welfare form of community justice'. The referral order is unique in that it allows for the young person's offending behaviour to be viewed within its social context. The causes of crime are recognized and the victim and wider community are involved in the process, and this all takes place within a legislative framework. By undertaking the referral order the young person will have to come face to face with what they have done. It could therefore be argued that through this legislation the aims of restorative justice are paramount in the government's vision for reducing offending and healing community wounds. The panels represent an alternative to other forms of sentencing and allow the courts to deal with the more severe and persistent offenders.

At the time of writing the referral orders have been running for just over two years and to date no re-conviction data have been provided. It will be interesting to see, even at this early stage, what the data indicate and whether the referral order is actually successful in preventing re-offending. The real political agenda will become apparent if the order has not been successful, as this will raise the question of whom to blame. I would suggest a scenario where in order to save face the Labour government will condemn the community panel members for their inability to produce a contract that can tackle offending behaviour. The failure of the order and the subsequent blaming of panel members would probably be welcomed by those youth justice professionals who have been less supportive of this process and who are not convinced by the principles of restorative justice. This disinterest on the part of youth justice professionals in restorative schemes is not a new issue and has been documented in relation to other interventions as well (McKenzie, forthcoming). Equally, however, there are professionals who have been very supportive of the processes and will no doubt offer their own critiques in the face of adversity.

The training for community participants is informative and provides a certain level of insight into the causes of crime, but it is limited and could be argued to be inadequate for some members of the community, who are to be entrusted with playing such an influential role within young people's lives. Initially many of the panels were reliant upon the YOT member to assist, significantly, in reinforcing the consequences of offending behaviour and fleshing out the causes of crime. However, the early days of 'fresh faced' panel members have now passed and at present experienced panel members are able to guide their newer colleagues through this transitory stage. It would be unreasonable for the government to blame panel members for the lack of success if the re-conviction data turn out to be poor. What they need to consider is whose responsibility it is to prevent re-offending, and also that the causes of community disturbance by youths can lie within social inequalities as well as with individual responsibility.

The crux is that there appears to be a difference between what practitioners understand by the term restorative justice and the nature of interventions the government wants practitioners to implement through restorative measures. However, it must also be acknowledged that although the government is concerned with outcome measurements it is also interested in developing good and effective practice, but as precursors to meeting its outcome focused targets.

The effective practice initiative introduced by the Youth Justice Board is intended to enable the service to work within the parameters of evidence-based practice. Effective practice comprises 15 key elements. These are:

- Assessment, planning interventions and supervision
- Education, training and employment
- Final warning interventions
- Intensive supervision and surveillance programmes
- Mental health
- Mentoring
- Offending behaviour programmes
- Parenting
- Remand management
- Resettlement
- Restorative justice
- Substance misuse
- Swift administration of justice
- Targeted neighbourhood prevention programmes
- Young people who sexually abuse.

Each of these key elements is supported by research source documentation to enable a process of effective practice quality assurance to take place within each youth offending team via a self-assessment process. The information gathered enables the Youth Justice Board to acquire a full picture of the work of the YOTs as it provides a qualitative context to the quantitative information collected through the routine data returns for each office (Youth Justice Board, nd). From this information effective practice can be assessed and disseminated. The Youth Justice Board has demonstrated a commitment to the effective practice process by developing, in conjunction with higher educational institutions, a professional certificate in Effective Practice (Youth Justice). This is offered to all youth justice practitioners with the aim of having 80 per cent of its workforce passed through this course by 2006. Although it is admirable that the youth justice board wishes to have its professionals educated in this way and has been forthcoming with developing a qualification framework for the youth justice sector, it has become apparent that financial support is less than forthcoming. Practitioners who wish to pursue continuing education along the qualification framework have found funding to be problematic and the support of management sporadic at best and non-existent at worst. In order for practitioners to feel compelled to further their education there simply needs to be more management, as well as government, support.

The Labour government appears to appreciate the importance of including the victim within the youth justice system and is truly willing to put the 'community' back into community justice, even if their motives are questionable. The youth justice system and youth justice professionals, with the aid of restorative justice, have demonstrated this commitment to victim inclusion and are eager to advocate equal opportunities and effective practice. However, the question that is still paramount is why, when victims are said to be an important element of the youth justice system, does there continue to be a lack of victim involvement? Although there is a greater emphasis on the role of the victim and an increased understanding that their needs are paramount (Zehr 1990), the government appears more concerned with the effect that restorative measures have upon the offending behaviour of the young person rather than the overall satisfaction of all parties with both the process and its outcomes. At times it seems that the rhetoric that victims should be at the centre of the criminal justice system (Blunkett 2002) is just that, without any real meaning behind it. In this light, it is a shame that society is unaware of what is actually taking place within the youth justice system and, consequently, seems to have little regard for it.

It is evident that, besides the continued view that new public managerialism is the best form of management, there have been great strides made to reforming the youth justice system. We should expect to see an increase in public confidence and understanding of youth justice. Both of these expectations are a requirement for engaging victims and the wider community in restorative and community interventions but so far they do not seem to have been forthcoming.

The Audit Commission's review 2004

The Audit Commission's review of the reformed youth justice system concluded that on the whole 'the new system is an improvement on the old one' (Audit Commission 2004: 2): effective, efficient and economic and therefore meeting new public management outcomes. In particular, improvements were made in relation to the structure of the system, young people were more likely to be involved in interventions following their conviction, and more reparation was made to victims and the community. There was also an improvement in relation to faster sentencing of young people following their arrest that has had the effect of reducing offending on bail: a drop from one in three to one in five. There has also been a fall of 5 per cent in known offenders re-offending and a lower reconviction rate after the new community penalties have been administered (Audit Commission 2004). These are all positive outcomes and all those involved should be applauded for the efforts made. However, it was indicated that there is a decline in public confidence regarding the criminal justice system's effectiveness in dealing with young offenders and in part this can be put down to a lack of popular understanding of the work that is done by youth offending teams. Indeed, in 2001/2002, one quarter of the general public thought that the justice system dealt effectively with young offenders; a year later only one in five felt the same. Three out of four people had never heard of YOTs (Audit Commission 2004).

The lack of public appreciation of the success of the youth justice system has important repercussions upon not just youth justice policy but on how young offenders and young people in general are treated. Simmons and Todd (2003) report that following the changes in the youth justice system there had been a fall in the public's confidence in the youth justice system from 25 per cent in 1999 to 21 per cent in 2003. Regardless of the fact that youth crime has not increased, Hough and Roberts (2003) state that three out of four people felt that crime had worsened over the past two years and that nine out of ten thought there was an increase in violent crimes. This, in conjunction with the Audit Commission's (2004) report that seven out of ten of the general public feel that the police and court are too lenient on young offenders, conjures up a worrying picture for the youth justice board and the labour government, primarily because general elections can be won or lost based on the public's confidence in law and order policy.

The vilification of young people

The Audit Commission (2004), through a contextual analysis of national and local papers, concluded that public opinion tended to reflect the negative interpretations of young people portrayed through the coverage in the national press. Young people, in some instances through no fault of their own, have become labelled as 'yobs' or 'thugs'. There has been a great deal of stereotyping of them as evil-doers who are a threat to the law-abiding society and who are out for what they can get. This is not a new concept, however, and much of this type of rhetoric can be traced back 100 years or more: 'The media have reported hooliganism – drunkenness, disorderly behaviour, assaults on police, street robberies and fighting. It was something like organized terrorism in the streets' (*The Times*, 17 August 1898, in Pearson 1983). As Muncie (1999) states, 'youth' and 'crime' and 'disorder' are all social constructions: they are what we say they are. Some behaviour demonstrated by young people must be seen as problematic, anti-social or simply unpleasant; however, it should be recognized when the behaviour is truly offensive to society and not merely a 'media-inspired term' (Muncie 2004: 39). It is clear that public tolerance of incivility has lowered, whilst the fear of young people has increased (Young and Matthews 2003). The Labour government, as a means of winning public votes, has seized upon this and through the introduction of the Anti-Social Behaviour Order has taken advantage. The order was introduced to combat troublesome and mischievous behaviour which was likely to cause harm and distress to the local community. These orders, as with some of the others introduced with the Crime and Disorder Act 1998, are aimed at managing the behaviour of pre-delinquents. However, they actually blur the distinction between crime prevention and crime control (Smith 2003: 61). What they also do is offer a false sense of community safety, as the anti-social aspect is based upon perceptions of rowdy and troublesome behaviour and all that is perceived to be wrong with youthfulness (Bland and Read 2000).

Rather than tackling the problems of our youth, ASBOs only perpetuate them as they continue to stigmatize the young to the extent that 'yob culture' becomes a self-fulfilling prophecy. As Muncie (2004: 117) states, 'it is the application of a stigmatizing label that is considered pivotal in informing future behaviour patterns'. Society also becomes increasingly fearful, suspicious of youths, which in turn means that they are more closely supervised by the police than other age group. This means that the focus is on the behaviour of young people rather than on the causes of their behaviour, and this is in direct conflict with Labour's rhetoric of being tough on the causes of crime. As a consequence of the increased use of ASBOs, young people are being criminalized much earlier and quite probably unnecessarily. Campbell (2002) states that in 2000, 74 per cent of ASBOs made were on the under-21s, with over half of those sentenced in court for breach receiving a custodial sentence. This suggests that ASBOs, though a civil measure, are accelerating routes into custody (Muncie 2004).

Finally, there should be concern about the amount of intervention that some young people find themselves on the receiving end of. A challenging adolescent may find themselves having agreed to comply with an anti-social behaviour order contract, an education contract and even a referral order contract, thus leading to contract confusion due to a cognitive inability to address all the interventions concurrently. The ASBO appears to be seen by the general public and the government as a means to cure all the ills of our out-of-control youth. However, it hardly seems supportive of young people and indeed it contravenes the restorative ethos of reintegration through its stigmatizing shaming effects, allegedly in opposition to the aspirations of the youth justice system.

It is important to emphasize the good news: the new youth justice system is beginning to accomplish the tasks set at its creation in 1998. However, the various views and influence of government, media and the general public are set to spoil the progress already made by the Youth Justice Board and Youth Offending Teams. We have already seen the government recommending an adulterated version of restorative justice in order to tackle youth offending and a media who constantly portray a negative image of young people and the youth justice system. Maybe the system would be better left to the guidance of the Youth Justice Board with the interferences from government kept to a minimum.

Conclusion

The development of the youth justice system is ongoing and the response from the government to the Audit Commission report (2004) is positive and realistic, envisaging the wider development of children and young people's services (Home Office 2004). The use of restorative justice to deal with youth offending should be considered as a progressive move towards offering proper community justice. However, while the media is portraying young people as evil and continuing to vilify them, and the government's response is to act in a manner that reinforces such assumptions, then the true meaning of community justice will be lost: we will be ostracizing our young people, the adult community of the future.

References

Ashworth, A. (2000) 'Victims' Rights, Defendants' Rights and Criminal Procedure', in A. Crawford and J. Goodey (eds), *Integrating a Victim Perspective within Criminal Justice*. Aldershot: Ashgate.

Audit Commission (1996) *Misspent Youth . . . Young People and Crime*. London. Audit Commission.

Audit Commission (2004) *Youth Justice 2004: A Review of the Reformed Youth Justice System*. London: Audit Commission.

Bazemore, G. and Walgrave, L. (1999) 'Restorative Juvenile Justice: In Search of Fundamentals and an Outline for Systematic Reform', in: G. Bazemore and L. Walgrave (eds), *Restorative Juvenile Justice: Repairing the Harm of Youth Crime*. New York: Criminal Justice Press.

Bland, N. and Read, T. (2000) *Policing Anti-social Behaviour*, Police Research Series Paper 123. London: Home Office.

Blunkett, D. (2002) *Keynote Address to the Conference of HM Inspectors of Prisons and Probation*, 21 March 2002.

Brown, S. (1998) *Understanding Youth and Crime*. Buckingham: Open University Press.

Campbell, S. (2002) *A Review of Anti-Social Behaviour Orders*. Home Office Research Study 236. London: Home Office.

Cayley, D. (1998) *The Expanding Prison: The Crisis in Crime and Punishment and the Search for Alternatives*. Cleveland, OH: Pilgrim Press.

Crawford, A. (2000a) 'Introduction', in A. Crawford, and J. Goodey (eds), *Integrating a Victim Perspective within Criminal Justice*. Aldershot: Ashgate.

Crawford, A. (2000b) 'Salient Themes Towards a Victim Perspective and the Limitations of Restorative Justice: Some Concluding Comments', in A. Crawford and J. Goodey (eds), *Integrating a Victim Perspective within Criminal Justice*. Aldershot: Ashgate.

Crawford, A. and Newburn, T. (2003) *Youth Offending and Restorative Justice: Implementing Reform in Youth Justice*. Cullompton: Willan Publishing.

Daly, K. (2001) 'Conferencing in Australia and New Zealand: Variations, Research Findings, and Prospects', in A. Morris and G. Maxwell (eds), *Restorative Justice for Juveniles, Conferencing, Mediation and Circles*. Portland, Oregon: Hart Publishing.

Erez, E. (2000) 'Integrating a Victim Perspective in Criminal Justice Through Victim Impact Statements', in A. Crawford, and J. Goodey (eds), *Integrating a Victim Perspective within Criminal Justice*. Aldershot: Ashgate.

Haines, K. and Drakeford, M. (1998) *Young People and Youth Justice*. Basingstoke: Macmillan.

Heffernan, R. (2000) *New Labour and Thatcherism: Political Change in Britain*. Basingstoke: Palgrave.

Home Office (1997a) *Tackling Delays in the Youth Justice System: A Consultation Paper*. London: Home Office.

Home Office (1997b) *No More Excuses: A New Approach to Tackling Youth Crime in England and Wales*, CM3809. London: Home Office.

Home Office (2004) *Government Response to the Audit Commissions Report – Youth Justice 2004: A Review of the Reformed Youth Justice System*. Available online: http://www.youth-justice-board.gov.uk/uk/NR/rdonlyres/pB8B6E2E-1265-4004-B821-47C988ABDD7A/109/AuditCommissionResponse.pdf, downloaded 23 December 2004.

Hough, M. and Roberts, J. (2003) *Youth Crime and Youth Justice: Public Opinion in England and Wales*, IPCR Research Paper 1. London: ICPR.

Johnstone, G. (2002) *Restorative Justice: Ideas, Values, Debates*. Cullompton: Willan Publishing.

Leng, R., Taylor, R. and Wasik, M. (1998) *Blackstone's Guide to the Crime and Disorder Act 1998*. London: Blackstone Press.

McKenzie, N. (Forthcoming) *Beyond the Fringe: Family Group Conferencing and its Relationship with the Criminal Justice Process*. Unpublished PhD Thesis, University of Portsmouth.

Morris, A. and Young, W. (2000) 'Reforming Criminal Justice: The Potential of Restorative Justice', in H. Strang and J. Braithwaite (eds), *Restorative Justice: Philosophy to Practice*. Aldershot: Ashgate.

Muncie, J. (1999) *Youth and Crime*. London: Sage.

Muncie, J. (2004) *Youth and Crime*, 2nd edition. London: Sage.

Nellis, M. and Gelsthorpe, L. (2003) 'Human Rights and the Probation Values Debate', in W.H. Chui and M. Nellis (eds), *Moving Probation Forward: Evidence, Arguments and Practice*. Harlow: Pearson Education.

Newburn, T., Crawford, A., Earle, R., Goldie, S., Hale, C., Masters, G., Netten, A., Saunders, R., Hallam, A., Sharpe, K. and Uglow, S. (2002) *The Introduction of the Referral Order into the Youth Justice System: Final Report*, Home Office Research Study 242. London: Home Office.

Pearson, G. (1983) *Hooligan: A History of Respectable Fears*. London: Macmillan.

Pickford, J. (ed.) (2000) *Youth Justice: Theory and Practice*. London: Cavendish Publishing.

Pitts, J. (2000) 'The New Youth Justice Under the Politics of Electoral Anxiety', in B. Goldson (ed.), *The New Youth Justice*. Lyme Regis: Russell House Publishing.

Raynor, P. (2001) 'Community Penalties and Social Integration: "Community" as Solution and as Problem', in A. Bottoms, L. Gelsthorpe, and S. Rex (eds), *Community Penalties: Change and Challenges*. Cullompton: Willan Publishing.

Reeves, H. and Mulley, K. (2000) 'The New Status of Victims in the UK: Opportunities and Threats', in A. Crawford and J. Goodey (eds), *Integrating a Victim Perspective within Criminal Justice*. Aldershot: Ashgate.

Savage, S.P. and Nash, M. (2001) 'Law and Order under Blair: New Labour or Old Conservatism', in S.P. Savage and R. Atkinson (eds), *Public Policy under Blair*. Basingstoke: Palgrave.

Shapland, J. (2000) 'Victims and Criminal Justice: Creating Responsible Criminal Justice Agencies', in A. Crawford and J. Goodey (eds), *Integrating a Victim Perspective within Criminal Justice*. Aldershot: Ashgate.

Simmons, J. and Dodd, T. (eds) (2003) *Crime in England and Wales 2002/2003*, Home Office Statistical Bulletin. London: Home Office.

Smith, R. (2003) *Youth Justice: Ideas, Policy, Practice*. Cullompton: Willan Publishing.

Straw, J. and Michael, A. (1996) *Tackling Youth Crime: Reforming Youth Justice*. Consultation Paper. London: HMSO.

Walgrave, L. (2000) 'Extending the Victim Perspective Towards a Systematic Restorative Justice Alternative', in A. Crawford and J. Goodey (eds), *Integrating a Victim Perspective Within Criminal Justice*. Aldershot: Ashgate.

Walgrave, L. (2001) 'On Restoration and Punishment: Favourable Similarities and Fortunate Differences', in A. Morris and G. Maxwell (eds), *Restorative Justice for Juveniles, Conferencing, Mediation and Circles*. Portland, Oregon: Hart Publishing.

Young, J. and Matthews, R. (2003) 'New Labour, Crime Control and Social Exclusion', in R. Mathews and J. Young (eds), *The New Politics of Crime and Punishment*. Cullompton: Willan.

Youth Justice Board (nd) *Effective Practice*. Available online: http://www.youth-justice-board.gov.uk/practitionersportal/practice, downloaded 23 December 2004.

Zehr, H. (1990) *Changing Lenses*. London: Herald Press.

Chapter 12

Community responses to hate crime

Nathan Hall

The last decade of the twentieth century saw an increasing political and social concern with criminal behaviour motivated by racism, and latterly by religious intolerance. In response to a perceived rise in racially motivated offending across Europe and a general shift in social attitudes regarding the abhorrence of crimes motivated by bigotry, the UK followed a number of other European countries by introducing specific legislation to combat it. The 1998 Crime and Disorder Act, later amended by the Anti-Terrorism, Crime and Security Act of 2001, contains provisions for additional penalties to be imposed by the courts to nine pre-existing offences where it can be proved that those offences were racially or religiously motivated or aggravated either in whole or in part. In other words, not only is the offence punished but also the specific motivation behind it.

More recently, however, the rather narrow focus on race has begun to widen to incorporate other aspects of diversity. Attention has begun to centre on the broader concept of 'hate crime'. The Criminal Justice Act 2003 allows for homophobic motivation and bias against disability to be taken into account by sentencers as aggravating factors in an offence, and the Serious Organised Crime and Police Bill contains a new offence of *incitement to religious hatred*. Whilst the law at present only recognizes *specific* offences motivated by racial or religious prejudice, for policing purposes the Association of Chief Police Officers (ACPO 2000: 13) define hate crime as 'a crime where the perpetrator's prejudice against any identifiable group of people is a factor in determining who is victimised', a definition that has also been adopted by the Association of Chief Officers of Probation.

Crimes motivated by prejudice and bigotry are obviously nothing new. However, recent official recognition of these offences as a distinct category of criminal behaviour has effectively presented the criminal justice system with a 'new' category of offender. Indeed, hate offenders present a unique challenge to the criminal justice system in that the law is concerned not only with the crime, but also with the specific motivation behind their offending. It establishes a need specifically to recognize and address the underlying prejudice that informs that behaviour.

This chapter will explore the challenge that hate offenders present. It will be argued that the prison system and traditional community punishments are relatively ineffectual in challenging hate-motivated behaviour. Instead, it is argued that for most hate offenders, community sentences that simultaneously punish the crime and challenge the offender's erroneous belief systems offer better potential for effective intervention. To this end the chapter will explore some of the unique characteristics and dynamics that relate to hate offenders before outlining some of the key limitations of traditional custodial and community sentences. The chapter will then examine recent developments in programmes designed for intervening in hate-motivated behaviour. The chapter concludes by arguing that whilst innovative community sentences undoubtedly hold the greatest potential, they are not a panacea, and the development of successful programmes is at best uncertain because of both the complex nature of hate and prejudice, and our relative lack of understanding of them.

Perpetrator characteristics

Before we can consider how we might best respond to hate offenders, it is important to examine what is known about them. This in itself is no simple task. Indeed, in his 1999 book *Violent Racism*, Ben Bowling was able to describe the perpetrators of race hate crime as 'devilish effigies' about which very little was known. Since then, however, a growing body of research has begun to emerge, and it demonstrates that hate offending is a complex and multi-faceted form of criminal behaviour.

In her review of the socio-psychological literature, Kellina Craig (2002) presents evidence from a range of disciplines that suggests that hate crime represents a unique form of aggression that has both symbolic and instrumental functions for the perpetrator and cannot be attributed to any one factor. Craig identifies that many hate offenders will carry a deep-seated resentment of minority groups and their members.

Committing hate crimes helps perpetrators to maintain a positive social identity by lauding their in-group through the denigration of an out-group. Thus, she suggests, victims will often be the targets of extreme negative stereotypes.

Craig also presents evidence to demonstrate that stereotypes and resentment may be fuelled by actual or imagined economic competition and frustration (social strain), the presence of certain religious values, the disproportionate presence of psychopathological traits among hate offenders as compared to other criminals, and the presence of authoritarian personality traits among a large number of haters. Hate crime perpetrators can effectively be motivated by one or more of a wide range of social, psychological, political, cultural and other factors. On the basis of Craig's research, the search for a single, universal causal factor for hate crime is likely to be fruitless. Rather, it is the interplay of a number of different factors that produces perpetrators.

This situation is recognized by Rae Sibbitt (1997) in her British study of the perpetrators of racial violence and racial harassment. Sibbitt suggests that there are essentially two strands of theories to explain why certain people commit racially motivated offences. The first, she argues, links racist behaviour to crime in general. The psychological and contextual factors that facilitate other types of criminal and anti-social behaviour will also facilitate racist behaviour.

The second approach suggests that racial harassment is a logical and predictable expression of underlying racism in society at large. In this sense then, prejudice is felt by a community towards a minority group, perhaps fuelled by perceptions of strain, but there is a context in which a minority of that majority will 'cross the line' and express their prejudice through harassment and violence. This approach assumes that the perpetrator is simply expressing the views and prejudices that are felt but not necessarily physically expressed by a wider community.

Sibbitt (1997) argues that it is the interplay of contextual factors, such as unemployment, economic hardship and/or deprivation, competition for scarce resources (for example, housing), and a lack of community facilities (particularly in relation to youth and leisure facilities), and the psychology of certain individuals that produces perpetrators. Offenders are also likely to be involved in other forms of criminal or anti-social behaviour, and operate with the passive support (or at least without the condemnation) of some sections of the wider community who share similar views. Sibbitt's work, and her discussion of the wider 'perpetrator community', produces some interesting implications for criminal justice practitioners responding to perpetrators of hate crime in that the individual's prejudice is likely to be entrenched in the wider community from which they were drawn, and to which they will likely return having served a sentence.

Research in the United States by McDevitt, Levin and Bennett (2002) has drawn upon the motives cited by police officials, victims as well as perpetrators themselves to produce a typology of hate offenders. Their research concluded that hate offenders can be placed into one of four motivational categories.

1   *Thrill* – Perpetrators in this category accounted for the majority of offenders (66 per cent of their sample). They commit hate crimes in order to create excitement for themselves and to strengthen their feelings of power over what they perceive to be subordinate groups.

2   *Defensive* – These offenders, comprising 25 per cent of the sample, see their crimes as a 'tool' to be used for the protection of what they perceive to be 'threatened' resources within society. Clearly this category has strong links with the notion of social strain and indeed is analogous to the comments often informally cited by people who oppose the influx of asylum seekers in to the UK (for example, 'they take all our jobs').

3   *Retaliatory* – Offenders in this category (8 per cent of the sample) commit hate crimes to avenge the perceived or real degradation of their in-group. They therefore respond when they perceive that members of another group have in some way 'attacked' their own group and some form of redress is required to secure revenge and to reaffirm dominant social hierarchies.

4   *Mission* – Perpetrators who fit this typology are generally rare (less than 1 per cent of the study) but are the most committed and prejudiced of all hate offenders. They see their role as 'crusaders' who are essentially cleansing the earth of a perceived evil rather than responding to any singular event. Thus, as McDevitt *et al* (2002) suggest, for a mission offender hate can be viewed as a 'career', whereas for the thrill offender, hate is something akin to a 'hobby'.

Whilst these typologies have been somewhat simplified here (see McDevitt *et al* 2002 for a comprehensive overview) and despite the study's methodological limitations, identifying perpetrators through these categories and their associated case files has provided some very interesting supplementary information, as illustrated in Table 12.1. We can see from this that the majority of hate offenders are young adults, as is the case for offenders generally. Also of interest is the suggestion that hate crime is often a group activity, involving whatever 'weapons' happen to be at hand, that occurs often with little or no victim–offender history. This supports the view that hate crimes are

Table 12.1 Characteristics of hate crimes by offender motivation

Attack characteristics	Thrill	Defensive	Retaliatory	Mission
Number of offenders	Group	Group	Single offender	Group
Age of offender(s)	Teens–young adults	Teens–young adults	Teens–young adults	Young adults–adults
Location	Victim's turf	Offender's turf	Victim's turf	Victims' or offender's turf
Weapon	Hands, feet, rocks	Hands, feet rocks	Hands, feet, sticks, guns	Bats, guns
Victim–offender history	None	Previous acts of intimidation	Often no history	None
Commitment to bias	Little	Moderate	Moderate	Full
Deterrence	Likely	Unlikely	Unlikely	Most unlikely

Source: McDevitt *et al* (2002: 311)

impersonal and that victims are interchangeable. The final point of note is a differential commitment to their prejudice. With the exception of thrill offenders, the offender's commitment to their hatred is a significant factor, particularly in relation to whether or not they can be deterred from their actions. The latter finding has important implications for responding to hate crime offenders, and we shall return to this in due course.

A punitive approach to hatred

Despite increasing interest in crimes motivated by hate, the term 'hate crime' does not specifically appear in any UK legislation and therefore does not officially exist as a distinct category of criminal behaviour in itself. Instead, specific legislation prohibits certain acts, which are already outlawed in other legislation, but allows for hate to be used as an aggravating factor.

The key piece of legislation in this respect is the Crime and Disorder Act 1998, which allows for enhanced sentencing for racially and religiously motivated assaults, criminal damage, public order offences and harassment. Under the Crime and Disorder Act (1998, Part 2, Section 28) an offence is racially aggravated if:

(a) at the time of committing the offence, or immediately before or after doing so, the offender demonstrates towards the victim of the offence hostility based on the victim's membership (or presumed membership) of a racial group; or

(b) the offence is motivated (wholly or partly) by hostility towards members of a racial group based on their membership of that group.

A 'racial group' refers to persons defined by reference to their race, colour, nationality or ethnic or national origins and in Section 28(3a) includes membership of any religious group.

The enactment of this legislation has effectively created nine 'new' racially/religiously aggravated offences based upon pre-existing offences contained in other legislation. The CDA allows for sentence enhancement for offences where it can be proved that racial/religious aggravation was present at the time of the offence, except where offences already carry a maximum life sentence. The Act also allows for the courts (with the exception of the magistrates' courts) to increase sentences for other non-specified offences aggravated by racial hostility. Thus, some offences that would normally be summary only have become either-way offences (magistrates are able to commit racist offenders to the Crown court for sentence), and maximum sentences have increased 'to the next level' on the sentencing tariff. In addition to longer custodial sentences, the provisions for enhanced sentencing also include increased fines, community sentences and compensation (Burney and Rose 2002), and require the courts to explicitly pronounce in open court that the offence was racially motivated.

The increasingly punitive approach to hate crimes and hate offenders through the imposition of enhanced sanctions for those convicted of specific hate-motivated offences makes it likely that the prison service will become more frequently involved with hate offenders. It is therefore important to consider the role of the prison service in responding to hate offenders and its role in preventing future offending.

Imprisonment of hate offenders raises a difficult dilemma. On the one hand there is the need to protect the public from dangerous offenders, but on the other there is the need to effectively address the underlying causes of the hate crime (i.e. the offender's prejudice) in order to prevent future offending. Prison may achieve the former (at least for the duration of the offender's incapacitation), but it tends to fall short on the latter.

The problems associated with imprisonment as a response to hate offenders are threefold. First, because the chances of being caught, convicted and ultimately sent to prison are remote for most hate offenders, the deterrent value of prison is weak at best. Second, prisons are often divided along racial and ethnic lines, and are therefore 'hotbeds' for prejudice, intolerance and hate group activity and recruitment (Gerstenfeld 2004). Third, simply punishing offenders is not enough. If future offending is to be prevented, then some form of rehabilitation that addresses the offender's prejudicial attitudes that caused the offence to occur in the first place is crucial. In an overcrowded prison system, where both effective rehabilitative programmes and the opportunities to implement them are relatively rare, it is unlikely that prison will offer any effective solution beyond simply removing them from society for a period of time. Indeed, Levin and McDevitt (2002) argue that imprisonment may in fact be counterproductive because hate-based views may be hardened whilst in prison, thereby increasing the likelihood that they will be physically expressed following release.

The best hope, it would seem, lies in a dual approach whereby offenders are rightly punished for their crime, but also in which their underlying prejudices are challenged. Rehabilitating offenders, as well as punishing them, would appear to hold the key to preventing future offending. The question, of course, is how do we respond to hate as a prejudice and rehabilitate offenders?

Clearly, much will depend on the type of offender involved. If we refer back to Table 12.1, showing the offender characteristics developed by McDevitt *et al* (2002), we can get some clues about the likelihood of influencing, deterring or indeed preventing future offending. From the evidence presented in the table, those offenders who commit hate offences for the 'thrill' hold the best hope for success in challenging their behaviour. Where the offenders are characterized as 'defensive', 'retaliatory' or 'mission', the chances of success in this respect become increasingly uncertain as the perpetrator's 'commitment to bias' increases. Fortunately, those motivated by the thrill are more common than the other types. Still, if the prison system fails to address effectively the offending behaviour of those that are convicted, then we need to consider employing alternative sentences to imprisonment. Perhaps, then, community sentences offer better prospects.

Some degree of success, particularly for first-time offenders, has been achieved in the United States through probation and community service sentences. Levin and McDevitt (2002) refer in particular to sentences consisting of probation including some form of community service to a local minority group or minority group organization. Based largely on contact theories, the intention here is that the offender will learn about the community they have targeted, whilst returning something positive to that community by repairing some of the damage and harm caused. Such an approach, however, is not always straightforward. As Levin and McDevitt (2002: 201) suggest:

A major limitation of the community service sentencing approach is its lack of formal treatment programs. Having a location for the assignment of offenders is one thing; putting together an effective program to reduce hatred is quite another. Having an offender paint the exterior of a synagogue that he has defaced might return something to the community he has harmed, but it is questionable that this activity alone would teach the offender why what he did was wrong. To do that, he would need a program that effectively addressed his misconceptions.

Similarly, writing of probation practice with regard to racially motivated offenders in the UK, Dixon and Court (2003) acknowledge the limitations of existing practices. Given the unique nature of hate offending, they suggest that generalist offender programmes are relatively ineffective because they fail adequately to address the dynamic risk factors that are, as we have seen, inherently associated with hate as a motivation for crime. Similarly, Dixon and Court suggest that general cognitive behavioural programmes for hate offenders are ineffective because they fail to impact upon the emotional aspects of this type of criminal behaviour. Echoing Levin and McDevitt, Dixon and Court (2003: 150) argue that the complex psychological processes and the wide range of risk factors that underpin hate offending can only be effectively dealt with by developing interventions specifically tailored to hate offenders.

But what elements might such interventions contain? In light of the problems associated with the prison system and community sentences that fail effectively to tackle the offender's underlying prejudice, Levin and McDevitt (2002: 203) make a number of suggestions for the content of such offender programmes, stating that:

> a model hate crime offender treatment or rehabilitation program must include the following elements: assessment, discussion of impact on victims, cultural awareness, restitution/community service, delineation of legal consequences, participation in a major cultural event, and aftercare.

For Levin and McDevitt (2002) each stage represents an important step in the rehabilitation of hate offenders. Based upon their offender typology, the assessment allows trained professionals to understand the type of offender they are dealing with, and the strength of their prejudicial attitudes. Such understanding will serve to guide the programme in the most suitable direction. Following the assessment, Levin and McDevitt point to the importance of explaining to the offender the harm they have caused to their victim. Many hate offenders see their victims as 'different', 'inferior' or 'inhuman', and reversing this dehumanization process is an important aim.

Furthermore, Levin and McDevitt suggest that many hate offenders readily accept false and negative stereotypes of their victim's group. Thus it is important to identify and challenge these misconceptions whilst simultaneously promoting the benefits and values of diversity within the community. Attempting to deconstruct stereotypes and misconceptions about a group is a crucial element of increasing an offender's cultural awareness.

In addition, the sentence should contain a genuine reparative and restitutive element. It should be related to the community harmed yet tailored to avoid resentment on the part of the perpetrator. In this sense, then, involving the offender in a major cultural event within the victim's community can help the offender to see the victim as a human being, thereby serving as both a reparative purpose to the victim and their community and an educative experience for the offender. In addition, the legal consequences of pursuing hate-motivated behaviour should be explained, particularly as many young hate offenders may be of the opinion that they can still 'get away with it', even if they are caught again.

A further suggested component of a rehabilitative programme involves 'aftercare' for the offender so that they can return to the programme to resolve any remaining issues if they feel they need to. Finally, Levin and McDevitt suggest, such offender programmes should be continuously evaluated and monitored, and amended as new and improved information about prejudice and hatred comes to light.

Such rehabilitative programmes may sound ambitious, possibly overly optimistic. There is little doubt that adopting such an approach for hardened hate offenders can be highly unsuitable. Nevertheless, for young, first-time or thrill offenders, a carefully designed and implemented programme containing these elements may prove to be of value. Therefore, whilst acknowledging that for hardened hate offenders the only realistic option may be incarceration, Levin and McDevitt (2002: 207) optimistically suggest that for other offenders:

> Intermediate sentences – less than prison but more than probation – are necessary for assuring that hate crimes are treated more seriously than ordinary offences. However, many hatemongers can be rehabilitated – if they are fortunate enough to benefit from a serious but humane and imaginative approach to criminality.

The question remains, however, as to what form this 'humane and imaginative' approach should take, and how realistic a proposition it really is. The remainder of this chapter will explore some of these issues.

Community approaches

The aims of probation work are to protect the public, reduce re-offending, properly punish offenders in the community, ensure offenders' awareness of the effects of crime on victims and the public, and to rehabilitate offenders. To this end, probation work broadly involves assisting sentencers through pre-sentence reports following an offender's conviction, combining the continuous assessment and management of risk and dangerousness with the provision of expert supervision programmes designed to reduce re-offending, and the supervision of offenders sentenced to unpaid work in the community through community punishment orders (NPS 2004). In the UK the probation service therefore occupies a unique position among criminal justice agencies in terms of working with hate offenders, and in particular race-hate offenders.

In 2000, following academic and professional criticism of the probation service's approach to racially motivated offenders (RMOs), the probation service's Accreditation Panel established a national sub-group specifically to identify and develop effective programmes of intervention with RMOs (Dixon 2002). Having conducted a literature review in an attempt to establish 'what works', a theory manual was published in 2001 with the purpose of assisting practitioners and informing future programme development. Ultimately the Accreditation Panel concluded that no firm decision could be made regarding the most effective way to deal with RMOs and recommended that a range of different approaches be piloted and evaluated in an attempt to uncover effective interventions (Dixon 2002).

On the basis of this recommendation, David Perry (2002) states that the National Probation Directorate identified three potential avenues to explore in relation to RMOs. The first is to test the impact of existing general offending behaviour programmes on RMOs. The justification for this approach is that in addition to the unique factors that influence hate offending, many RMOs also share similar criminogenic risk factors with other types of offenders, and therefore interventions that are already in place, if managed appropriately, may prove to be valuable with RMOs.

The second potential avenue for working with RMOs involves the development of a citizenship education module to be added to existing general programmes of intervention. Perry suggests that by developing an RMO's knowledge, skills and identity in the area of 'citizenship', the additional factors that specifically relate to racist offending may be challenged.

The third avenue involves the development of new programmes specifically for RMOs that draw upon existing knowledge about hate offenders and offending. David Perry argues that this option would only be pursued if the other two failed to work or when the dynamic risk factors alluded to above are conclusively identified. This approach mirrors that of the rehabilitative programme suggested by Levin and McDevitt but is also the most complex of the three approaches, given that the potential factors that combine to produce hate offenders are so many and varied. In many respects, this latter approach is really about finding out what works and what doesn't.

A number of probation areas have recently developed and piloted specific programmes of intervention for RMOs in an attempt to find out what works in practice. In reviewing this programme development, Dixon (2002) suggests that many probation areas have drawn on the 'From Murmur to Murder Manual' (Kay and Gast 1999), which emphasizes the need for effective interventions to address holistically issues of offender denial and minimization, enhance pro-social values, examine the basis of the offender's racism, raise awareness of the victim's perspective and help the offender develop new skills to reduce re-offending.

Dixon describes in further detail the Diversity Awareness Programme (DAP) piloted in the London probation area. The ultimate purpose of the Diversity Awareness Programme is to assist practitioners in challenging the prejudicial assumptions that inform hate offending with the aim of reducing re-offending.

> Crucially, the DAP seeks to expose the targeted nature of the offending by focusing on issues of race, cultural identity and the need to develop skills to manage anger and aggression on a single programme. It is thus informed by the research which suggests that cultures of violence and cultures of racism both need to be challenged. The programme works to help offenders develop a positive non-racist identity – it challenges the factors that inform racial violence and seeks to highlight their receptivity to some of the myths circulated in their communities. (Dixon 2002: 212)

In considering his experience of piloting the DAP, Court (2003: 56) states:

> I have been encouraged by the response of offenders participating in the programme, both in custody as well as in the community. The programme consists of seven modules that assess and explore socialization processes from childhood, moving onto the development of racial identity, attitudes, beliefs and values. The purpose is

to encourage the offender to consider how prejudicial attitudes have contributed towards their offending and how to develop the thinking skills and practice strategies to avoid offending in the future.

Dixon and Court (2003) further explain that the use of 'race diaries' as part of the programme has been a particularly effective way of engaging with hate offenders. Here, offenders are encouraged to record, consider and positively manage their thoughts and behaviour in relation to any interactions with members of minority groups. In describing the race diary as a 'powerful tool in prompting behavioural change', Court (2003: 56–57) further suggests that the programme enables participants to identify and disclose their racial prejudices and encourages them to take greater responsibility for the impact of these prejudices upon their behaviour both within the offence and in their lives generally. Court also suggests that when offenders have reached this stage of recognition, they are often more prepared to learn and develop the skills and strategies to manage their behaviour in a less offensive and more pro-social manner.

Whilst these are encouraging signs, this remains a developing area of intervention work and, given that the interventions involved are not universally used across all probation areas, it is difficult to draw firm and generalizable conclusions as to what might universally work. Nevertheless, this ongoing activity within the probation arena is clearly cause for a certain degree of optimism.

However, it is not just probation that is looking at innovative approaches to hate offenders. Gerstenfeld (2004) suggests that potential success in rehabilitating hate offenders might be found in restorative justice through victim–offender mediation. This approach, which has grown in popularity in recent times, seeks to actively involve the offender, the victim and the wider community in the justice process by bringing the victim and the offender together with the aim of achieving reparation and reconciliation. Under controlled circumstances the victim has the opportunity to explain to the offender the impact that the offence had on them and to ask questions of the offender. In response, the offender has the opportunity to explain their actions and to apologize for what they have done.

According to Shenk (2001) victim–offender mediation is ideal for responding to hate crimes for three reasons. First, because hate offenders often 'dehumanize' the objects of their stereotypes, coming face to face with their victim allows the offender to understand the harm they have caused and to view their target as an individual: as a human as opposed to a 'faceless' representative of a hated group. Such an experience can play an important role in deconstructing an offender's stereotypes. Second, both parties are afforded the opportunity for emotional release, an important factor in overcoming the effects of crime; and third, the experience may serve to encourage reporting of hate crimes by victims and curtail future offending by the perpetrator.

We might also reasonably add a fourth and fifth benefit to this list. First, such an approach places the victim at the centre of the delivery of justice (a situation hitherto largely avoided by the justice system; see Tapley, this volume) and signifies empowerment of the victim. Second, the use of victim–offender mediation does not necessarily mean that other more punitive approaches cannot be used as well (Gerstenfeld 2004).

Community sentences: limitations, problems and solutions

Despite these recent and ongoing developments there are a number of problems associated with the community punishment/rehabilitation approach to RMOs. The first and most obvious problem is that we still have remarkably little idea about what works when responding to hate offenders. This is a product of a number of factors, most notably the relative novelty of this type of offending (or at least of our interest in it) and the complexity of prejudice as a human emotion and as a motivational factor in criminal behaviour (Allport 1954). As we have seen, hate offending can be underpinned by one or more of a wide range of factors and thus developing effective interventions can never be a straightforward task. Of course, the only way to overcome this issue is for research into hate to continue, for interventions to be based on the findings of such research, and for those interventions to be tried and tested by practitioners in the field. We have already noted that this is already occurring, but we should be prepared for a long journey. This is not a problem that can be solved overnight.

In addition we are faced with a number of more specific problems. The first is that the probation service is at present largely dependent upon the courts to provide them with their clientele. The attrition rate for racially motivated offending within the criminal justice system is very high. Home Office figures (1996) suggest that in only 2 per cent of notifiable offences is an offender caught and convicted, and research suggests that this figure is even less for racially motivated crimes (Bowling 1999, Lemos 2000). Therefore relatively few hate offenders ever reach court for their offence, which means that the probation service will simply not have the opportunity to work with the vast majority of offenders.

Plea-bargaining offers a further obstacle. Because the hate element of a crime is often difficult to prove, research has demonstrated extensive plea-bargaining in cases whereby the 'racist' element of a crime is dropped before the case reaches court in order to secure a conviction of a lesser offence (Burney and Rose 2002). Because of this, those offenders are unlikely to be subjected to any specific 'hate' related interventions. In this sense, then, even where offenders do not slip through the net, the hate element does, unless of course the offender displays some form of hatred during the course of their supervision. Put simply, the high rate of attrition ensures that most hate offenders are never identified and officially labelled as such, in which case it is quite irrelevant how good any interventions might be.

It is of concern that the probation service and youth offending teams continue to rely on the courts to identify their racist offenders. Many racist offenders remain hidden from view and their underlying prejudices are therefore not addressed. The danger here is that the risk assessments carried out by probation officers may subsequently be inaccurate. Indeed, despite some positive progress, Court (2003: 58) concludes his evaluation of recent probation work in this field by stating:

> ...until the probation service and the youth offending teams develop the skills and confidence to explore racial hostility, in particular where the victim rather than the court alone have identified it, assessments of harm to the public can only be partial at best, and at worst dangerously misleading.

Such a proposition may well have merit. There might be a role for probation in identifying hate. The foundations are there because the probation service has adopted ACPO's definition of hate crime, whereby the hate element of an offence can be identified by anyone. If adequate screening for offenders can be implemented as part of their initial interview and assessment by probation officers, as is the case in parts of the London probation area, then perhaps the need to rely so heavily on the courts for identifying offenders can be lessened and more effective interventions can be made. This situation might be eased by, for example, closer liaison with court officials, improved assessment of offenders, and through the training of probation staff to identify confidently racist attitudes in offenders (Court 2003).

A resulting problem of failing to identify properly racist or hate offenders is that they will remain a tiny fraction of the probation service's caseload and may not be seen as a priority. In a bureaucratic world the logical follow-on is that if hate offenders are so small in their number then where is the urgency or need to devote finite resources to developing interventions for them? In reality the likelihood is that there are many more offenders under the supervision of the probation service who have racist or hateful tendencies, but that have just not been officially recognized.

It is telling that in her study of racist offenders and responses to them, Sibbitt (1997) found that very few of the probation officers she studied had experience of dealing with racist offenders and, where racist attitudes were expressed, few knew what to do about them. This was reflected in research by Lemos (2000). Offenders' racist tendencies either remained hidden from view or went unchallenged, which shows that without experience or training, probation workers appear ill-equipped to deal with hate.

As a related issue, Sibbitt suggests that part of the problem for the probation service has been that as an organization it has traditionally viewed offenders as needy and disadvantaged individuals in need of help and guidance. Sibbitt argues that racist offenders, like sex offenders and child abusers, do not neatly 'fit' this traditional image of the offender and therefore pose something of a unique but rare challenge to the cultural orientation of probation officers. Perhaps selecting 'specialist' probation officers to deal specifically with racist offenders might offer a solution here.

Despite its apparent benefits, we should not assume that the restorative justice approach will prove to be any kind of panacea for hate offending. There is an ongoing scholarly debate surrounding the practical efficacy of victim–offender mediation with its true value at present uncertain, particularly for hate offences where its success remains unproven (Gerstenfeld 2004). Furthermore, this approach is entirely dependent on the offender being caught and convicted, the victim wishing to meet them, and cooperation being established between the two parties. There may also be the possibility that the offender's hatred of the victim's group may be so strong as to render the process useless. As such, the cases suitable for mediation need to be chosen carefully.

Whatever approach we take, being able to explain to the offender *why* their actions were wrong is a key element. Sibbitt (1997) argues that when dealing with racist offenders (and therefore by analogy, hate offenders) agencies need to look beyond the offender and recognize both the relationship between the individual and the wider 'perpetrator community' from which he or she is drawn, and the function that the hatred serves for the individual offender. Attempts to combat hatred need to extend beyond the individual offender and also consider the social situation in which the hatred was fostered and shaped and the purpose it serves.

Once the importance of these two factors is recognized, Sibbitt argues, it will become easier to engage the offender in a constructive manner. She describes four responses that professionals might adopt in dealing with an offender's expressions of hatred. First, the professional may not respond at all, in which case the problem remains unchallenged. Second, the professional may respond with 'moral opprobrium', where the inappropriateness of the offender's views are explained and further sanctions threatened. Third, the professional may attempt to deconstruct and challenge the logic of the offender's arguments by pointing out the irrationality of their thinking, although Sibbitt cautions against making the offender feel intellectually inferior and appearing insensitive to what may be genuine underlying concerns on the offender's part. Finally, Sibbitt advocates the challenging of hatred in the context of a holistic approach in which perpetrators, potential perpetrators and the perpetrator community should be targeted.

With regard to individual perpetrators, Sibbitt suggests that the most appropriate intervention for the perpetrator will be dependent upon a number of issues, including their criminal history both specifically in racist activity and in anti-social behaviour more generally, the wishes of the victim, the risk posed to the public, the effectiveness or otherwise of previous attempts at intervention, and the perpetrator's personal circumstances. To this end Sibbitt highlights the importance of multi-agency information sharing, so that a comprehensive account of relevant information and related issues is kept and can be used to determine which agency is best suited to working with the offender, be it the police, the probation service, housing officers, or youth, community or social workers.

In addition to the provisions for racially and religiously aggravated offending, the Crime and Disorder Act (1998) includes a legal require-ment for local agencies and groups to work together to find solutions to local crime problems. Lemos (2000) suggests that multi-agency forums typically have three areas of concern when dealing with hate crime. First, they are responsible for developing and implementing a coherent strategy for preventing and dealing with hate crime, including the publication of targets and progress made towards those targets. Second, they are required to cooperate on policy and practice and third, they may cooperate in dealing with individual cases of hate crime. The emphasis is therefore on the forming of alliances with any group or individuals who are in a position to contribute information and intelligence, and who can assist in the development of strategies to combat hate crime in a community.

Such strategies might include the development of information-sharing protocols to identify effectively the nature of the local hate crime problem and to allocate appropriate resources where they are most needed. They might also include the creation of 'hate crime panels' to develop, implement and oversee anti-hate initiatives with offenders and the wider community. Alternatively, the development of informal or civil sanctions, for example through tenancy agreements, might prove more effective in certain cases than the traditional criminal justice approach (see ACPO 2000 for further examples of multi-agency partnerships and strategies). However, the existence of a legal requirement to tackle hate crime holistically is no guarantee of success, and neither is the mere existence of a multi-agency forum.

With regard to working with potential perpetrators, which Sibbitt defines as those who have not yet offended (or more to the point, have not yet been caught) but who are at risk of offending, the role of local community diversionary projects and schemes is advocated, particularly aimed at (disillusioned) youths. Agencies such as the police and probation service may play a part here by helping to identify where such schemes would be most beneficial and who might be best placed to run them. Sibbitt points to the apparent success of an established youth project in London that engaged youths on a housing estate and challenged their specific prejudices and general attitudes to criminality using a variety of methods (for a detailed account see Sibbitt 1997).

Finally, in respect of 'perpetrator communities', professionals may play a part by challenging inappropriate language or behaviour whenever it occurs in the course of their work by, for example, using one of the four strategies suggested for individual offenders, described above. Furthermore, Sibbitt outlines the positive benefits of community projects, where members of a community are required to work together to achieve a goal that is of mutual concern so that it becomes necessary to view each other in terms wider than just 'race' or 'religion' or 'sexuality' in order to achieve that common goal – for example, a youth club, the acquisition of leisure facilities, or through the formation of tenant associations on estates. Sibbitt points to the success of such schemes in various parts of inner London, Bristol and Leicester.

The (im)possibility of successful intervention

Despite this range of available options, and regardless of whether criminal justice agencies work individually or in partnership, there is a further issue that affects all interventions to hate crime, in England and

Wales, in that it is only possible to be convicted of a racially or religiously motivated or aggravated offence. Such a situation therefore at worst precludes, and at best hinders, other types of hate offending from being officially responded to by criminal justice agencies. For example, it is not possible to be convicted of a homophobically motivated offence, as one could be for a racially motivated offence, even though homophobia can be considered as an aggravating factor at sentencing. Such an offence is simply not on the statute books; it doesn't legally exist. Therefore, the impetus and necessity for agencies such as the probation service to develop interventions for such offenders isn't there. Interventions therefore understandably focus largely on issues of racism, and not on other forms of hatred.

It would require a change in the law to cover aspects of diversity other than just race, but such a move would open up a myriad moral and political dilemmas about exactly which prejudices to outlaw. Such a debate is beyond the scope of this chapter (see Hall, 2005: forthcoming). The practical alternative would be for the probation service and others to develop the skills and confidence to identify and challenge all negative prejudice as and when it surfaces in offenders.

The overriding problem here stems from the fact that hate crime is rarely about pure hate. As we saw from Levin and McDevitt's typology, *mission* offenders are rare. In reality the situation is considerably more complicated because hate crime as legally and practically defined is really about prejudice, and what we might perceive to be *real* hatred is just a small part. Prejudice is a broad and cloudy concept of uncertain origin about which we conclusively know relatively little other than that it is probably an unavoidable and universal human trait (Jacobs and Potter 1998). As Andrew Sullivan (1999) rightly points out, humans are social beings. We associate, and therefore we disassociate, and one cannot happen without the other.

Instead, we have adopted the word 'hate' as catch-all term for a bewildering range of human emotions that apparently require an official response to challenge them. In the case of clear, immutable hatred this is relatively unproblematic. But this is rare. Few offences are motivated solely by hate to the exclusion of all other motivational factors. Most 'hate' crimes are motivated by prejudice, and when we use the term hate, prejudice is usually what we mean. For example, in the Crime and Disorder Act the word 'hostility' is not explained, but the common dictionary definition of 'hostile' includes simply being 'unfriendly'. This is where the situation becomes complicated. Is being 'unfriendly' really the same as being 'hateful'? As Andrew Sullivan (1999) further suggests, there are so many different forms of hate and prejudice, some strong, some weak, some understandable and acceptable, some abhorrent and unacceptable, and all with different psychological dynamics under-pinning them. Like much human emotion, he argues, hate is often not rational but does have its reasons, and we cannot understand nor condemn it without knowing them.

Despite this, Sullivan suggests, both the notion and concept of hate crime take a psychological mystery and turn it into a facile political artefact, yet the boundaries between hate and prejudice, and prejudice and opinion, and opinion and truth are so complicated and blurred that really we should not be too surprised that we do not conclusively know how to respond effectively to hate offenders. The range of psychological emotions we have labelled under the word 'hate' is simply too wide, and no two 'hates' are the same. These are hardly solid foundations to build upon. Perhaps instead we should consider an alternative approach. Dampening the optimism of others, Sullivan (1999: 7–8) suggests:

> ... violence can and should be stopped. In a free society, hate can't and shouldn't be ... in an increasingly diverse culture it is crazy to expect that hate, in all its variety, can be eradicated. A free country will always mean a hateful country. This may not be fair, or perfect, or admirable, but it is reality, and whilst we need not endorse it, we should not delude ourselves into thinking we can prevent it. That is surely the distinction between toleration and tolerance. Tolerance is the eradication of hate; toleration is co-existence despite it. We might do better as a culture and a polity if we concentrated more on achieving the latter rather than the former. We would certainly be less frustrated.

Concluding comments

In this chapter I have presented a brief overview of existing and ongoing efforts to combat hate crime and the prejudice that underpins it. But despite recent advances the obvious question still remains: just how effective are these responses to hate? Unfortunately, as we have implied throughout this chapter, this is a question that is impossible to answer with any great degree of certainty at the present time. As Gerstenfeld (2004: 193), speaking primarily of efforts to combat hate crimes in the United States, suggests:

> There is no shortage of individuals and organisations that wish to combat hate crimes, but there is almost a complete lack of

assessment of their efforts. If we knew which endeavours work and which do not, these people could channel their energies and finances in much more useful ways. It will not necessarily be easy to determine what works, but, at this point, any addition to existing knowledge would be of great benefit.

The same can also be said for efforts here in the UK. It seems that the best we can suggest is that some techniques work better than others, depending on different circumstances and situations. The nature of the criminal justice system ensures that regardless of how effective criminal justice interventions may be, the majority of hate offenders will never be subjected to them, and even when they are the success of existing interventions and preventative methods are uncertain largely because we still do not know very much about this 'new' concept called 'hate' that has become the operative word.

What is certain, however, is that hate crime is here to stay. Criminal justice professionals and others seeking to combat hate are required to 'think outside the box' and be imaginative and creative in their approach when dealing with the perpetrators of hate crime in order to address the range of associated risk factors. Some issues can be relatively easily overcome. Others cannot. We also need to think a little more clearly about exactly what it is that we are trying to challenge: broad prejudice or narrow hatred? In a world where prejudice and hate are embedded in social structures, public discourse from neighbourly disputes to international relations, this is a moral, political and above all a social issue that transcends the concerns of criminal justice.

References

ACPO (Association of Chief Police Officers) (2000) *ACPO Guide to Identifying and Combating Hate Crime.* London: ACPO.

Allport, G.W. (1954) *The Nature of Prejudice.* Massachusetts: Addison-Wesley.

Bowling, B. (1999) *Violent Racism: Victimisation, Policing and Social Context.* New York: Oxford University Press.

Burney, E. and Rose, G. (2002) *Racist Offences: How is the Law Working?* Home Office Research Study 270. London: Home Office.

Court, D. (2003) 'Direct Work with Racially Motivated Offenders', *Probation Journal,* 50: 52–58.

Craig, K.M. (2002) 'Examining Hate-Motivated Aggression: A Review of the Social Psychological Literature on Hate Crimes as a Distinct Form of Aggression', *Aggression And Violent Behaviour,* 7: 85–101.

Dixon, L. (2002) 'Tackling Racist Offending: A Generalised or Targeted Approach?', *Probation Journal,* 49: 205–216.

Dixon, L. and Court, D. (2003) 'Developing Good Practice with Racially Motivated Offenders', *Probation Journal* 50: 149–153.

Gerstenfeld, P. (2004) *Hate Crimes: Causes, Controls, and Controversies.* Thousand Oaks: Sage.

Hall, N. (2005) *Hate Crime.* Cullompton: Willan.

Home Office (1996) *Action for Justice.* London: HMSO.

Jacobs, J.B. and Potter, K. (1998) *Hate Crimes: Criminal Law and Identity Politics.* New York: Oxford University Press.

Kay, J. and Gast, L. (1999) *From Murmur to Murder: Working with Racially Motivated Offenders.* West Midlands: West Midlands Probation Training Consortium.

Lemos, G. (2000) *Racial Harassment: Action on the Ground.* London: Lemos and Crane.

Levin, B. and McDevitt, J. (2002) *Hate Crimes Revisited.* Oxford: Westview.

McDevitt, J., Levin, J. and Bennett, S. (2002) 'Hate Crime Offenders: An Expanded Typology', *Journal of Social Issues*, 58: 303–317.

NPS (National Probation Service) (2004) *About Us: Our Aims.* Downloaded on 2 February 2005 from www.probation.homeoffice.gov.uk.

Perry, D. (2002) 'Racially Motivated Offenders: The Way Forward', *Probation Journal* 49: 305–309.

Shenk, A.H. (2001) 'Victim-Offender Mediation: The Road to Repairing Hate Crime Injustice', *Ohio State Journal on Dispute Resolution*, 17: 185–217.

Sibbitt, R. (1997) *The Perpetrators of Racial Harassment and Racial Violence*, Home Office Research Study 176. London: Home Office.

Sullivan, A. (1999) *What's So Bad About Hate?* Downloaded 31 January 2005 from www.andrewsullivan.com.

Chapter 13

Marginalized and disenfranchised: community justice and mentally disordered offenders

Jane Winstone and Francis Pakes

Mentally disordered offenders pose a unique challenge to the criminal justice system and have done so for some time. It was widely undisputed when Prins described the plight of this group on the fringes of society as 'the people that nobody owns' (Prins 1993: 152, 571–78). However, by 1998, Nigel Stone had made the claim that this was no longer the case, as a number of official reports had addressed this issue. These included official reports and guidance from the Home Office and the Department of Health, such as the Reed Report (1992), various committees of inquiry (e.g. Ritchie 1994 on the events leading up to the killing of Jonathan Zito by Christopher Clunis; Blom-Cooper 1995 on the management of Andrew Robinson at Torbay) and a flurry of other publications (e.g. Staite 1994, CLC 1994, Vaughan and Badger 1995). Stone claimed that all of these contributed to a concerted focus on mentally disordered offenders as a special challenge within the criminal justice system and a particular priority within mainstream health service provision (Stone 1998). However, the question is raised as to whether all this attention has meant that the marginalization of mentally disordered offenders has been properly addressed.

These publications were key to developing the proposed reform of the outdated and problematic Mental Health Act 1983. In 2000 a White Paper, *Reform of the Mental Health Act*, was introduced (DOH 2000) to wide critical comment and subsequently subjected to further consultation. However, its provisions were so broadly drafted that in the opinion of the *British Medical Journal* it 'threatens the civil liberties of the whole population and the professional boundaries of psychiatrists' (Kmieto-wicz 2002). This consultation subsequently resulted in the Mental Health Bill 2004. The Mental Health Alliance responded to the new Bill 2004 by stating:

> We have a Bill that is rooted in an out-dated, false stereotype that people with mental health problems are a danger to society and are unable to make their own decisions about care and treatment. The revised Bill remains objectionable in principle and unworkable in practice. (*Medical News Today* 2004)

If, before considering the Mental Health Bill 2004 in further detail, it is accepted that these responses from eminent bodies establish a *prima facie* case that the proposed reforms appear to exacerbate rather than resolve the undermining of the rights and liberties of mentally disordered offenders, then it is necessary to trace how the potential for such social exclusionary processes have taken root and exhibit themselves so manifestly at policy-making level.

We not do deny an association between certain forms of mental disorder and offending behaviour. However, as McGuire (2002) states, it is a misunderstanding of the relationship between the two that gives rise to fears out of all proportion to the risks posed. There is not a wealth of empirical research published in the area, however a recent study (Johnson and Taylor 2001) demonstrates that there are significantly lower reconviction rates for offenders who are mentally disordered compared to those with no mental disorder, matched for demographic factors and offence gravity. This study identified that between 1984 and the end of 1998, 1,846 patients were conditionally discharged for the first time. Fewer than one in ten (9 per cent) of those discharged were reconvicted of a standard list offence within two years of discharge. Included within this group were 1 per cent whose reconviction was for a grave offence. Since 1987 reconviction rates for this group have continued to be noticeably lower than the matched group, averaging 7 per cent for a standard list offence. Over a five-year period reconviction rates are 3 per cent for grave offences. For sexual offences the expected reconviction rate is 11 per cent and the actual reconviction rate for mentally disordered offenders convicted of a sex offence is 2 per cent or nine points lower than would be expected of discharged prisoners and those sentenced to community penalties who match the restricted patients on criminal history and demographic factors (Johnson and Taylor 2001).

This is convincing evidence that people categorized as mentally disordered offenders are significantly less likely to engage in repeat offending even where their conviction is for a serious offence; the rates of recidivism are significantly less than for their matched group without a mental health complication. Mentally disordered offenders can therefore be argued to pose less risk to the public than other offenders, which begs the question of how this group have become so stigmatized. Part of the problem must be the 'axe-wielding maniac' archetype of popular perception. The tendency to equate outbursts of violence with mental illness serves to highlight what is, in fact, quite a rare phenomenon, such as the case of Peter Bryan. In March 2005 Bryan was discharged from a psychiatric hospital and subsequently killed his friend and ate his brains. The impact of this type of event is that all potentially dangerous behaviour is linked to mental illness – and all people who are mentally ill become labelled as potentially dangerous. This is an image, we will argue, that is being perpetuated through the proposed reforms of the Mental Health Act.

Issues of definition

There is no widely accepted definition of mental disorder. This makes it difficult to decide what distinguishes it from the normal or healthy mental states that the term is intended to exclude. Legal definitions (Mental Health Act 1983) have given rise to a series of commentaries for guidance under the heading of mental disorder. One definition states that mental disorder is any illness with significant psychological or behavioural manifestations that is associated with either a painful or distressing symptom or impairment in one or more areas of functioning (see Davison and Neale 2000). It is immediately obvious that such a definition of mental disorder requires interpretation. On the other hand, the term 'mental illness' (as opposed to mental disorder) is the working tool of description of the health professions. Medical definitions of mental illness are also not absolute. This means that the diagnosis of mental illness becomes just as much of an art as a science with all the attendant diagnostic issues of differences between professional expertise and opinion. Not only therefore is mental disorder poorly defined legally, but the legal and medical professions do not work to the same definitions. In addition, for both legal and professional bodies, there is tension within and between regarding interpretation.

Attempting to define mentally disordered *offending* merely exacerbates the problem. With regard to mentally disordered offending, the search for a definition to inform this chapter produced no more satisfactory results than that for mental disorder, however a definition of mentally disordered offending is offered as follows:

> any offence where manifestations of mental disorder, which can be clinically diagnosed, are a contributory factor to offending behaviour. (Winstone 2004)

Labelling an individual as a mentally disordered offender requires both a psychiatric determination of disorder as well as a demonstration by a multi-agency panel that the disorder has contributed to the offending behaviour, before the court can make a decision to sentence under the provisions of the Mental Health Act 1983 (with provision for management as set out under the Criminal Justice Act 1991).

Such a range of professional perspectives, with the additional issue of competing multi-agency philosophies and aims, brings about a situation in which the implementation of community justice for mentally disordered offenders rests on, to put it mildly, less than firm foundations. The potential for getting it wrong is formidable and within this context there are various ways – through expectation and association, cultural norms and attitudes – in which unconscious stereotyping and bias in assessment can occur.

Certain behaviours do not by themselves signify a mental disorder but may simply be a form of social deviance on the individual's part (Davison and Neale 2000). For example, there are some offences so appalling that it is tempting to assume that the individual concerned must be mentally deranged, as in serial murder and child molestation. This was the case in the Soham (2003) murders of two young girls where the accused underwent intensive psychiatric assessment before it was decided that he was fit to plead under standard criminal justice provisions. However, the very fact that mental disorder and horrific behaviour are linked in this way suggests that there exists this association in the public and professional mindset: if a certain behaviour is deeply offensive then it is likely to be underpinned by a pathology. Such a link establishes a framework from which stereotyping can emerge, based on belief, normative social codes and individual experience – all of which promote unconscious bias in assessment processes.

With regard to cultural issues, specific definitions of mental disorder will vary slightly from culture to culture because of differing social and cultural norms. Cultural misconceptions can therefore confuse the ways in which the concepts of mental disorder and mentally disordered offender are applied. For example, in some cultures a normal display of grief is to rend clothing and express grief vocally and publically. This is seen as an act of respect upon the death of a loved one. In most European cultures such behaviour would be interpreted as excessive, suggesting that the bereaved had become mentally unstable as a result of grief and in need of psychiatric support.

Within a multi-cultural society such lack of awareness of different cultural norms can result in a misguided assessment of mental fitness and an unnecessary fear of the danger that an individual poses to themselves or others. Sentencing statistics do suggest a cultural bias in identification and application of the concept of 'mentally disordered' (Walton nd). This source quotes research that suggests that if a person is young, male and black they are more likely to be detained as a mentally disordered offender than a young, male, white counterpart. The BBC reported (BBC 2005) that black, male, mentally disordered offenders were significantly more likely to be subjected to physical restraint than their white counterparts. This highlights the fact that mental disorder is surrounded by a lack of clarity, and the risks that that poses: it further opens the door to introduction of bias in clinical assessment and management.

Badger, Nursten, Williams and Woodward (1999) produced additional empirical evidence that unintended bias in clinical assessment and professional judgement leads to an unrepresentative profile of mentally disordered offenders in the sentenced population. Psychotic remand prisoners are more likely to be black and older than other mentally disordered prisoners and these figures are particularly significant for women. Further findings were that non-white groups are over-represented in special hospitals, making up almost 20 per cent of the population. Schizophrenia makes a small independent contribution to the risk of acquiring a criminal record, but more substantial influences are gender, substance abuse, ethnicity and age of onset of criminal career (Badger *et al* 1999). Not only does this further confirm that mental disorder is not a substantial influence on the likelihood of attaining a criminal record, but it supports the claim that bias has been introduced in clinical risk assessment, which arises, partly, from a weak understanding of the risk that mentally disordered offenders pose.

Diagnosis and risk assessment

It should not be surprising that it is difficult to apply the concept of mental disorder to risk assessment. There is no rigorous actuarial risk assessment tool in use across the medical and criminal justice sectors for this group; professional assessment has to guide the process, despite the subjectivity of diagnosis and all the attendant evidence that clinical assessment introduces bias (Kemshall and Maguire 2001). This is a

223

situation that is unlikely to resolve itself without focused research, especially given the tensions in how diagnosis is arrived at.

The medical priority in the management of mental illness is to accurately diagnose and treat. However, mental disorders can vary greatly in their symptoms, in terms of their severity, course, outcome and amenability to treatment. They can adversely affect any and every aspect of a person's life, including his or her enjoyment, mood, attitudes, occupation or career, sexual functioning, family and marital life, other interpersonal relations, and the management of financial affairs (Davison and Neale 2000). As mentioned at the outset, there is no single comprehensive definition. The guide that medical experts use to distinguish between normal and abnormal behaviour is that abnormality is usually determined based on the presence of several characteristics at one time (Davison and Neale 2000). The best medical definition and determination of abnormal behaviour takes into account the characteristics of statistical infrequency, violation of norms, personal distress, disability or dysfunction and unexpectedness (Davison and Neale 2000). There is nothing clear-cut as to how these criteria are interpreted. It has already been demonstrated that personal distress is subject to variations in social and cultural norms. An individual may be experiencing a period of disruption in their lives and demonstrating chaotic behaviour as a result, but this does not necessarily imply mental disorder. The difficulties in diagnosis multiply when linked to classification. Davison and Neale (2000) set out a range of classifications that include anxiety disorders, somatoform and dissociative disorders, psychophysiological disorders, eating and mood disorders, schizophrenia, substance-related disorders, personality disorders, sexual and gender identity disorders, disorders of childhood and disorders of ageing. Each of these disorders has sub-categories, and presenting features and symptoms can vary in their severity and presence. The challenge to professional expertise in forming an accurate diagnosis is evident.

Mental disorder does not inevitably lead to mentally disordered offending, but offenders are found in each of the categories listed. Neither does it follow that the mental disorder has contributed to the offending or, as shown above, that because a person exhibits forms of anti-social behaviour with features of unexpectedness, that they are also mentally disordered. Therefore, without a reliable universal actuarial system for diagnosis, the classification of symptoms is a real and problematic issue. Some of the challenges faced by health professionals are that professional agreement is required between psychiatrists as to whether an offender is mentally disordered, their susceptibility to and type of treatment, the extent to which the disorder has contributed to an offence, and the likelihood of causing harm to self or others (now and in the future); or, alternatively, whether the individual is exhibiting anti-social behaviour that violates the socially constructed expectation of norms, but is not mentally disordered.

Intervention

Once a patient has been classified and diagnosed, a regime of management can commence. Intervention for mental disorder typically combines a therapeutic approach combined with a traditional medical model, which is the delivery of drug treatment to produce symptomatic control. Depending on the degree and severity of the symptoms and the nature of the risk posed by the individual, intervention can take place in the community, in halfway houses, in special hospitals or secure units, and in the case of the mentally disordered offender, in prison or under probation supervision with a multi-disciplinary input. Resourcing is an issue here, as provisions for the treatment and management of mentally disordered offenders remains limited compared to the demand. MIND (2004) claims that one in four people are turned away during a mental health crisis and that lack of resources to manage mentally disordered offenders in the community leads to the increasing use of prison, which is an inappropriate setting for the treatment of severe mental illness.

Programmatic approaches and mental disorder

The accredited programme initiative to address offending behaviour is based on the 'what works' research evidence and can be broadly understood as a clinical intervention. However, it does not appear to be widely recognized that such interventions are unsuitable for anyone with a mental disorder, whether or not this has been judged to be a contributory factor to the offending behaviour.

The guidance offered on the offending behaviour programmes (Offending Behaviour Programmes Unit 2005) is that clinical and therapeutic interventions should be recognized as differing in the following respects:

- Clinical (accredited) programmes are aimed at reducing crime, not at reducing distress or the symptoms or causes of mental disorder.

- Most therapeutic programmes run for mental health problems will run for much longer than the three months of accredited offending behaviour programmes.

- The clinical standards applied to 'consent' differ from those applied to therapeutic health interventions. Under the accredited Offending Behaviour Programmes, progress through, for example, the prison system, including transfer to more open conditions and access to release on parole, may be made conditional on a prisoner's agreement to attend a particular programme. Were a similar course (e.g. an anger management course) to be offered as a health care intervention, for consent to be valid in this context no such conditions could be attached to the offer.

- Offending Behaviour Programmes in prison are usually overseen by forensic psychologists, not clinical psychologists. In the community they will rarely be overseen by a psychologist at all, the responsibility for the supervision of the sentence being with the identified probation officer.

These guidelines, whilst applying to the prison environment, also apply to the delivery of community based accredited programmes for those offenders who are suffering from a clinically diagnosed mental health condition. However, the problems with accurate identification and diagnosis present the dilemma that individuals may be exposed to a programme of intervention that could exacerbate their mental health condition and to which issues of consent have been inappropriately applied.

The dilemmas for intervention with regard to symptomatic management is particularly acute in those patients where agreement cannot be secured as to whether the individual has a treatable disorder. If the disorder is not treatable then there is no current legal or medical mandate for detention or forcible intervention. The diagnosis and management of personality disorder illustrates the issues well.

Personality disorder

Personality disorders are a problematic diagnosis: a mental disorder that cannot be classified as either a psychosis or a neurosis. These are long-term, maladaptive accentuations of one or a set of particular personality traits (Davison and Neale 2000), which may first be exhibited in infancy or childhood. The heart of the dilemma for classification and diagnosis is the lack of specificity. It seems that patients with a personality disorder do not necessarily have traits different from the general population. Rather, they share tendencies but exhibit them *in extremis* (Clark and Watson 1999). Diagnosis may rely upon a detailed clinical and social history that is mainly interpretive. Symptoms may vary and traits may not be definite. To make matters worse, clinical literature distinguishes between various forms of personality disorder, sometimes referred to in shorthand as psychopathy, and the debate as to whether psychopathy actually represents a distinct form of personality disorder is far from settled (see Harris, Rise and Quinsey 1994).

The first example is the hystrionic personality disorder. Its dominant symptoms include excessive levels of egocentrism and insincerity. The anti-social type exhibits physical aggression and irresponsible attitudes towards money, work and other 'social bonds' including a notable absence of remorse, whereas the borderline personality disorder is characterized by affective instability and impulsivity (Blackburn and Coid 1998). The extent to which these disorders are distinct is quite possibly one of gradation and many of the symptoms are shared across types of personality disorders. Personality disorders are often established via the administration of questionnaires, such as Hare's Psychopathy Checklist (revised) (Hare 1991), or via structured interviews.

Blackburn and Coid (1998) assessed 167 violent male offenders who were either in prison or in a maximum-security mental hospital. They identified four factors that might underlie personality disorders, at least in the incarcerated population. These are impulsivity, detachment, sensitivity (or lack of it) and compulsivity. Particularly high scores on impulsivity related to their offending history, including age of first offence, as well as total levels of offending. Other factors, such as detachment and sensitivity, hardly correlate with offending at all. It again highlights the complex nature of the relationship between personality disorders and offending: frequency of personality disorders in prisons and secure mental institutions is high, but it is increasingly acknowledged that many who suffer from a personality disorder lead more or less successful lives (Board and Fritzon 2005).

Blackburn and Coid (1998), in debating the perplexing nature of identifying the various forms of personality disorder, suggest that in their mildest form these disorders relate most closely to anti-social behaviour, with reasons for anti-social behaviour that are commonly found in the normal offender population, for example cognitive distortions around victim empathy, which are the focus of cognitive behavioural work that is being disseminated across the National Offender Management Service. However, the nature and extent of the cognitive distortions of people with a diagnosis of mental disorder, including personality disorder, renders them unsuitable for this type of clinical programme – if indeed they have been accurately diagnosed before they come under the auspices of sentence management.

The sad news is that there is no medical intervention available to people with a diagnosis of personality disorder that can be demonstrated to ameliorate the symptoms reliably. So not only is the individual problematic to classify; once diagnosed, there is no treatment. This is the group, however, that comes before the court most frequently for sentencing under mentally disordered offender provision (Humphreys 1992 in Badger *et al* 1999). Humphreys further comments on the low priority of people with a dual diagnosis of personality disorder/offending behaviour with regard to admission and treatment statistics, being the group most rapidly discharged from psychiatric provision and the most likely to have unexplained delayed admission when their behaviour was considered life-threatening to themselves. This suggests that this group is being severely affected by the lack of clarity in diagnosis, the paucity of effective treatment regimes and the risk of being subjected to inappropriate clinical intervention. It would appear from the limited research available that they are either not being treated under the psychiatric provision but being sentenced under the normal criminal justice processes, or are rapidly discharged when they do meet the psychiatric services. In short, we do not know what to do with them, or what to do for them. This group clearly stands out as an example of the lack of resourcing in terms of community and health service arrangements, lack of understanding as a result of the limited research in this area and lack of clarity in legal arrangements.

In conclusion, personality disorder acutely typifies the dilemmas a sentencing court faces. A closer examination of the legal issues and priorities demonstrates the problems faced in the application of the current legislation.

Twenty-first century reforms: a bleak future for rehabilitation and human rights

It is important for the integrity of criminal justice that the purpose of punishment is seen to be upheld and to be different from the management of those before the court with a mental disorder and mentally disordered offending. The constitutional justification for punishment is the blameworthiness of an individual. However, an individual's insanity means that he is legally blameless, for he cannot possess *mens rea*, a guilty mind (Savage 2000). Furthermore, since punishment is unlikely to have any of its intended effects on a mentally disturbed person – that is, rehabilitation, deterrence, or retribution – it is ineffective at best and a miscarriage of justice at worst to inflict this upon a mentally disordered offender. Additionally, if there is no curative treatment available for a mentally disordered offender, there are no legal grounds to order treatment, as the provisions of the Mental Health Act 1983 require that the justification for health care intervention is that it can positively impact upon the condition.

The Mental Health Act 1983 deals with states of mental disorder. It specifies that people must not be deemed to have a form of mental disorder or mental illness by reason only of promiscuity or other immoral conduct, sexual deviancy or dependence on alcohol or drugs. In the past people have been brought into the psychiatric system because, for example, they have had a child outside marriage, or they engaged in adult homosexual practices, so this statement is an important safeguard. Use of alcohol and other substances might sometimes cause a mental disorder or mental illness, which is within the scope of the Act, but use of these substances in itself cannot be within the scope of the Act. Of the four sub-categories of mental disorder specified in the Mental Health Act 1983, one refers to arrested or incomplete development of the mind, psychopathic disorder and any other disorder or disability of the mind, two refer to mental impairment linked to a state of arrested or incomplete development of the mind, and the fourth to psychopathic disorders. This latter is taken to mean a persistent disorder or disability of the mind that results in abnormally aggressive or seriously irresponsible conduct on the part of the person concerned. This is linked to a range of disorders, including personality disorder, but in no way reflects the categories and sub-categories of medical classification and definition.

Definitions, the base for common understanding, are important when they are linked to risk assessment and disposals, and in the case of mentally disordered offenders, where there are legal and ethical problems around human rights and public protection. Davison and Neale (2000) argue that the management of mentally disordered offenders needs to address the following legal and ethical issues: that to detain a person who is mentally capable under mental health provisions is a grievous injustice and a label for life; to detain a person who is not mentally capable under mental health provisions may result in a longer period of detention where that person presents only the same or similar risk factor as a person who has committed the same act but is mentally stable; how to manage an individual who was mentally ill at the time the crime was committed but is no longer mentally ill at the time of sentencing or at the time of committal or shortly thereafter; that to fail to detain a person who is not mentally capable under mental health provisions may present a risk to the public that is unacceptable.

At present, people who are mentally ill but deemed untreatable by psychiatrists, such as people with personality disorders or psychopaths, cannot be detained under the Mental Health Act 1983. For example, if a person is convicted of murder with the disposal of a Hospital Order, but is deemed untreatable, they could be released, unless they are committed to a secure hospital or a prison such as Rampton. With regard to *mens rea,* that is, a disordered mind cannot be a guilty mind, Davison and Neale (2000) debate whether emotionally disturbed perpetrators are less criminally responsible than those who are not mentally disordered but commit the same crimes. They raise the question as to whether such individuals should even be brought to trial. Although efforts to excuse or protect an accused person by invoking the insanity defence or by judging him or her incompetent to stand trial are undoubtedly well-intentioned, invoking these doctrines can often subject those accused to a greater denial of liberties than they would otherwise experience. It is these dilemmas that mental health reform needs to address.

In their introduction to mental health reform, the Department of Health stated that the focus was upon people with personality disorder who at present cannot be compelled to take medication unless they are sectioned and remanded to a secure hospital. They estimated that there were just over 2,000 people who fall into the category of severe personality disorder who may cause harm to themselves or others. Of these, 98 per cent are men and at any time most are in prison or in secure hospitals (DOH 2000). The underpinning rationale for reform was that as the law stands at present it fails to protect the public from the danger that these people represent. The aims of reform would be:

the management of dangerous people with severe personality disorder; to strike the balance between the interests of individuals and society; meet the need of this group better than the present patchy provision; firmly ground in evidence from research and be capable of adapting over time as new research evidence comes forward; provide better value for money than the present arrangements; lead in time to a reduction in the level of the most serious offending by people with severe personality disorder, as better measures are identified and implemented and through the early identification and detention of those who are dangerous. (DOH 1999: 1)

In 2000 a White Paper was issued to reform the Mental Health Bill. It proposed to give doctors new powers to lock up patients and force them to have treatment, including the provision for people with severe and untreatable personality disorders to be detained indefinitely if experts considered an individual with this diagnosis to be a danger to the public – whether or not they had committed an offence.

The Home Office received over 2,000 responses to these proposals, which exhibit a sharp divide between public, expert and legal opinion. The Zito Trust, representing a voice for those concerned chiefly with public protection issues, broadly supported the proposals. The National Health Service Confederation objected to them on the basis that any legislation must be based on rigorous definitions of dangerous severe personality disorder as well as on sound data on treatability. Neither of these requirements was provided for. In addition, it argued that available provisions had to be consistent with the constraints imposed by the European Convention on Human Rights and the Human Rights Act 1998. Mental health professionals also objected to the proposals, reiterating the problems in the areas of diagnosis, treatment and risk assessment. They questioned how any system of justice could possibly justify indefinitely detaining a citizen who has committed no offence on the basis of poor diagnostics and flimsy evidence. It is to their credit that they are aware of the limitations of diagnosis and, whilst recognizing the need for reform, also require that reform should not be based upon bias and stereotyping. It is also to the credit of the Department of Health that it took the points raised so seriously as to delay proceeding with the legislation whilst they engaged in further consultation.

In 2004 the draft Mental Health Bill was published. The bill revises the definition of 'mental disorder' to cover 'a disturbance in the functioning of the mind or brain resulting from any disability or disorder of the mind or brain. Examples of a mental disorder include schizophrenia, depression or a learning disability.' The 1983 Act's condition of 'treatability' would also be removed so that there would be no exclusion of people who have a sole diagnosis of mental impairment or psychopathic disorder, as well as sexual deviants and those addicted to drugs or alcohol (*Guardian* 2005).

Whilst the government first announced plans to detain psychopaths who have not committed a crime, following the public outrage at the murder by Michael Stone of Lin Russell and her six-year-old daughter Megan in Kent in 1996, the proposals, without doubt, widen the net of those who can be assessed as mentally disordered – and indefinitely detained without ever having committed an offence. Compulsory treatment in the community is also proposed in order, it is claimed, to address the 'revolving door' of relapse and readmission because of failure to take medication. Powers to enforce both treatment and detention have therefore been extended.

These new proposals focus upon rights and compulsion. They appear to serve only to exacerbate further the issues of exclusion and marginalization of those who suffer from a mental illness. In response, MIND (2004) pointed out that in terms of treatment, current resourcing does not cope with current demand and therefore the right to treatment is not linked with the provision available. Furthermore, the term 'sufficient mental capacity' that underpins the assessment of whether an individual can exercise rights to refuse treatment, is poorly defined, unclear and open to abuse. MIND observes, with regard to community compulsion to treatment, that the constraints proposed are such that they suggest that if a person is *that* ill they should be treated in hospital. They criticize the reduced safeguards, which they claim weakens the role of non-medical and multi-agency staff, and note that there are insufficient arrangements for the right to advocacy at the beginning of the assessment process. The safeguards against people being given invasive treatment, including irreversible measures such as psychosurgery, are weak. By extending compulsion to people who are already in prison, it condones an inappropriate setting for the treatment of severe mental illness. MIND (2004) further claims that the proposals not only hinder the exercise of human rights for those with a mental disorder but particularly discriminate against people with a mental disorder who appear in court, suggesting an exponential disenfranchisement of this group. In terms of risk management it could be argued to uphold the principle of exclusion and herald the end of rehabilitation (Young 1999, Worrall 1997). Rather than balancing risks and right, the Mental Health Bill attempts to eliminate risk altogether – a futile venture (Hudson 2001, Fennell 2002).

The new reforms have united health professionals and medical practitioners in their condemnation of the proposals. The Mental Health Professionals (*Medical News Today* 2004) reiterated that detention was proposed without clear diagnostic rigour and upon people who have not contravened the law in any way. *Psychminded* (2004) (an online journal for psychiatrists) stated that the revision of the wording from 'for the health and safety of the patient' to 'for the protection of the patient from suicide, or serious self-harm, or serious neglect by him or his safety', poses risks to medical practitioners in determining treatment versus rights of the patients. The Mental Health Alliance (2004) responded that the 'definition of those who qualify for treatment against their will is far too broad, forcing professionals to bring too many people in for compulsory treatment and damaging the vital trust between doctor and patient'. The Royal College of Psychiatrists (2004) called the provisions 'unfair, stigmatising and dangerous', not just for patients with a clear diagnosis, but for any person exhibiting what could be interpreted as symptoms of mental confusion. The agreement across the professional spectrum is that the new legislation could lead to compulsion infringing upon human rights.

The professional bodies opposing the proposals argue that the bill's emphasis on managing risk will reinforce the public misconception that mentally ill people are dangerous. Richard Brook, chief executive of the charity MIND, stated that the proposed legislation 'risks introducing fear and coercion into what should be a purely therapeutic relationship. It risks driving those who most need care and treatment away from seeking help as and when they need it most' (MIND 2004).

The future looks bleak, with a Mental Health Act that threatens to focus excessively on control and repression, at the expense of treatment and rehabilitation. Ironically, to be mentally ill, whether of an episodic or long-standing nature, appears to be becoming an increasingly risky diagnosis, first, because of the high levels of victimization directed towards the mentally ill and second, because of the increased powers of the state to control the lives and movements of people with a diagnosis of mental disorder, without drawing upon sound evidence, or having appropriate resources or treatment to offer.

Conclusion: a missed opportunity

In conclusion, this chapter has explored whether mentally disordered offenders are marginalized and disenfranchised members of society. The sentencing profile confirms the *prima facie* case that current arrangements discriminate against offenders with a mental disorder and especially those from a minority ethnic group or from other than a Western European cultural background. The bias in sentencing statistics confirms the stereotyping and labelling based on misinformed public perceptions of risk and a poor legal conceptualization of complex medical issues, resulting in a blurring of the boundaries between risk management and human rights (see Gray, Laing and Noaks 2002).

Does this amount to marginalization? If to be assessed as mentally disordered means that an individual is perceived as posing a threat to society, that the lack of resources in this area means more limited opportunities for treatment than people with other diagnoses, that the individual is not a priority for treatment when treatment is sought, that appropriate care in the community and the supported housing stock for people with mental disorder is limited, then the answer to that question must be 'yes'. If this is the situation for people with mental disorder, how much more is it compounded if the label of mentally disordered offender has been applied?

Does the debate evidence disenfranchisment of people with mental disorder? The views of mental health professionals on the proposed legislation suggest that if disenfranchisement is taken to mean limited or obstructed access to human rights, rights of representation and equality of treatment and opportunity, then individuals with a mental disorder experience disenfranchisement under the current arrangements and the proposed arrangements perpetuate the social exclusion of this group, again exacerbated if the individual has acquired the label of mentally disordered offender.

Whilst the government has stated that reforms and future developments in the arena of mental health provision should be based on evidence and research, McGuire (2002) argues that even the limited research in this area produces ideologies and practices focusing on blame and risk avoidance. Any legislation that simply reflects back the power base in society to define and label stereotypically those members of society with the least powerful voice, arising out of poorly constructed definitions and prejudice based on misunderstanding and misplaced fear, is bound to perpetuate injustice. Should the Mental Health Bill (2004) become enshrined in law without significant and fundamental change, it will represent a lost opportunity to bring mental health provision into the twenty-first century, to shed outdated and historical attitudes and to bring justice to this group of people.

References

Badger, D., Nursten, J., Williams, P. and Woodward, M. (1999) *Systematic Review of the Internation Literature on the Epidemiology of Mentally Disordered Offenders*, CRD Report 125. Available online: http://www.york.ac.uk/inst/crd/report15.htm, accessed 18 February 2002.

BBC (British Broadcasting Association) (2005) *Today Programme*, 12 January.

Blackburn, R. and Coid, J.W. (1998) 'Psychopathy and the Dimensions of Personality Disorder in Violent Offenders', *Personality and Individual Difference*, 25: 129–145.

Blom-Cooper, L. (1992) *Report of Committee of Inquiry into Complaints about Ashworth Hospital*. London: HMSO.

Board, B.J. and Fritzon, K. (2005) 'Disordered Personalities at Work,' *Psychology, Crime and Law*, 11: 17–32.

Clark, L. and Watson. D. (1999) 'Personality, disorder, and personality disorder: towards a more rational conceptualization', *Journal of Personality Disorders*, 13: 142–151.

CLC (Children's Legal Centre) (1994) *Mental Health Handbook: A Guide to the Law Affecting Children and Young People*, 2nd edition. Essex: CLC.

Davison, G. and Neale, J. (2000) *Abnormal Psychology*, 8th edition. Chichester: Wiley.

DOH (Department of Health) (1999) *Executive Summary. Managing Dangerous People with Severe Personality Disorder: Proposals for Policy Development. July 1999*. London: DOH.

DOH (Department of Health) (2000) *Reform of the Mental Health Act – White Paper and Summary of Responses*. London: DOH.

Fennell, P. (2002) 'Radical Risk Management, Mental Health and Criminal Justice', in N. Gray, J. Laing and L. Noaks (eds), *Criminal Justice, Mental Health and the Politics of Risk*. London: Cavendish.

Gray, N., Laing, J. and Noaks, L. (eds) (2002) *Criminal Justice, Mental Health and the Politics of Risk*. London: Cavendish.

Guardian (2005) 'Draft Mental Health Bill', 29 March. Available online: http://society.guardian.co.uk/mentalhealth/story/0,8150,836476,00.html.

Hare, R.D. (1991) *The Psychopathy Checklist - Revised*. Toronto: Multi-Health Systems.

Harris, G.T., Rice, M.E. and Quinsey, V.L. (1994) 'Psychopathy as a Taxon: Evidence that Psychopaths are a Distinct Class', *Journal of Consulting and Clinical Psychology*, 62: 387–397.

Hudson, B. (2001) 'Punishment, Rights, and Difference: Defending Justice in the Risk Society', in K. Stenson and R. Sullivan (eds), *Crime, Risk and Justice: The Politics of Crime Control in Liberal Democracies*. Cullompton: Willan.

Johnson, S. and Taylor, R. (2001) *Statistics of Mentally Disordered Offenders 2000*. London: Home Office.

Kemshall, H. and Maguire, M. (2001) 'Public Protection, Partnership and Risk Penality: The Multi-agency Risk Management of Sexual and Violent Offenders', *Punishment and Society*, 1: 237–264.

Kmietowicz, Z. (2002) 'New Mental Health Bill, British Medical Journal', 325: 678. Available online: http://bmj.bmjjournals.com/cgi/content/full/325/7366/678/b.

McGuire, J. (2002) *Offender Rehabilitation and Treatment: Effective Programmes and Policies to Reduce Re-offending*. Chichester: Wiley.

Medical News Today (2004) 'Revised Mental Health Bill Must not Waste Opportunity'. Available online: http://www.medicalnewstoday.com, accessed 16 September 2004.

Mental Health Alliance (2004) Available online: http://www.mentalhealth.org.uk/page.cfm?pagecode=PRCMMH, accessed 16 September 2004.

MIND (2004) 'The new Mental Health Bill'. Available online: http://www.mind.org.uk, accessed 16 September 2004.

Offending Behaviour Programmes Unit (2005) *Offending Behaviour Programmes (Prison Service Accredited)*. London: Offending Behaviour Programmes Unit.

Prins, H. (1993) 'The People Nobody Owns', in W. Watson and A. Grounds (eds), *The Mentally Disordered Offender in an Era of Community Care: New Directions in Provision*. Cambridge: Cambridge University Press.

Psychminded (2004) 'Government Publishes Revised Draft Mental Health Bill', Pyschminded.co.uk, 9 September.

Reed, J. (1992) *Review of Health and Social Services for Mentally Disordered Offenders and Others Requiring Similar Services*. Cm 2088. London: HMSO.

Ritchie, J. (1994) *The Report of the Enquiry into the Care and Treatment of Christopher Clunis*. London: HMSO.

The Royal College of Psychiatrists (2004) *Draft Mental Health Bill: RCP Anxious about Civil Liberties, Ethics, Practicality and Effectiveness*, press release, 16 September.

Savage, S. (2000) 'An In-Depth Review of Mentally Disordered Offending', in J. Winstone and C. Dixon (eds), *Strategies for Tackling Offending Behaviour*. Portsmouth: ICJS, University of Portsmouth.

Staite, C. (1994) *Diversion from Custody for Mentally Disordered Offenders*. Harrow: Longman.

Stone, N. (1998) *A Companion Guide to Mentally Disordered Offender*. West Yorkshire: Owen Wells.

Vaughan, P. and Badger, D. (1995) *Working with Mentally Disordered Offenders in the Community*. London: Chapman and Hall.

Walton, M. (nd) *Mentally Disordered Offenders*. Available online: http://www.mark-walton.net/mdo/index.asp, accessed 15 January 2005.

Winstone, J. (2004) *Are Mentally Disordered Offenders Marginalised and Disenfranchised?* Unpublished Paper, ICJS student conference. University of Portsmouth, Feburary 2004.

Worrall, A. (1997) *Punishment in the Community*. Harlow: Addison Wesley Longman.

Young, J. (1999) *The Exclusive Society: Social Exclusion, Crime and Difference in Late Modernity*. London: Sage.

Chapter 14

Improving confidence in criminal justice: achieving community justice for victims and witnesses

Jacki Tapley

One of the most profound influences upon criminology and criminal justice policy during the last two decades has been the significant shift in emphasis from an offender-focused criminal justice system to the unprecedented focus now being placed upon the victims of crime. Whilst two centuries ago victims of crime were the main protagonists in criminal matters, the emergence of a complex modern criminal justice system resulted in the overriding issues of deterrence, detection, prosecution, punishment and reform of the offender usurping the once prominent role of the victim. The rise in the professional administration of criminal justice by judges, lawyers, the police and criminal experts, led to a decline in the role of the victim in criminal proceedings, with the concerns of the wider public interest subsuming the more particular needs of the victim (Christie 1977, Fattah 1986). As a consequence, the relationship between the offender and the state came to dominate all developments in criminal justice prosecution, punishment and rehabilitation, to the exclusion of the relationship between the victim and the state (Ashworth 1983).

However, this re-emergence of victims of crime as a legitimate third party in the criminal justice process, and the long overdue recognition of victims as vital participants for the efficient and effective administration of criminal justice, has not been an accomplishment easily attained. Instead, the achievements made so far have been the gradual culmination of a number of factors – historical, social, political and criminological. Further improvements to the status of victims in the criminal process will require continued vigilance to ensure that the current populist political rhetoric, pledging to 'rebalance the criminal justice system in favour of victims' (Home Office 2002: 2) is actually converted into the reality of victims' experiences, by respecting the rights of victims, whilst continuing to acknowledge the rights of the defendant.

It is now widely acknowledged that for too long both academic and professional concerns have focused too narrowly on the offender (Christie 1977, Cayley 1998, Fattah 2000). Explanations regarding the causes of crime have swung from biological to psychological and sociological and back again, whilst questions of what to do with the offender have alternated regularly between punitive and rehabilitative models. This has left us at the beginning of the twenty-first century with an apparently uneasy compromise between the two, influenced strongly by social, political and economical factors, and reflected in the return to criminal justice policies which now emphasize a community justice approach. However, the use of the term 'community' during the last two decades has become politically expedient, and as a result what is meant exactly by the term depends heavily upon the political motivations at any particular time. Both the previous Conservative government and the New Labour government emphasize the role of communities in relation to reducing crime. The Conservatives attached great importance to the concept of 'active citizenship', which placed increasing responsibilities upon individuals, whilst reducing the role of the state (Heater 1990, Rose 2000). This notion of individual responsibility for preventing both crime and victimization has continued under the Labour government, transferred without difficulty into 'New Labour's rights and duties communitarianism' (Driver and Martell 1997: 38). This concept reflects earlier right-wing policies which reduced the role of the state: a shift from a benevolent welfare state built upon social-liberal notions of citizenship, towards the embracement of free-market principles with an increasingly influential 'duties discourse' based upon the notion of active citizenship and obligations and rights (Lister 1997: 19).

This chapter will first explore briefly some of the important contributory factors that have placed victims' issues so predominantly on the political agenda. This will provide a broad understanding of the contemporary and often controversial debates concerning the status of victims of crime in the criminal process. The chapter will then examine some of the major initiatives that have been introduced to improve public confidence and encourage the public to participate in the criminal process, as part of the Labour government's agenda to modernize the criminal justice system. Crucially, the stated aims of these reforms are to improve access to justice for both victims and communities. Therefore, this chapter will explore what the concept of community justice means from a victim perspective.

The re-emerging victim

The relatively recent rediscovery of crime victims has been well documented by commentators, tracing the emergence since the 1960s of increasingly well-organized groups set up to assist or campaign on behalf of victims (Mawby and Gill 1987, Rock 1990). The subsequent collection of groups with diverse interests and aims later became commonly and conveniently known as the 'victims' movement'. However, this term gave a misleading impression of unity and has been more accurately described by Van Dijk (1988: 126) as 'ideologically heterogeneous'. As such, the 'movement' remains a loose association of groups and individuals supporting different aspects of victimization, ranging from far right groups to feminist groups and with some enjoying far greater political and financial support than others. For example, the compatible philosophy and politically neutral stance originally adopted by Victim Support helped it to gain prominence and assisted in attracting increasing financial support from the Conservative government in the 1980s (Williams 1999a). However, it has been argued that this has been at the expense of those groups whose philosophies challenge conventional thinking, particularly those from a feminist perspective, e.g. Rape Crisis, and, as a consequence, these groups have become the 'hidden wing' of the victims' movement (Williams 1999a). Despite their diversity, however, it is clear that the increasing combined influence of these groups during the last 30 years has contributed towards the raising of public, political, media and criminological concern for victims of crime.

A favourable factor coinciding with the emergence and development of victim interest groups during the 1970s was the growing dissent regarding the effectiveness of interventions with offenders based upon models of 'rehabilitation' and 'training', sparking off what later became commonly known as the 'nothing works' debate (Priestly and Maguire 1995). As described by Brody (1976) and Bottoms (1977), we had entered a period of 'penological pessimism', a demise of faith in the ability of the criminal justice system to rehabilitate offenders. Thus, 'the 1970s ended in a pervasive sense of crisis with the Conservative opposition proposing new "tough" measures in which questions of law and order featured prominently' (Jefferson and Shapland 1994: 266).

Subsequently, the Conservative election victory in 1979 heralded the advent of two complementary ideologies – monetarism and authoritarian populism, marking a fundamental departure from the post-war welfare consensus governing state economic and social policy (Phipps 1988). Public sector reforms governed by the ideology of the free-market extended to the criminal justice system, with the subsequent implementation of new managerialist principles, based on cost efficiency and service effectiveness, largely borrowed from the private sector (Hood 1991, Stewart and Walsh 1992). Subsequently, responsibility for the administration of criminal justice was devolved to the criminal justice agencies and, in line with market-style reforms, such agencies became responsible to the 'consumers' of their services. However, it has been argued that this was a subversive strategy in so far as it involved a redefinition of criminal justice as a service industry concerned with customer care, rather than as a regulatory function of government:

> The idea of consumers of the criminal justice system is one of the more important initiatives of the 1980s. Agencies, for the first time, are being conjoined to care about lay people using their 'services'... Consumerism has also had a certain pay-off economically. If the cost of controlling a rising crime rate were apparently spiralling out of reach, demonstrating consumer satisfaction might just prove a more feasible (cheaper) alternative. (Jefferson and Shapland 1990: 12, cited in Mawby and Walklate 1994: 81)

Thus, it was this apparent acceptance of the ineffectiveness of rehabilitating offenders that attention started to focus on the *effects* of crime and those who had suffered the *real* injury – the victims and the communities in which crime occurred. As observed by Grimshaw (1989), an important factor in the regeneration of criminological concern for victims of crime was the development of national and local crime surveys during the 1980s, which started to reveal the true extent of victimization and provided an alternative source of information to official statistics. In 1982, the findings of the first national British Crime Survey (BCS) in the UK concluded that for every offence recorded, four were actually committed (Hough and Mayhew 1983), thus revealing the greater extent of victimization which was previously unknown. Further national surveys were conducted biannually from 1988 and since 2000 the BCS has moved to an annual cycle with interviews taking place throughout the year. This reflects the government's increasing use of the BCS as a tool to judge public opinion and to inform criminal policy, particularly in relation to identifying patterns of victimization.

However, the methodologies of such large-scale studies as a means of understanding the processes of victimization has been subjected to a number of criticisms, in particular their focus on conventional crimes, for example, street crime, whilst being unrepresentative of victims of more serious crime (Zedner 1994). Hidden violence, as characterized by Stanko (1985, 1988), including cases of domestic violence and sexual assault, is likely to be grossly undercounted, as the technique of data collection does not lend itself to gaining information concerning sensitive areas of victimization. Therefore, it is argued that the aggregate results produced 'tend to wash or attenuate the overall effects of crime' (Lurigio 1987: 456).

In an attempt to rectify the failings of the mass survey techniques, smaller-scale, qualitative studies began to focus on specific victim groups and more serious types of crime. By doing so, academic research emerging during the 1980s, particularly from a feminist perspective, began to highlight the acute stress and adverse physical, practical effects and financial hardship suffered by many victims of crime (Zedner 1994). This not only suggested that victimization entailed greater costs to victims than the mass crime surveys had implied, but also began to provide evidence that the pendulum had swung too far in favour of the offender (Maguire and Bennett 1982). As observed by Van Dijk (1988), there was a growing realisation that society was more concerned with rehabilitating the offender than with rehabilitating the victim. Whilst the reform period of the 1960s and 1970s had done much to ensure better rights for the defendant, based predominantly on a welfare model of justice, they occurred without any consideration for the victim. Subsequently the research had discovered that victims were being exposed to insensitive treatment by the criminal justice process, resulting in what has now become commonly termed as 'secondary victimization' by the system itself. Instead, what was needed was research from the victims' perspective.

Victim research and reform

In an attempt to remedy this apparent lack of knowledge, Shapland, Willmore and Duff (1985: 4) undertook a longitudinal study aimed at providing a 'victim's eye view' of the experiences of victims as their cases passed through the whole of the criminal justice system. Among the most significant findings to emerge from the Shapland *et al* (1985) study was the attitude of the police as a prime determinant of victim satisfaction. The study concluded that victims' problems with the criminal justice system seemed to stem from their lack of an accepted role within it and the fact that the system was not geared to the perspective of the victim. The victims' experiences demonstrated the presence of a paradox within the criminal justice system, highlighting in particular: 'the contradiction between the practical importance of the victim and the ignorance of and ignoring of his [*sic*] attitudes and experiences by the professionals within the criminal justice system' (Shapland *et al* 1985: 177).

Further studies supported the findings of the Shapland *et al* (1985) research. Such studies focused on the effects of crime (Janoff-Bulman 1985, Maguire and Corbett 1987), the treatment of victims by the criminal justice system (Adler 1987) and the needs and services for crime victims (Mawby and Gill 1987, Shapland and Cohen 1987). The sheer consistency of the findings meant that the experiences of victims could no longer be overlooked, creating a surge of interest in crime victims, including increasing international pressures (United Nations 1985, Council of Europe 1985). Eventually, the Home Office began to develop an interest in the victims of crime, awakening to the realization that being seen to be doing something for victims had potential political benefits. As a consequence, the 1990s witnessed a rapid politicization of victims' issues supported by a plethora of initiatives and reforms aimed at improving services to victims of crime (Tapley 2003).

However, these developments led commentators to argue that victims of crime had come to serve a political purpose for New Right politicians wishing to shift the agenda away from the rehabilitation of offenders towards their punishment. In particular, they were seen to encourage harsher sentencing and to bring criminal justice professionals under firmer central government control (Phipps 1988, Elias 1993). Victims, it was argued, filled a vacuum and distracted attention away from the growing penal crisis and the rapidly expanding expenditure on prisons, both in Europe and America. The purpose of this, as described by Phipps (1988: 180), was 'to invoke outrage and sympathy on behalf of crime victims ... to excite hostility against the offender and to discredit the "softness" of the criminal justice system'. Thus observers were led to comment that the rediscovery of crime victims had been motivated primarily, not by a new-found compassion for victims, but to mask a hidden political agenda aimed at promoting tougher law and order policies to appease the populist vote (Fattah 1992, Henderson 1992).

Fattah (1997) warns of the dangers of creating a false contest between the rights of offenders and victims and discusses this further in an article tracing the history and development of victimology (Fattah 2000). He describes the transformation of victimology 'from an academic discipline into a humanistic movement, the shift from scholarly research to political activism' (Fattah 2000: 25) and warns of the implications of this 'metamorphosis' on criminal justice policy. Whilst Fattah (2000) is right to criticize the use of emotive rhetoric relating to victims to provide ammunition to implement punitive political agendas, what he fails to acknowledge is the dissatisfaction caused by the lack of status and entitlements afforded by the state to victims within the criminal justice process. It is this imbalance, which denies recognition and redress for the harm suffered, whilst acknowledging the rights of those who have inflicted the harm, that needs to be addressed in order to achieve a fairer system (Tapley 2003).

However, contrary to Fattah's fears, research undertaken in the United States indicates that the introduction of legislative reforms can have surprisingly little impact upon the criminal justice system. In particular, it found that implementation depends primarily upon the attitudes of criminal justice professionals and that the lack of legal sanctions often results in victims' rights remaining privileges to be granted or denied (Kelly 1990, Kelly and Erez 1997). This demonstrates that legislative changes will have little impact unless accompanied by attitudinal changes within organizational cultures, which later research has proved to be a far more difficult task to achieve (Tapley 2003).

The Victim's Charter and its impact

Whilst none of the reforms in the UK were legislated for, the stated aims and purposes underpinning these reforms contributed further to the growing awareness concerning the needs and rights of victims. As a consequence, during the 1990s the terminology of rights became synonymous with victims of crime. Perhaps the most significant of victim reforms was the Victim's Charter initiative, which refashioned victims of crime as the consumers of criminal justice services (Crawford and Enterkin 1999). This consumerist perspective conformed to the wider Citizen's Charter initiative, introduced in 1988 by John Major's Conservative government. The Citizen's Charter aimed not only to improve service delivery, but additionally to impose a new culture upon public sector agencies, one of 'customer service' (Bellamy and Greenaway 1995: 479).

The first Victim's Charter was published in 1990 (Home Office 1990). Whilst it was acknowledged as a significant move in the right direction, commentators concluded that the lack of legislative backing undermined its presentation as a *statement of rights*. Instead, they argued that the Charter represented more accurately a code of practice, i.e. a statement of 'moral rights' rather than legal ones (Spicker 1988, cited in Mawby and Walklate 1994: 171). The lack of accountability should any agency fail to meet its responsibilities was a further limitation to the effectiveness of the Charter, as was the failure of the government to provide any additional resources with which to facilitate the shift in practices required.

Fenwick (1995) therefore argued that whilst recent years had seen a number of developments which gave rise to the notion that in some sense victims have 'rights', these were 'seriously misleading, merely providing minimal, inexpensive and unenforceable entitlements' (Fenwick 1995: 845).

In fact, the criminal justice agencies were under no legal duty to ensure that victims had access to the services under the Charter and there was no recourse for victims should they be breached. Of course, a necessary prerequisite of exercising one's rights is having knowledge of them in the first place. As previously observed by Marshall (1975: 207, cited in Williams 1999: 74): 'Citizens only have rights if they are aware of what these rights are, believe in the authenticity of such rights and have the skills needed to exercise them.' Therefore, having the knowledge and ability to complain is based upon the assumption that victims are aware of the existence of such entitlements. However, as noted by Williams (1999b), although the Charter is available on demand from Victim Support schemes, police stations, the Home Office and more latterly the internet, its existence and purpose are not widely known outside these agencies. Consequently, as observed by Ashworth (1998: 64), when right-holders are not informed of their rights, 'it undermines the very value that the right was intended to respect'.

This increasingly political and controversial debate concerning victims' rights during the 1990s subsequently made the politically neutral stance adopted by one of the UK's most influential victim interest groups, Victim Support, harder to maintain. Whilst Victim Support welcomed the intentions outlined in the Victim's Charter, it proposed that a series of important questions remained unanswered, and subsequently adopted a more assertive strategy concerning not only the needs of victims, but also directly addressing the issue of victims' rights. With the publication in 1995 of its policy paper entitled *The Rights of Victims of Crime* (Victim Support 1995), Victim Support committed itself to the view that affording victims rights would assist in improving and protecting their position in the criminal justice process. As such, the policy document contains a statement of the rights to which Victim Support believes all victims of crime are fundamentally entitled. By focusing on the experiences of crime victims and witnesses within the criminal justice system, it concludes:

> The state's concern to deal with the offender while at the same time protecting his/her human rights needs to be matched by a similar concern for the victim. The loss of public confidence in the criminal justice system depends mainly on the way people are treated when they are required to take part in the criminal justice process, and it is here that there is particular scope for improvement. (Victim Support 1995: 4)

As a result of the growing momentum in favour of victims and in response to criticisms of the first Victim's Charter, the government published a revised version in 1996, re-entitled *A Statement of Service Standards for Victims of Crime* (Home Office 1996). Whilst its provisions are more extensive and specific than its predecessor it is important to note the subtle change in terminology adopted by the revised Charter, from 'a statement of *rights*' to 'a statement of *service standards*'. In particular, this bestows upon victims a status not as citizens with *rights*, but as consumers of *services*, thus subtly weakening their access to these entitlements. This, Fenwick (1997) argues, reveals the apparent paradox of the current rights-based approach, in that it still denies the possibility of individual action as a means of enforcing the rights. Although the revised Charter does include a general grievance procedure, this advises victims to complain directly to the agency with which they have a complaint. However, it could be argued that expecting already disempowered individuals to complain about the services of a powerful criminal justice institution is unrealistic, especially when they are confused as to what those services should be and what exactly their entitlements are. This is indicative of a process that intentionally constructs victims as 'passive consumers', whilst the political rhetoric expressly intimates their status as citizens with enforceable entitlements (Tapley 2003).

It can be argued that the terminology of the Victim's Charters, switching from one of advocating rights to that of providing service standards, reflects the lack of theoretical coherence underpinning the reforms and the redefinition of victims as consumers not citizens. As a consequence, attempts to implement the reforms have been ambiguous and slow, relying on the discretion of those agencies involved and a competition for scarce resources between achieving organizational needs under new managerialist principles and attending to the needs of victims. Instead of reforms being based upon clear theoretical principles, with victims regarded as citizens with valid entitlements to justice, they were imposed upon the principles of managerial justice, whereby victims are regarded as the passive consumers of discretionary and unaccountable services (Tapley 2003).

In an attempt to explore the impact of these reforms, I undertook a qualitative, longitudinal study, focusing on the ability of the criminal justice agencies to fulfil their responsibilities towards victims, as outlined in the Victim's Charter and the associated documents (Tapley 2003). The study focused on the experiences of victims of violent crime and revealed that whilst 73 per cent of the research population were satisfied with their initial contact with the police, lack of information as their cases progressed through the criminal process remained the primary cause of victim dissatisfaction (Tapley 2003). In particular, the research found that the information victims require falls into two main categories: (1) practical information and advice about the criminal justice process itself and the procedures involved; (2) specific information relating to their case.

The importance victims attach to being kept informed has been well documented in the studies of victims' needs since the mid-80s (Maguire and Bennett 1982, Shapland *et al* 1985). The main problems cited by victims have included lack of contact with the police, lack of information and a general feeling of being accorded low status by the criminal justice authorities (Victim Support 1995). In particular, victims of violent crime and crimes against the person have been found to experience further stress if they are not kept fully informed as to what is happening and why at all stages of the criminal process, both pre- and post-trial (Newburn and Merry 1990).

As identified earlier by Shapland *et al* (1985: 92), people's attitudes and judgements of satisfaction are based on expectations and these, in turn, are to some extent a product of their own prior knowledge about what may happen. The lack of knowledge concerning the criminal justice system found in the earlier and more recent study illustrates clearly the need for the police and the courts not to presume that victims will know what may happen and what his/her part in the proceedings will be.

Although the Home Office published its first *Victims of Crime* leaflet in 1994 (Home Office 1994), which provided a condensed version of the Victim's Charter and has since been regularly revised, together with a number of other leaflets providing information to victims and witnesses about different aspects of the criminal justice process, it is questionable as to how helpful these are to people who may be suffering from the initial trauma of victimization or the longer-term psychological effects (Zehr 1990, Norris, Kaniasty and Thompson 1997).

As acknowledged by Williams (1999b: 389): 'It is difficult to imagine distressed victims and survivors turning to this turgid, bureaucratic prose for relief.' This raises the important issue as to how information can best be effectively conveyed to victims, as the research highlights this as a substantial problem throughout the process. As acknowledged by Ashworth (1998: 64), greater attention needs to be devoted to techniques of communication, as 'being told is not the same as being caused to understand'.

By utilizing a qualitative longitudinal research design, necessitating repeat in-depth interviews at each stage of the criminal justice process, it was found that the greatest frustration experienced by the research participants was the inability to obtain information from the relevant agencies when it was needed (Tapley 2003). Consequently, there needs to be better communication between the different agencies concerned, but more importantly it needs to be clarified as to who is responsible for informing victims at the different stages of the case and that this responsibility be held accountable. This empirical study found that specific responsibilities become submerged beneath a hierarchy of bureaucratic documents, procedures and priorities. As a consequence, this bureaucratic response fails to acknowledge the victims' needs, focusing instead on organizational needs.

The study identified a need not only for more basic information about the criminal process and their case, but for the level of communication to be based upon a more humanist approach. Crucially, victims required somebody to talk to, an interactive response to assist them in their understanding of the complex legal processes involved. Whilst information leaflets can be a helpful additional tool, they do not provide an opportunity for an exchange of information. Most importantly, they cannot offer often anxious victims reassurance that their case is being dealt with and that somebody cares enough to be doing something about it (Tapley 2003).

Beyond the rhetoric

Despite two decades of increasing political rhetoric and reforms, the research found that victims were continuing to suffer secondary victimization by the process itself, due to their redefinition as consumers and the lack of status this provides within the criminal justice process. The study concluded that what victims require is information to be provided by a consistent, professional source that can be contacted and relied upon to provide up-to-date and accurate information when required. This suggests the need for one designated point of contact for victims, to be provided by individuals who are specifically trained to work with victims and have an understanding of both the impact of victimization and a thorough knowledge of the criminal justice process. This service could provide the bridge between the two parallel discourses identified between criminal justice professionals and victims, and would provide victims with access to a fair and balanced criminal justice process (Tapley 2003). Indicative of the research participants' lack of confidence in the CJS was their response when asked if they would report an offence again. No less than 84 per cent of the participants stated that they would only report an offence to the police again if it were very serious. The definition of 'serious' used by the participants tended to imply serious physical injury, which raises serious concerns bearing in mind that all the participants in the study were already the victims of a violent crime.

The apparent failure of reforms to be implemented based upon the provision of service standards indicates the need for victim entitlements to be placed upon a statutory footing that holds the different criminal justice agencies accountable for their specific roles. As observed by Rock (1999), up until now reforms have been more aspirational than practical in character.

This evidence supports the arguments of those who have suggested that the politicization of victims' issues has been a relatively cheap and convenient ploy to divert attention away from the other failings of the criminal justice system. However, whilst this may have been the original motivation, the ploy has certainly backfired over recent years due to an increasing demand for victims to be accorded legislative rights. Instead of pacifying victim advocates, the increasing focus on victims has drawn even greater attention to the distinct imbalance between the rights of defendants and the absence of rights for victims, contributing to the growing public dissatisfaction with the CJS as a whole.

Despite statistical evidence that crime rates are falling (Dodd, Nicholas, Povey and Walker 2004), fear of crime among individuals and communities remains high, further evidenced by research that indicates a lack of public confidence in the CJS. Measures of public confidence are taken by the BCS, which in 2000 found that although 69 per cent of respondents were confident that the system respects the rights of the accused and treats them fairly, only 26 per cent were confident that it meets the needs of victims. Furthermore:

> Having been a victim of crime reported to the police at some time is highly related to a lack of confidence that the criminal justice system meets the needs of victims or delivers justice. Generally, having had contact with the system at some time appears to decrease confidence. (Mirrlees-Black 2001: 6)

Research undertaken by the Institute of Public Policy Research (2001), entitled *Reluctant Witness*, revealed a shocking apathy towards the CJS. The study found that one in ten Britons would not even bother to report a murder they had witnessed, 69 per cent would not call the police if they heard screaming from their neighbours and 70 per cent would not report a street brawl. The report stated that people are frightened of retribution, anxious about how police and the courts would treat them, and did not actually fancy the inconvenience (Institute of Public Policy Research 2001).

Thus, despite a plethora of initiatives introduced to improve the services offered to victims of crime, victims feel unsupported and alienated by the whole process, illustrating that whilst possible solutions have been produced *rhetorically*, these have not resulted in an increased responsiveness to victims' needs in *reality* (Tapley 2003). These findings have been supported by the Audit Commission, in which their report found public confidence is continuing to fall. In 2002/2003 only 30 per cent felt that the system met the needs of victims, compared with 34 per cent in 2001/2002 (Audit Commission 2003).

As a consequence of this evidence, the true extent of victim and witness dissatisfaction has now gained some political acceptance, with the realization that the CJS relies on the goodwill of members of the public, and in particular victims, to apprehend, prosecute and punish those who commit criminal offences. The now apparent unwillingness of victims and members of the public to participate in the criminal justice process and an acknowledgement of the importance of their role was finally recognized in the objectives outlined in the *Criminal Justice System Strategic Plan 1999–2002* (Home Office 1999: 1):

> The criminal justice system stands or falls on whether it jointly meets what people can reasonably expect of it – victims, witnesses, jurors and the wider public – whose confidence and trust need to be earned, and interests respected.

Addressing the needs of victims and witnesses is now routinely recognized as a central objective of the criminal justice system, outlined by Tony Blair in his foreword to *Cutting Crime, Delivering Justice: A Strategic Plan for Criminal Justice 2004–08* (Office of Criminal Justice Reform 2004: 5):

> We start with one overriding principle – that the law abiding citizen must be at the heart of our criminal justice system. For too long, that was far from the case. The system seemed to think only about the rights of the accused. The interests of victims appeared to be an afterthought, if considered at all. This whole programme amounts to a modernising and rebalancing of the entire criminal justice system in favour of victims and the community.

It can be argued, therefore, that steadily declining public confidence in the ability of the criminal justice system to deal effectively with crime and, in particular, to assist those most affected by it, has caused the state to reflect quite intently upon its own policies and practices. This has been evidenced in a number of important documents published, all of which focus on attempts to reform and modernize the criminal justice system. These include the Narey Report (1997), the Glidewell Report (1998), the Halliday Report (2001) and the Report by Lord Justice Auld (2001). Auld (2001) acknowledges that whilst the rights of the defendant as a citizen must be protected, the current system pursues this without due consideration for the rights and protection of the victim.

In response to the recommendations of Lord Justice Auld's Report (Auld 2001), ACPO launched an initiative entitled *The Search for the Truth* (ACPO 2002). This describes the culture of the criminal trial as a tactical game played between lawyers rather than a search for the truth, with the cumulative effect of providing a hostile environment for victims and witnesses. It is this emphasis within the courts and legal culture that is blocking current attempts to integrate a victim perspective, and thus contributing to the implementation failure of reforms (Tapley 2003).

In addition to these wider attempts to modernize the criminal justice system, reports have also been published focusing specifically on victims and witnesses. These include the report on the treatment of vulnerable or intimidated witnesses (Home Office 1998), the introduction of special measures in courts by the Youth Justice and Criminal Evidence Act (1999), the introduction of Victim Personal Statements (Home Office 2001), a new role for the CPS involving direct communication with victims (CPS 2001a, 2001b) and, finally, a consultation paper reviewing the Victim's Charter (Home Office *et al* 2001).

The review of the Victim's Charter initiatives summarized what it somewhat optimistically described as the 'progress' the government has made so far in providing better services to victims and stated its intention to look to the future by considering further improvements (Home Office 2001). These included the possible introduction of statutory rights for victims and the establishment of a Victims' Ombudsman to investigate complaints and to champion victims' interests. Professing 'greater awareness of the rights, duties and expectations of victims of crime' (Home Office 2001: 4), the document set out what the government believed should be the guiding principles of the new Charter, together with the responsibilities of the relevant agencies. In addition, the document responded to criticisms of the format of the previous Charter and suggested ways in which this could be improved.

The government further announced its intentions with the publication of the White Paper *Justice for All* the aims of which are 'to rebalance the system in favour of victims, witnesses and communities and to deliver justice for all, by building greater trust and credibility' (Home Office 2002: 1). The proposals included the establishment of a Victims' Commissioner, supported by a new National Victims' Advisory Panel, and the introduction of more measures for vulnerable and intimidated witnesses.

This was followed by the publication of a national strategy to deliver improved services to victims, entitled *A New Deal for Victims and Witnesses* (Home Office 2003a). The strategy incorporates the two Public Service Agreement targets for the criminal justice agencies, to bring more offenders to justice and to improve public confidence, stating that improving services to victims and witnesses is key to delivering both these targets.

To achieve these targets and as part of its wider process of reforms to modernize the criminal justice system, the government published a national framework document in 2003 entitled *Improving Public Satisfaction and Confidence in the Criminal Justice System* (Home Office 2003b). This document acknowledges that low confidence means that the public are less likely to report crimes, lack of local intelligence makes it harder to detect crime, victims and witnesses are less willing to give evidence in court, and the recruitment and retention of criminal justice professionals is made more difficult when the agencies are not held in high esteem. The document identifies key points that affect satisfaction and confidence and outlines five performance areas that Local Criminal Justice Boards are responsible for improving. These comprise staff engagement, community engagement (with a focus on race issues), communications, increasing victim and witness satisfaction and increasing overall public confidence.

Local Criminal Justice Boards (LCJBs) were newly formed in April 2003, replacing the Trials Issues Groups. The 42 boards represent a multi-agency approach to improving the criminal justice process locally and in each area consist of all the chief officers in every criminal justice agency, including the police, the CPS, the Crown and magistrates courts, probation, prisons, the Witness Service and Victim Support. Each LCJB has been tasked to increase confidence and satisfaction locally by raising the standards of each agency, improving provision of services and in commissioning services to meet the needs of victims and the local community. Very recently I undertook research on behalf of one LCJB to assist in the development of its delivery plan, as required by the Home Office (2003b). The research involved an audit of victim and witness services provided by local statutory and voluntary agencies, and a witness satisfaction survey (Tapley 2005a; 2005b).

A recent initiative to improve victim and witness satisfaction, following on from the recommendations of earlier research (Tapley 2003) is the establishment of Witness Care Units. These are to be introduced nationally in 2005, following five pilot studies under the *No Witness, No Justice* project, (Criminal Justice System 2004). The main aim of the Witness Care Units is to provide one point of contact for victims and witnesses who are required to attend court to ensure that their needs are met and to enable more victims and witnesses to give evidence. The project involved five pilot areas and, although a final evaluation of the scheme was still pending, additional funding was announced in February 2004 so that the Witness Care Units could be introduced nationally in 2005. This further reflects the haste with which some initiatives are announced, without due consideration of the full costs and implications for those agencies required to implement them.

To improve public confidence and encourage wider community engagement, the criminal justice agencies are also being required actively to consult and communicate with local communities. Some local partnerships have already been achieved through the creation of local Crime and Disorder Reduction Partnerships, introduced by the Crime and Disorder Act (1998), which placed a responsibility upon local authorities to reduce crime in local communities (see Loveday, this volume). Figures have recently been published detailing the performance of the LCJBs one year on, with the Attorney General, Lord Goldsmith (2004) claiming:

> The LCJBs are the visible proof of the criminal justice agencies working effectively together to make communities safe. The Boards have made significant progress over the last year, helping to bring more offences to justice and fewer ineffective trials.

These initiatives should now be further strengthened by the changes in legislation being introduced by the Domestic Violence, Crime and Victims Act, which gained Royal Assent in November 2004. Focusing on domestic violence, the government claims that this Act will overhaul domestic violence law, providing the police and the courts with tougher powers to protect victims and prosecute the perpetrators (Tapley 2005a). Section 13 of the Act requires the Home Secretary to publish a Code of Practice for victims. This outlines the obligations of the CJS agencies and, where a victim's right under the Code is breached, it details the complaints procedure and referral to the Independent Commissioner for Victims and Witnesses, an appointment established by the bill to give a voice to victims in Parliament.

At the time of writing, the Code of Practice remains an indicative draft, awaiting the outcome of the consultation process. However, the responsibilities place a considerable burden upon all the criminal justice agencies and will have serious implications for additional training and resources. Earlier research has demonstrated that failure to implement previous initiatives has been due to the haste with which they have been introduced and a lack of necessary resources to support them, thus seriously undermining the abilities of the relevant agencies to implement the required practices (Tapley 2003). Whilst concerns have already been raised by criminal justice professionals regarding their ability to meet the requirements of the Code within existing resources, little response has been received from the central government. That casts doubt upon the government's commitment to ensuring that victims and witnesses really are to be placed at the centre of the criminal justice system.

Conclusion

As this chapter has demonstrated, there has been a plethora of initiatives and reforms aimed at improving services to victims and witnesses. The government now accepts that the CJS relies on the goodwill of the public, as victims and witnesses, to report and assist with the investigation and prosecution of offenders. By improving the experiences of victims and witnesses, the government is hoping to improve public confidence and satisfaction, to ensure that individuals and communities have access to justice. However, the research has indicated that the CJS still expects a great deal from victims and witnesses, whilst offering little in return. To ensure that community justice is achieved from a victim perspective, an improved criminal justice response is required, supported by sufficient resources and provided by a range of agencies, within the CJS and the wider community. The Domestic Violence, Crime and Victims Act (2004) promises to provide better protection and support to victims of crime, including better access to health services, housing and financial support. However, to succeed it is essential that the process not only considers the rights of the offender and organizational needs, but also respects the rights of the victims and witnesses and strives to ensure that justice can be accessed by all. The Code of Practice introduced by the new Act will provide the necessary framework outlining the statutory responsibilities of each agency. However, to be successful, a significant change in criminal justice professional cultures is still required, supported by the necessary resources to ensure that their responsibilities can be fulfilled. Continual monitoring and evaluation will be required to ensure that individuals and communities are aware of their statutory entitlements, thus ensuring that community justice is achieved – not just rhetorically, but in reality.

References

ACPO (2002) *The Search for the Truth,* ACPO Media Initiative, London, 10 January.

Adler, Z. (1987) *Rape on Trial.* London: Routledge and Kegan Paul.

Ashworth, A. (1983) *Sentencing and Penal Policy.* London: Weidenfeld and Nicholson.

Ashworth, A. (1998) *The Criminal Process.* Oxford: Oxford University Press.

Audit Commission (2003) *Victims and Witnesses: Providing Better Support.* London: Audit Commission.

Auld, Lord Justice. (2001) *Review of the Criminal Courts.* Available online: www.criminal-courts-review.org.uk.

Bellamy, R. and Greenaway, J. (1995) 'The New Right Conception of Citizenship and the Citizen's Charter', *Government and Opposition,* 30, Autumn: 469–91.

Bottoms, A.E. (1977) 'Reflections on the Renaissance of Dangerousness', *Howard Journal of Criminal Justice,* 16: 70–96.

Brody, S.R. (1976) *The Effectiveness of Sentencing: A Review of the Literature.* Home Office Research Study 35. London: HMSO.

Cayley, D. (1998) *The Expanding Prison: The Crisis in Crime and Punishment and the Search for Alternatives.* Cleveland, OH: Pilgrim Press.

Christie, N. (1977) 'Conflicts as Property', *British Journal of Criminology,* 17: 1–15.

Council of Europe (1985) *Recommendation No. R (85)11 of the Committee of Ministers to Member States on the Position of the Victim in the Framework of Criminal Law and Procedure.* Strasbourg, France: Council of Europe.

Crawford, A. and Enterkin, J. (1999) *Victim Contact Work and the Probation Service: A Study of Service Delivery and Impact.* Leeds: Centre for Criminal Justice Studies, University of Leeds.

Criminal Justice System (2004) *No Witness, No Justice,* CPS/ACPO/OPSR Victim and Witness Care Project. London: Criminal Justice System.

Crown Prosecution Service (2001a) *Strategic Plan 2001–04: Business Plan 2001–02,* London: Crown Prosecution Service.

Crown Prosecution Service (2001b) *CPS Gets Closer to the Community.* Available online: http://tap.ccta.gov.uk/cps/infoup, accessed 2 October 2001.

Dodd, T., Nicholas, S., Povey, D. and Walker, A. (2004) *Crime in England and Wales 2003/2004,* Home Office Statistical Bulletin 10/04. London: Home Office.

Driver, S. and Martell, L. (1997) 'New Labour's Communitarianisms', *Critical Social Policy,* 17: 27–46.

Elias, R. (1993) *Victims Still: The Political Manipulation of Crime Victims.* Newbury Park: Sage.

Fattah, E.A. (ed.) (1986) *From Crime Policy to Victim Policy.* London: Macmillan.

Fattah, E.A. (1992) *Towards a Critical Victimology.* London: Macmillan.

Fattah, E.A. (1997) 'Toward a Victim Policy Aimed at Healing, Not Suffering', in R.C. Davis, A.J. Lurigio and W.G. Skogan (eds), *Victims of Crime,* London: Sage Publications.

Fattah, E.A. (2000) 'Victimology: Past, Present and Future', *Criminologie,* 33: 17–46.

Fenwick, H. (1995) 'Rights of Victims in the Criminal Justice System: Rhetoric or Reality?' *Criminal Law Review:* 843–853.

Fenwick, H. (1997) 'Procedural "Rights" of Victims of Crime: Public or Private Ordering of the Criminal Justice Process?' *The Modern Law Review,* 60: 317–333.

Glidewell, I. (1998) *The Review of the Crown Prosecution Service: A Report,* Cmnd. 3960. London: HMSO.

Goldsmith, P. (2004) *Local Criminal Justice Boards Continue to Make Progress Against Key Government Targets.* Available online: cjsonline.gov.uk/the_cjs/whats_new/news_3044.html, accessed 27 October 2004.

Grimshaw, R. (1989) 'Booktalk: Policing', *Network* (BSA Newsletter), January: 13–14.

Halliday (2001) *Review of Sentencing.* Available online: www.homeoffice.gov.uk/cpg/halliday.htm.

Heater, D. (1990) *Citizenship: The Civic Ideal in World History. Politics and Education.* London: Longman.

Henderson, L.N. (1992) 'The Wrongs of Victims' Rights', in E.A. Fattah (ed.) *Towards a Critical Victimology.* London: Macmillan.

Home Office (1990) *Victim's Charter: A Statement of the Rights of Victims.* London: HMSO.

Home Office (1994) *Victims of Crime.* London: HMSO.

Home Office (1996) *Victim's Charter: A Statement of Service Standards for Victims of Crime.* London: HMSO.

Home Office (1998) *Speaking Up for Justice.* London: HMSO.

Home Office (1999) *Criminal Justice System Strategic Plan 1999–2002.* London: Home Office.

Home Office (2001) *The Victim Personal Statement Scheme: Guidance Note for Practitioners or Those Operating the Scheme.* London: HMSO.

Home Office (2002) *Justice for All,* White Paper. London: Home Office.

Home Office (2003a) *A New Deal for Victims and Witnesses: National Strategy to Deliver Improved Services.* London: Home Office.

Home Office (2003b) *Improving Public Satisfaction and Confidence in the Criminal Justice System.* London: Home Office.

Home Office, Lord Chancellor's Department and the Attorney-General (2001) *A Review of the Victim's Charter.* London: Home Office.

Hood, C. (1991) 'A Public Management for All Seasons?' *Public Administration,* 69: 3–19.

Hough, J.M and Mayhew, P. (1983) *The British Crime Survey: First Report,* Home Office Research Study 76. London: Home Office.

Institute of Public Policy Research (2001) *Reluctant Witness.* London: Institute of Public Policy Research.

Janoff-Bulman, R. (1985) 'The Aftermath of Victimization: Rebuilding Shattered Assumptions', in C. Figley (ed.), *Trauma and its Wake: The Study and Treatment of Post-traumatic Stress Disorder.* New York: Bruner/Mazel.

Jefferson, T. and Shapland, J. (1994) 'Criminal Justice and the Production of Order and Control: Criminological Research in the UK in the 1980s', *British Journal of Criminology,* 34: 265–290.

Kelly, D.P. (1990) 'Victim Participation in the Criminal Justice Systems', in R.C. Davis, A.J. Lurigio and W.G. Skogan (eds), *Victims of Crime: Problems, Policies and Programs.* Newbury Park, CA: Sage.

Kelly, D.P. and Erez, E. (1997) 'Victim Participation in the Criminal Justice System', in R.C. Davis, A.J. Lurigio and W.G. Skogan (eds), *Victims of Crime,* 2nd edition. Newbury Park, CA: Sage.

Lister, R. (1997) *Citizenship: Feminist Perspectives.* London: Macmillan.

Lurigio, A.J. (1987) 'Are all Victims Alike? The Adverse, Generalised, and Differential Impact of Crime', *Crime and Delinquency,* 33: 452–467.

Maguire, M. and Bennett, T. (1982) *Burglary in a Dwelling.* London: Heinemann.

Maguire, M. and Corbett, C. (1987) *The Effects of Crime and the Work of Victim Support Schemes.* Aldershot: Gower.

Mawby, R.I. and Gill, M. (1987) *Crime Victims: Needs, Services and the Voluntary Sector.* London: Tavistock.

Mawby, R.I. and Walklate, S. (1994) *Critical Victimology.* London: Sage.

Mirrlees-Black, C. (2001) *Confidence in the Criminal Justice System: Findings from the 2000 British Crime Survey,* Home Office Research, Development and Statistics Directorate, Research Findings 137. London: Home Office.

Narey (1997) *Review of Delay in Criminal Justice System.* Available online: www.homeoffice.gov.uk/cpd/pvu/crimerev.htm.

Newburn, T. and Merry, S. (1990) *Keeping in Touch – Police–Victim Communication in Areas,* Home Office Research Study 116. London: HMSO.

Norris, F.H., Kaniasty, K. and Thompson, M.P. (1997) 'The Psychological Consequences of Crime: Findings From a Longitudinal Population-Based Study', in R.C. Davis, A.J. Lurigio and W.G. Skogan (eds), *Victims of Crime.* London: Sage.

Office of Criminal Justice Reform (2004) *Cutting Crime, Delivering Justice: A Strategic*

Plan for Criminal Justice 2004–08. London: Home Office.

Phipps, A. (1988) 'Ideologies, Political Parties and Victims of Crime', in M. Maguire and J. Pointing (eds), *Victims of Crime: A New Deal?* Milton Keynes: Open University Press.

Priestly, P. and McGuire, J. (1995) 'Reviewing "What Works": Past, Present and Future', in J. McGuire (ed.), *What Works: Reducing Re-offending: Guidelines from Research and Practice.* Chichester: John Wiley and Sons Ltd.

Rock, P. (1990) *Helping Victims of Crime: The Home Office and the Rise of Victim Support in England and Wales.* Oxford: Clarendon Press.

Rock, P. (1999) 'Acknowledging Victims' Needs and Rights', *Criminal Justice Matters,* 35: 4–5.

Rose, N. (2000) 'Government and Control', in D. Garland and R. Sparks (eds), *Criminology and Social Theory.* New York: Oxford University Press.

Shapland, J. and Cohen, D. (1987) 'Facilities for Victims: The Role of the Police and the Courts', *Criminal Law Review:* 28–38.

Shapland, J., Willmore, J. and Duff, P. (1985) *Victims in the Criminal Justice System.* Aldershot: Gower.

Stanko, E. (1985) *Intimate Intrusions: Women's Experience of Male Violence.* London: Virago.

Stanko, E. (1988) 'Fear of Crime and the Myth of the Safe Home: A Feminist Critique of Criminology', in K. Yllo and M. Bograd (eds), *Feminist Perspectives on Wife Abuse.* London: Sage.

Stewart, J. and Walsh, K. (1992) 'Change in the Management of Public Services', *Public Administration,* 70: 499–518.

Tapley, J. (2003) *From 'Good Citizen' to 'Deserving Client': The Relationship Between Victims of Violent Crime and the State Using Citizenship as the Conceptualising Tool.* Unpublished PhD Thesis, University of Southampton.

Tapley, J. (2005a) 'Political Rhetoric and the Reality of Victims' Experiences – Findings from a Witness Satisfaction Survey', *The Prison Journal,* 158: 45–52.

Tapley, J. (2005b) 'Public Confidence Costs – Criminal Justice from a Victim's Perspective', *British Journal of Community Justice,* 3.2. pp. 25–37.

United Nations (1985) *Declaration of Basic Principles of Justice for Victims of Crime and Abuse of Power.* New York: UN Department of Public Information.

Van Dijk, J. (1988) 'Ideological Trends Within the Victims Movement: An International Perspective', in M. Maguire and J. Pointing (eds), *Victims of Crime: A New Deal?* Milton Keynes: Open University Press.

Victim Support (1995) *The Rights of Victims of Crime.* London: Victim Support.

Williams, B. (1999a) *Working with Victims of Crime: Policies, Politics and Practice.* London: Jessica Kingsley.

Williams, B. (1999b) 'The Victim's Charter: Citizens as Consumers of Criminal Justice Services', *The Howard Journal of Criminal Justice,* 38: 384–396.

Zedner, L. (1994) 'Victims', in M. Maguire, R. Morgan and R. Reiner (eds), *The Oxford Handbook of Criminology.* Oxford: Clarendon Press.

Zehr, H. (1990) *Changing Lenses: A New Focus for Crime and Justice.* Scottdale, PA: Herald Press.

Chapter 15

Is research working? Revisiting the research and effective practice agenda

James McGuire

Many academics and researchers hope that their findings will be of practical value and will inform the work of practitioners and policy-makers. Conversely, many of the latter look to the research community for information that will answer their questions or help to guide their decisions. But the process goes further than that; the traffic in ideas is not all one-way. Practice also guides research. Not only do its outcomes yield findings of interest to everyone involved, the resultant activity generates new questions. This happens in general terms, by placing certain themes or issues on the agenda. It also happens more specifically through the commissioning of particular projects. Such a reciprocal or symbiotic pattern typifies a large number of the advances made in many fields of inquiry.

This system of apparent shared benefit between what used to be called the 'pure' and 'applied' sectors of a field has been known by different names at different times. In recent years it has gone under the collective rubric of 'evidence-based practice'. It has attained high status in medicine and healthcare, and more recently in many sectors of social science, public policy and service provision. In my own profession of clinical psychology, a variant of the model known as the *scientist practitioner* has been regarded as a core value since the time of a landmark conference held in Boulder, Colorado in 1949 (Barker, Pistrang and Elliott 2002, Barlow, Hayes and Nelson 1984). Whilst it is not without its critics (Pilgrim and Treacher 1992) the model, similar to that of the *researcher practitioner* promoted for probation officers by the Home Office, remains central to the activities of many professionals, most of whom are not directly engaged in research.

So far so good: it looks like researchers and practitioners often enjoy a mutually beneficial relationship. However, attempting to discern the pathways of interaction between research findings and policy changes is a far from easy task. Close inspection shows that there is a plethora of interwoven complexities and crossover strands, and (to continue the weaving metaphor) untidy tangles, occasional knots, and broken threads. And then, of course (to do the metaphor to death), there are those who never wanted the carpet in the first place.

This chapter is focused on the question of how research evidence is used, with particular reference to the 'what works debate' as it has come to be familiarly known in the field of criminal justice. Perhaps now it is less of a debate than an 'agenda', as surely very few remain who doubt that there is convincing evidence of the possibility of reducing recidivism among persistent offenders. Nevertheless, several possibilities continue to raise questions and cause concern: that it has become a new orthodoxy with a restrictive focus (Rex 2001), that it represents an insidious form of social control (Kemshall 2002), that it is intrinsically oppressive (Boone 2004), and that maybe it does not work anyway (Merrington and Stanley 2004). Other chapters of this book have dissected various aspects of these criticisms. The objective of the present one is to consider gaps and obstacles in transferring research findings into practice, and where feasible, consider ways of overcoming them.

It is possible to approach this in several ways, and in what follows, we will begin by asking how we got where we are now. This entails a brief résumé of the background to the current usage of research findings in community justice, referring most closely to the United Kingdom. However, many of the considerations also apply to other countries where similar questions have arisen. Of necessity within the confines of a book chapter written by one individual, this account is highly condensed and subjective. The second main section of the chapter will examine some specific dimensions of the research–practice relationship that may help to furnish an answer to the question of whether research is 'working' as best it might.

Applying research in community justice

Leading reviewers of the history of penology in western societies have noted that for a period of 150 years or more – from approximately the early nineteenth century to the last quarter of the twentieth – it was thought possible to 'reform the offender' (Gaes 1998). This is in contrast to the prevalent ethos of the preceding era, during which the concept of retribution predominated (Walker 1991). Then, the social order was maintained through the ritualized, public infliction of pain and humiliation. At the beginning of the nineteenth century, in conjunction with many other social changes, a new epoch arrived, focused on restricting the freedom and controlling the activities and daily routines of those who had broken the law – usually by incarcerating them in large institutions (Foucault 1977). Towards the beginning of the twentieth century, a further evolution took place, to rescue offenders from the hardships of imprisonment, and help them with the problems that were thought to have driven them to crime, a movement that has been called 'penal welfarism' (Bottoms, Rex and Robinson 2004).

Research reviews and penal policies

During the twentieth century a growing number of studies appeared, reporting on evaluations of the impact of various interventions designed to reduce criminal recidivism. That work was extensively reviewed for the first time on any sizeable scale during the third quarter of the century. In the United States, the government of New York State commissioned a report on the effectiveness of rehabilitation with offenders. Although work towards this began in 1968, its final version incorporating the findings of 231 outcome studies was not published in book form until the mid-1970s (Lipton, Martinson and Wilks 1975). At approximately the same time, the Home Office in the United Kingdom undertook a similar project to review the outcome of 100 studies on the effectiveness of sentencing (Brody 1976).

The authors of both reviews found the research to be plagued with problems, with poor-quality designs and insufficient information on the nature of interventions. They felt compelled to conclude that little or nothing had been shown to work to achieve the intended objectives of rehabilitation or reducing criminal recidivism. The absence of clear, easily interpretable findings notwithstanding, these reviews were massively influential. Many commentators attribute the farthest-reaching influence to a journal paper by Martinson (1974). Although some researchers challenged its negative conclusions, and drew attention to positive findings that had been neglected (Gendreau and Ross 1980), neither their objections nor Martinson's (1979) later withdrawal of those conclusions had any impact on the direction of public policy, which appeared wholeheartedly to absorb the 'nothing works' dictum.

Gaes has described the publication of the Martinson (1974) paper as 'a watershed event' (Gaes 1998: 713). On the basis of the bleak claims made within it, the idea of rehabilitation was, if not entirely banished, at least relegated in the scale of priorities in the minds of many practitioners and academics (Bottoms and McWilliams 1979, Raynor and Vanstone 1994, Vanstone 2000). The ensuing period was marked by a pronounced trend towards more punitive sentencing, resulting in a dramatic rise in the usage of imprisonment, most meteorically in the United States (Wacquant 2005, Zimring and Hawkins 1994).

Among many liberal thinkers, it has become customary to place the blame for the escalating harshness and 'penal nihilism' of the subsequent era on these research reviews. But the dynamics of that process and the pattern of influences at work may not be quite so simple. First, contemporaneously with the above reviews, another significant book also appeared in the mid-1970s. This reported on the work of the United States Committee on the Study of Incarceration (von Hirsch 1976). Approaching the field from a different perspective, its authors too concluded that offender rehabilitation or 'treatment' were failed endeavours. The Committee advocated a justice policy based on desert and deterrence, and forwarded a series of arguments for the application of proportionality in sentencing. The key message widely perceived to be emanating from it, however, was that positive efforts to reduce criminal recidivism were fruitless.

But second, and in contrast to the standard view that the growth of punitive sanctions and a general 'get-tough' ethos was the result of the conclusion that nothing works, Andrews and Bonta (2003) have contended that the real culprit of the time was the then pervasive 'theoreticism' of sociological criminology. By this they mean the intensely intellectualized focus on linguistic and cultural analysis of deviance, coupled with a relentless re-examination and rejection of conventional definitions of crime, and exploration of how such constructions and categories are a product of wider social processes. For several decades from the 1970s onwards, the mainstream sociological study of deviance had at best a distant relationship with everyday events, whether outside on the streets or inside the criminal justice system. This profound disconnection and that vacuum, argue Andrews and Bonta, had as much to do with the authoritarian direction of penal policy as the evidence that was assumed to show that 'nothing works'.

There is another paradox in the supposed impact of these reviews. Both Martinson (1974, 1979) and von Hirsch (1976) made it quite clear in their writings that imprisonment did not work. Neither saw any advantage in increased use of it. The former concluded firmly that there was no evidence of an association between recidivism and the length of prison sentences. The latter strongly recommended 'stringent limitations' on the usage of imprisonment. It is salutary to note that this conclusion has been repeated with almost unremitting monotony since the very arrival of the modern prison. Foucault (1976: 264) has described how, after its introduction in France, 'the prison, in its reality and visible effects, was denounced at once as the great failure of penal justice'. Critiques of its methods and its effects appeared very early on, during the period 1820–1845. Given that reports on this matter have now been conveying the same essential message for over 180 years, the powers-that-be in society seem chronically prone to highly selective listening.

The re-emergence of 'rehabilitation'

Following the gloomy conclusions of the 1970s outlined above, the 'official' rediscovery of the possibility that offending behaviour could be reduced was a gradual, halting process. From the mid-1980s onwards, however, the balance of evidence slowly began to shift more strongly towards the view that beliefs in the failure of rehabilitation had been misplaced. Today, recurrent critiques and some disappointing results notwithstanding, we can be more confident than ever about the basic thesis that 'offender rehabilitation has been, can be and will be achieved. The principles underlying effective rehabilitation generalize across far too many intervention strategies and offender samples to be dismissed as trivial' (Gendreau and Ross 1987: 395).

This evidence has been surveyed and consolidated in a number of places as it has continued to accumulate (e.g. Andrews and Bonta 2003, MacKenzie 2002, McGuire 1995a, 2002, 2004, Motiuk and Serin 2001) and will be discussed only briefly here as a context for other points to follow. As must by now be well known, an important factor in bringing about change was the application of meta-analytic review to the relevant research literature from 1985 onwards. Findings are now available from no fewer than 52 meta-analyses, and numerous primary studies and several new integrative reviews are published every year. With the advent of the Campbell Collaboration, concerted efforts are under way to synthesize findings from the most rigorously designed studies in more precisely delineated areas (Farrington and Petrosino 2001). Nevertheless some authors have continued to regard the empirical base with disbelief and derision (Mair 2004) and dismissal of it has been enshrined in resolutions at the annual conferences of the National Association of Probation Officers. According to more detached assessments, however, 'the extreme scepticism still shown by some commentators...can no longer be regarded as realistic' (Raynor 2004a: 199).

Impact on community sentencing

These disputes supply a broad framework within which the movement of probation services towards the use of research evidence has taken place. But we need also to locate them within a political context, with particular reference to England and Wales. From approximately 1990 onwards, the probation service there found itself in a gradually more threatened position. The Conservative government had come to power in 1979 with a mandate to reduce taxation and cut public expenditure. Its monetarist economic policies resulted in detailed scrutiny of all elements of government spending and a radicalized emphasis on achieving 'value for money'. One by one, major services were either sold to the private sector or required to make 'efficiency savings'. The turn of the probation service came with the publication in 1989 of a report by the Audit Commission, a semi-autonomous agency that monitors the spending of local government departments. This was in many respects a decisive moment in the service's history. The report concluded that:

> While there is a striking variety of probation schemes in operation involving much vision, creativity and imagination, these schemes must be evaluated and their impact on offending behaviour assessed. It is unsatisfactory that at present considerable sums are spent with relatively little understanding of the effects achieved. (Audit Commission 1989: 2)

During Michael Howard's tenure as Home Secretary between 1993 and 1997, the probation service reputedly came close to extinction. It was widely rumoured that he thought private security companies could perform its key tasks both more effectively and more economically. The core issue was the lack of any evidence that probation provided a good public service, and Howard believed that whereas prison 'worked', probation did not. It is easy to say that such arguments should have been resisted: many attempts were made to do so. But the strong ideological drive was not to be diverted. If the then Chief Inspector of Probation, Sir Graham Smith, had not defended probation by drawing on the 'what works' research, the service might well have been abolished.

Findings from the latter research were highlighted through a series of conferences known by the title 'What Works' which began in 1990 with a regional event in the north-west of England. This was followed by national conferences, with speakers from both the UK and overseas, in 1991, 1992, 1994, 1996 and 1998. All were held in Manchester though an additional conference on a slightly different theme, entitled 'Does Punishment Work?' was held in London in 1995. These events were not, as some believe, sponsored by the Home Office as part of a 'top-down' process of persuading probation officers to change their practices. Quite the reverse: the entire initiative was practitioner-led. Membership of the conference planning group evolved over successive years but consisted almost entirely of probation or social work staff.

One objective of the conferences was to try to integrate research and practice, usually combining keynote speeches by leading researchers with practice workshops exemplifying activities that had been or were being evaluated. Another objective was to influence the criminal justice establishment towards applying the available evidence: hence the publication of various conference proceedings in book form (McGuire 1995a, McGuire and Rowson 1996, Rowson and McGuire 1991, 1996). For the 1996 conference, possibly a high-water mark, keynote speakers included the then Chief Inspector of Probation (Sir Graham Smith), the Director-General of the Prison Service (Richard Tilt), and the Shadow Home Secretary (Jack Straw) who was widely expected, as it turned out correctly, to take up the substantive post were Labour to win the 1997 general election.

During the later 1990s a considerable amount of energy was expended within the Home Office to weigh up the mounting research and distil its messages into implications for policy. This may also have been influenced by an earlier, penetrating analysis of reconviction data showing no evidence of differential effectiveness of different types of sentences for adults (Lloyd, Mair and Hough 1994). Reviews of the 'reducing re-offending' research literature and of specific forms of intervention were carried out. One focused on direct work with offenders (Vennard, Sugg and Hedderman 1997). Another spanned a wider range of criminal justice activities, including police work, using a series of presentations at a specially convened seminar held, for the convenience of international contributors, in a hotel at Heathrow airport (Goldblatt and Lewis 1998).

Subsequently, the embryonic National Probation Service commissioned literature and 'best practice' reviews of its own (Underdown 1998) and also sought to discern implications for practice (Chapman and Hough 1998). The net result of these and other deliberations was the commencement of the Effective Practice Initiative, the inception of the Crime Reduction Programme and, at an operational level, the advent of the 'Pathfinder' programmes (formally announced at the 1998 What Works conference, the last run by the original planning group). There were subsequent consultations of a more organizational nature, on the possible (as of 2004, actual) convergence of the prison and probation services, together with reviews of sentencing, which are the concern of other chapters in this volume (see Lewis this volume, Gough, this volume).

The above is an over-simplified, perhaps even crude rendering of the events through which research findings were absorbed into policy formation, and it departs from other versions of what occurred at that time. For example, the sequence can be portrayed as a process of 'appropriation by the centre' of the outcome evidence, 'to legitimise and operationalise a risk-management approach' (Robinson 2001: 244). That may have been partly, maybe even solely, driven by a quest for more efficient resource management. In turn it had deeper implications for the balance of 'technicality' versus 'discretion' in the professional role of the probation officer and the possibility that this was to be reduced to that of a 'competent functionary'.

But like any other large-scale developments in government policy, the more sweeping changes in organizational structures and in sentencing policy and practice were influenced by many factors. Given their scope, it seems unlikely that the research evidence on reducing recidivism played a particularly significant part in them. It is far more likely that they were driven by broader considerations, including perceived public opinion, and pressures from the media. From approximately the year 2000 onwards, community sentences for offenders were subject to probably the largest experiment of its kind ever undertaken: as Raynor aptly depicts it, 'recent history's most spectacular example of a wholesale conversion to evidence-based practice' (2004b: 161). Alongside many other innovations, four novel types of intervention were implemented on a hitherto unprecedented scale, and research commissioned to evaluate them (Hollin *et al* 2002, Hollin *et al* 2004, Lewis *et al* 2003, McMahon *et al* 2004, Rex *et al* 2004). At the time of writing, portions of that work are still in progress.

Dimensions of the research–practice relationship

The foregoing narrative illustrates some of the vagaries of translating a body of research findings into usable 'messages' for practice and policy. Let us consider the central theme of this chapter from a different standpoint. What factors influence the way research is used, with special reference to the above background? There are of course many possible answers to that question. The second half of this chapter will focus on just four principal dimensions of them. They comprise first, limitations in the evidence base underpinning 'what works'; second, the problem of implementation; third, a mixture of myths and misunderstandings over the nature of the basic ideas; and fourth, a cluster of more diffuse problems that I will place under the collective heading of cultural and ideological resistance.

Limitations of the evidence base

A first obstacle to applying research to practice is that, at any given point in time, any field of research and the 'body of knowledge' associated with it are likely to have helped answer some questions but not others. The accumulation of systematized knowledge and understanding is a tentative, painstaking process. This applies even more in the social than in the physical, biological or environmental sciences. To begin with, the resources available for social research are paltry by comparison with the sums spent in the so-called 'hard' sciences. It is inconceivable in social science that hundreds of millions of pounds could be written off at a single stroke as has happened more than once with the explosion of *Ariane* satellite-bearing rockets.

From a context in which the officially and widely held view was that 'nothing works' to reduce re-offending, the initial priority was to communicate the finding that it is possible to support and engender change in individuals who have repeatedly broken the law. The dismissal of that possibility has profound implications for how justice is administered. When the findings of meta-analytic reviews first began to be disseminated therefore, researchers themselves pointed out that conclusions gained from the technique were typically 'general and broadbrush, as is appropriate from a meta-analytic base which aggregates over a wide range of studies' (Lipsey 1995: 78).

The clearest and most consistent trends to emerge from the earlier meta-analytic reviews established first, that rehabilitative efforts generally 'worked' as a means of reducing offender recidivism, and second, that certain methods were more reliable for achieving this than others. Drawing these results to the attention of the probation community, some crucial assumptions were made. The most important was that, having been (up to that point) primarily trained in social work, and thereby in the process of engaging with individuals and building working alliances with them, probation officers would use the more effective approaches as an adjunct to their existing skills. The methods would, in other words, constitute an extension of or an addition to their repertoire. No one anticipated that the delivery of programmes could somehow replace professional skills and expertise. Competence in relating to others was viewed as vital to the application of effective interventions (Gendreau 1996).

Understandably, once having taken the broad findings seriously, many managers and practitioners wished to interrogate the research for more finely tuned indicators. From a very early stage research was sometimes criticized as inadequate, as it could not specify 'what works with whom under what conditions', or other details, in all the requisite permutations. If a given method had never been tested in a particular setting, as was often the case, there was no information with a direct bearing on the question of whether it would 'work'. It might be possible to extrapolate to some extent from available studies, but that had to be done with caution. In the absence of firm guidance from research, an alternative direction would have been for practitioners to carry out their own evaluative work (McIvor 1995) but the extent to which that option was taken up remained limited.

In the intervening period, however, many more studies have been published and meta-analysed, and this has led to further refinements in the evidence base. Reviews are now available covering a wide range of types of offences separately or in combination (generic offending, drink-driving, violence, domestic violence, sexual assault, substance abuse), the effects of variations among participants (with respect to age, gender and ethnicity; see below), and on different methods of intervention (cognitive skills training, interpersonal skills training, anger management, relapse prevention, family-based work, therapeutic communities, educational and vocational programmes, school-based programmes, restorative justice, and deterrence).

Implementation

In another respect, however, the findings of the large-scale reviews and the process of trying to apply them to practice revealed a sizeable gap. Most of the primary studies that supported conclusions regarding 'what works' were essentially tests of various methods of intervention. They often contained other types of information, for example on the characteristics of the participants, on intermediate variables such as attitudes or skills, or on duration or intensity of services. Often, though, their main focus remained the 'treatment modality' (Lipsey 1995).

Thus the second obstacle to applying research findings was that by comparison, there was a relative dearth of evidence on the process of implementation. How do we transfer lessons learnt from research into practical settings, taking into account the influence of the local context on how work progresses, and on its likely outcomes? The importance of this issue was realized by Martinson: 'The critical fact seems to be the *conditions* under which the program is delivered' (1979: 254, italics in original).

Although Gendreau, Goggin and Smith (1999) acknowledged that this issue was neglected, it had not been entirely ignored, and progressively more attention has been paid to aspects of it. Roberts (1995) proposed a framework for locating the more intensive offending behaviour programmes alongside other types of service provided to offenders on probation. Palmer (1996) forwarded evidence-based proposals concerning the need to attend to offender characteristics, staff–client interactions, and agency settings when delivering programmes, and advocated a stepwise approach to the process of doing so. Harris and Smith described a series of 'conditions conducive to effective implementation' (1996: 191) that distinguished success from failure when absorbing and applying messages from research and engendering change in agencies. Gendreau, *et al* (2002) have reviewed a wide range of literature relevant to this and strengthened and augmented these sets of advice. The series of specifications or recommendations made by Andrews (1995, 2001) has also evolved and expanded over time.

Some authors have presented models of the connections that need to be made between programmes and other aspects of an agency's work if research-based knowledge is to be deployed appropriately and effectively. Bernfeld, Blase and Fixsen (1990) outlined a 'behavioural systems perspective' that entails considering four aspects of innovation and evaluation of effectiveness: client, programme, organization, and society. Further, it is imperative to view these system components as engaged in dynamic interaction over time. In implementing 'what works' findings in the UK, it may be that the second element has been highlighted at the expense of the other three. Harris and Smith (1996) developed a model of the 'mutual adaptation' process that needs to occur as a programme interacts with its organizational environment. More recently, Bernfeld, Farrington and Leschied (2001) have published an edited volume containing several illustrations of the difficulties likely to arise during implementation. Drawing on the benefits of practical experience, this also yields guidance regarding how to address such problems and where possible to surmount them.

However, these aspects of the outcome research played little or no part in the major departures that were made in probation in England and Wales at the turn of the century, the sheer magnitude of which took virtually everyone by surprise. For example, it is reported that the Home Office's then Director of Research and Statistics, who convened the 'Reducing Offending' review groups mentioned above, was 'stunned' (Cavadino, Crow and Dignan 1999, cited in Robinson 2001); and certainly members of the What Works conferences planning group were taken aback at the proposed scale of things to come. Seasoned observers such as Merrington and Stanley (2000) forewarned of likely difficulties, and more recently Raynor (2004b) has commented that the pace of implementation ran far ahead of the research. Overall, 'The evidence suggests that implementation problems are likely to have affected the success of offending behaviour programmes in reducing re-offending', most likely due to three factors, 'the rapid expansion of programmes; targeting programmes ineffectively; higher than expected attrition rates' (Debidin and Lovbakke 2005: 48, 49).

On that basis, the enormous and rapid expansion in Pathfinder programmes was clearly very adventurous. It would have been more judicious to proceed on the grounds of limited but better controlled studies, taking note of local and contextual variations. Leschied, Bernfeld and Farrington (2001: 8) have proposed an inventory of 'critical elements in dissemination' for agencies contemplating innovations such as the implementation of structured programmes. They recommend a sequence of activities flowing from the decision at senior level that sustained effort is needed. It is crucial first to foster multi-level ownership of innovation, and it will be preferable to 'seed' the service system with pilot projects rather than pursue full-scale 'roll-out' from the outset. Alongside this, senior staff should ensure that demonstration projects have long-term financial support, and try as far as possible to retain stable leadership, and to neutralize internal resistance and what McCarthy (1989, cited in Leschied *et al* 2001: 8) called the 'forces of counter-control'. More widely, efforts should be made to build community investment in the innovation, and there should be 'top to bottom' training of staff. It might be added that if practitioners and managers are given new tasks to embark upon, there should be commensurate relief from previous ones. Where workloads become too onerous, the quality of implementation of any new agenda is likely to suffer.

As Ogloff and Davis (2004) have observed, there is a great deal at stake in the current investment in rehabilitative activities; and the outcomes of the enterprise are not yet clear. It may be that if readily visible effects are not achieved from the present period of experimentation, the metaphorical law-and-order pendulum will once again swing back to an exclusively punitive ethos. Having apparently been tried and found wanting, 'rehabilitation' could lose all credibility and be permanently rejected as a goal.

Demonstration and practical programmes

There is another facet of everyday delivery of research-based interventions that often gives rise to difficulty. In healthcare services, there is a well-established difference between outcomes obtained in specially designed experiments and those obtained in the 'real world' of service provision. These different estimates are respectively known as efficacy and effectiveness. *Efficacy* refers to the outcome of an intervention evaluated in a specially designed research trial. Investigation of it often involves the use of 'manualized' interventions, careful selection of participants, random assignment to treatment and comparison groups, special training for staff, and close monitoring by researchers. *Effectiveness* by contrast refers to the outcome of an intervention in a practical service setting. Generally, the process of achieving this has to be much more responsive to the ongoing demand of referrals or allocations. There is typically less control over the pattern of delivery, and resources are usually more limited. It is scarcely surprising, therefore, that on average these types of evaluations yield lower effect sizes than for efficacy studies.

Lipsey (1999) has analysed the importance of this difference in criminal justice evaluations, using the terms 'demonstration' and 'practical' projects to denote the efficacy/effectiveness distinction. He collated data from 196 practical programmes from his larger database of over 400 outcome studies. The mean effect size was only half of that for demonstration programmes. Yet this still represented significant mean reductions in recidivism among programme participants, despite the finding that fewer than one in five of the projects he examined had characteristics generally associated with higher effect sizes in the 'what works' literature. Thus in everyday, practical application, we may well expect outcomes to be less impressive than those found in elegantly designed research. Larger effects were associated with attendance being 'court-mandated' (i.e. subject to legal compulsion); with use of a delivery site that was not a law enforcement facility, but where the programme was coordinated by a criminal justice agency, such as probation or other community-based services for offenders.

Myths and misunderstandings

A third category of obstacles to more widespread acceptance of the 'what works' findings and associated practice and policy initiatives is that, regrettably, there are several ways in which the research informing the advent of these departures in criminal justice has been misunderstood. Some of them are so pervasive as virtually to have the status of myths. Since its inception, the idea that it could be helpful to work with offenders in specific ways guided by research has been exposed to a steady stream of disparagement. It is difficult to identify a segment of it that has not given rise to some complaint. It has been alleged that the existing research was all North American, therefore not applicable elsewhere, particularly the UK (as we never follow American trends?). It was all a technical quick fix, based on the error-prone, if not actually smoke-and-mirrors, exercise of meta-analysis. No account was taken of the diversity of client populations; it was a case of 'one size fits all'. The whole thing was an iniquitous scheme devised by cognitive-behavioural psychologists, who alongside psychiatrists have a key role in disciplining the population (Foucault said it, so it must be right). It was founded on a denial of the influence, maybe even the existence, of social environments.

The nature of programmes

Some of the reservations may be rooted in the use of the word 'programme'. Many practitioners automatically recoil from it, assuming it implies an activity that is highly prescriptive, allowing little room for manoeuvre on the part of either probationers or practitioners. But programmes can be conceptualized in various ways, and the core concept is simply that there be something that provides a sequence of opportunities for learning, planned in advance so that certain parts of it can be replicable (McGuire 2001). Programme manuals can take a variety of forms, and while some are very prescriptive as to contents, others are much more open and flexible (McMurran and Duggan 2005). Furthermore, it is important to bear in mind that all structured programmes in current use were intended to be 'integrated into the overall objectives of supervision' (Rex 2001: 69). For example, the individual sessions that follow the group programme in 'Think First' are designed as a vehicle through which the case manager becomes familiar with the issues raised by a participant during the group sessions, and which will become the foci of the remaining period of supervision.

The alleged absence of theory

Another objection to 'what works' research and a barrier to acceptance of its findings is the notion that it is based on a simple-minded input-output ('black box') model, so that even where interventions are effective it is impossible to answer the question 'why?' (Rex 2001). It is difficult to identify the original source of this supposition but it may be that any corpus of empirical findings is likely to be represented within certain standpoints as unavoidably positivist and atheoretical. From self-styled 'critical' and 'deconstructionist' perspectives, for example, any attempt to comprehend the variations in involvement in criminality between individuals is inherently and deeply suspect (see McGuire 2004 for fuller discussion).

On the contrary, the types of interventions that (to date) have been most consistently effective are anchored in theories of persistent offending as an acquired pattern of behaviour. Judging by the data obtained from longitudinal studies, such a pattern is often linked to other difficulties in individuals' lives. The most prominent explanatory model is cognitive social learning theory and its variants, which are integrated in a broader account that also identifies the role of environmental and societal variables (McGuire 2004). The theoretical concepts underpinning this are wholly distinct from those of rational choice theory, which Kemshall (2002: 48) mistakenly describes as the 'cornerstone' of cognitive-behavioural programmes.

For structured offending behaviour programmes to be accepted for dissemination by the Correctional Services Accreditation Panel, they had to be accompanied by a 'theory manual' specifying the ways in which the methods employed in a programme were hypothesized to engender change in participants. This stipulation is not congruent with a view that such initiatives are judged solely by their capacity to produce results, in the absence of any understanding of how that will occur, and 'why' an intervention 'works'.

A further oddity within this is that amidst the objections that are often raised against structured programmes, many authors unquestioningly endorse the use of pro-social modelling (Trotter 2000), which is the subject of almost ubiquitous approval. But the concept of pro-social modelling also derives from social learning theory, just like the much less wholesome programmes, and has been consistently recommended as an essential element of interactions both in programme delivery and other encounters between practitioners and their clients.

The 'denial' of diversity

Another prevailing misconception is that structured programmes are only suitable for white adult male populations, and it has been widely presumed that they were designed mainly with that group in mind. Certainly, as most programmes stand they are not available in a multiplicity of forms tailored for different sections of the community. On the other hand, programmes are generally designed to incorporate the principle of *responsivity*, whereby the detailed ways in which sessions are run should be adapted to the needs of those participating (Andrews 1995, 2001). Kemshall, Canton and Bailey (2004) protest that this simply displaces the onus to take action onto the individual practitioner's skill and competence.

But many of the research studies on which 'what works' recommendations are based were carried out with samples that included members of different ethnic groups. That is scarcely surprising as the majority of the studies were done in the USA where African Americans and other minorities are disproportionately represented in the criminal justice system (Miller 1996).

Several meta-analyses have been reported on the differential effects of key demographic variables on the outcomes of structured interventions. With regard to age, Cleland *et al* (1997) found that there were larger effect sizes for adolescent than adult offenders, with weaker effects for young adults. But cumulatively, the evidence to date indicates that similar basic approaches work across diverse populations. On gender, Dowden and

Andrews (1999) discovered that the 'human service principles' advocated as yielding the strongest effects for male offenders were equally applicable to females. For ethnicity, Wilson, Lipsey and Soydan (2003) analysed outcomes from 305 studies divided according to the proportions of offenders from different ethnic groups. 'Mainstream' interventions showed positive effects with ethnic minority participants (on both offending behaviour and a range of other outcomes) and programmes were equally effective regardless of the ethnic group with whom they were used.

Undoubtedly these are aspects of responsivity that require fuller research. But there is a difference between not having developed exact specifications to ensure that programmes meet the needs of different sections of the community, and being 'insensitive' to those needs as alleged by Rex (2001: 70), or attempting to render diversity 'invisible' as averred by Kemshall, Canton and Bailey (2004: 349). As the latter authors admit, there is virtually no evidence concerning differences in needs that could inform such developments. For all the furore that has been raised in conjunction with this issue, it is clear that neither research nor practice in either criminal justice or social work had previously done much that was meaningful to address it, but it has been a very useful stick with which to beat the installation of programmes.

Even were that not the case, if in England and Wales most 'volume crime' is committed by young white males, who thereby form the majority of the repeat offender population, would it not be at least defensible to have begun with activities that were judged usable with that group? More recently, specific recommendations have been made concerning adaptations that may be required for work with black offenders and women offenders. For the former it is important to acknowledge the complex links that may exist between experiences of discrimination and offending (Durrance and Williams 2003, Kemshall, Canton and Bailey 2004). For the latter it is proposed that there may be aspects of both dynamic risk factors and responsivity that previous interventions have failed to encompass (Harper *et al* 2004).

With reference to the separate issue of the literacy demands of the offending behaviour programmes in most widespread current use, Davies *et al* (2004) have examined the materials in some depth, and the National Probation Service's Change Control Panel has stipulated amendments that need to be made to address the points so raised. These initiatives have proceeded at different rates, which with reference to some projects could have been faster, but the processes involved have often entailed wide consultation. The contention that the underlying mission that propels the use of structured programmes is one of social exclusion (Kemshall 2002) is hard to reconcile with the considerable efforts that have been made to adapt programmes for a variety of client needs.

Cultural and ideological resistance

As previous sections have shown, there may be several legitimate and well-founded criticisms to make of the dissemination of research-based practice in probation, most forcefully with respect to the speed, scale and manner of implementation, and range of applicability of what was known. But beyond the kinds of objections just listed, there are others that stem from a deeper opposition that might best be called cultural or ideological resistance. They revolve around the notion that the background research has been seized upon and has become a tool in the hands of the state in its efforts to control the population, and variations on that theme. There are several separate but interconnected features of this.

Individual 'versus' social factors

One much-rehearsed starting point for dismissal of interventions that focus on helping offenders to change is that they address internal, intra-individual processes and actions. That is often taken to imply that they locate the causes of crime entirely within persons. Such a stance is in turn equated with ignoring the environmental, structural and political forces that contribute to crime, a fatal flaw that from the standpoint of those who understand crime purely as a socially determined phenomenon, automatically discredits the whole enterprise.

However, the insistence that attempting to work with individuals means that their backgrounds have no relevance is simply invalid. In the explanatory models on which effective interventions are based, crime is conceptualized as a net product of many factors: not only within individuals, but also in their immediate circumstances, life histories, and wider social environments (Andrews and Bonta 2003, McGuire 2004). Yet it is individuals who are found guilty of crimes; and historically, the function of the probation service has been to supervise those who have community sentences imposed on them as a result. Its capacity to reach much beyond this is very limited. Given convincing evidence that re-offending is associated with the experience of other kinds of difficulties and with unsuccessful efforts to deal with them (see, for example, Zamble and Quinsey 1997), there is ample justification for offering, even mandating, the most appropriate and best validated forms of help. Other kinds of preventive work are invaluable, within schools, families and communities (Farrington and Coid 2003, McGuire 2002, Sherman *et al* 2002), but those tasks are done by other agencies. Because a particular kind of work is focused on a specific objective that is a given organization's remit does not mean that other facets of the total picture are considered immaterial.

In other words, as Raynor (2004b) aptly notes, it is a false dichotomy to suggest that researching how better to work with individuals or engaging in practice informed by that research *ipso facto* constitutes a rejection of the importance of social change. Pursuing one is not incompatible with advocating the other. To the extent that social factors play a part in crime, there is unquestionable justification for taking action to address them. Whether that can be accomplished from within the *probation service* might be a different matter, and raises fundamental questions regarding its role as criminal justice agency.

Technicality

Some critics have expressed fears that the advent of 'programming' means that there has been a significant shift in the role of the probation officer, whose interpersonal and social work skills are devalued as a result. For Robinson (2001: 243) this is manifested in a gradual trend away from the 'indeterminacy' of the practice of the autonomous professional to a situation where many more tasks are marked by the 'technicality' of fixed routines. This terminology is adapted from Jamous and Peloille (1970, cited in Robinson 2001), who hypothesize that there is an inverse relationship between these two features of occupations. In a position where all tasks are prescribed, and 'treatment integrity' is monitored, practitioner independence is thereby undermined. That in turn is a component of a general movement towards managerialism and the furtive widening of state power. But it is difficult to see why increased technicality should be thought to demean professionalism or reduce status. The most prestigious (and on average, most highly paid) profession there is, medicine, is associated with a high level of technicality, some exceedingly routinized tasks alongside a sizeable amount of indeterminacy. The history of professions shows that they establish themselves by demarcating areas of specialized knowledge and skill (Johnson 1972).

It may be a more powerful argument to suggest that probation should invent a novel and potentially more advantageous balance between autonomy, discretion and technicality. A similar approach has been well rehearsed by Gendreau and his colleagues (2002), who have urged that criminal justice agencies should employ 'credentialled people', by which they mean individuals with appropriate qualifications in relevant social sciences. In a recent meta-analytic review, Dowden and Andrews (2004) have examined the importance of core staff skills and the quality of staff-client relationships, which among other factors were significantly correlated with outcome effects. These associations emerged most clearly among interventions that adhered to the other 'human service principles' proposed by Andrews (1995, 2001) and his co-workers. This provides a firm empirical basis for the claim that staff skills are a crucial ingredient of effective practice, and amplifies suggestions made some time ago by (among others) Priestley and McGuire (1983).

Community justice and social control

Recently Kemshall (2002) has argued that there is a 'hidden agenda' in the drive towards effective practice. This is to inculcate a sense of personal accountability within individuals and thereby induce them to be controlled from inside themselves, doing society's job for it, so to speak. The argument draws on the concept of the 'responsibilization agenda' borrowed from Rose (1996, cited in Kemshall 2002). The net effect of this is to institute a process by which the work of the state can be done, as it were at arm's length. Hence structured programmes like 'Think First' are intended primarily as a form of 'moral engineering' (Kemshall 2002: 51), through which individuals become practised in a process of 'self-surveillance', monitoring themselves on a frequent basis to certify they are complying with the law.

Whilst there are many valuable points made in these and other critical papers, this seems a curious argument. First, that it is one objective of structured programmes to secure self-motivated avoidance of crime is scarcely 'hidden'. It is explicitly stated in numerous training manuals, policy documents, and publicity leaflets. Second, has something similar not been a key aim of probation for a very long time? Were probation officers of a bygone era sublimely unconcerned when those whom they sought to 'advise, assist and befriend' felt better, but kept turning up in court? Accompanying the traditional social welfare objectives of proba-tion there was an assumption that helping to improve an individual's circumstances would facilitate personal change, including a greater likelihood of staying out of trouble with the law. According to the studies of Rex (1999), based on fieldwork carried out in 1994 (well before the Effective Practice Initiative), supervisory activity was replete with discourse concerning maturity, individual autonomy, or appealing to a sense of responsibility. It is similarly espoused in the projected new paradigm of 'desistance-focused' probation. Is entertaining such thoughts not a form of self-surveillance? Third, it is through a protracted process partaking of some features of self-surveillance that citizens pass examinations, secure university degrees, stick at jobs and, among other possible options, become professors of criminal justice. If this helps people to succeed in life, is it not worth imparting to others? The discovery that societies seek to instil self-control in their citizens is usually attributed to Jean-Jacques Rousseau (1712–1778), so it is hardly new; nor is it especially well hidden.

Expanding on this concept, Kemshall (2002) depicts the probation service as a key agency of social control. According to the British Crime Survey, in 2003 there were 11.7 million crimes committed in England and Wales, 5.9 million of them officially recorded (Home Office 2005a). Just over two million people were prosecuted, of whom 107,000 were sentenced to custody, and 191,000 given community sentences. Among the latter, 35,270 were placed on offending behaviour programmes, with only 13,136 completing them (National Probation Service 2004; note that these figures relate to the fiscal year 2003–2004). But whereas those imprisoned served an average of 12.6 months fully deprived of their liberty, attendance at even the most demanding probation programme entails a total of three days (72 hours) of contact time. Finally, taking the financial year 2000–2001 as an example, probation services accounted for just 4.5 per cent of expenditure on the criminal justice system (Home Office 2005b). It is difficult to see how these figures correspond to Kemshall's (2002) Orwellian vision. Although a character in *The Archers* radio series was given a community sentence with a requirement to attend an offending behaviour programme, there is a long way to go before such happenings attain the potency of Dartmoor Prison in the collective imagination.

Harsher penal environment

For other writers, the sequelae of applying conclusions based on 'what works' literature is a net increase in repressiveness. Boone (2004) has argued that the research findings have been readily taken up because they converge with a utilitarian approach to penology that conveniently serves the interests of the modern state. Proponents of rehabilitation were assimilated into this, inadvertently providing governments with a new apparatus for social control. In countries such as the UK and the Netherlands this was accompanied by increases in the numbers sentenced to prison. Boone argues that that was no coincidence, and through a subtle conflation of argument casts not only usage of the research, but the research itself as sinister. Yet reviewers of it (Andrews 1995, Andrews and Bonta 2003, Gendreau 1996, McGuire 1995b, 2004, McGuire and Priestley 1985) have often also adduced evidence that punitive sanctions are valueless, attempting to do so on scientific grounds because of a (possibly naive) belief that this would be much harder to dispose of than an ideological challenge.

With reference to increasing punitiveness, many factors influence the rate of imprisonment in a society. Most observers ascribe the upturn in its use in England and Wales to the impact of the horrific murder of Jamie Bulger in 1993. The prison population was certainly rising steadily for some time before the advent of effective practice and allied initiatives. Across those countries where outcome research has had some prominence there are large variations in rates of imprisonment. In England and Wales, the new Criminal Justice Act (2003) incorporates many changes that if properly implemented should help to reduce the prison population (Taylor, Wasik and Leng 2004).

Conclusion

All of these challenges notwithstanding, evidence-based criminal justice has become influential in a number of countries. It is no longer restricted to those places in which the original research to evaluate interventions was carried out. To date, its propagation could be said to have had a primarily 'North Atlantic' emphasis, reflecting developments mainly in the United Kingdom and Canada. Despite the fact that the bulk of the research findings emanated from the United States, for various reasons take-up there has been more sporadic. Is this work culture-bound to these locations, and unsuitable for application elsewhere?

Certainly in the research published to date, English is the dominant language and most studies and changes in practice have been situated in the justice systems of Anglophone nations. But in the largest meta-analysis so far conducted, the CDATE project, among nearly 10,000 documents collected, 14 languages other than English were represented (Lipton *et al* 2002). The research base, though predominantly North American, is by no means exclusively so (Redondo, Sánchez-Meca and Garrido 2002). Projects based on the findings, sometimes at local and sometimes at governmental level, have been instigated in a number of countries including Ireland, Sweden, Norway, Finland, Netherlands, Germany, Spain, Israel, Hong Kong, Australia and New Zealand. All of those are of course industrial, high technology, westernized countries. Given global diversity in language, culture, beliefs, and community, not to mention criminal justice systems, there are limits to how far any findings in social science are likely to be disseminated and applied.

References

Andrews, D.A. (1995) 'The Psychology of Criminal Conduct and Effective Treatment', in J. McGuire (ed.), *What Works: Reducing Re-offending: Guidelines from Research and Practice*. Chichester: John Wiley and Sons, pp. 35–62.

Andrews, D.A. (2001) 'Principles of Effective Correctional Programs', in L.L. Motiuk and R.C. Serin (eds), *Compendium 2000 on Effective Correctional Programming*. Ottawa: Correctional Service Canada, pp. 9–17.

Andrews, D.A. and Bonta, J. (2003) *The Psychology of Criminal Conduct*, 3rd edition. Cincinnati, OH: Anderson Publishing Co.

Audit Commission (1989) *The Probation Service: Promoting Value for Money*. Abingdon: Audit Commission Publications.

Barker, C., Pistrang, N. and Elliott, R. (2002) *Research Methods in Clinical Psychology: An Introduction for Students and Practitioners*. Chichester: John Wiley and Sons.

Barlow, D.H., Hayes, S.C. and Nelson, R.O. (1984) *The Scientist Practitioner: Research and Accountability in Clinical and Educational Settings*. New York: Pergamon.

Bernfeld, G.A., Blase, K.A. and Fixsen, D.L. (1990) 'Towards a Unified Perspective on Human Service Delivery Systems: Application of the Teaching-family Model', in R.J. McMahon and R. DeV. Peters (eds), *Behavioral Disorders of Adolescence*. New York: Plenum Press, pp. 191–205.

Bernfeld, G.A., Farrington, D.P. and Leschied, A.W. (eds) (2001) *Offender Rehabilitation in Practice: Implementing and Evaluating Effective Programs*. Chichester: John Wiley and Sons.

Boone, M. (2004) *Does What Works Lead to Less Repression? The Justification of Punishment According to What Works*. Paper given at the Societies of Criminology 1st Key Issues Conference, Paris.

Bottoms, A. and McWilliams, W. (1979) 'A Non-treatment Paradigm for Probation Practice', *British Journal of Social Work*, 9: 159–202.

Bottoms, A., Rex, S. and Robinson, G. (2004) 'How Did We Get Here?', in A. Bottoms, S. Rex and G. Robinson (eds), *Alternatives to Prison: Options for an Insecure Society*. Cullompton: Willan Publishing, pp. 1–27.

Brody, S. (1976) *The Effectiveness of Sentencing*, Home Office Research Study 35. London: HMSO.

Chapman, T. and Hough, M. (1998) *Evidence Based Practice: A Guide to Effective Practice*. London: Home Office.

Cleland, C.M., Pearson, F.S., Lipton, D.S. and Yee, D. (1997) 'Does Age Make a Difference? A Meta-analytic Approach to Reductions in Criminal Offending for Juveniles and Adults'. Paper presented at the Annual Meeting of the American Society of Criminology, San Diego, California.

Davies, K., Lewis, J., Byatt, J., Purvis, E. and Cole, B. (2004) *An Evaluation of the Literacy Demands of General Offending Behaviour Programmes*, Findings 233. London: Home Office Research, Development and Statistics Directorate.

Debidin, M. and Lovbakke, J. (2005) 'Offending Behaviour Programmes in Prison and Probation', in G. Harper and C. Chitty (eds), *The Impact of Corrections on Re-offending: A Review of 'What Works'*, Home Office Research Study 291. 2nd edition London: Home Office Research, Development and Statistics Directorate, pp. 31–54.

Dowden, C. and Andrews, D.A. (1999) 'What Works for Female Offenders: A Meta-analytic Review', *Crime and Delinquency*, 45: 438–452.

Dowden, C. and Andrews, D.A. (2004) 'The Importance of Staff Practice in

Delivering Effective Correctional Treatment: A Meta-analytic Review of Core Correctional Practice', *International Journal of Offender Therapy and Comparative Criminology*, 48: 203–214.

Durrance, P. and Williams, P. (2003) 'Broadening the Agenda Around What Works for Black and Asian Offenders', *Probation Journal*, 50: 211–224.

Farrington, D.P. and Coid, J.W. (eds) (2003) *Early Prevention of Adult Antisocial Behaviour*. Cambridge: Cambridge University Press.

Farrington, D.P. and Petrosino, A. (2001) 'The Campbell Collaboration Crime and Justice Group', *Annals of the American Academy of Political and Social Science*, 578: 35–49.

Foucault, M. (1977) *Discipline and Punish: The Birth of the Prison*. Harmondsworth: Peregrine Books.

Gaes, G.G. (1998) 'Correctional Treatment', in M. Tonry (ed.), *The Handbook of Crime and Punishment*. Oxford: Oxford University Press, pp. 712–738.

Gendreau, P. (1996) 'The Principles of Effective Intervention with Offenders', in A.T. Harland (ed.), *Choosing Correctional Options That Work: Defining the Demand and Evaluating the Supply*. Thousand Oaks, CA: Sage Publications, pp. 117–130.

Gendreau, P., Goggin, C., Cullen, F.T. and Paparozzi, M. (2002) 'The Common-sense Revolution and Correctional Policy', in J. McGuire (ed.) *Offender Rehabilitation and Treatment: Effective Programmes and Policies to Reduce Re-Offending*. Chichester: John Wiley and Sons, pp. 359–386.

Gendreau, P., Goggin, C. and Smith, P. (1999) 'The Forgotten Issue in Effective Correctional Treatment: Program Implementation', *International Journal of Offender Therapy and Comparative Criminology*, 43: 180–187.

Gendreau, P. and Ross, R.R. (1980) 'Effective Correctional Treatment: Bibliotherapy for Cynics', in R.R. Ross and P. Gendreau (eds), *Effective Correctional Treatment* Toronto: Butterworths, pp. 3–36.

Gendreau, P. and Ross, R.R. (1987) 'Revivification of Rehabilitation: Evidence from the 1980s', *Justice Quarterly*, 4: 349–407.

Goldblatt, P. and Lewis, C. (1998) *Reducing Offending: An Assessment of Research Evidence on Ways of Dealing with Offending Behaviour*, Home Office Research Study 187. London: Home Office.

Harper, G., Taylor, S., Man, L-H. and Niven, S. (2004) 'Factors Associated with Offending', in G. Harper and C. Chitty (eds), *The Impact of Corrections on Re-offending: A Review of 'What Works'*, Home Office Research Study 291. London: Home Office Research, Development and Statistics Directorate, pp. 17–30.

Harris, P. and Smith, S. (1996) 'Developing Community Corrections: An Implementation Perspective', in A.T. Harland (ed.), *Choosing Correctional Options That Work: Defining the Demand and Evaluating the Supply*. Thousand Oaks, CA: Sage Publications, pp. 183–222.

Hollin, C.R., McGuire, J., Palmer, E., Bilby, C., Hatcher, R. and Holmes, A. (2002) *Introducing Pathfinder Programmes to the Probation Service*, Home Office Research Study 247. London: Home Office.

Hollin, C.R., Palmer, E.J., McGuire, J., Hounsome, J., Hatcher, R., Bilby, C. and Clark, C. (2004) *Pathfinder Programmes in the Probation Service: A Retrospective Analysis*, Home Office On-Line Report 66/04. London: Home Office Research, Development and Statistics Directorate.

Home Office (2005a) *Sentencing Statistics 2003, England and Wales*. London: Home Office Research, Development and Statistics Directorate.

Home Office (2005b) *A Guide to the Criminal Justice System in England and Wales*.

London: Home Office Research, Development and Statistics Directorate.

Johnson, T.J. (1972) *Professions and Power*. London: Macmillan.

Kemshall, H. (2002) 'Effective Practice in Probation: An Example of "Advanced Liberal" Responsibilisation?', *Howard Journal of Criminal Justice*, 41: 41–58.

Kemshall, H., Canton, R. and Bailey, R. (2004) 'Dimensions of Difference', in A. Bottoms, S. Rex and G. Robinson (eds), *Alternatives to Prison: Options for an Insecure Society*. Cullompton: Willan Publishing, pp. 341–365.

Leschied, A.W., Bernfeld, G.A. and Farrington, D.P. (2001) 'Implementation Issues', in G.A. Bernfeld, D.P. Farrington and A.W. Leschied (eds), *Offender Rehabilitation in Practice: Implementing and Evaluating Effective Programs*. Chichester: John Wiley and Sons, pp. 3–19.

Lewis, S., Maguire, M., Raynor, P., Vanstone, M. and Vennard, J. (2003) *The Resettlement of Short-term Prisoners: An Evaluation of Seven Pathfinder Programmes*, Findings 200. London: Home Office Research, Development and Statistics Directorate.

Lipsey, M.W. (1995) 'What do we Learn from 400 Studies on the Effectiveness of Treatment with Juvenile Delinquents?', in J. McGuire (ed.), *What Works: Reducing Re-offending: Guidelines from Research and Practice*. Chichester: John Wiley and Sons, pp. 63–78.

Lipsey, M.W. (1999) 'Can Rehabilitative Programs Reduce the Recidivism of Juvenile Offenders? An Inquiry into the Effectiveness of Practical Programs', *Virginia Journal of Social Policy and the Law*, 6: 611–641.

Lipton, D.S., Martinson, R. and Wilks, J. (1975) *The Effectiveness of Correctional Treatment: A Survey of Treatment Evaluation Studies*. New York: Praeger.

Lipton, D.S., Pearson, F.S., Cleland, C.M. and Yee, D. (2002) 'The Effects of Therapeutic Communities and Milieu Therapy on Recidivism', in J. McGuire (ed.), *Offender Rehabilitation and Treatment: Effective Programmes and Policies to Reduce Re-Offending*. Chichester: John Wiley and Sons, p. 39–77.

Lloyd, C., Mair, G. and Hough, M. (1994) *Explaining Reconviction Rates: A Critical Analysis*, Home Office Research Study 136. London: HMSO.

MacKenzie, D.L. (2002) 'Reducing the Criminal Activities of Known Offenders and Delinquents: Crime Prevention in the Courts and Corrections', in L.W. Sherman, D.P. Farrington, B.C. Welsh, and D.L. MacKenzie (eds), *Evidence-Based Crime Prevention*. London and New York: Routledge, pp. 330–404.

Mair, G. (ed.) (2004) 'The Origins of What Works in England and Wales: A House Built on Sand?', in G. Mair (ed.), *What Matters in Probation*. Cullompton: Willan Publishing, pp. 12–33.

Martinson, R. (1974) 'What Works? Questions and Answers about Prison Reform', *The Public Interest*, 10: 22–54.

Martinson, R. (1979) 'New Findings, New Views: A Note of Caution Regarding Sentencing Reform', *Hofstra Law Review*, 7: 243–258.

McGuire, J. (ed.) (1995a) *What Works: Reducing Re-offending: Guidelines from Research and Practice*. Chichester: John Wiley and Sons.

McGuire, J. (1995b) 'The Failure of Punishment', *Science and Public Affairs*, Winter: 37–40.

McGuire, J. (2001) 'Defining Correctional Programs', in L.L. Motiuk and R.C. Serin (eds), *Compendium 2000 on Effective Correctional Programming*. Ottawa: Correctional Service Canada, pp. 1–8.

McGuire, J. (ed.) (2002) *Offender Rehabilitation and Treatment: Effective Practice and Policies to Reduce Re-offending*. Chichester: John Wiley and Sons.

McGuire, J. (2004) *Understanding Psychology and Crime: Perspectives on Theory and Action*. Maidenhead: Open University Press/McGraw-Hill Education.

McGuire, J. and Priestley, P. (1985) *Offending Behaviour: Skills and Stratagems for Going Straight*. London: Batsford.

McGuire, J. and Rowson, B. (eds) (1996) *Does Punishment Work?* London: Institute for the Study and Treatment of Delinquency.

McIvor, G. (1995) 'Practitioner Evaluation in Probation', in J. McGuire (ed.), *What Works: Reducing Re-offending: Guidelines from Research and Practice*. Chichester: John Wiley and Sons, pp. 209–219.

McMahon, G., Hall, A., Hayward, G., Hudson, C. and Roberts, C. (2004) *Basic Skills Programmes in the Probation Service: An Evaluation of the Basic Skills Pathfinder*, Findings 203. London: Home Office Research, Development and Statistics Directorate.

McMurran, M. and Duggan, C., (2005) 'The Manualisation of Offender Treatment', *Criminal Behaviour and Mental Health*, 15, pp. 17–27.

Merrington, S. and Stanley, S. (2000) 'Doubts About the What Works Initiative', *Probation Journal*, 47: 272–275.

Merrington, S. and Stanley, S. (2004) 'What Works? Revisiting the Evidence in England and Wales', *Probation Journal*, 51: 7–20.

Miller, J.G. (1996) *Search and Destroy: African-American Males in the Criminal Justice System*. Cambridge: Cambridge University Press.

Motiuk, L.L. and Serin, R.C. (eds) (2001) *Compendium 2000 on Effective Correctional Programming*. Ottawa: Correctional Service Canada.

National Probation Service (2004) *Annual Report for Accredited Programmes 2003–2004*. London: National Probation Service for England and Wales.

Ogloff, J.R.P. and Davis, M.R. (2004) 'Advances in Offender Assessment and Rehabilitation: Contributions of the Risk-needs-responsivity Approach', *Psychology, Crime and Law*, 10: 229–242.

Palmer, T. (1996) 'Programmatic and Nonprogrammatic Aspects of Successful Intervention', in A.T. Harland (ed.), *Choosing Correctional Options That Work: Defining the Demand and Evaluating the Supply*. Thousand Oaks, CA: Sage Publications, pp. 131–182.

Pilgrim, D. and Treacher, A. (1992) *Clinical Psychology Observed*. London: Routledge.

Priestley, P. and McGuire, J. (1983) *Learning to Help: Basic Skills Exercises*. London: Tavistock.

Raynor, P. (2004a) 'Rehabilitative and Reintegrative Approaches', in A. Bottoms, S. Rex and G. Robinson (eds), *Alternatives to Prison: Options for an Insecure Society*. Cullompton: Willan Publishing, pp. 195–223.

Raynor, P. (2004b) 'Seven Ways to Misunderstand Evidence-based Probation', in D. Smith (ed.), *Social Work and Evidence-Based Practice*. London and Philadelphia: Jessica Kingsley Publishers, pp. 161–178.

Raynor, P. and Vanstone, M. (1994) 'Probation Practice, Effectiveness and the Non-treatment Paradigm', *British Journal of Social Work*, 24: 387–404.

Redondo, S., Sánchez-Meca, J. and Garrido, V. (2002) 'Crime Treatment in Europe: A Review of Outcome Studies', in J. McGuire (ed.), *Offender Rehabilitation and Treatment: Effective Programmes and Policies to Reduce Re-offending*. Chichester: John Wiley and Sons, pp. 113–141.

Rex, S. (1999) 'Desistance from Offending: Experiences of Probation', *Howard Journal of Criminal Justice*, 38: 366–383.

Rex, S. (2001) 'Beyond Cognitive-behaviouralism? Reflections on the Effectiveness

Literature', in A. Bottoms, L. Gelsthorpe, and S. Rex (eds), *Community Penalties: Change and Challenges*. Cullompton: Willan Publishing, pp. 67–86.

Rex, S., Gelsthorpe, L., Roberts, C. and Jordan, P. (2004) *What's Promising in Community Service: Implementation of Seven Pathfinder Projects*, Findings 231. London: Home Office Research, Development and Statistics Directorate.

Roberts, C. (1995) 'Effective Practice and Service Delivery', in J. McGuire (ed.), *What Works: Reducing Re-offending: Guidelines from Research and Practice*. Chichester: John Wiley and Sons, pp. 221–236.

Robinson, G. (2001) 'Power, Knowledge, and "What Works" in Probation', *Howard Journal of Criminal Justice*, 40: 235–254.

Rowson, B. and McGuire, J. (eds) (1991) *What Works: Effective Methods to Reduce Re-offending*. Manchester: What Works Planning Group.

Rowson, B. and McGuire, J. (eds) (1996) *What Works: Making it Happen*. Manchester: What Works Planning Group.

Sherman, L.W., Farrington, D.P., Welsh, B.C. and MacKenzie, D.L. (eds) (2002) *Evidence-Based Crime Prevention*. London and New York: Routledge.

Taylor, R., Wasik, M. and Leng, R. (2004) *Blackstone's Guide to the Criminal Justice Act 2003*. Oxford: Oxford University Press.

Trotter, C. (2000) 'Social Work Education, Pro-social Orientation and Effective Probation Practice', *Probation Journal*, 47: 256–261.

Underdown, A. (1998) *Strategies for Effective Offender Supervision: Report of the HMIP What Works Project*. London: Home Office.

Vanstone, M. (2000) 'Cognitive-behavioural Work with Offenders in the UK: A History of Influential Endeavour', *Howard Journal of Criminal Justice*, 39: 171–183.

Vennard, J., Sugg, D. and Hedderman, C. (1997) *Changing Offenders' Attitudes and Behaviour: What Works?* Home Office Research Study 171. London: HMSO.

Von Hirsch, A. (1976) *Doing Justice: The Choice of Punishments. Report of the Committee for the Study of Incarceration*. New York: Hill and Wang.

Wacquant, L. (2005) 'The Great Penal Leap Backward: Incarceration in America from Nixon to Clinton', in J. Pratt, D. Brown, M. Brown, S. Hallsworth and W. Morrison (eds), *The New Punitiveness: Trends, Theories, Perspectives*. Cullompton: Willan Publishing, pp. 3–26.

Walker, N. (1991) *Why Punish? Theories of Punishment Reassessed*. Oxford: Oxford University Press.

Wilson, S.J., Lipsey, M.W. and Soydan, H. (2003) 'Are Mainstream Programs for Juvenile Delinquency Less Effective with Minority Youth than Majority Youth? A Meta-analysis of Outcomes Research', *Research on Social Work Practice*, 13: 3–26.

Zamble, E. and Quinsey, V. (1997) *The Criminal Recidivism Process*. Cambridge: Cambridge University Press.

Zimring, F.E. and Hawkins, G. (1994) 'The Growth of Imprisonment in California', *British Journal of Criminology*, 34 (Special Issue): pp. 83–96.

Chapter 16

Community justice in a safety culture: probation service and community justice in the Netherlands

Miranda Boone

It seems rather ironic to be asked for 'the Dutch perspective' in a predominantly British book on community justice. After all, most of the Dutch developments in this field were inspired by the British (and Canadian) model. One could even argue that this already started with the foundation in 1823 of the Dutch Fellowship for Moral Reformation of Prisoners (*Het Nederlands Genootschap tot Zedelijke Verbetering der Gevangenen*), an event that was undeniably influenced by the establishment of the British Society for the Reformation of Prison Discipline and the Reformation of Juvenile Offenders' in 1816. The British reader therefore will have a feeling of *déjà vu* sometimes, although some of the developments I describe are typical for the pragmatic Dutch law culture that so easily leads to indifference (Van de Bunt and Leuw 1995, Van Koppen 2003). On the other hand, some of the developments in the field of community justice that are already fully implemented in the United Kingdom, for example What Works, have only just started in the Netherlands.

In this contribution I will describe recent history of both community sentences and the probation service in the Netherlands. Although these developments could also be analysed apart from each other, the interesting aspect they have in common is their emphasis on quantity instead of quality. Above all, community sentences have become – at least on a macro level – the cheapest way to express and expand the culture of safety that has also infected the Netherlands. The probation service has been pushed to become part of the criminal justice system and in that position it is expected in particular to 'produce' as many social enquiry reports on offenders and to carry out as many community service orders as possible. In this contribution I will defend the point of view that the emphasis on quantitative growth has had the consequence that serious rehabilitation efforts are reserved for a motivated category of offenders that already have good perspectives to succeed. I will illustrate this with the outcomes of a research project on the probation service and ethnic minorities.

Community sanctions are defined as those sanctions or part of sanctions that are carried out in the community and contain a restriction of liberty because certain obligations or restrictions are imposed on the offender. Although probation in the Netherlands is comprised of different organizations and has had different names, I will simply refer to it as the probation service.

Community sentences: expansion in a punitive society

The renewed topic was intensively discussed at the end of the nineteenth century on the initiative of the *Internationale Kriminalistische Vereinigung* debate on community sentences as an alternative to prison sentences started in the mid-1960s. The terms in which the topic was discussed were typical for that era. Retribution as an aim of punishment was heavily rejected and there was widespread belief that both society and the delinquent profited from the rehabilitation of the offender. Behavioural changes and conflict solution were seen as the most important goals of criminal justice intervention, goals to which a prison sentence did not contribute at all. On the contrary, exclusion and stigmatization were seen as harmful side-effects of the prison sentence, that qualified it as an inhumane reaction that should only be used very selectively. Besides financial penalties and increased use of suspended sentences, unpaid labour for the sake of the community was proposed as an alternative for imprisonment (Commissie Vermogensstraffen, 1969, 1972, Mulder and Schootstra 1974). Its alternative character was taken very seriously.

The imposition of unpaid labour was allowed only under the condition that it was 'almost certainly applied as an alternative for a short prison sentence' (Commissie Alternatieve Strafrechtelijke Sancties 1979). This condition can be characterized as rather naive since the first evaluation of the British community service order showed that this sentence replaced prison in only 40–50 per cent of the cases (Pease, Billingham and Earnshaw 1977), a fact that the committee that prepared the introduction of the Dutch community service order was informed about (Commissie Alternatieve Strafrechtelijke Sancties 1979). Times had changed as the first experiments with unpaid labour finally started in the beginning of the 1980s. Prison rates had started to rise and for the first time the Dutch government was confronted with a lack of prison capacity. From that time onwards other arguments in favour of community sentencing were also brought into the discussion, the shortage of cells in particular.

Soon after its official introduction in the sanction system, the implementation of unpaid labour increased dramatically. In the first year of its existence (1981) only 213 unpaid labour penalties were enforced; by 1985 this had increased to almost 3,000, and nowadays almost 31,000 work sentences per year are applied on adults alone. Very rapidly, it also became clear that the sentence was not solely applied as an alternative for prison. Research indicated that offenders on whom unpaid labour was imposed showed more similarities with offenders on suspended sentences than with offenders on whom an unconditional prison sentence was imposed (Spaans 1995). From the political corner, however, no one seemed to be particularly worried about this development, on the contrary, the spectacular growth of unpaid labour was seen as a sign of its success. This particularly became clear from the influential policy document *Society and Criminality* (*Samenleving en Criminaliteit*, Ministerie van Justitie 1985), which states that the aim is to expand unpaid labour up to 4,000 cases per year. Similar aims are expressed in the subsequent policy document, *Justice on the Move* (*Recht in Beweging*, Ministerie van Justitie 1990) and in successive explanatory memoranda on justice budgets.

While net-widening effects were initially rejected, community sentences soon became an important instrument to reinforce the credibility of the criminal justice system. In cases where a criminal justice response had failed to occur or was considered too weak, community sentences were seen as a cheap and appropriate tool to 'fill up the lack of the criminal justice enforcement' (Commissie Heroverweging Instrumentarium Rechtshandhaving 1995).

As a result of the quantitative growth of community sentences, the original goal, rehabilitation, seems to have become less important. Research shows that results from community service orders are not much better compared to prison sentences (Spaans 1995) in terms of reducing offending. For a further expansion of community sentences, however, it is sufficient that the results are not any worse either (*Substitutie van Vrijheidsstraffen*, Ministerie van Justitie 1997). After the introduction of unpaid labour as a third formal sentence (beside prison and financial penalties) in the Penal Code for adults in 1989, public dissatisfaction focused on the supposed lack of a punitive element within community sentences. Community sentences were seen to be too lenient to be imposed, for example, on a drunk driving offender. As a solution for both the quantitative growth and the demand for harsher sentencing in the community, group projects emerged in which offenders had to work in the woods to cut down trees, for example. Rehabilitation as an aim of sentencing has since shifted again, this time onto the upcoming educational sentences. The changes that alternative sentences have undergone are perfectly expressed in the terminology that is used in new legislation: task sentences. This jargon was already in use in 1996 to note the fact that the alternative period of the sentence had come to an end, according to the Minister of Justice at that time (*Beleidsnota Taakstraffen* 1996: 4).

In 2001 the legal framework of community sentences changed again, primarily to enable growth. Besides the community service order, educational sentences also obtained a legal basis in the Penal Code. Combinations of community service orders, educational sentences and prison sentences were made possible and the maximum number of hours that can be imposed was doubled to 480. One of the most important changes under the new law, however, is the possibility for the prosecution service to impose a community sentence as a condition of a *transactie* (out-of-court settlement by the Public Prosecutor) with the offender, a possibility that was still unthinkable under the 1989 Act because of 'the supposed punitive character of community sentence orders'.[1]

Nowadays 31,000 community sentences a year are imposed on adult offenders and another 17,000 on juvenile offenders. Only a small number of those are educational sentences: 1,331 for adults in 2003. Recent data for youngsters are not available, but the share of educational sentences on the total amount of community sentences certainly exceeds that of adults (Leertouwer *et al* 2004).

To accommodate these large numbers, community service orders are mainly implemented in group projects. Besides, educational programmes are developed by the probation service, which can be implemented in different judicial modalities and in different stages of the criminal law process. Some can be imposed as a formal educational sentence by the judge, others as a special condition of a suspended sentence. For the benefit of the introduction of What Works in the Dutch sanction system (see below), all existing programmes were recently screened in light of a list of quality criteria. One of the problems was that none of the programmes could be judged by its effectiveness, simply because no evaluative research had been pursued. Nevertheless, from the over 200 programmes that were developed up and down the country in recent years, 25 were selected of which 11 can be imposed as a formal sentence by the judge. Those 25 programmes are carried out on a national scale according to uniform guidelines (Boone and Poort 2002).

This overview of community sentencing in the Netherlands needs to be supplemented with one more development. From the middle of the 1980s onwards, alternatives were sought not only for the imposition of prison sentences, but also for the way in which they are carried out. This resulted in the introduction of 'penitentiary programmes' in the Penitentiary Principles Act 1999. These programmes may start a year before the anticipated date of early release and participators effectively leave prison and work or follow educational activities during the day and stay at home in the evenings and at night. As with community sentences, application of penitentiary programmes should contribute both to the rehabilitation of the offender and to the reduction of the shortage of cells.

From a doctrinal point of view it seems rather strange that programmes that are quite similar with respect to content, must sometimes be considered as a community sentence, sometimes as a prison sentence. To stress the punitive character of penitentiary programmes, electronic monitoring is almost invariably used to control the prisoner in the first phase of the programme. Another difference with community sentences is that the prisoner has to participate in the programme for the full remainder of the prison sentence. In that period they are allowed to work or to follow a rehabilitation programme, whereas other freedoms are assigned in phases. In 2004, 767 offenders participated in a penitentiary programme, of which 629 were (partly) supervised by electronic monitoring, according to the automatic data system of the probation service on 19 November 2004. The fact that these numbers are rather disappointing is mainly attributed to the strict selection procedure and the preference of many detainees for open prison regimes without electronic monitoring (Reidnied 2001, Laemers *et al* 2001).

The Dutch probation service: from sandals and woolly socks to a businesslike organization

The introduction of community sentences in the Dutch penal law system has had enormous consequences for the probation service. From the beginning it has been clear that the probation service was the intended organization to implement and supervise community sentences. It even seems plausible that the substitute and rehabilitative character of community sentences was initially emphasized to convince the probation service of the extent to which this extension of tasks fitted its core objectives. That the organization has been under pressure to accept this

287

new task becomes clear from the explanatory memoranda on the justice budgets in that period. In the Budget of 1982, threatening phrases were uttered: 'in the light of the current economic situation it has to be considered if certain probation activities can be intensified while other, less important tasks can be decreased or brought to an end'.[2] A year later the Minister of Justice concluded with relief: 'Although there has been some hesitations within probation with respect to unpaid labour, it seems to have become convinced that this sanction is a good alternative for unconditional imprisonment.'

Actually, the probation service was bitterly divided on the issue. In an early letter to the Secretary of Justice, the organization agreed on preparing and accompanying unpaid labour, but refused to control and report failures to the prosecution service.[3] Persisting in this refusal, however, would have been the starting point of the dismantling of the organization (Heinrich 1995: 255). So in 1986 the preparing, implementing and controlling of unpaid labour was added to the Probation Bill as a new task. In a latter stage, the implementation of penitentiary programmes and the controlling of electronic monitoring were also added to the probation tasks.

To understand the primary resistance and current situation of the probation service, it may be significant to go one step back in history and examine the period preceding the introduction of community sentences, the 1960s and 1970s. Probation work had undergone a professional development by that time. Professional schooling of probation workers even became a condition for government subsidy, a measure that resulted in a disappearance of voluntary workers and the education of probation workers as social workers in so-called 'social academies', institutions for the training of social workers. These academies fostered the typical anti-authority mentality of this era. In addition, they were taught that a professional relationship with the client needed a basis of trust, a condition that was difficult to combine with the judicial tasks that require enforcement. The changing attitude towards crime and the criminal complicated the already difficult relationship with central government and the position of the probation service in the criminal justice system even more – a relationship that had always been difficult, given the particular character of the probation service (Janse de Jonge 1991, Heinrich 1995). Causes for crime were no longer sought in the individual-psychological circumstances of the offender, but in the structure of society and social circumstances, an analysis that asked for much broader action than could be justified by the much more limited goals of the Ministry of Justice (Heinrich 1995). Nevertheless, the Ministry did accept the more autonomous position of the probation service, resulting in a decrease of supervision tasks and an increase of means available for care and assistance. To give an example: in order to give probation officers full freedom in the shape of the contact with their clients, the range of possible conditions that could be linked to a suspended release was reduced to only one, namely probation contact, whatever form that might take.

Although this era in Dutch probation history was rather short, it still has a major influence on the character and (self-)image of probation. From this period also dates the label 'woollen goat socks organization', an expression that is difficult to translate into English, but raises the image of an overly lenient organization with too much idealism and a shortage of results.

Bearing this preceding period in mind, one can imagine that the hard-handed involvement of the probation service with the carrying out of community sentences came as a shock for the organization and most probation workers. Still, the full dependency of governmental subsidies did not give any counteroffensive much of a chance (Heinrich 1995). One further circumstance contributed to the vulnerability of the probation service, one that unfortunately still exists. That is the fact that there has never been a serious investigation into the results of probation work in general. The involvement with community sentences can be seen as the starting point of increasing governmental interference; a development that has gathered a great deal of momentum since. This increasing interference has had two eye-catching consequences: first, the service has changed from a social welfare organization into one fully managed by production numbers. Second, closely connected to the first, this development caused divisions within the organization, a serious identity crisis from which it has not fully recovered. This second development will be discussed below.

The first development is already illustrated by the emphasis on the quantitative growth of community sentences as described above. The production-oriented attitude of the service becomes particularly visible in the characteristics of the reorganization of 1995. Besides an organizational change, this reorganization intended to bring about a new method of working and a cultural change in the service. From being a social welfare organization, the probation service was forcibly transformed into a businesslike organization. These efforts were mostly inspired by the need to economize. Not that the content of the work changed, but it had to be performed in a more efficient way. For this reason, the probation service started to work with target groups. In the first instance, these target groups also included more problematic categories of offenders, namely drug addicts and homeless offenders. At a latter stage the service was put under (political) pressure to prefer clients with high potentials above the most problematic groups (NFR 1991).

The reorganization also resulted in an alteration to the division of the budget among the three main tasks of the probation service. Most money was reserved for community sanctions. The second main task, social enquiry and advice, had to be carried out in a more efficient way, a goal that could be achieved by introducing structured questionnaires and by strictly adhering to the target group policy. Early interventions were allowed only if they could contribute to the diagnosis of a client and in cases of crisis-intervention. Counselling and aftercare had to bear the biggest loss. Not only did the budget for these tasks decrease, from now on they had to be carried out in a much more structured and efficient fashion.

The more businesslike way of working has become most visible in the far-reaching automatic data processing systems that are implemented. One of them is a registration system, called the Client Follow System (Client Volg Systeem, CVS), in which all activities that are developed with probation clients are recorded on a national scale. Even more radical has been the transformation of the service into an output-guided organization. For this operation it was necessary to classify all probation activities under a restricted number of probation products that the Ministry of Justice was prepared to pay for. This resulted in the definition of 11 products, these excluded a number of activities that were also important in the view of probation officers, for instance, offering assistance inside prison, attending cases of clients in court hearings or visiting a demoralized client to give them support. Subsidy is totally based on the output system. Each year an agreement is made between probation service and the Ministry of Justice on the numbers of products to be supplied per year. Those agreements may not be exceeded. The probation service is paid by the number of products produced in one year, multiplied by the cost price. Those agreements influence the whole organization, of course. Production numbers are passed on to the different departments and also, on a more informal level, to individual probation officers.

Because of its predictable consequences, the choice for an organization managed by production numbers is still difficult to understand. One of the few contemporary academic writers, who publishes on the Dutch probation service, Geert van der Laan warned back in 1994 that a more businesslike way of working would not lead to a more normative orientation on probation work, as was suggested in the policy documents underlying the reorganization. 'To be able to reject behaviour not only in judicial terms, but also on moral grounds in front of their clients, probation workers need to be prepared to take risks and be willing to confront clients with their failures', he stated. Therefore they need management support. One-sided emphasis on output is likely to lead to calculation and avoidance of risk. The unwanted consequence of a market-oriented organization can be that probation workers choose to play it safe: 'as long as I achieve my production numbers, nobody can criticise me' (Van der Laan 1994). Such targets have become detached from 'doing a good job' from a traditional probation point of view. In a volume published in 1998 on the occasion of the 175th anniversary of the probation service, the authors reached the conclusion that the reorganization and new methods of working had led to an exclusion of problematic groups of probation clients (Schuyt and Kommer 1998). In the next section I will illustrate how those methods of working have similar results for clients from ethnic minorities.

Selectivity as a result: consequences for ethnic minorities

The consequences of the developments described above are illustrated by a research project I carried out in 2002 on probation work and ethnic minorities (Boone 2002). I interviewed probation officers, observed interactions between probation officers and clients with different cultural backgrounds, attended meetings and studied over 100 pre-sentence reports. The two main results were that the organization is both less accessible for ethnic minority clients and offers poorer quality of service to them. In this chapter I will only look at the problem of accessibility, because it is a clear illustration of the consequences of the current organization of probation service.

The theoretical framework used for this study is the concept of 'street level bureaucracy', a term coined successfully by Michael Lipsky in 1980 (Lipsky 1980). Typical of such an organization is the intrinsic tension between production demands of management and the desire of officials to give good quality to their individual clients. Lipsky argues that the various ways in which officials cope with this situation will disadvantage clients of difficult groups. It is no surprise that the transformation of the probation service into an organization that is assessed only on its production numbers would encourage these harmful mechanisms.

Also, clients deriving from ethnic minority groups (clients were assigned to an ethnic minority group in cases where at least one of the parents was born in a foreign country) are relatively likely to have characteristics that distinguish them as 'problematic clients'. I will discuss the most important. Language and cultural context problems obviously catch the eye. In more than half of the conversations I attended, language problems affected the conversation a great deal. Probation officers do not often make use of interpreters or the interpreter's telephone, because according to them, this only worsens the problem. Besides, language is not only a verbal, but also a cultural or contextual skill. For instance, probation officers have considerable difficulty explaining the nature of their work to people who never heard of an organization such as the probation service before. Probation officers also tend to use complicated names for other typical Dutch organizations. Sometimes they check that the client understands the nature of that organization, but often that is forgotten as well. In addition, any information the client gives, however, must be put into the right context. For example, a Dutch probation officer will have an image of a school for children with educational problems and the consequences the attendance at such a school can have for the social life of a child. However, understanding the impact of having attended a Koran school is a different story. Because most regular probation officers will not know much about such an institution it is hard for them to offer assistance on a similar professional level, for example by asking appropriate questions to get deeper into the story of the offender.

A second factor that complicates interaction with clients of ethnic minority groups is the large number of suspects denying that they have committed the crime. For probation officers, a confession represents an important starting point for assistance: 'How can I help somebody to stop re-offending if he or she did not do anything (or so they say)?' Results of earlier research also pointed out that suspects from a Moroccan or Antillean background deny their crimes more frequently (Klooster, Van Hoek and Van't Hoff 1999), although this result is refuted in another study (Wartna, Beijers and Essers 1999). A third problem is the accessibility of the clients themselves. Clients of the probation service do not shine in reliability and punctuality in general, but those deriving from minority groups are even less likely to keep their appointments. This is a problem, because of the typical Dutch method of making appointments: probation officers invite their clients in writing and expect them at the office at a fixed time. Finally, it is much more difficult to motivate clients for a behavioural skill programme if their behaviour derives from or is justified by standards that differ from those on which the violated rule is based on. This problem expresses itself in particular in cases of domestic violence.

Bearing the theory of 'street level bureaucracies' in mind, these characteristics arouse the expectation that the probation service is less accessible for clients deriving from ethnic minority groups, and this turned out to be the case.

Typical of early intervention is that the supply of potential clients is almost endless. For that reason, probation officers are forced to make choices. Every morning, information about suspects in custody is faxed to a probation unit from the nearest police station. Probation officers have to decide whom they are going to visit. Although officially a target group policy exists, probation officers use other criteria in practice. Inability to speak Dutch, the lack of a residence permit and denial of the crime are important indications *not* to offer early intervention. I do not have to point out that all of these factors disadvantage clients of ethnic minority groups. Probation officers found justifications for those decisions in high production demands and the time-consuming administration system. One probation officer told me: 'If you visit a client in the police station and you come to the conclusion that you have no possibility to offer an early intervention, you still have to fill in six pages in the administration system. You are better off calling the police and ask who's in. Does he admit it? Does he speak Dutch? OK, in that case I'll come and visit him.'

Denials also influence the decision of probation officers to write a social enquiry report. Many probation officers refuse to write an enquiry report about offenders who do not confess they have committed the crime. Alternatively they may write a report about the social circumstances of the offender, but refuse to advise the judge about the most appropriate penalty; as a consequence of the judge not being offered an alternative, it is more likely that a prison sentence will be imposed. These attitudes disadvantage clients deriving from ethnic minority groups in particular. Out of a sample of 100 social enquiry reports, probation officers gave penalty advice in twice as many cases of Dutch clients as they did in cases concerning ethnic minority clients.

Refusal to confess was the most common explanation for the lack of penalty advice given in the enquiry reports. Closer investigation, however, showed that this qualification is very subjective. On the one hand, the crime was also (partly) denied in half the cases in the sample where a penalty advice was given. On the other hand, in one third of social enquiry reports which lacked a penalty advice because of the supposed negation of the client, the client admitted the crime at least partly.

Some training programmes for clients organized by the probation service demand that participants have control of the Dutch language, admit the offence, are motivated to change their behaviour and are able to keep appointments. For some programmes this is understandable, but for others it seems more logical that participants acquire these very skills during the course. It is obvious that these criteria particularly affect clients of ethnic minority groups. In the interviews, probation officers admitted that they had difficulties in getting this category of offenders accepted for training and treatment programmes. If this observation is correct, the conclusion must be that 'creaming' ethnic minority clients has already become institutionalized.

The problems described above are partly compensated for by the enthusiasm of a group of probation officers who are trying to break down barriers, despite the domineering production culture. They visit clients at home if they do not appear on their appointments, communicate with offenders and their families in all possible ways, and try to find ways of helping offenders, even those who do not fully admit the offence. However, the organization does not reward or facilitate these extra efforts. Instead, they may be disciplined for failing to achieve their production target.

Recent developments: What Works and more economics

The state of affairs so far is that community justice in the Netherlands has expanded enormously, but most of all in a quantitative way. The increase in community sentences is closely connected to the recent history of the probation service and in this organization a major emphasis on production numbers has become visible in recent years. Although on a local level new programmes are continually being invented of which the creators are convinced of their rehabilitative potential, on a national level rehabilitation is no longer seen as the major goal of community sentencing and probation activities. This conclusion can be derived from the fact that proper research on good practices of probation has hardly been conducted in the Netherlands, and disappointing results on the effects of, for instance, community service orders have never stood in the way of more growth. Of course, the search for effective interventions was encouraged, but even without those effects, community sentencing was seen as a visible and not too expensive governmental reaction to crime, particularly in cases where a visible reaction had been lacking before. Considered in this way, both community sentences and probation activities have contributed particularly to the security doctrine that has become dominant in the Netherlands (Van Swaaningen 2004, Pakes 2004).

As already indicated, the growing interference of government with probation and its transformation into an output-guided organization has burdened the probation service with both a serious image problem and an identity crisis. Since its establishment, but most particularly in the era preceding the introduction of community sentences, the probation service profile rested heavily on support for, even solidarity with, the offender. Interventions were aimed primarily at the well-being of offenders. As a result of the increasing interference of government, the probation service was confronted with the question of priorities: was it working for the offender or the Ministry of Justice (Van Swaaningen 1995, Boone and Uit Beijerse 1995)? As can be read in successive annual reports (SRN 2001, 2002), the answer of probation service has been: for the benefit of society's. Its main aim is not the rehabilitation of the offender, but the contribution to the safety of society. Although both the offender and society can be served by diminishing recidivism, this is, of course, an important change of perspective, one that not only does not distinguish probation from the other organizations in the criminal justice system, but is not understood very well both inside and outside the organization.

Outside the organization, criticism is threefold. First, that the probation service has simply betrayed its roots and its traditional solidarity with the offender by becoming so closely tied to the Ministry of Justice (Janse de Jonge 1993, Van Swaaningen 1997, Kelk 2004). A second criticism takes issue with the narrow aims of modern probation (reducing recidivism) and questions if any results can be reached by an organization that offers only superficial programmes to relatively privileged groups of clients (Van der Laan 1994, 2004, Ridder-Padt 2002, 2004, De Jonge 2002, Boone 2002, Boone and Poort 2002). And despite all the organizational changes, the service still has to fight the strong public image of the woollen goat sock, at least according to the manager-director in a recent interview (Boone and Poort 2004).

Within the organization, different categories of probation workers can be distinguished. A first group were educated as social workers, started their career long before the main organizational changes took place and are in general rather bitter and frustrated by the changes and the way they are implemented. A second group of probation workers tries to combine the production demands of the organization with their own ideals, without gaining much credit for these extra efforts. And a third, compliant group comes disturbingly close to the description Van der Laan gave in 1994: meet your targets, avoid criticism. In general, however, probation workers complain about the lack of possibilities they have to give their clients the support they think is necessary to keep them from re-offending (Boone 2002, Ridder-Padt 2002).

These criticisms finally resulted in renewed attention to the quality and content of probation work, a change of perspective that will certainly have been stimulated by the exit of the manager-director responsible for the reorganization. This quality-impulse has expressed itself in, for instance, training programmes for probation officers to improve the quality of work with clients from different cultures. Most important, however, are the development of a diagnostic instrument and a specific method of working for probation officers, 'assisting in an enforcement capacity'. A scientific panel of all kind of disciplines supervises both developments. The method of working has recently been laid down in a handbook that has been issued to all probation workers (Menger and Krechtig 2004). The development of a diagnostic instrument is part of the introduction of a Dutch version of What Works, termed Push Back Recidivism (*Terugdringen Recidive*), in the Dutch sanction system. As with its Canadian and English counterparts, it aims to treat offenders on more scientific grounds, mainly based on the work of the Canadian scholars Andrews and Bonta (e.g. Andrews *et al* 1990, Andrews, Bonta and Hoge 1990, Bonta 2002). Therefore all existing educational programmes of the service are screened (see above), a diagnostic instrument is developed for both prison and probation services and a new rehabilitation programme is developed on the foundation of What Works, called enhanced thinking skills.

At this crucial stage of improvement, however, the Minister of Justice decided to cut back dramatically the organization's funding. In the following year, the organization had to economize by 30 million euro – no less than a quarter of its total budget. Although members of parliament and other individuals and various organizations protested against these plans, the probation service holds a very weak position because of its inability to show that many of its efforts actually have an effect. Moreover, the cutbacks were highly specific, meaning that long-term counselling (*trajectbegeleiding*) and assistance on a voluntary basis were totally abolished, with more money being reserved for supervision and training programmes. Savings also had to be realized by more efficient methods of working. Interventions have to be selective and effective, which means, according to the Minister, that interventions can only be offered to a selective group of offenders of whom good results can be expected.[4]

In this climate and under these circumstances it can be seriously questioned if the implementation of What Works will improve the quality of probation work. The British example shows that too high expectations and a lack of attention to implementation problems can lead to disappointing results (Mair 2004). In an earlier publication I defended the argument that What Works could even contribute to more repression due to the scientific expectations it arouses and to the fact that the blessings of What Works are totally formulated in terms of the risk to society that can easily lead to a loss of proportionality (Boone and Poort 2002). These worries increase as a consequence of the emphasis that is put on selectivity and efficiency of the project. In many policy documents concerning Push Back Recidivism, emphasis is put on the select use of the available programmes. In a letter accompanying the government paper *To a Safer Society (Naar een veiliger samenleving)*, the Minister of Justice states this intention. Only if offenders are willing and able to change their behaviour, or can be motivated to do so, will they be offered participation in a rehabilitation programme.[5] The same intention becomes visible in the opening note of the project Push Back Recidivism. 'Reintegration programmes will only be started if a real expectation exists that it will contribute to a reduction of recidivism' (Ministerie van Justitie 2002). And in a recent paper, the programme manager of the project describes the central message of the project as 'to concentrate interven-tions on those convicts that are expected to succeed and to enlarge quality of the interventions what will result in increased effectiveness' (Van der Linden 2004).

What this selectivity will contain exactly is not very clear yet, but the principal question is, of course, who decides on which criteria who can be motivated and how much efforts (and money) is allowed to be spent. Fear seems justified that only offenders who have good opportunities to succeed will be selected for rehabilitation programmes. These offenders, of course, do not validate the success of these programmes: they would probably not have re-offended regardless of what treatment they were given.

This fear is also connected to a second characteristic of the Dutch version of What Works: the emphasis on efficiency. Implementation of the project should not only contribute to more effectiveness in sentencing, but should also do so against lesser costs. This aspect is also highly stressed in the United Kingdom where a cost-benefit analysis aimed at achieving a 5 per cent reduction in that rate between 2001 and 2004 has been the decisive argument for the implementation of What Works (Perry 2002). Cost reduction for an offender with a medium risk of recidivism turned out to be £1.26 for every invested pound and therefore worth a try. Although it became clear that the high expectations have led to disappointment in the United Kingdom (Mair 2004) so far, this model is also adopted in the Netherlands and the research centre of the Ministry of Justice is at present developing a cost-benefit analysis for criminal interventions.

Conclusion

The recent history of community sentences is closely connected to that of the probation service. Both developments are characterized by the emphasis on quantitative growth. Apart from its rehabilitative potential, the growth of community sentences has been stimulated to reduce the pressure on prison capacity and to contribute to the reinforcement of the credibility of the criminal justice system. Heavy-handed involvement in the probation service with the implementation and supervision of community sentences has been a starting point for growing govern-mental interference, finally resulting in an organization that is totally guided by production numbers.

Successive research has shown that one consequence of these developments is that promising rehabilitation programmes are reserved for motivated and high-potential candidates, while problematic categories of offenders are excluded of these efforts. Whilst that helps the probation service meets its targets, it is hardly the best way forward towards a safer society. Clearly, what is at stake is not just the probation service; the very idea of probation has been substantially eroded.

Continuous criticisms from both outside and inside the probation service have renewed attention on the quality and content of probation work. The introduction of What Works in the Dutch sanction system can reinforce those developments, but can also have the opposite effect, in particular since the implementation will be accompanied by drastic cutbacks.

Notes

1 Kamerstukken II 1978/8720074, nr. 6, p.8.
2 Kamerstukken II 1981/82, 17100, hoofdstuk VI, nr. 2, p. 35.
3 Letter of 31 January 1978. Also: Kamerstukken II 1978/1979, 15300, hoofdstuk VI, nr. 2. p. 34.
4 Letters of the Minister of Justice, Kamerstukken II, vergaderjaar 2003–2004, 28290, nr. 1 and Kamerstukken II, vergaderjaar 2003–2004, 29270, nr. 3.
5 Kamerstukken II, 02/03, 28600 VI, nr. 8, p. 4.

References

Andrews, D.A., Bonta, J. and Hoge, R.D. (1990) 'Classification for Effective Rehabilitation: Rediscovering Psychology', *Criminal Justice and Behavior*: 1719–52.
Andrews, D.A., Zinger, I., Hoge, R.D., Bonta, J., Gendreau, P. and Cullen, F. (1990) 'Does Correctional Treatment Work? A Clinically-relevant and Psychologically Informed Meta-analysis', *Criminology*, 28: 369–404.
Beleidsnota Taakstraffen (1996) *Voor straf werken en leren*. The Hague: Ministry of Justice.
Bonta, J. (2002) 'Recidivepreventie bij delinquenten; een overzicht van de huidige kennis en een visie op de toekomst', *Justitiële Verkenningen*: 2820–36.
Boone, M. (2002) *Leren Diversifiëren: Reclassering en culturele diversiteit*. Utrecht: Willem Pome Instituut voor Strafrechtswetenschappen.
Boone, M. and Poort, R. (2002) 'Wat werkt (niet) in Nederland', *Justitiële Verkenningen*, 28: 48–64.
Boone, M. and Poort, R. (2004) 'Schakel in justitieketen of geketend aan Justitie: Interview with Van Gennip, Director Reclassering Nederland', *Proces*, 83: 261–268.
Boone, M. and Uit Beijerse, J. (1995) 'Vernieuwing van het werk van de reclassering: trafrechtelijke mogelijkheden en beperkingen', *Proces*, 74: 43–49.
Commissie Alternatieve Strafrechtelijke Sancties (1979) *Dienstverlening (interimrapport)*. The Hague: Ministry of Justice.
Commissie Heroverweging Instrumentarium Rechtshandhaving (1995) *Het recht ten uitvoer gelegd. Oude en nieuwe instrumenten van rechtshandhaving*. The Hague:

Ministry of Justice.
Commissie Vermogensstraffen (1969) *Interimrapport*. The Hague: SDU.
Commissie Vermogensstraffen (1972) *Eindrapport*. The Hague: SDU.
De Jonge, G. (2002) 'De erfenis van de reclassering', *Proces*, 81: 180–183.
Heinrich, J.P. (1995) *Particuliere Reclassering en overheid in Nederland sinds 1823.* Arnhem: Gouda Quint.
Janse de Jonge, J.A. (1991) *Om de persoon van de dader, Over straftheorieën en voorlichting door de reclassering*. Arnhem: Gouda Quint.
Janse de Jonge, J.A.. (1993) 'Om het behoud van de reclasseringsgedachte', in J.A. Janse de Jonge, M. Moerings and A. van Vliet (eds), *Binnen de steen van dit bestaan: Over rechtsbescherming en totale instituties*, Utrecht: Willem Pompe Institute, pp. 51-71.
Kelk, C. (2004) 'Reclassering nu', *Proces*, 83: 242–243.
Klooster, E.M., Van Hoek, A.J.E. and Van't Hoff, C.A. (1999) *Allochtonen en strafbeleving, een onderzoek naar de strafbeleving van Antilliaanse, Surinaamse, Marokkaanse en Turkse jongens*. The Hague: Ministry of Justice.
Laemers, M., Vegter, P. and Fiselier, J. (2001) *Evaluatie Penitentiaire Beginselenwet en Penitentiare Maatregel*. Nijmegen, ITS.
Leertouwer *et al* (2004) *Sanctiecapaciteit 2008*. The Hague: WODC, Onderzoek en Beleid 221.
Van der Linden, B. (2004) 'Terugdringen Recidive', *Proces*, 83: 94–102.
Lipsky, M. (1980) *Street Level Bureaucracies: Dilemmas of the Individual Public Services.* New York: Russell, Sage Foundation.
Mair, G. (2004) 'The Origins of What Works in England and Wales: A House Built on Sand?, in G. Mair (ed.), *What Matters in Probation*. Cullompton: Willan Publishing, pp. 12–34.
Menger, A. and Krechtig, L. (2004) *Het delict als maatstaf: Methodiek voor werken in een gedwongen kader*. Stichting Reclassering Nederland: SRN.
Ministerie van Justitie (1985) *Samenleving en Criminaliteit: Een beleidsplan voor de komende jaren*. The Hague: SDU.
Ministerie van Justitie (1990) *Recht in Beweging. Een beleidsplan voor justitie in de komende jaren* (1990). The Hague: SDU.
Ministerie van Justitie (1997) *Substitutie van Vrijheidsstraffen, Interdepartementaal beleidsonderzoek substitutie van vrijheidsstraffen door taakstraffen*. The Hague: IBO-ronde 1996, report no. 8.
Ministerie van Justitie (2001) *Nota Effectieve Reïntegratie: Een gemeenschappelijke uitdaging voor de reclassering en het gevangeniswezen*. The Hague: DPJS.
Ministerie van Justitie (2002) *Bouwstenen van het programma Terugdringen Recidive: Startnotitie*. The Hague: Ministry of Justice.
Mulder, G.E. and Schootstra, H. (1974) *Prae-advies over de voorwaardelijke veroordeling.* Handelingen 1974 der Nederlandse Juristen-Vereniging, deel I, tweede stuk. Zwolle: Tjeenk Willink.
NFR (Nederlandse Federatie voor Reclasseringsinstellingen) (1991) *Taken en Prioriteiten Reclassering*. 's Hertogenbosch: NFR.
Pakes, F. (2004) 'The Politics of Discontent: The Emergence of a New Criminal Justice Discourse in the Netherlands', *Howard Journal of Criminal Justice*, 43: 284–298.
Pease, K., Billingham, S., and Earnshaw, I. (1977) *Community Service assessed in 1976*, Home Office Research Study 39. London: HMSO.
Perry, D. (2002) 'Bewijsgerelateerde praktijk en bewijsgerelateerd beleid; moder-

nisering van de reclassering in Engeland en in Wales', *Justitiële Verkenningen*, 28: 36–48.

Reidnied, J. (2001) 'De doelgroep en doelstelling van het penitentiair programma onder de PBW', in M. Boone en G. de Jonge (eds), *De Penitentiaire Beginselenwet in werking*. Deventer: Gouda Quint, pp. 35–59.

Ridder-Padt, M.S.H. (2002) 'Doet de reclassering goede dingen? Over de effecten van de Nota Effectieve Reïntegratie en het project Outputsturing', *Sancties*, 2002: 178–184.

Ridder-Padt, M.S.H. (2004) 'Nieuwe perspectieven voor de aan het strafrecht gerelateerde hulpverlening', *Proces*, 83: 220–226.

Schuyt, K. and Kommer, M. (1998) *Niet bij straf alleen, de spanning tussen idealisme en realisme in het reclasseringswerk*. Amsterdam: University Press Amsterdam.

Spaans, E.C. (1995) *Werken of Zitten: De toepassing van werkstraffen en korte vrijheidsstraffen in 1992*. Arnhem: Gouda Quint.

SRN (Stichting Reclassering Nederland) (2001) *Van helder naar transparant*, jaarverslag 1999/2000. Utrecht: SRN.

SRN (2002) *Werken aan de basis*, jaarverslag 2001. Utrecht: SRN.

Van de Bunt, H.G. and Leuw, E. (1995) 'Gedogen als zelfkant van de rechtshandhaving?', *Justitiële Verkenningen*, 21: 65–75.

Van Koppen, P.J. (2003) *Verankering van rechtspraak: Over de wisselwerking tussen burger, politie, justitie en rechter*. Amsterdam: Inaugural lecture at the Free University.

Van der Laan, G. (1994) 'De nieuwe normen van de reclassering', *Tijdschrift voor de Sociale Sector*, 11: 24–29.

Van der Laan, G. (2004) 'De metamorfose van de reclassering als teken des tijds', *Proces*, 83: 233–242.

Van der Linden, B. (2004) 'Terugdringen Recidive', *Proces*, 83: 94–102.

Van Swaaningen, R. (1997) 'De reclassering als flexibel en marktgericht productie-bedrijf', *Proces*, 76: 193–198.

Van Swaaningen, R. (2004) 'Veiligheid in Nederland en Europa, een sociologische beschouwing aan de hand van David Garland', *Justitiële Verkenningen*, 30: 9–24.

Wartna, B.S.J., Beijers, W.M.E.H. and Essers, A.A.M. (1999) *Ontkennende en bekennende verdachten: Over de proceshouding van verdachten van strafzaken tijdens het politieverhoor*. The Hague: Ministry of Justice, WODC.

Index

Added to a page number 'f' denotes a figure and 't' denotes a table.